"Most of us can't give our daughters enough money for lifetime security. So give this book. Read it—discuss it—together. It could even change your life for the better."
—Joyce Lain Kennedy, syndicated careers columnist

"Concrete and realistic ideas and guidelines to help our daughters reach their full potential."
—Vicki Lansky, author of such books as Feed Me, I'm Yours and Practical Parenting Tips

"[This book] will be an important contribution to girls and their parents. If all the parents in the United States applied the teachings of this book to themselves and their daughters, this would be a much more hospitable place for girls and young women to live and succeed."
—Heather Johnston Nicholson, Ph.D., Director,
Girls Incorporated National Resource Center

"A superb road map for a successful future . . . Today's yellow brick road can only be successfully traveled with a suitcase filled with a strong sense of self and critical thinking skills. What better gift can a parent give?"
—Connie LaFace Olson, Los Angeles Unified School District, Career Equity Services

"Confirming what so many women have known and felt, this amazing and insightful guide provides a framework for changing the lives of their daughters. A must for anyone raising a daughter, soon to be a woman, partner, worker, and parent."
—Penelope C. Paine, Contract Consultant, California Department of Education,
Office of Gender Equity

"Every parent should keep this book handy over the child-rearing years. Its analysis is sound and followed by down-to-earth advice clearly expressed. Don't plan just to read it through— you'll want to have it at the ready and take its advice. Life will be better for your daughter, your family, and yourself."
—Mildred Kiefer Wurf, Washington, D.C., Representative, Girls Incorporated

PENGUIN BOOKS

THINGS WILL BE DIFFERENT FOR MY DAUGHTER

Mindy Bingham is an author, educator, and publisher with more than twenty years' experience working with girls and young women. She is the author or co-author of sixteen books, including *My Way Sally* (with Penelope Colville Paine), recipient of the Ben Franklin Award. She lives in Santa Barbara, California.

Sandy Stryker holds a degree in journalism from the University of Minnesota and has been an advocate for girls' and women's rights since 1975. Her first children's book, *Tonia the Tree*, received the Merit Award from the Friends of American Writers. She lives in St. Paul, Minnesota.

Bingham and Stryker have collaborated on eight other books, including the best-selling *Choices: A Teen Woman's Journal for Self-awareness and Personal Planning*, which is now required reading in hundreds of junior and senior high schools, and *Career Choices: A Guide for Teens and Young Adults*, currently being used in more than five hundred secondary schools and more than one hundred job readiness programs.

Mindy Bingham *and* Sandy Stryker

WITH SUSAN ALLSTETTER NEUFELDT, PH.D.

Produced by Alison Brown Cerier Book Development, Inc.

penguin books

Things will be different for my daughter

A PRACTICAL GUIDE TO BUILDING HER SELF-ESTEEM AND SELF-RELIANCE

PENGUIN BOOKS
Published by the Penguin Group
Penguin Books USA Inc., 375 Hudson Street,
New York, New York 10014, U.S.A.
Penguin Books Ltd, 27 Wrights Lane,
London W8 5TZ, England
Penguin Books Australia Ltd, Ringwood,
Victoria, Australia
Penguin Books Canada Ltd, 10 Alcorn Avenue,
Toronto, Ontario, Canada M4V 3B2
Penguin Books (N.Z.) Ltd, 182–190 Wairau Road,
Auckland 10, New Zealand

Penguin Books Ltd, Registered Offices:
Harmondsworth, Middlesex, England

First published in Penguin Books 1995

3   5   7   9   10   8   6   4   2

Produced by Alison Brown Cerier Book Development, Inc.,

AUTHORS' NOTE
To preserve privacy, the names and some of the identifying characteristics of the individuals
depicted in this book have been changed. Their stories, however, are true.

Grateful acknowledgment is made for permission to reprint the following copyrighted works:

Excerpt from "Mindworks" column, Minneapolis Star-Tribune. Used with permission.
AAUW's recommendations to National Education Goals from "Restructuring Education:
Getting Girls into America's Goals," published by the American Association of
University Women (AAUW), 1111 16th Street, N.W., Washington, D.C. 20036.
Used with permission.
Excerpts from "An Action Agenda for Equalizing Girls' Options" and "Tips for Parents to
Build Girls' Interest in Science and Math" published by Girls Incorporated. Used with permission.

LIBRARY OF CONGRESS CATALOGING IN PUBLICATION DATA
Bingham, Mindy, 1950–
Things will be different for my daughter : a practical guide to
building her self-esteem and self-reliance / Mindy Bingham and Sandy Stryker : with
Susan Allstetter Neufeldt.
p.   cm.
Includes bibliographical references and index.
ISBN 0 14 02.4125 6
1. Parent and teenager—United States.   2. Teenage girls—United
States—Psychology.   3. Teenage girls—United States—Growth.
4. Self-esteem in adolescence—United States.   5. Self-perception in
adolescence—United States.   I. Stryker, Sandy.   II. Neufeldt,
Susan Allstetter.   III. Title.
HQ799.15.B56   1995
649´.125—dc20   94-18517

Printed in the United States of America
Set in Goudy
Designed by Claire Naylon Vaccaro

Book design by Claire Naylon Vaccaro

Contents

iii. *What's a parent to do?*

iv. *Everybody's daughter*

Foreword

Today there is a growing recognition of the hurdles girls confront and of the need to remove those hurdles to enable girls to succeed. At Girls Incorporated we understand the challenges and joys of growing up female in America. In our centers across the country we have helped girls grow strong, smart, and bold by teaching them to confront gender stereotypes and develop their own interests and skills. We know that when environments are carefully conceived to provide opportunities, girls grow into confident and capable adults. And we know that creating these environments is not easy.

Raising your daughter to be confident, successful, and strong is a complicated assignment. *Things Will Be Different for My Daughter* can offer you valuable support all along the way. Mindy Bingham and Sandy Stryker, along with Susan Neufeldt, have assembled a toolkit of facts and activities for parents who want to support and empower girls. They tell how to teach girls, from infancy to teens to beyond, the skills they need for today's world.

While there are many books devoted to parenting and child development, few focus on helping girls succeed in spite of the challenges they face. Through this book, parents and others can make things different for girls. If every parent reads this book and applies its teachings, the world will be a much more hospitable place for girls to live and to succeed.

Amy Sutnick Plotch
Director of Communications
Heather Johnston Nicholson
Director, National Resource Center
Girls Incorporated

Preface

During the winter of 1991, when Alison Brown Cerier asked us if we'd be interested in writing this book, we were intrigued by the theme. Alison, concerned about the report issued by the American Association of University Women (AAUW) stating that American girls' self-esteem seems to plummet as they move through childhood and into adolescence, wanted to produce a book that would help turn around this unhappy situation. A professional acquaintance at the Carnegie Foundation who knew our work suggested us for the job.

We have been reading, writing, and speaking about women's issues throughout our adult lives, going back to our college years in the late 1960s. Working within community organizations, women's groups, and educational institutions, we sought to understand the special problems facing women and began to develop programs that we hoped might be of some small assistance.

For example, when it became clear to us that the key to happiness and success for women was economic and emotional self-sufficiency, we co-authored *Choices: A Teen Woman's Journal for Self-awareness and Personal Planning*, which was published in 1983. It started as a modest effort, but it seemed to hit a nerve. When an article about the book from the *Los Angeles Times* was picked up by newspapers around the country, bookstores were plagued by phone calls from parents and other adults looking for this revolutionary text. Although it continues to sell well among individuals, the book has had its greatest impact through school programs. More than half a million young people have now been exposed to the materials in *Choices* and *Challenges*, the companion book for boys published a year later.

Encouraged by our success, we decided to address other issues. We wrote *Changes* for women reentering the workforce after a period of absence and *More Choices: A Strategic Planning Guide for Mixing Career and Family*.

Wherever we turned our attentions, however, the same stumbling block appeared: By the time young women reach high school, they have already developed some damaging attitudes and thought patterns. With this in mind, we designed a Mother-Daughter Choices project for small groups of sixth-grade girls and their mothers. This program attempts to establish open communication between mother and child and, we hope, help the young women get over that bumpy stretch of life known as adolescence with a minimum of pain and anguish for themselves and their families. It, too, became successful on a national level, as did our Women Helping

Girls with Choices program, which involved encouraging women's service organizations to become advocates for girls in their communities.

In 1987 Mindy organized a conference entitled Focus on Equity, paid for by funds the books had earned for their sponsoring organization, the Girls Club of Santa Barbara. At this conference, thirty-five leaders from national girls' and women's organizations and educational specialists in gender equity from many states came together to explore the problems facing girls, envision their solutions, and raise these issues to national prominence. As the three-day meeting concluded, Sarah Harder, then incoming national president of the AAUW, made a commitment to the group that advocacy for girls would become the focus issue during her term in office.

The rest, as they say, is history. Few Americans are unfamiliar with the AAUW studies published between 1990 and 1993. The needs of girls and the importance of self-esteem are now widely recognized throughout the country.

Meanwhile, we were looking more closely at the issue of identity. There is a direct relationship, we found, between being "identity achieved" and maintaining a high level of self-esteem. Identity also has an impact on economic self-sufficiency, and with these concepts in mind, in 1990 we published *Career Choices*. This innovative curriculum for young people of both sexes is now being used in more than five hundred schools.

So when Alison asked if we'd like to take on *this* project, we felt confident of our ability to write a practical, easy-to-use manual and make it accessible to a wide audience. Our previous work, we thought, would serve as a guide: If a woman is to lead a happy and successful life, she needs to be emotionally and economically self-sufficient. In order to do that, she must somehow maintain high self-esteem during adolescence, something she is more likely to be able to do if she becomes "identity achieved" in late childhood and early adolescence.

No problem, we told Alison. We would probably have a manuscript ready in six months. That was in May 1991.

As we became fully immersed in the project, we got the feeling that we were missing something. Our understanding didn't go deep enough. Then we read Suzanne Kobasa Ouellette's work on the hardy personality. Here was the base on which all of our other goals for girls must be founded. We identified eight key skills that a girl must develop if she is to form a hardy personality, and these are, you'll see, the cornerstone of this book.

That was nearly three years ago. What was to be a short book grew and grew. Making choices about what we could include and what must be left out became a difficult task. We apologize for our regrettable, yet unavoidable, omissions. We could not focus attention on special groups of girls, special interests, or even much on diverse cultures or ethnic groups. These must wait for another book.

With that in mind, we want to encourage other researchers, authors, and program developers to use our model of the special development stages of girls to further develop their own studies, projects, or programs. We believe that grass-roots efforts can draw national attention to an issue, and we would take great satisfaction in seeing others expand on our work.

We have been pleased to have the input of Dr. Susan Neufeldt, director of the Ray E. Hosford Clinic in the Counseling/Clinical/School Psychology Program in the Graduate School of Education at the University of California at Santa Barbara. Previously in private practice as a psychologist, she returned to academic life to pursue her interest in training psychologists and counselors, and is the author of a manual for supervising beginning therapists. She has been married for more than twenty years and is the mother of a teenage daughter. As a counseling psychologist, she focuses her efforts toward the development of people's strengths and talents. Susan reviewed and supplemented the text for us from a psychologist's perspective. Also, throughout the book you'll find many insightful stories Susan shared with us about her own experiences and those of her daughter.

So after thirteen years of writing books for girls and young women, we bring our work full circle by addressing you, the parents. You have the power to make a tremendous impact on your daughter, and it is our best hope to assist you in that all-important job.

Using this book

We encourage you to pick up pen or pencil and make your reading an interactive process. You'll find questions, activities, and planning guides sprinkled throughout the text. Argue with us in the margins or underline points you want to come back to. This is important to the self-discovery process that awaits you.

The book is divided into three sections relating to our philosophy about change.

In part 1, chapters 1 to 8, we will offer you a working definition of self-esteem, help you evaluate your own attitudes, discuss the term *femininity* and how it affects your daughter's attitude toward achievement, discuss some theories of identity formation, and suggest how you might help your daughter become "identity achieved."

Chapter 6, "Developing a Hardy Personality," is perhaps the most important chapter in the book. In it we identify attitudes and behaviors commonly encouraged in females that must be changed if our daughters are to become unique, independent, self-sufficient individuals.

In chapter 7 we present our model of the special development stages of girls. It will help you develop your strategy for raising your daughter, whether she's an infant or an adolescent. Particularly if your daughter is older, it may save you some frustration by demonstrating the *order* in which developmental tasks should be accomplished.

We conclude this section in chapter 8 with an overview of parenting roles and a discussion of how you can bring about change.

Parts 2 and 3 of the book get more specific. Here you will start to develop your own plan for your daughter and, perhaps, for your own behavioral changes. We aim to help you by, first, discussing the general issues that come up at different points in your daughter's life and then, in part 3, addressing such specific concerns as books, toys, and the media; math, sports, and school in general; appearance, relationships, and sexuality; career planning and exploration; and becoming an independent adult. All of these chapters include specific advice and things you can do to avoid, get through, or solve the problems that often arise.

In the last section of the book, we look at institutionalizing change—making things better for everyone's daughters.

At the end of many chapters is a box that will send you to "Your Plan" at the back of the book. In these pages, beginning on page 455, you can record, as they develop, the messages you plan to send your daughter at various ages—on careers, relationships, appearance, sports, and other specific issues, as well as notes to help her develop the hardy personality traits that you will have learned about in chapter 6.

Think of this book as "Raising a Daughter 101." We've provided an overview of the most important issues, but because they are so complex, you may want to delve deeper into topics of particular concern. Since we have necessarily had to limit our discussion to problems endemic to all females, you will probably want to consult other resources if your daughter's personal situation or her cultural or ethnic group presents its own obstacles to her success.

While many challenges lie ahead for you and your daughter, we hope that together you will be able to keep always before you a vision of the woman she can become. Often in this book we will need to talk about the disadvantages of being female, so it's important to keep in mind that in spite of everything, being a woman is something to celebrate, not something to overcome. Today a woman has the freedom to explore every corner of her consciousness and embrace every part of the personality she finds there. Not confined to be either/or, contemporary woman can be beauty and businesswoman, mother and scholar, lover and friend. We want your daughter to relish being a girl and look forward to becoming a woman. While we can't ignore the challenges ahead, we hope that as you read you will be able to see beyond the immediate problems to that place of infinite possibilities, and that this is the vision of womanhood you will pass on to her.

I am not afraid of the storm, for I am learning how to sail my ship.
— *Louisa May Alcott*

Mindy Bingham and Sandy Stryker
March 1994

Acknowledgments

We would first like to thank Alison Brown Cerier, the godmother and guardian angel of *Things Will Be Different for My Daughter*. It was Alison who had the original idea to write a practical book for parents about girls and self-esteem and who recruited us to take on the project. Over the past three years she has served as agent, adviser, editor, and cheerleader, attempting with unflagging good spirits to keep us on track and on schedule. Without her the book would not exist.

Special thanks, too, to our editor, Mindy Werner, whose belief in the project kept it alive. We appreciate her understanding and support, her insight and intelligence, and her commitment to the topic.

Dr. Susan Neufeldt joined our team after we'd completed the first draft and devoted hundreds of hours to helping us crystallize our thoughts and more clearly present the theories behind the practical advice. We gratefully acknowledge her huge contribution of insight, expertise, and personal experience as well as the energy and dedication she brought to the project.

Dr. Robert Shafer once again served as adviser, sounding board, and devil's advocate and helped to stimulate and steer the thoughts behind much of the material in the book, for which we are greatly appreciative.

Our dear friends Penny Paine and Betty Shepperd were ongoing sources of assistance and encouragement. Their relentless enthusiasm and commitment to girls has kept us going through the difficult parts of numerous projects, especially this one.

Many thanks to Dr. Heather Johnston Nicholson and Amy Sutnick Plotch for reviewing the manuscript from their vantage point as experts on girls and all the facts that add to or detract from their growth, equity, and self-esteem. Their comments made this a richer book.

Special thanks to Mildred Wurf and Margaret Gates of Girls Incorporated, whose active support for our work has helped to spread its influence. To Jane Quinn, thanks for recommending us for the project.

Our gratitude to the American Association of University Women for their foresight and dedication to advocacy for girls everywhere.

We have been fortunate to have input from numerous experts and advocates, many of them our friends and mentors. Their observations and insights are woven throughout the text. Sincere thanks to Becky Cabaza, Dr. Sally Archer, Jan Roberta, Judy Cobbs, Linda Wagner, Dr. Joan Lipsitz, Martha Bernstein, Betty Stambolian, Connie Gibson, Mary Wiberg, Sarah Harder, Jan Fritzen, Dr. Lillian Carson, Jenny Erwin, Beverly Burns, Dr. Ken Hoyt, Mary Ann Etu, Bernie Burley, Connie LaFace Olson, Dr. Doug Larche, Joyce Lain Kennedy, Elizabeth Mehren, Barbara Miller, Emily Card, Christine Smart, Mardena Fehling, Fiona Hill, Michelle Jackman, Hillary Kline, Nancy Marriott, Carl Lindros, Dr. Edith Phelps, Lucile Graham, Elenor Van Cott, Rebecca Dedmond, Dr. Lois Phillips, Rose Allen, Alice Halberstadt, Lucinda Gatch, Vicki Lansky, Lynn Jaffe and the Melpomene Institute for Women's Health Research, Cynthia Gerdes and the staff at Creative Kidstuff, the staff at the Red Balloon, and the many parents and daughters who shared their stories with us, including Conner Kilbourn, Julie Gibson, Shelley Honigbaum, Stacie Hill, Chasta Suazo, Vanessa Martinez, Jody Kaufman, Barclay DeVeau, Kate Shanahan, Nicole Talley, Gina Grandi, Diane Talley, Stephanie Ortale, Diana O'Keefe, Denise Adams, Carol Scott, Annette Sorel, Sara Lykken, Sue Beauchamp, Pamela Brandt, Mary Schwind, Kathy Kisch, Wendy Pederson, Kristen McCarthy, and Ann Ricketts.

Thanks to those in our lives who were unavoidably neglected or who had to pick up the pieces when manuscript pressures made us physically or emotionally unavailable: Shirley Cornelius, Jim Johnson, Chris Nolte, Itoko Maeno, Dan Poynter, Shirley Myers, Socorro Avila, and Cliff Pederson.

Wendy Bingham was actively involved in this project from the beginning, conducting surveys, organizing brainstorming sessions, gathering data, and providing a reality check. She deserves double thanks—as contributor and inspiration.

Finally, and especially, thanks to the men in our lives: Jim Comiskey, who moved to Santa Barbara to help out for the duration of the writing of this book and ended up staying for good; and Bill Stryker, defender of just causes, booster of low spirits, and clipper of relevant articles. Their love and support are cherished and reciprocated.

i.
Awareness of the issues

chapter one

Self-Esteem:
A Key to Unlocking
Your Daughter's Future

*U*ntil recently, if you had written a fairy tale about the lives of girls and women, it might have started something like this: "Once upon a time there was a magic castle, surrounded by a high stone wall and a moat and jealously guarded by nasty dragons instructed to keep all females outside, where they could only dream about the treasures within."

Today's story would need some revision. The castle might still be there—and the wall and the moat—but the villains would have to be replaced, perhaps by well-meaning but shortsighted dragons who, going about their daily tasks as they have always done, fail to see that even though the doors have been unlocked and the drawbridge lowered, the little girl stands and waits on the other side.

In our new story you are the hero, the one who can help the child—your daughter—cross the moat, open the door, and choose for herself the ultimate treasure: writing and living her own story, with no constraints or limitations.

As you read and work through this book, you will learn that no single key can unlock that door. There are skills to teach her, personality traits to encourage, an identity to explore and develop. And there is self-esteem, so important for your daughter to build and hold on to as she moves into adulthood. Let's start our discussion by considering what it is, where it comes from, and how it grows.

In 1991 the American Association of University Women

Love yourself first and everything else falls into line. You really have to love yourself to get anything done in this world.

— Lucille Ball

(AAUW), a national service organization dedicated to the education of women and girls, brought the nation to attention with the release of its report on girls and self-esteem. Suddenly the topic was of great importance to the media, cultural leaders, government officials, and other molders of public opinion. By bringing long overdue attention to this serious problem, the AAUW performed a valuable national service, for which it must be commended. At last, it seemed, we understood why, in spite of drastic societal change and twenty years of "equal opportunity," so many girls and young women were clearly not working up to their potential or achieving their dreams.

The AAUW national self-esteem survey of three thousand children in grades four to ten, conducted in 1990, gave us a good indication of the depth and the scope of the problem. Its key findings were as follows:

> 1. In elementary school, 60 percent of girls and 67 percent of boys say they are "happy the way I am." Among middle-school students, however, only 29 percent of the girls still feel good about themselves.

Self-esteem for boys also decreases, but not nearly as much: 46 percent manage to hang on to their high self-esteem. The gap between the genders increases, from seven to seventeen points. The sharpest drops in self-esteem occur in the years "between elementary school and middle school," according to the report.

> 2. Aware that the culture values them less and grants them fewer choices for their future, girls need to have more self-esteem than boys in order to aspire to a nontraditional career (that is, one not traditionally held by a member of that sex).

There are more male engineers than female engineers, so engineering is considered a nontraditional career for women. Nontraditional careers for women usually offer high pay and more autonomy. With less confidence in their abilities than boys, girls are also more prone to say that they are "not smart enough" or "not good enough" to achieve their highest ambitions.

For boys, confidence and self-esteem are related to "doing." They feel good about their achievements, and many report that their talents are what they like best about themselves. For girls, self-esteem is related more to "being": their appearance and their pleasing personality. It's no coincidence that as physical appearance and popularity become more important to a girl, her self-esteem begins to tumble. Beginning junior high is a crisis point.

It's important to note that trends in self-esteem differ by race as well as gender. African American girls start out feeling better about themselves than white girls do (65 percent of elementary school girls have high self-esteem), and most of them retain that feeling. The survey found only a seven-point drop in esteem level among older girls. Hispanic girls start out with the highest level of self-esteem of any female group (68 percent) but also record the biggest drop—thirty-eight points between elementary and high school (they still feel better about themselves than white high school girls, however).

3. *Parents and teachers have the power to build a young woman's self-esteem—or to tear it down.*

Unfortunately, too often they do the latter. Because of age-old notions that females are not as capable as males, society has lower expectations for females. For girls, this can lead to a vicious downward spiral. Because those they look up to and admire—parents and teachers—indicate they don't have high expectations for them, many girls do not take the risks required to achieve.

It is only by achieving that they can acquire a feeling of success. Self-esteem is built upon the experience of success. With each success self-esteem grows and new goals can be taken on. Think of it as a circular process. When an individual experiences success, she grows in self-confidence. As her self-confidence grows she feels empowered to try new challenges. As she succeeds with each challenge, she develops the sense that she can cope with whatever life throws her way, and that feeling leads to self-confidence, self-reliance, and self-esteem.

4. *There is a strong correlation between math and science and self-esteem.*

The ability to excel in math and science is empowering. It is a critical filter that separates economic classes, particularly in a technological society. It is not surprising, then, that those who like these subjects have higher self-esteem, are more likely to aspire to careers as professionals, and cling more stubbornly to those aspirations than those who don't like math or science.

Studies show that young women who like math and science are more confident in general, and also feel better about the way they look than any other group of either sex. In addition, they are less concerned about being liked by others.

❧ Let's consider that third point again. Parents and teachers, not peers, are the biggest influence on a young woman's self-esteem and aspirations. Your task, then, is to build those characteristics as best you can.

Before you can do that, though, you need to have a pretty good notion of what the term *self-esteem* really means. In recent years it's become one of those overused buzzwords, applied so often that it's come to mean almost anything—or practically nothing. We've tried to make things a bit clearer here by offering an explanation of the term as we see it, followed by some hints on recognizing it and a discussion of its sources.

What is self-esteem?

The eighteenth-century French philosopher Jean-Jacques Rousseau may have been one of the first to attempt a definition of self-esteem. He called it self-love and said it is "the only natural passion of man." To Freud it was the "ego ideal," to Oscar Wilde "the beginning of a lifelong romance." According to a February 1992 cover story in *Newsweek*, "Self-esteem is clearly a product of today's relentless search for ever more fundamental and unifying laws of nature."

Most people have some idea of what the term means, and if you want a short, snappy definition, you can find dozens of them. If you're looking for something more meaty, you could read a few of the many books on the topic. Today you can look to the National Council for Self-Esteem for assistance, as well as to state and regional groups like the California Task Force to Promote Self-Esteem and Personal and Social Responsibility.

We've read as much as we could find and evaluated all that we've read, and we've come to a few conclusions.

Self-esteem is not something your daughter initially learns for herself, like walking or tying her shoes, although she can learn to do things that help her build or maintain her self-esteem in later life. It is something you can help her acquire, by loving and valuing her, and by showing respect for women at large. It is perhaps the most valuable gift she will ever receive. Of course, this is one gift you can't just pay for with a check, tie up with a ribbon, and present as you would a sweater. Giving this gift will take some effort on your part.

As for a definition of self-esteem, one of the best we found comes from Dr. Nathaniel Branden's book, *The Power of Self-Esteem*. According to Dr. Branden, "Self-esteem is

1. *confidence in our ability to think and to cope with the challenges of life.*
2. *confidence in our right to be happy, the feeling of being worthy, deserving, entitled to assert our needs and wants and to enjoy the fruits of our efforts.*"

Positive self-esteem operates as, in effect, the immune system of the spirit, providing resistance, strength, and a capacity for regeneration.

—Dr. Nathaniel Branden, *New Woman*, January 1993

The signs of high self-esteem

How can you tell if someone has high self-esteem? Here are a few things to watch for.

1. Someone with high self-esteem does not give up easily, even after failure, but is able to persist and to learn from the effort.

For a child, the opportunities to learn from failure begin early, with such tasks as learning how to walk. Is she allowed to fall down and pick herself up and fall down again? Or does someone rush in to make sure she doesn't get hurt? If parents are too eager to rescue a child, she will learn to doubt her ability to master new tasks, and her self-esteem will suffer. If she is allowed to fail or succeed on her own, she will learn to accept new challenges with enthusiasm, an attitude that, in itself, is likely to lead to more success and greater levels of self-esteem.

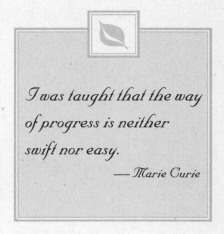

I was taught that the way of progress is neither swift nor easy.

— *Marie Curie*

2. A person with high self-esteem is willing to take risks.

As we've just seen, someone with low self-esteem has much more to lose from failure than an individual who thinks well of herself. It isn't surprising, then, that the former is likely to shy away from new adventures and experiences. If she doesn't do well, her already fragile sense of self will suffer further damage. The person who has had the opportunity to fail and to survive failure is much more likely to embrace changes and challenges, knowing that she is capable and that, even if she fails, her failure has no bearing on her value as a human being.

3. Someone with self-esteem will know what she wants and have enough confidence to ask for it.

A child who is encouraged to suppress her own wishes in order to meet someone else's expectations is in danger of becoming a chronic "people pleaser." She may grow to believe that she has no right to her own preferences and opinions, if she can even remember what those might be. As she repeatedly beats down her own sense of identity, her sense of self-esteem, too, grows dimmer and dimmer.

The child who knows who she is and feels valued for her unique self feels entitled to have what she wants and is not afraid to ask for it and pursue it, despite obstacles.

*I cannot give you the for-
mula for success, but I
can give you the formula
for failure, which is—
try to please everybody.*
— *Herbert Bayard Swope*

*Do not rely completely on
any other human being,
however dear. We meet
all life's greatest tests
alone.*
—*Agnes Macphail*

*4. A person with high self-esteem is discriminating in her
relationships.*

She can trust her own judgment and choose close friends and
romantic partners who interest her, who like her and support
her values, enthusiasms, and abilities, and who make her laugh.
She is not limited to choosing people with perceived high status
in her peer group as friends and romantic partners, nor is she
likely to stay in relationships that are abusive.

An individual with a strong sense of self does not find it necessary to sacrifice her own standards or values in a desperate
need to avoid being alone. While she considers the opinions of
others, other people's approval and disapproval do not define
who she is. She can be comfortable alone, or she can enjoy the
company of others.

*5. An individual with high self-esteem can be connected
to others while maintaining her own sense of self.*

For most people, a committed relationship with mate, children,
family, friends, or even employers and employees is one of the
most important elements of a good life.

The drive to bond with others at an intimate level is
strong—but the possibility of hurt or pain is very real. The person with high self-esteem is not afraid to make these kinds of
commitments because of her confidence and self-knowledge, her
capacity to be her own person and bounce back if the relationship goes wrong.

What are the sources of self-esteem?

According to Dr. Jennifer James, author of *Women and the Blues*, four factors play a
large part in determining self-esteem.

1. Fate or culture.

This includes such things as the place and time of your birth, your sex, race, health
or disability, appearance, intelligence, and so on. At least initially, these are beyond

your control. You may be able to modify them later on, but they will never completely disappear from your image of yourself. For example, someone born in poverty may achieve great wealth in later life, yet she may never get over the stigma of being poor. Similarly, an unattractive child may grow into a beauty and yet always feel somewhat insecure about her looks.

2. The family.

Since that's basically what this book is all about, we'll leave it at that for now.

3. Experience.

What you do, how you're treated, whether your life is blessed by fate or marked by tragedy, will affect the way you feel about yourself. Teachers, friends, spouses, employers, and other significant people in your life can make you feel better—or worse. The more positive experiences you have and the more positive people you surround yourself with, the better you're likely to feel.

Even if you had many negative experiences in the past, you can overcome their effect on your self-esteem by changing the quality of new experiences. As an unemployed woman, without close friends, in a bad marriage to a man who continually told her how worthless she was, Natalie "had just enough self-esteem left to know I needed help." She sought counseling and, within a year, landed a job she was good at, found a group of supportive friends, and ended the marriage. "The bad memories didn't go away," Natalie says now. "For a while I really couldn't stand to think about the past. But I kept piling up the good stuff through new experiences and little successes, and eventually this new self-image took root. It still amazes me, but there it is!"

4. Perspective.

How do you view the things that happen to you? This relates to chapter 6, "Developing a Hardy Personality," and the feeling of being in control of your life. Dr. James states, "Perspective is learned from our family or culture (like optimism or pessimism), but there are many people who seem to create their own. They decide to interpret their life events in terms of challenges and possibilities, not losses and injustices."

Is this something a person can learn? Psychologist Martin E. P. Seligman thinks so. His book *Learned Optimism* is all about how it can—and why it should—be done. This is not a "feel good" book, but one based solidly on years of clinical research. It includes a chapter entitled "Helping Your Child Escape Pessimism," and for that reason we highly recommend it.

How does self-esteem develop?

Self-esteem depends on the development of a healthy sense of self, a person's own understanding and acceptance of who she really is. A sense of self begins to develop almost from birth. If a child is able to master the appropriate tasks for her age in a positive way (without being neglected, threatened, or humiliated, for example), and if her development is acknowledged and appreciated, she begins to feel a sense of mastery and self-confidence.

Note that it is not achievement alone that leads to self-esteem; it is acknowledgment of that achievement. Sally Archer, professor of psychology at Trenton State College, says that in her observations girls do achieve—at an early age and often at a higher level than boys. "When I take my kids to the pool," she told us, "I see the little girls jumping right in while the boys are more likely to cling to their moms." Archer says that girls seem to have fewer problems adjusting to school than boys, and they are consistently better students. But these are not the accomplishments girls tend to be rewarded and recognized for. Instead they are rewarded for their appearance, for "being a good little girl," for playing "nicely" with the other children. These are all achievements based on the perceptions or approval of others, what someone else considers "nice" or "pretty," which might change the next day. To make sure she is considered "nice," a girl must keep checking to see if the adults think she is nice. A strong sense of self comes from achievements that the girl can measure herself, like learning to jump off the diving board, and that others also value.

If they are unable to find recognition in the larger world, girls and women tend to seek acceptance on a smaller scale by becoming determined "people pleasers," by looking for recognition from others that they are worthwhile human beings. If different people have conflicting ideas about what she should do, whom does she decide to please and whom does she disappoint? Either way, can she avoid feeling guilty?

In an effort to find an identity, which is a healthy impulse, they do what anyone without much of a sense of self does: they take on the identity of someone close to them as a substitute for having an identity of their own. But this doesn't work, either. If Maria's only identity is being Bobby's girl, who is she when Bobby goes away?

Fortunately, parents who are aware of these dilemmas and willing to take the time can make a real difference in their daughter's life. Contrary to popular opinion, kids do value their parents' opinions, even during adolescence, when they're not supposed to want anything as totally uncool as a close relationship with Mom and Dad. If you can recognize your daughter's achievements—not instead of, but along with her relationship skills—she will be able to incorporate those accomplishments into her self-image. If you encourage her to pursue all of her interests and not just those that may be considered "appropriate" for girls, and if, at the same time, you exhibit and express respect for women and all the tasks traditionally assigned them, you can help her feel valued by, and valuable to, the world around her. (Please don't assume, because this book focuses heavily on the importance of achievement, that we are in any way denigrating relationships or traditional female roles. But our society is very good at passing on traditional messages, and you probably don't need to be overly concerned about reinforcing them. What you can do—*must* do—is to instill the qualities less emphasized for females in our culture that will help your daughter become a confident and self-sufficient adult. Helping you do that is our main goal.)

Do you know it when you see it?

In order to build a good sense of self-esteem, a child must accomplish certain developmental tasks. As we see it, these are the six qualities to watch for and to nurture to the best of your abilities.

   1. A child must feel autonomous.

She must have the sense that she can accomplish on her own, that she is in control of her destiny. This sense of control can be developed by allowing your daughter to start making simple choices for herself as soon as she exhibits an interest in doing so. If she can decide what to wear, which game to play, whom to play it with, and so on, she will feel empowered. She will know you think she can make good decisions, that she knows her own mind best. If you or someone else makes all these decisions, she will come to feel helpless and passive, and she will learn to doubt her ability to take charge of her life.

   2. A child must develop the capacity to be self-sufficient.

Generations of women brought up to believe in fairy tales learned to see themselves as victims needing to be rescued by a prince, a fairy godmother, or even a couple of white mice masquerading as coachmen. Millions of American women and children now living in poverty are testimony to the folly of this approach. A girl who is raised from an early age to believe that she will be responsible for taking care of herself and, perhaps, a family as well can expect a brighter future, both financially and in terms of her self-esteem.

   3. A child must feel that she is competent and that she can master new skills.

Whether she is learning to walk or to dress herself, to ride a bike or to puzzle out a problem in math, a girl is also learning that she can "do"—that she can act in the world. When well-meaning parents, teachers, or other adults rush in to help a girl—

One of the strongest messages I received from my mother was that I had to be prepared to take care of myself. Of course, she always added the amendment, "in case you are someday left a widow." But it was good advice nonetheless. I took it to heart, and I've always been grateful.

—*Woman, 42*

I was the only one in my Scout troop to get the handywoman's badge. I had to repair a pane of glass, tie a parcel, and change a fuse, among other things. Unfortunately, when the time came, my leader, a friend's mom, wasn't capable of giving me the examination. Both the skills and knowledge I could learn from these kinds of tasks came in handy later, when my husband and I did much of the work in building our own house.

—*Woman, 45*

usually much sooner than they would offer the same assistance to a boy—she learns that she is not competent, and her self-esteem suffers accordingly.

4. A child must develop character, or backbone—that quality that enables her to make wise choices and then know she has the willpower to follow through on the projects she undertakes.

Unlike temperament, which, for the most part, is inborn, character is something a person must develop. It comes out of knowing who she is, what she wants, and what she believes. Someone with character is likely to use such phrases as "I want this," "I can do that," or "this I will not stand for." Again, these are not statements that girls are traditionally rewarded for making. Instead, they are encouraged to ask questions or ask permission: "What do you want me to do?" "Is it okay if I do that?" Assertions and ultimata are mostly male prerogatives.

Then she must develop the willpower to follow through even under difficult circumstances. Once she knows that she is capable of facing challenges and forcing herself to "hang in there" and seeing a project through to the end no matter how challenging, her self-confidence will soar. If she doesn't feel she has willpower and discipline, it is likely she won't even try new tasks.

5. A child must know who she is and be true to her authentic self.

Expectant parents who think they will be able to train their child or mold her into their own ideal are often surprised to find that one tiny baby is quite different from another. A baby's unique personality emerges shortly after birth. How she develops will, to a large extent, depend on how her parents respond to her unique needs.

Stella Chess, M.D., and Alexander Thomas, M.D., in their book, *Know Your Child,* call this principle the "goodness or poorness of fit." Goodness of fit exists when she is allowed to be herself, and healthy development can be expected to follow. But if a parent's demands and expectations are too high and not compatible with the child's temperament or personality, developmental problems may arise.

Though there is a tendency among parents to have certain expectations for children of both sexes, boys are usually allowed more room to express their unique personalities. Since the roles of women in our society have been traditionally narrow, a girl tends to be given less latitude. If she is too daring, she gets rescued and lectured about being careful. If she is too active, she is dressed in ruffles and frills that restrain her movement. If she shows too much interest in climbing trees or catching frogs, she has dolls pressed upon her. As a result, says Sally Archer, many girls learn to depend on other people to define them instead of developing a strong, internal identity and sense of self. Since they can hardly be true to something they lack, they have little chance of meeting this requirement for developing healthy self-esteem.

6. *A child must feel valued by friends, family, and society.*

Often it's not that a girl isn't valued by her family or in her community; it's just that boys are valued more. It's interesting to note that many successful women were either only children or came from families where all the siblings were female. Were they raised differently from the way they would have been if they'd had brothers? Or could it be that they were simply spared the consequences of observing the different ways boys and girls are treated? We don't

My mother wants to know why I can't settle down. I'm afraid to. Every time I fall in love, I find myself giving up my self. We only talk about his interests, his life, his problems. I find myself working on his projects, his hobbies, and his passions. I feel consumed. It isn't long before I resent it, it puts a crimp in the relationship, and we drift apart. I'd rather be alone than be engulfed.

— Woman, 35

We decided to allow our daughter to choose what she would wear from the time she was very young. One day while in grade school she decided to wear her pajamas to school. I recall getting a few odd looks from some of the other parents after that day, but Edie's grown up to be a very strong woman with a mind and a will of her own.

— Mother of daughter in her twenties

know, but it's interesting to speculate. What happens when a young woman sees her brother being allowed more freedom or having his opinion taken more seriously in family discussions? How does she feel when her parents have higher expectations for his future? Miranda, an editor for a New York publisher, had two extremely successful older brothers. While she feels her parents perhaps had fewer expectations for her, they did try to treat her equitably. She recalls vividly, however, asking her high school math teacher why she received an A– on her report card when she'd had all A's in class. "Because," he said, "you'll never be as good as your brothers." Since you can't keep incidents like this from happening, it's essential that you make sure your daughter feels valued at home and empowered to fight injustice at school!

If you think you are a second-class citizen, you are.

—*Ted Turner*

Later in this section you'll see how building your daughter's self-esteem relates to forming her identity, seeing herself as an achiever, and developing the skills of a hardy personality. Each of these achievements builds on the foundation of the one before: using the fundamental skills of a hardy personality, a girl can form an identity as an achiever, and that in turn is the basis of self-esteem. These are too many terms and concepts to grasp all at once, but know that the chapters to come do build one upon the other. Each chapter is a step inward, toward the most fundamental needs of your daughter. We're going to tackle one level at a time in the following chapters, and then in chapter 7 ("Where to Start?") you will be able to analyze where your daughter is right now on the road to self-esteem and an adult future of satisfaction and inner peace. Then you'll know where to start to make a difference.

But before we turn to your daughter, let's begin by thinking about where *you* are.

Again, here are the six developmental tasks a child must accomplish in order to have self-esteem. Refer to this checklist as you develop your plan for your daughter.

In order to have self-esteem, a child must:
1. Feel autonomous, yet have the ability to connect.
2. Be self-sufficient.
3. Feel she can master new skills.
4. Build character and willpower.
5. Be true to her authentic self.
6. Feel valued.

chapter two

What Attitudes, Experiences, and Feelings Do You Bring to Parenting?

Consciously or unconsciously, like it or not, most people raise their children in the same way they were brought up—unless they make a deliberate and determined effort to do it differently. "Recently," said Marietta, "I asked my parents what I was like as a little girl. My mother said her most vivid recollection was that I always had my arms up—I always wanted to be held and cuddled. It's not that Mom and Dad were cold or neglectful, it's just that they were busy and not overly affectionate, I guess. I always thought I'd do things a little differently with my own daughter. Now she's almost grown, and it didn't occur to me until I had this conversation with my folks that I'd done the same thing they did. I hadn't been as affectionate with Lucy as she would have liked. I parented her as I was parented."

Children who received love and respect become nurturing and loving parents, while abused children often become abusive parents, and the overprotected tend to become the overprotective. This fact powerfully demonstrates the futility of following that favorite old parental maxim, "Do as I say, not as I do." If you want to bring up a daughter with a strong self-image, "you can't just talk the talk—you have to walk the walk." As a parent, your cliché of choice should be "Actions speak louder than words."

So if your parents did a terrific job, you can feel confident that you'll be as successful in raising your daughter, right? Unfortunately, no. It's not quite that easy. Because of the dramatic changes—cultural, political, and economic—that have taken place in our society over the past two decades, family life has

Setting an example is not the main means of influencing another, it is the only means.

— *Albert Einstein*

Children have never been very good at listening to their elders, but they have never failed to imitate them.

— *James Baldwin*

My mother's attitude was something like "Always remember you're not as worthy or as good as other people." As you might imagine, my self-esteem level was somewhere near the South Pole, and I nearly ruined my life before I got help from supportive friends, mentors, and a therapist and was able to turn things around. At first I put all the blame on my mom, but then I started to think about her own background. She'd been raised to think that she was unworthy.

—*Speech pathologist*

been forever altered. The future for contemporary young women looks very little like the one most of us were brought up to expect. Today every young woman needs to grow up assuming that she will have to be economically self-sufficient. She will probably be working for pay at the same time she's raising her children—perhaps without a spouse or support of any kind. This is a lesson many women, through no fault of their own, had to learn the hard way, with huge emotional and financial consequences for them and their children.

If you are in your thirties or forties, you are probably already aware that the world your daughter inhabits bears little resemblance to the place where you grew up. In fact, over the last twenty years societal changes have come about so rapidly that even young parents need to make some major attitude adjustments or, at least, take the time to rethink parenting strategies.

So before you begin developing an action plan for raising your daughter, it's important to evaluate your own attitudes and experiences. In this chapter the spotlight will be on you. How were you raised? What is your level of self-esteem? Do you have any notions about the proper way for girls to behave? Do you believe in equal opportunities for women? The following activities, questionnaires, and self-assessment exercises will help you examine your own experiences, thoughts, and actions.

If your children have contact with their other parent—or a stepparent—ask that person to go through the exercises, too. Your daughter will benefit most if all of her parents and stepparents are committed to helping her achieve healthy self-esteem.

What about your own self-esteem?

It's extremely difficult for parents with low self-esteem to raise children who think positively about themselves. Young people learn more by example than they do from what they're told, and low self-esteem usually exhibits itself in a variety of unhealthy behaviors, ranging from putting everyone else's needs ahead of one's own, to workaholism, to substance abuse, to violence. While most adults have a fair idea of their level of self-esteem, the activity "How's Your Own Self-Esteem?" may help you make a more accurate assessment.

How's your own self-esteem?

Answer the following questions by circling the number of the answer that fits you the best.

(1) When I admire people's accomplishments or appearance, I compliment them.
   1. Almost never
   2. Seldom
   3. More than half the time
   4. Usually

(2) My facial expression and body movements reflect how I feel.
   1. Almost never
   2. Seldom
   3. More than half the time
   4. Usually

(3) When someone asks me to do something I don't want to do, I tell them that I would rather not do that.
1. Almost never
2. Seldom
3. More than half the time
4. Usually

(4) When people criticize me, I listen to what they say and then decide for myself whether it is true.
1. Almost never
2. Seldom
3. More than half the time
4. Usually

(5) If I make a mistake, I make every effort to correct it, and then I don't worry about it further.
1. Almost never
2. Seldom
3. More than half the time
4. Usually

(6) When I am faced with a problem, I believe that I can figure out a solution, and I do.
1. Almost never
2. Seldom
3. More than half the time
4. Usually

(7) When someone compliments me, I am pleased, and I thank them graciously.
1. Almost never
2. Seldom
3. More than half the time
4. Usually

(8) When a close friend or relative does something that hurts my feelings, I tell them about it without attacking them.
1. Almost never
2. Seldom
3. More than half the time
4. Usually

(9) I look forward to new experiences.
1. Almost never
2. Seldom
3. More than half the time
4. Usually

(10) I believe that I have friends, colleagues, and/or relatives who like and respect me.
1. Almost never
2. Seldom
3. More than half the time
4. Usually

(11) When I think about my future I feel confident that I can take care of myself, by my-self, if the need arises.
1. Almost never
2. Seldom
3. More than half the time
4. Usually

(12) I feel worthy of love and happiness.
1. Almost never
2. Seldom
3. More than half the time
4. Usually

(13) I believe that I can bounce back from adversity. I can face whatever crisis comes my way.
1. Almost never
2. Seldom
3. More than half the time
4. Usually

(14) I believe I have the willpower to follow through with any task I choose to undertake.
1. Almost never
2. Seldom
3. More than half the time
4. Usually

(15) I feel in control of my destiny. I am the author of my own life.
1. Almost never
2. Seldom
3. More than half the time
4. Usually

Add up the numbers you have circled. The highest-possible score is 60 points. The higher the score, the higher your self-esteem is at this time.

Don't despair if you feel your score is too low. Self-esteem can be improved. Your awareness and your willingness to change make all the difference. If your score was lower than you would like, you may want to consider readings, a workshop, or therapy. Change is not easy, but it is certainly worth the effort—for your sake as well as your daughter's.

There are two important points to keep in mind. First, we are not born with a set level of self-esteem. (If we were, it would be pointless for us to write this book or for you to read it.) We may be born with a temperament and particular traits, such as introversion and extroversion, but how we feel about ourselves and what we can do is learned. Self-esteem is something we begin developing at an early age and must continue to nurture throughout our lives. If you learned to devalue yourself, you can learn to value yourself. If your own level of self-esteem is low, wanting to change is taking a step in the right direction. In order for real change to occur, studies show, this desire must be accompanied by the belief that you can change. In other words, you must feel that you are in control of your life, not that others control you or that you are a victim of fate or circumstance.

Changing from a "they control me" person to an "I control me" individual is a big job, but it begins with simple awareness, and it can progress through a series of small steps. For years writer and women's advocate Gloria Steinem has been encouraging her audiences to bring about personal and social change by committing one "outrageous act" every day. She is quick to explain that an act can be outrageous merely by being unexpected. Many women, for example, finally got their families to pitch in with the housework when they let the dirty socks and wet towels remain on the floor until someone else noticed. A man who's always shown only his "macho" side might give him-

Take charge of your thoughts. You can do what you will with them.
— *Plato*

self permission to enroll in a cooking class that interests him. Taking the time to do something nice for yourself can be an outrageous act, as can writing a letter to the president of a company whose ads you find offensive. All these actions say "I count." They help you take control of your own life, and they will also make you a more effective role model for your daughter.

There are some excellent books on self-esteem in adults that you might find helpful if yours requires more than a minimal lifting. A few are listed at the end of this book, and you'll find others at your library or bookstore. Or consider attending some lectures or classes or getting into individual or group therapy.

Bill Stryker, who has produced college textbooks for eighteen years, has seen changes come about in his profession and credits them to a process of "learned sensitivity." When he started out on the job, he says, it was still possible to find sociology textbooks in which most of the African Americans pictured were either servants or basketball players. Like gender stereotypes today, racial stereotypes were so entrenched that most people didn't even notice. Even authors and publishers, who are supposed to be on top of these things, were insensitive to the implications of their actions. They may have been embarrassed when the situation was brought to their attention, but this new awareness enabled them to make the needed changes.

In similar ways we will be drawing your attention to potential problems throughout this book. Again, we are not saying that you are a failure as a parent. We don't believe that for a minute! Please bear with us, don't take offense, and remember that we're on your side—and your daughter's.

Messages from the past

As children, we all receive spoken and unspoken messages from parents and other significant adults concerning who we are, what we should be doing, and how we measure up to some real or imagined ideal. Some messages are hard to miss. Elinor, a math teacher and mother of a daughter and two sons, remembers the day her father gave her a copy of *How to Win Friends and Influence People* and encouraged her to put more effort into improving her social life. (She was an honor student, but he didn't mention that. A message received!) More subtly, a parent who always stepped in to help finish your homework or rewashed the floor as soon as you put your mop away made it apparent that you were not sufficiently competent to complete these tasks yourself.

It is hard to fight an enemy who has outposts in your head.

— *Sally Kempton,*
American writer

Fortunately messages can be positive and empowering as well. If an important person in your life let you know that you were smart and competent, you probably still put that belief to good use every time you need to solve a problem.

Whether they were positive or negative, it's important to recognize the messages you received because they are powerful and pervasive and because they have a way of coming back to help or haunt you throughout your life. They may well be affecting your daughter's future as well.

"A Journey Back to Your Childhood" and "The Message Center" may help you get in touch with some of the messages you once received.

A journey back to your childhood

Find a comfortable chair in a quiet room and close your eyes for a few minutes. Breathe deeply and let your body relax. Think back to the years when you were growing up. See the face of your mother, the face of your father. Look around the home you grew up in. What does your living room look like? Your kitchen? See your bedroom. In your mind's eye, look into a mirror and see yourself as a five-year-old, a nine-year-old, as you were at thirteen and seventeen.

What messages did you receive from the significant people in your life? Think about it for a moment. What did they tell you about the importance of an education, your appearance, your intelligence, your relationships, a career?

Here are three examples:
Your appearance: "My brother never let an opportunity pass to tell me I was fat and ugly."

Your future: "My father always said that since I didn't want to be a nurse or a teacher, he didn't see much point in my going to college."

The importance of education: "A good education is the best ticket to a happy future."

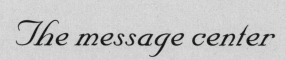

The message center

Think back to the past again. What did the significant people in your life say about your future? Imagine them leaving their messages on a telephone answering machine in the bedroom of your childhood. Write what you remember them saying.

Hello, you have reached _____'s [your name] message center. What would you like to tell me about my future? *Beep!*

Mother's message:

Father's message:

Teacher's message:

Other significant adult's message (coach, mentor, boss, relative):

Best friend's message:

Girlfriend's or boyfriend's message:

Messages come from other sources as well. In fact, some of the strongest messages we receive come from our society and its cultural expectations. Sex, age, race, nationality, religion, physical appearance, physical or intellectual abilities, financial status, social class—any of these can be the basis for taunts and jeers or praise and affection, great expectations or limited hope. What messages did society give you?

Example: As a female, I learned from society that my body was more important than my brain and that only certain career paths were open to me.

Society's message:

Now go back and circle the messages that were limiting or negative. How much influence have they had on your life up until now?

"The Message Center" is meant to help you remember and be impressed by the power parents and other significant people in our lives have—often without even realizing it—over the way young people view themselves. It's an awesome responsibility and one we hope you'll keep in mind as you begin to develop your parenting strategies and plans.

Now: How much power do you want those old messages to have over your future? Why not try to erase those old tapes by recording some new ones, in "New Messages"?

The power that drives us

The unconscious mind is a powerful force on your feelings and, therefore, your behaviors and attitudes. Those of you familiar with computers might want to think of it as your DOS, your disk operating system. The DOS of a computer, loaded when the machine is new, defines the environment and tells the other programs how to behave. Similar to a computer's DOS, your unconscious mind will give directions to your conscious mind, allowing you to start, stop, or continue a task. Much of the unconscious was "loaded" during your infancy and childhood, but new experiences throughout your life will add to it.

New messages

Think of some positive statements to give yourself and write them in the spaces below. You may want to use the same format that is used for affirmations. The rules for this include putting your name in the statement, making it positive rather than negative, and writing it as though it is already true. (Example: "I, Charlotte, am a capable decision maker," not "I, Charlotte, plan to stop making stupid decisions as soon as I get my degree.") Recite them to yourself often. Or read them into a tape recorder and listen to them while you're puttering around your home or relaxing.

Examples:
I, Sheila, am an attractive woman.
I, Darlene, can be anything I choose.
I, Barbara, value my mind as well as my body.

1.
2.
3.
4.
5.
6.

Go back and read your own positive messages one more time. Would these be appropriate beliefs to instill in your daughter?

How powerful is your unconscious mind? Have you ever found yourself reacting inappropriately to a given situation? When you can't explain your feelings or actions intellectually, they may be driven by your unconscious. For example, while having her car washed out of town recently, Mindy was physically assaulted by one of the attendants. It was very frightening, but it was only a brief episode, so she tried to forget the incident quickly. Though she was enraged, she told herself she was a strong person and could get over it.

She enjoys having a clean car, so having her car washed every time she fills it with gas is one of her small luxuries. For the next two months, though, she let this practice slide. She was simply too busy working on this book, she told herself, and didn't give the situation much thought until her mother needed to borrow the now filthy car on short notice.

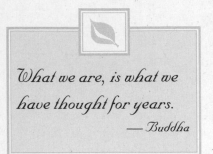

What we are, is what we have thought for years.

— *Buddha*

She raced to her regular car wash, but when she stopped at the pumps, she began to experience what felt like the beginning of a panic attack. Her heart started to pound, her palms began to sweat, and she felt sick to her stomach. In a panic, all she could think of was her need to get out of there.

She looked around and suddenly thought, Car wash! Then she remembered the assault. She stopped short. That brief but powerful experience had left its impression on her unconscious. She quickly reminded herself that this was not where the incident had taken place and that she was safe here. As quickly as the feeling had come upon her, it went away.

Because the incident at the car wash had occurred recently, Mindy was able to recall it and lessen its effect on her feelings and actions. But the experiences of infancy and childhood are often not that easily remembered. You may not understand why you react the way you do in certain circumstances even though consciously you know you would rather react differently. This phenomenon makes changing your behavior all the more difficult.

This book is about change: change in the way we think about our daughters, change in the way we parent them, and change in our feelings about what women can and can't do or be. In order for real change to occur, two things must happen first: a change in attitude, followed by a change in behavior; only then will we experience a change in our deepest feelings.

ATTITUDE

Reading this book may be enough to help you change any limiting attitudes you have about raising a daughter in today's world. We will present the facts and arguments for raising girls with hardy personalities who see themselves as capable and lovable human beings, and hope that you, too, will become strong proponents for this philosophy (if you aren't already).

BEHAVIOR

An attitudinal change alone will not make this happen. It might allow you to "talk a good game," but, as we said earlier, actions speak louder than words. If you really want things to be different for your daughter, you will probably have to change some of your behaviors as well. You will need new parenting strategies and techniques.

It will take energy, effort, planning, and persistence to change your behavior, but we have faith in you. We know you can do it. Expect to regress into old ways occasionally—everybody does, particularly early on in the process or when you're operating under stress—but don't give up. It's worth the effort.

And it will give you practice in the persistence you'll need to make the most difficult change of all, a change in the way you feel.

FEELINGS

Changing your feelings is a process of exploration, dialogue, and self-discovery. That is why we recommend various group activities throughout this book. Some people can go through uncomfortable feelings and transform themselves because they love someone else: perhaps your love for your daughter will be enough to see you through this challenging situation without help from anyone else. Others may choose to seek out professional help or counseling.

You may not be able to change your deepest emotional reactions. Your own past experiences may have made such a strong impression on you that no matter how well you understand the problem intellectually, you will not be able to overcome your feelings of anger, distrust, anxiety, or whatever. For your daughter's sake, though, we hope you will continue to modify your behavior. It will be a struggle for you, but we urge you to keep your goal in mind and keep trying.

Know, too, that promoting new attitudes and behaviors in your daughter is likely to feel uncomfortable at first, but remind yourself that what you are doing is in her own best interest.

I blew up at my daughter last night. I want her to be an independent woman who can make her own decisions, but when she came home late from her date I just lost it. I was a young man myself once, and memories of my own past behavior make me feel extremely protective of my daughter, so when she showed up late, I lost my temper instead of calmly pointing out that being late has certain consequences in our family.

— *Father of a teen*

In all affairs, love, religion, politics, or business, it's a healthy idea, now and then, to hang a question mark on things you have long taken for granted.

—*Bertrand Russell*

It was almost like a little bell went off in my head every time I heard my daughter react in an assertive manner to me. I actually had a physical reaction and felt a slight shock. I was raised never to talk back to my parents. Each time I had to control my automatic response, remind myself that this was not talking back, but rather a carefully crafted assertive response. It wasn't easy. I don't think I can ever change my feelings on this, but I do know I can change my behavior and I've worked hard to do it.

— Parent, 40

We hope we haven't made this all sound too daunting. It isn't easy, but the world your daughter faces is very different from the one you grew up in. To fail to give her the skills and attitudes required could greatly hinder her ability to experience a life of peace and satisfaction. For that reason it is extremely important that you persevere.

How do you feel about ...

Let's look at your feelings about equity for women, examine the facts about women and the world we live in, and then try to imagine the consequences of not changing to meet these challenges and not putting in the effort required to change your parenting strategies. Do the activities "Agree or Disagree?" and "Everyone Knows That . . ." (pages 29 and 30) before reading on.

Just the facts, please

If you marked "false" before each of the statements in "Everyone Knows That . . . ," give yourself a hand. You're better than most people at seeing the world the way it is. The media, politicians, employers, and others often, for their own purposes, present a different story, however. Not everyone has heard the facts.

The following statements and figures, each tied to one of the entries in "Everyone Knows That . . . ," are drawn from the latest available surveys and statistics.

1. Have women really made great strides toward equality? Hardly. As Susan Faludi says in her book Backlash: The Undeclared War Against American Women *(1991), "the last decade has seen a powerful counterassault on women's rights, a backlash, an attempt to retract*

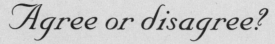

Agree or disagree?

The sentences below reflect some of the issues that will affect your daughter's life. What are your feelings about them? If you agree with them, mark them "A"; if you disagree, mark "D"; and if you are undecided, mark "U."

__ 1. Women should receive equal pay for equal work.

__ 2. An employer's parental leave policy should apply equally to men and women.

__ 3. Girls' athletics should receive the same attention and financial support as boys' athletics.

__ 4. Young people of both sexes should make career decisions based on their own abilities, values, and desires. The gender of most people currently employed in the occupation of choice is totally irrelevant.

__ 5. It is acceptable for either a man or a woman to stay home and provide primary care for the children.

__ 6. Whether or not a political candidate is qualified for office has nothing to do with his or her gender.

__ 7. Men and women have an equally important role to play in the raising of their children.

__ 8. Men and women should have an equally important role in financial support of the family.

__ 9. It is just as acceptable for a man to reveal his emotions as it is for a woman.

__10. Women should have as much opportunity as men to exercise personal power.

__11. Children should be encouraged and supported in their educational goals based on their desires, abilities, aptitudes, and commitment rather than on their gender.

__12. Laws should apply equally to men and women.

__13. Girls must be prepared to be economically self-sufficient and able to support a family on their own, if need be.

__14. I believe more choices for women will mean more choices for men.

If you agreed with all of the statements in "Agree or Disagree?" you believe in the political, economic, and social equality of women. Your attitudes will help build your daughter's self-esteem. If you disagreed with any of the statements, read "Everyone Knows That . . ." and "Just the Facts, Please."

Everyone knows that . . .

Indicate whether you think the statements below are true or false.

Everyone knows that:

T F 1. Women have made great strides in their fight for equality.
T F 2. The salary gap between men's and women's wages has been largely bridged.
T F 3. Women have moved out of traditional female occupations in huge proportions.
T F 4. Most employers are committed to women's advancement.
T F 5. The schools have come a long way toward achieving equal education for female students.
T F 6. Men are much more involved with their children and more helpful around the house than they used to be.
T F 7. Women are really more concerned about their personal life than they are about their work.
T F 8. Most women have not personally experienced sex discrimination on the job.
T F 9. Nearly all of the homeless people in the United States are men.
T F 10. The laws requiring divorced men to pay child support have been more stringently enforced in recent years, and as a result, single mothers can expect to receive more financial assistance from their ex-mates.

the handful of small and hard-won victories that the feminist movement did manage to win for women."

During the 1980s the Equal Rights Amendment was defeated, though national polls showed that nearly 60 percent of American women favored its adoption. In addition, there were serious reductions in a woman's right and access to reproductive choice, though it was supported by a majority of both sexes. Appointments of women to posts in the federal government decreased. Laws supporting maternal and child care were repeatedly defeated or vetoed.

Sexual violence, discrimination, and harassment increased dramatically, while funds to counteract these trends were cut. And there's more. Read on.

2. Women in this country face the "worst gender-based pay gap in the developed world," according to Faludi. According to Working Woman magazine, women earned 70 cents for every dollar earned by men in 1991. While the Economic Policy Institute reported that women's salaries equaled 77 percent of men's by 1993, the closing of the gap is attributed mostly to the fact that the average man's earnings fell by 10 percent between 1987 and 1993. More than four of every five women working at full-time jobs earn less than $20,000 a year. Only about half as many men fall into this category. Unless things change, your daughter will need a college degree just to be assured of earning as much as a man who only graduated from high school. With just a high school diploma, she will probably make less than a male high school dropout.

> *Modern poverty is not the poverty that was blessed in the Sermon on the Mount.*
> — George Bernard Shaw

In 1988 women could expect to earn the following figures for every dollar earned by their male counterparts: women college graduates—.59; black women—.59; older women—.58; Hispanic women—.54. Even when they work in the same occupations as men, women earn less. It seems, too, that as more women go to work in certain fields, the wage gap between the sexes actually gets wider. Working Woman magazine reported that since 1983 the gap has widened significantly among physicians, lawyers, financial managers, and other jobs traditionally held by men.

3. About 80 percent of working women in America still work as secretaries, administrative "support" workers, salesclerks, nurses, and teachers. The 1980s experienced an increase in the percentage of women in traditionally female-dominated fields, including retail sales, cleaning services, food preparation, bookkeeping, secretarial, administrative, and reception work. Women make up less than 8 percent of all federal and state judges, less than 6 percent of all law partners, and less than .5 percent of top corporate managers. According to the 1990 U.S. census, women constitute 97.8 percent of preschool and kindergarten teachers but just 22.6 percent of college economics instructors; 94.3 percent of registered nurses and 5.2 percent of mechanical engineers; 98.3 percent of dental hygienists and 12.8 percent of dentists. Women are 81.3 percent of apparel salespeople, but just 10.6 percent of the sales force for cars and boats. They are 3.6 percent of our airplane pilots, 15 percent of our architects, 12.9 percent of our physicists and astronomers, and 14 percent of our electrical technicians.

The figures, combined with the ones concerning the pay gap, illustrate *one of the central points of this book: Young women must take seriously the fact that they will need to work. Even with career training, women are paid less than men. Without training they are relegated to the "pink-collar ghetto," where they can expect to earn the minimum wage, where they will have little autonomy and next to no chance for advancement.*

4. Employers give lip service to women's advancement, but when human resource officers at Fortune 1000 companies were surveyed regarding their priorities in 1990, women's advancement was at the bottom of the list. Employers show their concern—or lack of it—in more concrete ways as well. Only 1 percent of private companies offers child care for its employees.

Perhaps this situation will have changed by the time your daughter enters the workforce, but for now it looks as though she will be largely on her own. Again, her career choice and training will have implications for her ability to have or care for a family.

5. According to a 1989 study, there is still sex discrimination in three-quarters of our high schools, despite a federal law banning the practice. Women receive less financial aid than male students in college, and although Title IX legislation demanding equity in school programs came into being twenty years ago, some colleges still spend as much on their football programs as they do on all women's sports combined.

Academic discrimination can be more subtle, but it is damaging nonetheless. Boys often "take over" the computer lab, and many girls are sufficiently intimidated to stay away. Girls may also be gently steered away from advanced math and science classes and channeled into more "feminine" pursuits. Teachers may tend to call on boys more often and challenge them to reason out the correct reply, while "rescuing" girls and providing the answers for them or giving neutral responses. If you make a habit of talking about school with your daughter, you may be able to discern whether any of these things are happening to her.

6. Men have received a lot of publicity over their supposedly renewed commitment to home and family, and we commend them and encourage them to keep it up, but, in fact, 70 percent of the housework is still done by women. Making an effort to distribute the work more equitably among everyone in your home could be beneficial for all. It will make life easier for the mom of the house, of course, but it will also communicate to children of both sexes that women are members of the family with equal rank, not servants.

This should help build your daughter's self-esteem and will earn you the undying gratitude of your future daughters-in-law as well. In addition, men who take on their share of the load become positive role models and demonstrate their respect for women and for the caregiving tasks too often devalued when performed by women.

7. Despite all the talk about man shortages, ticking biological clocks, infertility, and "the new traditionalism," when women are asked what issues concern them most, again and again they put equality on the job and in the home at the top of the list. Women want respect, and they want to be paid as men are—equal pay for equal work.

Once again, the political and economic consequences of being a woman come into play. In our society women are underpaid and undervalued. If they feel valued by their families, if they can come to value themselves, and if they are prepared to do a job that pays a living wage—even to women—things may work out well for them. If they do not learn to value themselves, however, they face difficulties in their futures. If they cannot support themselves financially, there are few safety nets in place to catch them. Perhaps that is why low-income women are more likely to support a women's rights agenda than are women with higher incomes.

8. Eighty to 95 percent of women workers indicate that they have been victims of sex discrimination and unequal pay.

Charges of sexual harassment, by the way, increased 70 percent during the last decade. Rape charges, too, have increased dramatically, though this is still alleged to be a greatly underreported crime.

With all this in mind, do you really want your little girl to be submissive and compliant?

9. The percentage of women among the homeless is growing faster than any other group. Why do women become homeless? Nearly half have taken to the streets to get away from domestic violence. (Funds for shelters have been cut dramatically in the past decade.) When you take this into consideration, along with the fact that many women do not have the skills that would allow them to earn a living wage, it's not surprising to learn that two-thirds of the poor adults in this country are women. When you're living on the edge, even a small push can have drastic consequences.

10. There was about a 25 percent decline in child support payments between the late 1970s and the mid-1980s. The average payment is $140 a month, less than an average car payment for most noncustodial parents. If half of all marriages end in divorce (they do) and 87 percent of single parents are women (they are), what are the chances that a woman unprepared to support herself will end up living in poverty? Better than you'd like to think.

Read these facts again, and imagine it's your daughter working for less pay, perhaps at a job well below her abilities, your daughter being denied that promotion, your little girl being sexually harassed or living in a cardboard box to escape the beatings of a violent partner. Then go back and reexamine the statements in "Agree or Disagree?" Changed your mind about anything?

How do you feel about feminism?

Quickly write your definition of feminism here:

What is your emotional reaction to the term? Circle how you feel.

Positive Negative Secure Anxious Supportive Angry Proud Threatened Determined Empowered Other _____

Do you agree or disagree with the following statement:

Women should have political, economic, and social rights equal to those of men.

Agree   Disagree   Undecided

The f-word

In a 1992 article for *The Washington Post*, writer Sally Quinn first defined feminism as "the principle that women should have political, economic, and social rights equal to those of men," which seems reasonable enough. She went on, though, to call it "a fringe cause, often with over-tones of lesbianism and man-hating." For the purposes of this book, we accept the first definition and consider the second assertion total nonsense. It is unfortunate that Quinn and others have helped to create a situation where many men and women who are in complete agreement with the sentiments of feminism are reluctant to use the word or accept the title. The fact that Susan Faludi's book *Backlash* was a major best-seller in 1992 is one indication that the issues are still relevant and concern is still strong among the public at large, whatever individuals choose to call themselves.

First person: "You aren't one of those feminists, are you?"
Second person: "Yes, I am."
First person: "Gee, you look so normal."
—Overheard conversation

Did you agree or disagree with the statement that women should have equal political, economic, and social rights? If you agreed, in theory you are a feminist. It's too bad that certain words have become so emotionally charged that their real meanings are lost or abandoned. Two words that have suffered a similar fate are "masculine" and "feminine."

How are men and women different?

A January 1992 cover story in *Time* magazine posed that ever-interesting question "Why are men and women different?" After eight pages of speculation, the article bravely concludes that "in the final analysis, it may be impossible to say where nature ends and nurture begins because the two are so intimately linked." In other words, we don't really know why men and women are different. Indeed, except in the most obvious biological ways, we aren't even sure that they are.

Still, most of us have some ingrained and socially sanctioned ideas about the character traits of a typical man or woman. What are yours? Do the activity "Typical Male, Typical Female" (pages 36 and 37).

Do all your charts look different? All the same? Any two the same? When psychologists Inge and Donald Broverman and their co-workers had seventy-nine psychologists complete a similar exercise (the results were published in the *Journal of*

Typical male, typical female

Below, we've listed a dozen characteristics in the left-hand column and the opposite traits in the column on the right. There are seven spaces between each pair of attributes, allowing you to indicate how you feel a typical man and women would rate on this scale. If you feel strongly that a typical male is independent rather than dependent, put a check in the left-hand column provided on the male chart. If you strongly believe that the opposite is true, make your mark in the far right-hand column. If you think the answer lies somewhere in between, mark what you believe to be the appropriate column.

How would you rate a typical male? Indicate your beliefs below.

TYPICAL MALE

Independent	_ _ _ _ _ _ _	Dependent
Self-reliant	_ _ _ _ _ _ _	Subservient
Aggressive	_ _ _ _ _ _ _	Submissive
Assertive	_ _ _ _ _ _ _	Yielding
Stoic	_ _ _ _ _ _ _	Emotional
Risk taker	_ _ _ _ _ _ _	Cautious
Competitive	_ _ _ _ _ _ _	Cooperative
Leader	_ _ _ _ _ _ _	Supporter
Strong	_ _ _ _ _ _ _	Gentle
Decisive	_ _ _ _ _ _ _	Indecisive
Forceful	_ _ _ _ _ _ _	Soft-spoken
Individualistic	_ _ _ _ _ _ _	Conformist
Analytical	_ _ _ _ _ _ _	Intuitive

TYPICAL FEMALE

Complete this chart to indicate how you would rate a typical female.

Independent	_	_	_	_	_	_	_	Dependent
Self-reliant	_	_	_	_	_	_	_	Subservient
Aggressive	_	_	_	_	_	_	_	Submissive
Assertive	_	_	_	_	_	_	_	Yielding
Stoic	_	_	_	_	_	_	_	Emotional
Risk taker	_	_	_	_	_	_	_	Cautious
Competitive	_	_	_	_	_	_	_	Cooperative
Leader	_	_	_	_	_	_	_	Supporter
Strong	_	_	_	_	_	_	_	Gentle
Decisive	_	_	_	_	_	_	_	Indecisive
Forceful	_	_	_	_	_	_	_	Soft-spoken
Individualistic	_	_	_	_	_	_	_	Conformist
Analytical	_	_	_	_	_	_	_	Intuitive

Okay, let's do this one more time, but with a slightly different angle. Complete the chart below in the same way, this time indicating how you believe a healthy adult would rate.

HEALTHY ADULT

Independent	_	_	_	_	_	_	_	Dependent
Self-reliant	_	_	_	_	_	_	_	Subservient
Aggressive	_	_	_	_	_	_	_	Submissive
Assertive	_	_	_	_	_	_	_	Yielding
Stoic	_	_	_	_	_	_	_	Emotional
Risk taker	_	_	_	_	_	_	_	Cautious
Competitive	_	_	_	_	_	_	_	Cooperative
Leader	_	_	_	_	_	_	_	Supporter
Strong	_	_	_	_	_	_	_	Gentle
Decisive	_	_	_	_	_	_	_	Indecisive
Forceful	_	_	_	_	_	_	_	Soft-spoken
Individualistic	_	_	_	_	_	_	_	Conformist
Analytical	_	_	_	_	_	_	_	Intuitive

[If I were a girl] I would become less out-going and more polite. I may become shy and be looked upon as a fragile glass doll.

—Boy in sex-role socialization study

Every time we liberate a woman, we liberate a man.

— Margaret Mead

Consulting and Clinical Psychology in 1970), they found that most participants—men and women alike—rated the typical male and the healthy adult very much the same. A typical woman, however, was rated more dependent, more passive, and more submissive. If your charts agree, your thinking is in line with what many psychological professionals thought in 1970.

But think about the message this sends to your daughter. If she senses (and she will) that you have one standard for women and another for mature, healthy adults, she is likely to be confused about your expectations for her. If she can't be both a woman and a mature adult, which one is she supposed to be? To be successful as a woman, must she stop striving to be independent, achieving, and strong and become submissive, supporting, and soft-spoken instead? What must it do to a young woman's sense of self-esteem when she's told to behave in a certain way when it's clear to her that these behaviors are the direct opposites of the traits valued by society?

Our co-author Susan was thirty-two years old when she said to her father, "I'd like to stop caring what you think, but I still care. And I know that you admire assertive, independent people, but you don't think women should be too assertive and independent, and I get very confused about that." Susan says her father did listen to that; he had to take a walk around the block to think about it, perhaps because he got a little tearful, and of course, he couldn't show her that!

Have you learned anything about yourself from this chapter? As you instigate your plan for your daughter, remember that if things are going to be different for her, they may have to be different for you as well.

chapter three

Redefining Femininity

What is your definition of femininity?

Write it below.

Where did your definition come from? Who or what influenced your thinking?

What is your definition of masculinity?

Who or what influenced your thinking about it?

Femininity is simply the quality or condition of being womanly, of conducting oneself in ways considered appropriate for women. Characteristics considered appropriate for women have varied, depending not only on what people have observed about women, but also on the needs of society at that time.

Definitions of femininity can be traced back thousands of years, to a time when women's role as childbearer, along with their smaller size, made them less suited than men to be hunters. Early men needed to feed their families; they wandered for days in search of game and killed large animals and dragged them home. Early women needed to nurture the next generation, so they remained close to home. They were also the primary gatherers of plant foods and were probably the inventors of agriculture and pharmacy. Both men and women contributed to the survival of the family and the tribe.

Times changed, but gender roles did not. In fact, among Europeans and their descendants in America, they became more constricting. With the rise of a large middle class during the nineteenth century, it became fashionable for newly prosperous men to imitate the upper classes by imposing "the ideal of the aristocratic, leisured lady on women of its own kind," according to Susan Brownmiller, author of *Femininity*.

It should be noted that lower-class women continued to work, as they had always done, and upper-class women still relegated most child care and many other "feminine" tasks to their servants. It was the new middle-class model that took hold, however, and philosophers and psychologists from Sigmund Freud to Erik Erikson have tried to prove that this man-made creation is, in fact, innate and unchangeable.

It seems likely, however, that what has been considered gender-role identification is really gender-role socialization. When girls and boys see adult women and adult men behaving in different ways, they learn what females and males are supposed to be like.

In order to develop an identity as a male or female, children imitate the behaviors of their same-sex parents or other same-sex role models. In addition, if young children are expected to exhibit certain personality traits, and if they are rewarded for doing so, they are likely to take on those characteristics as part of their identity. These are important points to keep in mind, beginning in your daughter's infancy.

Modeling and rewarding the limited gender roles of an earlier time effectively keeps women from controlling their own lives in today's world. It's really quite cruel, because if women feel compelled to live up to the old models of behavior, they will give up the right to be assertive, intelligent, or independent. Once that's happened, they are left without access to high-

I remember when my brother Billy saw a man smoking and said, in horror, "Men don't smoke! Ladies smoke!" He was four, and he'd only seen my mother smoke.

— Woman, 51

paying jobs or positions of power and authority. And we all know the consequences of that.

Traditionally, femininity has been categorized around the following themes:

1. *Giving service*
2. *Developing a nonthreatening personality*
3. *Cultivating beauty and sex appeal*

Did your definition of femininity match or have examples with these three themes? What other themes did your definition include?

Listed below are some of the earlier experts in gender-role identity, along with their definitions of masculinity and femininity. Keep in mind that these are the "experts" who probably influenced the way you were raised and therefore the way you think. Do you think these are still commonly held beliefs? How will your daughter's future be limited if she is expected to live within these definitions?

PARSON & BALES, 1955

Masculinity: An instrumental orientation that gets the job done or problem solved.

Femininity: An expressive orientation concerned with the welfare of others and the harmony of the group.

ERIKSON, 1964

Masculinity: A fondness for what works and for what man can make, whether it helps to build or destroy.

Femininity: A more "ethical" feminine commitment to resourcefulness in peace-keeping and devotion to healing.

BAKAN, 1966

Masculinity: A concern for oneself as an individual.

Femininity: A concern for relationships between oneself and others.

Like the term *feminist*, the meaning of the word *feminine* has become muddled. Did you have trouble coming up with definitions? Historically people associated it with everything sweet and soft-spoken, gentle and trusting, but in fact, it means

Crude classifications and false generalizations are the curse of organized human life.

—*H. G. Wells*

A foolish consistency is the hobgoblin of little minds.

—*Ralph Waldo Emerson*

nothing of the kind. It simply means the activities and characteristics of females.

Every person needs to develop a gender identity, a sense of herself or himself as female or male. Part of gender identity for women involves valuing her female body as it is different from a male body.

But by definition everything a female person does or is capable of doing can be considered feminine. If your daughter wants to paint her toenails, fine. That's a feminine thing to do. But why limit femininity? Scaling a mountain, fixing the plumbing, or flying to the moon can be equally feminine if your daughter chooses to do them.

But traditional ideas of sex differentiation held that the sexes ought to be as different psychologically as they are physically. Yet the "Typical Male, Typical Female" survey described in the preceding chapter ("What Attitudes, Experiences, and Feelings Do You Bring to Parenting?") reported that the characteristics of a healthy person in this society are not those traditionally considered feminine.

Therefore, in today's society a woman needs the instrumental traits traditionally described as masculine, such as assertiveness, independence, the ability to defend one's own beliefs, analytical skill, self-reliance, and decision-making competence. However, you will rightfully argue, doesn't she also need some of the expressive traits traditionally described as feminine, such as sensitivity, compassion, loyalty, warmth, love of children, and concern for others? And doesn't a man need these traits, too?

So what is a strategy for developing new ideals of womanliness and manliness, ideals that move in the direction of adopting all the human traits necessary for survival of our children and of all humankind?

Is androgyny the answer?

"Androgyny" has had the misfortune of being another one of those words most people reject without understanding. It seems to have become associated with some fuzzy notions of appearance: women with facial hair and men wearing eye makeup and the like. Truthfully, though, it has nothing to do with hermaphrodites or neutered beings of any kind.

Androgyny is a combination of instrumental (traditional masculine) and expressive (traditional feminine) characteristics within one person. It has nothing to do with appearance but pertains only to behaviors one displays.

It is a condition—an ideal, perhaps—allowing both men and women more flexibility in the roles they play and the characteristics they embody.

Androgyny means that any action or trait is not limited to a particular sex, and that an individual may or should—at different times and under different circumstances—exhibit either or both expressive and instrumental traits. An ordinarily independent and self-reliant man, for example, may become totally dependent on his wife's care in the event of a serious illness. A woman who sensitively nurtures her children at home can be tough enough to police the streets, prosecute criminals, or stand up to an exploitative boss.

Truthfully, haven't we moved strongly toward adrogyny in recent years? A century ago it was unthinkable for a women to enter the professions or to vote, much less to run for political office. And when did it become acceptable for men—professional athletes and coaches, at that—to show emotion or even to cry on national TV? The changes go much deeper, of course. In today's society there are thousands of roles to fill, and you have probably taken on several of them. Think about it. Do you behave the same way with your employer as you do with your spouse? Chances are a certain amount of androgyny has crept into your life already.

It may seem more natural to promote only traditionally "feminine" behavior in your daughter, but there's powerful evidence that this is not in her best interest. Numerous studies, most of them conducted in the 1960s, before the second stage of the feminist movement, showed that women who rate high on the traditional scale of femininity suffer from high anxiety, low self-esteem, and low social approval. Moreover, women who exhibit androgynous traits tend to have a higher self-esteem and better mental health than their stereotypically feminine sisters. In light of these facts it seems reasonable to believe that your daughter will be happier and more successful if she incorporates the "masculine" instrumental traits into her personality along with the "feminine" expressive ones.

The truth is, a great mind must be androgynous.
— Samuel Taylor Coleridge

What is most beautiful in virile men is something feminine; what is most beautiful in feminine women is something masculine.
— Susan Sontag

The Bem studies

In 1974, also in the *Journal of Consulting and Clinical Psychology*, Dr. Sandra Bem, a Stanford University psychologist, proffered some interesting new ideas based on her own survey, known as the Bem Sex-Role Inventory. She began by asking panels of men and women to rate lists of characteristics according to their desirability in men and in women, and her results were quite similar to the Brovermans'. She was able to identify twenty personality characteristics defined as masculine by men and twenty defined as feminine by women.

What follows is a sampling of the lists of masculine and feminine characteristics Dr. Bem noted in her surveys. Her survey presents both the feminine and masculine characteristics as positive domains of behavior.

MASCULINE CHARACTERISTICS

Acts like a leader
Ambitious
Assertive
Competitive
Defend my own beliefs

Independent
Individualistic
Self-reliant
Self-sufficient
Willing to take risks

FEMININE CHARACTERISTICS

Affectionate
Cheerful
Gentle
Gullible
Loyal

Sensitive to the needs of others
Shy
Soft-spoken
Understanding
Yielding

But Dr. Bem took her study a step farther. She asked individuals to rate their own personal preferences and tendencies. The results were astounding at the time, though they make sense in retrospect. While people are quite prepared to stereotype others by saying that women are one way and men are another, they do not stereotype themselves.

Men who rated high on the "masculinity" scale might also have such "feminine" traits as being gentle and understanding. Women, too, could be both tender and aggressive, dependent and independent, in turn. Others had insisted on an "either/or" definition of masculine or feminine. The terms—and all of the personality traits associated with them—were considered mutually exclusive. Dr. Bem's study showed that there are two independent personality dimensions involved here, and it is very possible for people to embody many traits from both sides. Those who have both masculine and feminine traits, in fact, are likely to be better adjusted and to have higher levels of self-esteem than those who are weighted in one way or the other. Dr. Bem called these people psychologically androgynous.

In further studies she set out to discover whether and how gender roles affect behavior. Bem defined participants in these experiments as feminine women and men (those scoring high on the feminine scale but low in masculine traits), masculine women and men (who rated high on the masculine scale, low on the feminine side), and androgynous men and women (who rated high on both scales).

The first experiment involved asking subjects to perform a variety of tasks under the pretense that photographs were needed for a different study. Participants were allowed to choose between pairs of activities and were offered payment for each— but the pay was always higher for the activity that went against his or her stereotypical sex role. For example, a feminine woman was offered more money to nail two boards together than she would receive for ironing napkins.

Even though subjects were assured that they needn't be competent at any task they selected, and that no one they knew was likely to ever see the photographs, even though instructions were available for each activity and participants were encouraged to perform a wide variety of tasks, the masculine men and the feminine women tended to stick with the activities they viewed as appropriate for their gender, even when it cost them money. Neither the androgynous participants nor the feminine men and masculine women responded in this way.

When these subjects were told which activities to perform, the feminine women and masculine men again indicated discomfort in cross-sex roles. According to Bem, "It would appear . . . that traditional sex roles do produce an unnecessary and perhaps even dysfunctional pattern of avoidance for many people."

In another study, this one designed to measure independence, Bem told subjects that they were taking part in an experiment on humor. Participants were asked to rate the funniness of a series of cartoons that had actually been selected by independent judges as being either very funny or not at all funny. Before stating their evaluations, participants heard what they believed were the reactions of others, each giving a false response, saying the funny cartoons were not funny, and vice versa.

Feminine males and females tended to conform to group opinion, while androgynous and masculine subjects retained their independence.

In order to study nurturing, Bem observed participants who were left in a room with a kitten and told to interact with it in any way they liked. Here, androgynous women were most responsive to the kitten, feminine women were least responsive, and masculine women rated somewhere in the middle. Bem concluded, "It is the feminine woman who, at this juncture, appears to be the most restricted."

To give these subjects an opportunity to prove her wrong, Bem conducted two more studies. One asked participants to interact with a baby, the other study had them listen to fellow students who were expressing their unhappiness and discussing their problems.

While the feminine women expressed more interest in nurturing the baby, Bem found that they were no more affectionate than the masculine or androgynous women in their actions. When it came to responding to another student, however, the feminine women were better listeners than anyone else. This seemed to verify Bem's hunch that "feminine women might simply be insufficiently assertive to act out their nurturing feelings in a situation where they must take responsibility for initiating and sustaining the interaction, and that they might display much greater nurturing if they were permitted to play a more passive or responsive role."

Here are descriptions of the six types of individuals Bem studied:

Androgynous man: He functions well in all areas of his life.
Feminine man: He functions well in relationships, less competently in
    other aspects of his life.

Masculine man: Here is your standard "macho" male, good at performing
    tasks but unable to function well in relationships.

Which of these men would you want as your employer or employee? Which would you choose as a spouse or partner?

Androgynous woman: Like her male counterpart, she functions effectively
    in all areas of her life.

Masculine woman: She, too, is competent in both domains. "This suggests
    that growing up female in our society may be sufficient to give virtually
    all women at least an adequate threshold of emotional responsiveness,"
    according to Bem.

Feminine woman: Here is your conformist, your "people pleaser." As Bem
    reports, "The major effect of femininity in women—untempered by a suf-
    ficient level of masculinity—may not be to inhibit instrumental or mas-

culine behaviors per se, but to inhibit any behavior at all in a situation where the 'appropriate' behavior is left ambiguous or unspecified."

Feminine women play it safe. They take no risks that might elicit criticism from their peers. The consequences of this conforming behavior can include avoiding challenging subjects in school; giving in to peer pressure regarding drug use, sexual activity, and the like; setting lower standards for academic and professional achievement; or failing to leave an abusive boyfriend or husband.

As we said earlier, androgyny is not as popular a concept as it was in the 1970s. Perhaps all those negative associations got in the way, or maybe it was simply too threatening for traditionalists. Some studies suggest that certain "masculine" traits are a better predictor of psychological well-being than is androgyny.

But the concept of behavioral or psychological androgyny still seems eminently useful to us for the purpose of helping you raise your daughter in today's world, and we hope that you will include the encouragement of androgynous traits as a part of the action plan you will outline for your daughter at the back of this book. What we're talking about, really, is simply the ability to develop a range of behaviors (not based on gender stereotypes) and then choose a behavior that is most appropriate in a given situation. Simply by being aware of these concepts, you, as a parent, are in a good position to promote a wide range of behaviors in your daughter. We hope you will give her permission to explore all parts of her personality, beginning now, whatever her present age. How do you do that? Throughout the rest of this book we will give you suggestions on how to help your daughter develop the full range of characteristics.

One way at home, one way at work

There's yet another study that reports some interesting observations about stereotypically masculine and feminine behavior. This one, conducted in Australia, found that the most successful people on the job, male or female, were those who could respond from their "masculine" side. This was not surprising. More interesting was the finding that couples in which each partner rated high on the feminine scale (high feminine female or male or androgynous individual) reported the happiest relationships and highest life satisfaction.

Let's look at a list of personality traits. Before reading on, circle those traits you can identify as your own.

1. self-reliant
2. independent
3. assertive
4. commanding
5. analytical
6. risk-taker
7. self-sufficient
8. aggressive
9. a leader
10. competitive
11. ambitious
12. physically energetic
13. adaptable
14. conscientious
15. reliable
16. trusting
17. yielding
18. cheerful
19. supportive
20. affectionate
21. loyal
22. sympathetic
23. nurturing
24. compassionate
25. diplomatic
26. tender
27. loves children
28. sincere

The first twelve items are the instrumental traits formerly considered "masculine" and, therefore, would be used most appropriately on the job. Items thirteen through sixteen are associated with both sexes (neuter) and could probably be used profitably both on the job and in private. The remaining traits are expressive traits, usually categorized as "feminine," and could be used effectively by both men and women in building and maintaining personal relationships.

In her work as a therapist, Susan has found that many men run into trouble at home, and many women on the job, because they are trying to act the same in both places. Women frequently complain that men don't take time to enjoy the process of conversation or of love-making; they want to get to the point. Men, on the other hand, complain that women on the job act as if the process of working hard is as important as the result. Neither has learned to vary their behavior to suit the environment.

Review your responses. Which of these traits did you use to describe yourself? They are all positive characteristics for both sexes, so why not try to expand your repertoire?

The strategy of being one way at work and another at home has been important to Mindy and Jim, both high-energy entrepreneurs. When they first started going out, they worked up a plan to temper their "strengths," as they both tended to display mostly masculine traits. They decided, for example, that each time they got together they would make it a point to remember and try to display appropriate relationship (feminine) characteristics. They would remind each other when either slipped into a

When she stopped conforming to the conventional picture of femininity, she finally began to enjoy being a woman.

— Betty Friedan

more achievement-oriented mode. Today the ability to switch gears has become especially important to them because, besides living together as husband and wife, they also work together as publishers of textbooks dedicated to educational reform. While they are in the office or a work situation they can be aggressive, decisive, individualistic, forceful, and independent, even with each other. But at home both rely on their relationship side—empathizing, listening, communicating, and sharing. It took awareness, then understanding, and then trial and error to change their behaviors, but they feel that the happiness and satisfaction they have gained made their efforts well worthwhile.

You and your partner might benefit from trying a similar experiment—and so will your daughter. By modeling these behaviors yourselves, you will have a powerful effect on her perception of what it means to be a woman and what it means to be a couple in today's society, with its more egalitarian ideal.

What's appropriate?

Need some practice? The following exercise might help. Consider the following situations and check the most appropriate response. Can you see how a behavior or response that is entirely appropriate at home is inappropriate at the office, and vice versa?

AT HOME

Your spouse takes up golf so you can spend more time together. On the course you are:

Competitive: Everytime you play, you play to win.

Supportive: You play to the level of your partner and provide any assistance needed.

AT WORK

You've been asked to bid an important job. You know the company in competition with you is new in town. Your bid is:

Competitive: You do everything you can to make sure you get the job.

Supportive: You bid so that the other company has an equal chance at getting the job. After all, they're new in town and could probably use the work.

AT HOME

Your "all thumbs" spouse tries to fix the sink. The pipe breaks and the kitchen is flooded. Your reaction is:

Analytical: "Lee, you don't know anything about plumbing. Why didn't you call the plumber?"

Diplomatic: "Well, at least you tried. Let's call the plumber."

AT WORK

Your "all thumbs" employee tries to fix the computer. As a result, the mother board is destroyed. Your reaction is:

Analytical: "Lee, you don't know anything about fixing computers. Why didn't you call the repair service?"

Diplomatic: "Well, at least you tried. Let's call the repair service."

AT HOME

You need your spouse to be more helpful with family responsibilities and household chores. While you work, your spouse spends the evening in front of the television. Should you be:

Aggressive: "I am feeling taken advantage of and this has got to stop."

Diplomatic: "Sweetheart, I know you need your rest, but do you think it's fair that I don't get any?"

AT WORK

You need more help from your co-workers on a team assignment. While you've been staying at work through the evening for weeks, everyone else goes home on time. Should you be:

Aggressive: "I am feeling taken advantage of and this has got to stop."

Diplomatic: "Hey guys, do you think we can share the workload more fairly?"

AT HOME

While you are visiting a large city, your car is broken into and your spouse's luggage is stolen. Included in the luggage are important family heirlooms. Should you be:
Analytical: "You should have known better than to leave your luggage in full view."
Nuturing: "I'm so sorry. I know how important those pieces were to you."

AT WORK

While your employee is visiting a large city, the company car is broken into and the luggage is stolen. Included in the luggage are important business records. Should you be:
Analytical: "You should have known better than to leave your luggage in full view."
Nuturing: "I'm so sorry. I know how important those items were."

Think back to a recent incident at work or with your partner in which your manner of communication didn't seem to work. Review the list of personality traits. What style were you using? Are you beginning to see why it's important for your daughter to develop both sides of her personality? Keep these traits in mind as you read the next chapters on helping your daughter become an achiever, build a strong identity, and develop a hardy personality.

What traits do you most want to encourage in your daughter?

List them below and make them part of your game plan. (Hint: In most cases you can count on peer pressure and popular culture to push for the "feminine" traits. You will have to provide more support for her to develop the others.)

I would like my daughter to develop the following traits:

1. _____

2. _____

3. _____

4. _____

5. _____

6. _____

7. _____

8. _____

9. _____

10. _____

11. _____

12. _____

Resolving the Conflict
Women Feel Between
Femininity and Achievement

*I*n the spring of 1969, as a San Diego State University freshman, Mindy was directed to write an essay for English class on the issue that most troubled her. She was shocked at the title that instantly came to her. Though she'd never heard of the women's movement or of Betty Friedan or Simone de Beauvoir, she sat down to write a paper entitled "The Conflict Between Femininity and Intelligence."

As she explored her thoughts and feelings, she realized that she had downplayed her intelligence and creativity so she would not appear unfeminine. Somehow she had received the message that she could not be both brainy and womanly. Mindy decided to reject that idea. From that point on, her grades soared, as did her self-esteem and ambitions for the future. She changed her major from elementary education to preveterinary medicine and went on to earn a bachelor of science degree.

Looking back at her past, Mindy can see where she first started feeling the conflict between femininity and achievement. Until sixth grade she was quite proud of her straight-A average. Then she started to notice boys and was soon going steady . . . the "in" thing to do. Her boyfriend was good-looking and the best athlete in the class, what was called "a real catch," and she enjoyed the status that seemed to confer on her. He was also not a very good student. One day her closest girlfriend took Mindy aside and told her that according to her older sister, it wasn't very wise to be smarter than your boyfriend. She warned Mindy she would probably lose her boyfriend if she didn't change her ways.

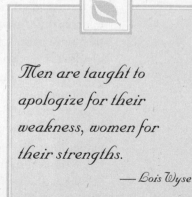

Men are taught to apologize for their weakness, women for their strengths.

— Lois Wyse

He did break up with her, and it didn't take long for Mindy to figure out that the girls who got the attention of the boys were pretty, pleasing, and passive. The smart girls were thought of as geeks and not feminine. Well, she was bright enough to be dumb. By the time she left junior high school, her grades were only average.

In burying her intelligence, Mindy was in good company. A 1960 study on bright children who become underachievers found that girls who don't work up to their potential had, in the first grade, a higher grade-point average than any other group. They tended to do well throughout grade school. Then, at about the time they entered junior high, their grades began to fall and fell consistently throughout the remainder of their high school careers. On the other hand, the achievement of the girls who were average students held steady, and some even grew academically. More recent studies confirm that not much has changed.

The struggles of adolescence

As adults, we can read the evidence in chapter 3 ("Redefining Femininity") and conclude that, indeed, our daughters need to develop both traits considered masculine and those considered feminine in order to thrive in today's world. Our daughters, however, cannot just look dispassionately at the evidence and come to logical conclusions. When they reach adolescence, they are faced with a peer culture that demands more conformity to stereotypical male and female roles than at any other time in their lives.

Adolescence is a time for all young people, male and female, to come to terms with their identities. Young males are particularly anxious and uncertain about their masculinity. As they struggle with their feelings about what it means to be a man, they tend to seek young women who are stereotypically "feminine." The passive, dependent, supportive female complements, bolsters, and does not challenge their aggressive, independent, masterful ways.

Equally important, young females enforce conformity among themselves. In Mindy's story above, it was a girl who told Mindy to get her act together and fit in. It was a girl who indicated that having a certain boyfriend was more important than achieving.

Consciously or unconsciously, young women are very much aware of what's considered more important. As we've seen, the brighter girls in grade school are the ones most likely to abandon their achievement-oriented behavior in secondary school.

Even those who disagree with the system have a hard time standing up to it. When Susan's daughter was twelve, they went to hear Naomi Wolf talk about her book *The Beauty Myth*, which says that girls grow up to believe image is more important than substance (we'll talk about this book more in chapter 19, "Mirror, Mirror, on the Wall"). Carla loved the lecture and agreed with everything Wolf said. But on the way home she suddenly began crying and said, "I want to think the way she does, but I can't right now."

Either / or thinking

Unless you have been careful to teach your daughter otherwise, she is likely to think of traditional "feminine" and "masculine" qualities in either/or terms, rather than as characteristics that can peacefully exist side by side in one person. Even if she knows, like Susan's daughter, that a variety of characteristics is desirable, she may feel alone and afraid no one will like her if she continues to display that variety. Wanting to be liked by other girls and to attract boys, she may be tempted to give up all of her achievement-oriented behaviors at precisely the time she will need to select school courses and make plans that will determine her future as a self-sufficient adult.

If your daughter gives up her achievement-oriented behaviors, it could have dire consequences for her future happiness. As they enter ninth grade, for example, a large percentage of talented and bright young women elect not to take the school courses that will lead to a career that will allow them to be economically independent. Many girls affect their future by choosing not to take higher-level math. This simple choice eliminates more than half of the possible college majors. Those majors could lead to potential careers from which young women may someday want to choose, including most higher-paying jobs.

If your daughter is more concerned about fitting in with girls and appealing to boys than she is about her studies, her life script may be written much too early.

Dad's role in supporting his daughter's achievement-oriented behaviors

As the most important man in your daughter's life to date, your assurance that she is feminine and attractive will go a long way. If she doesn't get your attention and approval, she is likely to seek it among boys her own age, perhaps at the cost of giving up her goals for achievement.

Susan's father helped her continue to excel in school throughout adolescence. While his reasoning offends her now, it probably helped her then. He said that it was important that she do well in school and go on to Stanford because she would need to be able to talk with the man she married. By implication, he told her that men wanted women who were their intellectual equals.

Fathers who were raised to be achievement oriented are excellent at modeling achievement. By becoming actively involved with her education, encouraging her accomplishments, and serving as her mentor, Dad, you can demonstrate that not all males expect her to be helpless and incompetent.

Don't try to tell her that boys are not important or that they don't care what she looks like. If you try to do that, she is likely to distrust all other things you have to say on the subject. Don't make her choose between love and achievement; encourage her to have both. Like Susan's father, you can show that she actually needs brains to get along with a man. Being intelligent and accomplished is attractive to an accomplished and intelligent male.

You can start by changing the clichés we use to describe our daughters. Next time your daughter is introduced to a new adult, note what that person says to her in welcome. What you are most likely to hear is something like

"Oh what a lovely little girl [or young woman]."
"Aren't you cute!"
"Isn't she sweet?"
"What gorgeous red hair you have."

If you hear a statement that recognizes only her appearance or personality, jump in with approval for other characteristics such as

"Yes, and she is smart and strong as well."

"Yes, and she's very clever and creative."

"Yes, and she's a really great chess player."

Your daughter *can* have it both ways. Next time she comes running into your arms, besides saying "Don't you look pretty," add a statement that recognizes her achievement capabilities, such as "And that's a terrific model airplane you just made." This will help her recognize that she can be competent and achieving as well as pretty and appealing.

Changing our language and labels

"Feminine," "masculine"—these are emotionally charged words. Challenging someone's femininity or masculinity is a sure way to cause an upset. We talk about "real" men and "real" women, as if some of us—the "real" ones—actually exist and the rest of us are mere illusions. We ask if someone is "man enough" or "woman enough" when we want to suggest that he or she is in some way inadequate.

When we do these things, we are usually not talking about sex at all, but rather about outmoded gender roles. It is "masculine" to be aggressive, logical, and ambitious; it is "feminine" to be submissive, emotional, dependent. Dr. Sandra Bem has suggested (wisely, we think) that "the best gender-role identity is no gender-role identity."

It is important, then, to stop using the words *feminine* or *masculine*, the phrases *woman enough* or *man enough*. Instead use terms that describe specific traits, defusing the emotions connected with these terms.

Sometimes, though, you may want a word to describe a whole category of behaviors. Look back at the Bem list of masculine and feminine characteristics, in the last chapter ("Redefining Femininity"). If you were in charge of coming up with replacement words for "masculine" and "feminine," what would you use?

A number of other ways have been suggested to describe these characteristics. They include

Instrumental and expressive
Professional and personal
External and internal
Logical and emotional
Achievement and relationship

You decide which terms work best for you. For the purpose of this book, we will refer to them from this point forward as achievement (masculine) traits and relationship (feminine) traits.

Your job, if you hope to raise a daughter who will resist the pressure to give up her achievement-oriented behavior in favor of her relationships, is to help her understand that she has a full complement of characteristics from both lists from which to draw. The important thing for her to consider is not whether a particular quality is masculine or feminine, but whether it is appropriate for the circumstance. To demonstrate this fact, discuss with her how she would react to the situations in "What to Do?" on page 59.

If you can convince your daughter to value and use all of her traits and talents, she is sure to have a fuller, more rewarding life. How will you convince her of this? By your actions as well as your words. Start now to let go of any gender-role stereotypes you've previously endorsed.

Overcoming gender-role stereotyping

It's a bit confusing, but basically here is the difference between a gender role and a sex role: Gender roles are those that our culture tells us are correct for men or women, respectively. Sex roles, on the other hand, have to do with the biological differences between males and females. Gender roles are learned and quite often are based on gender stereotypes. Many people still believe that gender roles are based on biology, but there is little basis for that in fact.

(We're talking about gender-role identity and stereotyping, not sexual identity. Sexual identity—the healthy awareness of being biologically male or female—develops by the time a child is three years old. A girl should be comfortable with her body and her sex as part of a healthy sexual identity. Neither you nor she should confuse her social behaviors with her sexual identity.)

What to do?

How would your daughter say she should proceed in these situations?

If she's home alone when the family dog is hit by a car, it would be best to
  a. stop where she is and cry helplessly.
  b. think the situation through and call the animal hospital, then assertively ask the neighbors for a ride.

If she wants to get a job at the public library, it would be most effective to
  a. give in to her shyness and sit quietly at home.
  b. overcome her shyness and ask for the job.

If her best friend is brokenhearted about losing her boyfriend, it would be most helpful to
  a. be forceful and tell her to stop feeling sorry for herself.
  b. be sympathetic and try to cheer her up.

What would be the appropriate *qualities* to draw on in the following situations? (See the list on page 48 for suggestions.)

Walking alone across a dark parking lot late at night

Caring for a newborn infant

Receiving an offensive phone call

Trying out for the basketball team

Visiting a sick friend

Getting a roommate to do her share of the chores

Ending a relationship

While attempting to attract a mate is a primal, basic instinct associated with sexual identity, the gender-role identity young women assume is not biologically determined. It is based, instead, on centuries of conditioning and cultural mandates. In the past, survival of the species depended on a population of strong men—hunters who were often away from home for extended periods of time—and nurturing women who, by default, were left alone to care for their children and devote themselves totally to their infants' needs, putting their own needs aside. At that time women often started bearing children at puberty and continued giving birth regularly throughout their own short adult lives. Few women had opportunities to do more.

While most experts still agree that during infancy a child's needs must come before those of its parents, today the average American family has only two children. The amount of time required for nurturing infants and toddlers has shrunk to a small percentage of one's life. The average life span, on the other hand, has increased dramatically—to about seventy-eight years for women. Since most families now need two wage earners to support a middle-class life-style, the need and opportunity for women to develop and use their achievement skills is undeniable. For a contemporary mother, part of caring for her children is functioning effectively in the work world as well as at home.

Likewise, fathers need to nurture at home as well as produce at work, because the attention of both parents is important to children's healthy development. For both sexes today it is imperative to be less gender stereotyped and more psychologically androgynous.

But old habits are hard to break. What makes it so difficult for your daughter to display her talents for achievement along with her talents for relationship? Children of both sexes learn at an early age that

women are primary caretakers _ _ _ _ _ _ _ _ men are primary breadwinners
women are submissive _ _ _ _ _ _ _ _ _ _ _ _ men are aggressive
women serve _ _ _ _ _ _ _ _ _ _ _ _ _ _ _ _ _ _ men lead
women cry _ _ _ _ _ _ _ _ _ _ _ _ _ _ _ _ _ _ _ men yell
women wield mops_ _ _ _ _ _ _ _ _ _ _ _ _ _ men wield power
women are valued for their appearance _ _ _ men are valued for what they do

Do gender-stereotyped roles still reign in your household? Take "The Thanksgiving Test."

The Thanksgiving test

Think back to a recent Thanksgiving dinner, then read the following paragraph and circle the parenthesized words that most closely relate to your experience.

The day started early for (Mom) (Dad), who got up to put the turkey in the oven while the rest of the family took advantage of the holiday and slept late. When the guests arrived, the (women) (men) gathered in front of the TV to watch football while the (women) (men) set the table and finished making dinner. As ceremonial head of the family, (Mom) (Dad) carved the turkey, but (Mom and Grandma) (Dad and Grandpa) did most of the actual serving. (Aunt Eunice) (Uncle Elmo) told an off-color story, and (Aunt Eunice) (Uncle Elmo) was mortified, but (Mom) (Dad) just laughed and (Mom) (Dad) tried to make everyone have a third helping of potatoes. After dinner (Aunt Eunice) (Uncle Elmo) passed out cigars and the (women) (men) went back to the TV. The (girls) (boys) went out to play touch football, and the (girls and women) (boys and men) cleaned up and did the dishes.

Under each statement below, give an example of how girls today learn these gender-role stereotypes. Then think of how you could show your daughter some other possibilities.

Women are primary caretakers.   Men are primary breadwinners.

_____   _____

Women are submissive.   Men are aggressive.

_____   _____

Women serve.   Men lead.

_____   _____

Women cry.   Men yell.

_____   _____

Women wield mops.   Men wield power.

_____   _____

Women are valued for their appearance.   Men are valued for themselves.

_____   _____

Have some warning lights gone off in your head? Now's the time to put some of those alternative messages to use.

A new feminine identity

Despite the need for attention to their own goals as well as those of others, young women still learn to be more "in touch" with other people's feelings and needs than they are with their own. If they don't have infants to care for, they devote the same kind of nurturing to their mate or to other friends and family members, seldom stopping to think whether their own needs are being met. They measure their worth entirely in terms of their responsiveness to others.

A woman can do anything. She can be traditionally feminine and that's all right; she can work, she can stay at home; she can be aggressive, she can be passive; she can be any way she wants with a man. But whenever there are the kinds of choices there are today, unless you have some solid base, life can be frightening.

—Barbara Walters

Consequently, too many young women grow up without boundaries or self-defined limits, and this can get them into trouble. If their friends' wishes come before their own, and if their friends want them to skip school or forget about that nerdy calculus class, they do what their friends want. If their boyfriends' needs come first, and their boyfriends want them to have sex, it is almost impossible for them to say no. (We'll address this later when discussing the hardy personality.)

A young woman whose only identity is the traditional feminine one learns to dismiss those qualities in herself that do not fit into that limiting mold. Unfortunately, they are the very characteristics necessary for lifelong achievement, self-esteem, and self-sufficiency. A woman who identifies herself solely on the basis of her relationships to others is, by definition, "nobody" when she is by herself. And, sooner or later, everyone is alone.

According to Professor Sally Archer, females are socialized to be what they think others want them to be. Thus the mixed messages they receive about what is appropriate behavior for them is a major problem as they strive to develop their identity. Trying to be "good girls," they seek the approval of others and define themselves accordingly. But using external standards to determine their self-worth is a losing game that leaves them empty inside. Instead of building an inner sense of who they are, they become people pleasers, and when they inevitably discover they can't please everyone, they become frustrated and discouraged. The result for these young women, says Archer, is that their "internal core of self is never going to be strong enough."

When parents and others begin to recognize their daughter's achievement ("masculine") characteristics—her skills and accomplishments—they provide another path, however. The mixed messages may still be coming in from society at large, but receiving recognition for her successes at home helps to lessen their effect. Archer points out that the problem is not that girls are not achieving, but that they receive praise and recognition mostly for their other traits. "It's not that they aren't performing," she says, "but that they don't use that performance to define themselves."

This does not mean that they should abandon their feminine selves and become honorary males. Girls and women can still be nurturing and empathetic, but they can be much more. The historical reasons for men to be "manly" and women to be "womanly" are no longer valid. The modern world has presented us with a wonderful opportunity for everyone to have and to use a full spectrum of behaviors. Just as no one should have to deny a loving nature, everyone should be free to embrace the desire to scale mountains, build bridges, or conquer disease.

Once we encouraged young women to base their identities on their gender roles. Our new goal must be to help our daughters find their identities as individuals—to see relationships and achievements not as limitations, but as parts of who they know themselves to be.

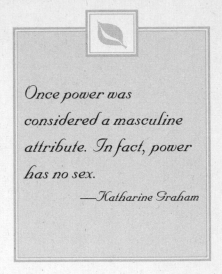

Once power was considered a masculine attribute. In fact, power has no sex.

—Katharine Graham

chapter five

Forming an Identity as an Achiever

By now you've probably noticed that certain terms keep popping up in our discussion. Achievement, identity, self-esteem—all are crucial to your daughter's physical and emotional well-being. Although we're explaining each of them separately, they really build on each other. Achievement helps consolidate identity, with self-esteem the end result. We will demonstrate how this works more fully in chapter 7.

When we speak of identity, we are talking about the steady, durable core of a person, who she is internally and how she understands herself in relation to others. A stable identity includes the basic goals, values, and beliefs that allow a woman to make decisions about herself and take action in the world with some consistency.

According to developmental psychologists, people are supposed to explore possibilities and consolidate their identities during their adolescence. They recognize that they are no longer children and search to discover who they will be as adults. For many young women, however, part of the identity search—the exploration of possibilities—is cut off. Instead of testing themselves physically and intellectually, instead of practicing skills that will enable them to prosper in the work world and develop satisfying relationships, they stop. They are women, and everyone knows what that means: to society, their worth depends not on their intelligence or their achievements, but only on their ability to attract men. So they limit their practice to one small arena. Junior high school girls, for instance, try out makeup and hairstyles to get junior high school boys interested. However, they fail to practice ways to negotiate with them so

Know thyself.

— *Socrates*

that their relationships can be balanced and satisfying. And they often neglect completely the skills necessary to compete in the work world.

In place of experimenting with a variety of roles, the adolescent female often settles for the stereotypical feminine role and searches for a male. Once attached to a male, she assumes *his* identity, abandoning her own goals and dreams in the process. It is at adolescence that young women are likely to start neglecting their schoolwork, downplaying their intelligence and achievements, giving up former ambitions for their future, and, not coincidentally, losing their self-esteem. Little wonder, then, that psychologists report most women who enter therapy at midlife are finally looking to answer the questions "Who am I, and what do I want?"

Dr. Sally Archer has done extensive research and written widely on the topic of female adolescent identity. In order to achieve an identity, she wrote in *Interpersonal and Identity Development, New Research Directions* that a person must

- *explore*
- *experiment*
- *contrast self with others*
- *sort through identifications*
- *choose those that seem to fit*
- *discard those that don't*
- *integrate the identifications into a unique individual*

It quickly becomes apparent that, traditionally, men have had an advantage in this process. Given more freedom to explore and experiment than women, they have also been able to choose from a much wider range of possibilities. Being husbands or fathers does not significantly alter their identity. Women who see themselves as wives and mothers, on the other hand, tend to think that many other traits are incompatible with their domestic roles.

It is especially important for females, therefore, to go through a formal identity search, preferably with outside help and support, and to develop a personality strong enough to withstand peer and societal pressures to conform. Her parents are the best mentors for this process.

Let's start with a look at your own identity. Complete "The Party" activity.

While the boys were learning to make go-carts and competing in soapbox derbies, we were learning to walk while balancing coins on the tops of our shoes and books on the tops of our heads.

— *Woman, 44*

The party

Imagine attending a party with one hundred strangers. As you arrive, you are told to mingle with the other guests, introducing yourself *without mentioning what you do*—your career, your hobbies, and so on. What would you say? Take some time to think about it, then write about two minutes' worth of conversation below, describing who you are.

Hello, I am . . .

Did you find "The Party" difficult? Men, especially, tend to think of themselves in terms of their activities and accomplishments and so find it hard to talk about themselves in other terms.

Did you describe yourself as Sam's wife, Donna's husband, Melissa's mother or father, Julie's daughter or son, or Maria's best friend? If you are a woman, it's likely that you did. Women are more likely to define themselves in terms of their relationships.

What adjectives did you use in your introduction? Were they primarily feminine, masculine, or neutral? (Review the Bem list in chapter 3, "Redefining Femininity.")

At a gathering in 1989 we actually staged this activity with one hundred people who knew each other by reputation but had never met. It was surprisingly difficult for nearly everyone. Some became frustrated, some retreated to the sidelines, and most eventually gave up the effort and began conversing about their jobs and roles. Most wanted to introduce themselves in terms of their accomplishments and titles and did not feel comfortable talking about who they were in terms of their passions, values, and personalities.

Have you ever gone through a formal search for your own identity? Can you talk about your values, beliefs, and personal goals and dreams? Can you list your strengths and your weaknesses? What are your dominant personality traits? Can you quickly enumerate your skills and aptitudes? What are your passions—those things for which you have boundless enthusiasm? What makes you laugh? What brings you joy?

By understanding the qualities that make you unique, you are in a better position to make better choices for yourself in such important areas as selecting a career, finding a mate, developing a life-style, or making a change.

How well do you think you know yourself? Take some time to fill in the bull's-eye diagram "Getting to Know *You*," on page 68.

To illustrate the importance of this process, let's look at the responses of a fictional individual who is considering a career change. Currently this person owns and manages apartment complexes.

Passions: Fly fishing, classical music, Oriental rugs, deep conversations
Values: Independence, helping others, creativity, knowledge
Personality: Leader, thorough, serious, thoughtful
Skills and Aptitudes: Problem solver, teacher, communicator
Roles: parent, child, spouse, business owner

This person might consider a career as a college professor, therapist, writer, or something that would tap into her characteristics more than staying in the apartment business. She might go to work for the local symphony as the executive director or as the person in charge of fund-raising. What other careers might she consider that would bring a life of satisfaction and fulfillment?

In filling in the "Getting to Know *You*" bull's-eye, you have completed a rudimentary identity survey.

Take another look at your answers. Which qualities mean the most to you—those that are often associated with someone of your gender or those that are unique to you?

During your daughter's adolescence and young adulthood, she will begin making commitments (career, life-style, mate, family, etc.). The better she knows herself and her possibilities, the wiser these decisions are going to be. If she bases them on a narrow definition of being female, it is highly unlikely that the decisions will be the best she could make.

How identity is formed

Initially people define themselves as male or female, and then they select from the possibilities they believe are offered to them. How does a child learn what possibili-

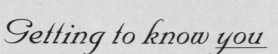

Getting to know you

Write your name in the center of the diagram, then add as many words as you can that describe your own passions, values, strengths, and so forth. As you fill out your diagram, keep in mind that everyone has many different sides; don't worry if some of your answers seem incompatible with others.

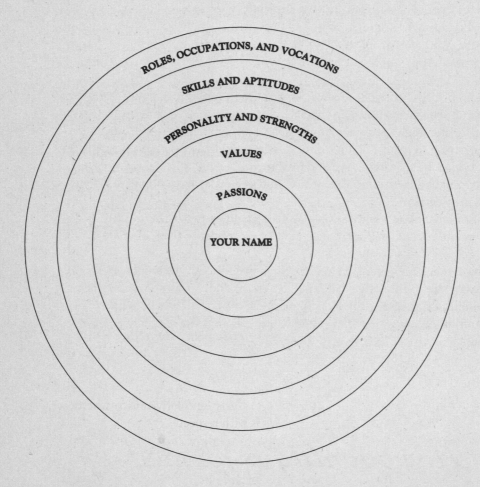

ROLES, OCCUPATIONS, AND VOCATIONS

SKILLS AND APTITUDES

PERSONALITY AND STRENGTHS

VALUES

PASSIONS

YOUR NAME

ties are offered to a woman in our society? Several theories have been advanced, but none seem to fully explain the process. It is more likely that some combination of the following three general forces is at work, teaching your daughter what is appropriate for her to be or do.

REINFORCEMENT

The first generally accepted theory holds that children learn in part by being rewarded for behaviors considered appropriate for their sex and by being punished for unacceptable behavior (reinforcement can be either positive or negative). For example, if a little girl gets her way more often by crying than by asking for what she wants, she soon learns how to turn on the tears. If she is scolded for getting dirty but admired for sitting quietly in her party dress, she learns it's best for her not to be active. If she's praised for being pretty and popular, while the good grades she gets in math are overlooked, she learns it's more important for girls to be liked than to be smart.

Reinforcement is strengthened when the same messages are received time and time again, but sometimes a single powerful event makes a lasting impression. Former AAUW national president Sarah Harder, for example, recalls how, at her eighth-grade graduation, she and her classmates were asked to tell the audience their career plans. When she announced that she planned to be the curator of the butterfly collection at the Field Museum in Chicago, the room rocked with laughter. "I laughed along with them," she says, "and it wasn't a conscious decision, but I never considered that goal again. I stopped taking science classes and concentrated more on English."

MODELING

The second process by which children are thought to acquire some of their gender role identity is, basically, imitation. Mary sees her mother put on lipstick, so she wants to wear lipstick, too. Modeling is a bit more complicated, however, in that it can also involve noting what happens when people behave in a certain way or taking symbolic meaning from pictures or stories. Children notice if their older sister is praised for making dinner while their older brother is ridiculed for taking an interest in cooking. They take note, too, when the male characters in their picture books act while the females stand back and wait or admire. Girls especially notice whether their fathers treat their mothers' ideas and opinions with respect.

It is often assumed that children model themselves only after people of the same sex, but this does not seem to be the case among preschoolers. Children of both sexes may be equally interested in playing dress-up or "fixing" the car, as they've seen their parents do. If the boy is given a toy tool set and the girl a pretend makeup kit, however, both will learn what their parents consider appropriate behavior for members of their sex.

This is an important point to remember since, as we said earlier, your daughter's future happiness and success may rest on her ability to claim for herself both relationship ("feminine") and achievement ("masculine") behavioral styles. She may be interested in car repair, she may be capable of learning to do it, but if she does not see this as an acceptable interest for girls, she will abandon it. The wider the variety of actions you, as parents, can model for your daughter, the better her chances of incorporating the attitudes and behaviors that will benefit her in the future. You can reinforce these behaviors by the gifts you give and the praise you hand out. Why shouldn't she have trucks, blocks, and tool sets in addition to dolls and stuffed animals?

THE COGNITIVE-DEVELOPMENTAL THEORY

A child observes her world and, from what she sees, develops a set of rules that she can apply to a wide array of situations. Remember, it's what she sees that matters here, whether or not it holds true in the world at large. You've probably heard the story about the little boy whose mother was an attorney: when asked if he wanted to be a lawyer when he grew up, he said, "No, only mommies are lawyers."

When Susan was about thirteen, she looked around and noticed that many of the girls she knew were getting better grades than the boys. She asked her parents about that, and they said, "Oh, yes, girls usually get better grades in the early years, but by the time they reach their junior year in high school, boys start passing up the girls." Guess how her performance changed in relation to that of the boys!

Children are looking for structure in their lives and so are likely to embrace and uphold gender stereotypes, but as they mature they generally learn to revise their views, if given an opportunity to do so. Rebecca, who has no children of her own, recalls being upset by the actions of both her nephew and her niece when they were about three or four. Her nephew had developed an elaborate set of rules about where people would sit, the order in which they would be served at the dinner table, and so on. The only constant was that his mother always came last. Rebecca's niece, on the other hand, was determined to wear nothing but pink and ruffles, no matter how many sweatshirts and dungarees her aunt foisted upon her. The children's parents weren't terribly concerned, and in the end Rebecca had to admit they were right. Both children outgrew their stereotypical behavior and became "pretty terrific kids," she says.

People often assume that girls automatically identify with their mother and boys with their father, but this doesn't seem to be the case in gender roles. Since most children still spend more time with their mothers than with their fathers, both boys and girls tend to identify with her throughout their childhood, though boys generally do not pick up sex-typed behaviors from her.

As they enter childhood, girls are often able to experiment with being like a boy. In studies of adult women, from 20 to 31 percent remember wishing they were boys at some time in their childhood. Only about 2.5 to 4.0 percent of men say that they recall wanting to be girls. This seems understandable for two reasons. First, girls perceive at an early age that the accepted "feminine" role offers fewer options for them and that they are less valued by society than their male counterparts. Second, it is more acceptable for them to exhibit "masculine" traits. Being a "tomboy" is acceptable, at least until they enter puberty. Girls are allowed to wear sneakers and jeans, to climb trees and play soccer, but boys get the message that it is definitely not okay for them to traipse around in high heels or play with baby dolls.

It's not fair to assume, therefore, that there is one "correct" identity for girls, and that your daughter will learn it automatically from her mother. Your daughter may identify with either or both parents. If you want her to develop the wide range of personality traits that characterize a healthy adult, both achievement ("masculine") and relationship ("feminine"), it's beneficial for both of you to demonstrate as many of those characteristics as possible.

Carolyn Heilbrun wrote in *Reinventing Womanhood* that women of achievement are most likely to identify with a "masculine" father rather than a "feminine" mother, which gives credence to the Broverman study we discussed earlier. A 1973 study determined that the highest-functioning girls identified most with dominant fathers, while the lowest-functioning daughters identified with a passive, retiring mother. Today, of course, gender roles are less rigidly defined, so that it matters less which parent a daughter identifies with than which behaviors she adopts. If you are a single mother, this should be good news—providing you demonstrate both the nurturing traits usually associated with women and the competencies usually associated with men. If you find that you are unable to do so, we suggest that you find your daughter role models who do exhibit the characteristics you see lacking in yourself.

Mixing career and family—a complication in a girl's search for identity

For males, the traditional family role is that of provider; therefore the more ambitious career goals a man has, the better for his family. There is no conflict between expectations at home and on the job.

Young women, too, have serious career goals these days, but when they look around they see that females are still responsible for most child care and household tasks. They see, too, that most adult women work at low-level, low-paying jobs. There are few models to demonstrate successful mixing of career and family. Little advice on the subject is forthcoming to them. Young women are left alone, then, to work out their own solutions. Since most females value relationships more than career, and since they fear pursuing career goals that may endanger those relationships, many opt to lower their professional ambitions.

Those who do appear to maintain professional ambitions often have no realistic sense of what is required. Some young women resort to fantasy. A subject in one study reported that she planned to "go to med school, have a baby when I finish, stay home a couple years, start my career, have another baby, stay home a couple more years before I finally start my practice," apparently without considering how likely the medical profession would be to adjust itself to her plans.

Other young women redirect their goals and decide to achieve in the personal rather than professional realm. They often select careers that require less training and offer easy reentry after taking time out for child rearing, such as retail sales or secretarial work.

The problem with these solutions is that they do not provide for the likely event that a woman will need to be the financial support for her family at some time (even in lasting marriages, chances are good that the man will lose a job or be unable to work for a period of time). Young women need strategies and ideas to cope with the complexities of their dual identities.

One important component in the successful mixing of career and family is to delay parenting. Having a child at an early age makes life in today's world much more difficult. You can help your daughter see the importance of this fact by taking her through a comprehensive life planning process, beginning before she enters adolescence. You'll find more information on balancing career and family needs when you get to chapter 25, "Strategies for Mixing Career and Family."

Before adolescence

It is important to your daughter's future and her self-esteem that she comes to think of herself as an achiever while she's still a preadolescent. As we've already seen, at puberty she will almost certainly be pressured by her peers to pay more attention to her relationships and her "femininity" than to her other successes and accomplishments. Before she reaches this point, she must come to see herself as a full-fledged individual who will become an independent and economically self-sufficient adult.

If this is to happen, she must learn not only to be an achiever, but to achieve for the right reasons—for her own intrinsic satisfaction. Males are often motivated to achieve for the sheer pleasure of succeeding or doing something well and to rank themselves in their male peer group. Females, on the other hand, often skip over the pleasure of accomplishment and depend only on external rewards: the approval and recognition their achievements bring from parents, friends, and teachers. At adolescence, particularly late adolescence, that approval may no longer be forthcoming from important people in their lives, such as boyfriends and peers. Without some sense of satisfaction in her own competence that is validated by others, the motive to achieve ceases to exist.

Problems may also arise if your daughter has adopted the traditional definition of femininity. Since achievement is not considered feminine, she may abandon her efforts for fear that they will make her seem less attractive to males. Similarly, if she is concerned only with her relationships, she is likely to be less willing to postpone marriage and parenting in order to get the education and training required for high achievement.

The idea that identity is consolidated in adolescence comes from psychoanalyst Erik Erikson, whose 1963 book, *Childhood and Society*, outlined the "eight stages of man." These are the psychological stages of personality development, which unfold in sequential fashion, with each stage building on the ones preceding.

According to Erikson, puberty marks the beginning of the fifth stage, identity versus identity confusion. During this time the individual develops "a sense of self

I grew up in a small midwest town where there were dozens of "characters," but I only recently realized that they were all men. These guys could do anything, say anything, dress any way they pleased, and no one got terribly excited about it. "That's old Joe for ya," they'd say. They might be shaking their head, but they'd be smiling, too. The women, though, seemed to have adopted a traditional role. They showed little fluctuation in personality or behavior. For them, the word <u>different</u> was a sort of code for the word <u>wrong</u>.

—Woman, 43

To be nobody but yourself—in a world which is doing its best, night and day, to make you everybody else—means to fight the hardest battle which any human being can fight, and never stop fighting.

—e. e. cummings

that is reliable and consistent, both for oneself and for others." This is followed, he says, by the sixth stage, intimacy versus isolation. At this point an individual develops "commitment and the ethical strength to abide by such commitments."

It should be noted that Erikson's theories are based entirely on studies of males. For females, the sequence and/or the amount of time spent in each stage appears to be different. Some researchers believe that females either flip-flop the identity and intimacy stages, putting intimacy ahead of identity, or stay for such a short time in the identity stage that the process is not completed. As a result, they will give up this fragile identity when they form an intimate relationship, either taking on the identity of their significant other or defining themselves in ways approved by their mate.

The earlier you can help your daughter start to think of herself as an achiever, therefore, the more solid this identity is likely to be when she begins her search for intimacy.

Why boys are likely to have a stronger identity and higher self-esteem

Ever since people started to worry about such things, it seems, the term *man* has been synonymous with *human*. Just as Erik Erikson did, theorists studied males and decided that what was true of, or normal for, them was true and normal, period. From birth to death, males are valued for their achievements. Our societies are designed to maximize and celebrate male accomplishments. Little wonder, then, that men can forge strong identities.

Females, on the other hand, sense from an early age that their value comes from pleasing others and their identity is what other people tell them it is. While boys have a wide range of role models, most girls identify with their mothers, who are likely to exhibit traditional female roles at home and on the job.

Boys achieve to gain mastery; girls achieve to gain approval. Sensing that the ultimate approval will come from their eventual mate, they may put off establishing their own identity so they can more easily adapt to what the males want them to be. When the approval disappears, so does their self-esteem and self-definition.

Boys and girls are still being socialized to fit the gender roles required by conditions in the distant past.

In the next chapter, "Developing a Hardy Personality," we will discuss the skills you can help your daughter master from her earliest years so that she will avoid this fate and decide for herself who she is, take pride in her own achievements, and hang on to her self-esteem.

From clique to individual

If you're ever observed a group of adolescents, you know they don't look like young people trying to find their individual identities. They look more like an experiment in cloning gone awry: same hair, same jeans, same shoes. They walk alike, talk alike, and probably chew the same brand of gum. What's going on here?

As they leave childhood and start to become adults, young people go through a period in which they begin to separate from their families by identifying strongly with their same-sex peer group. This is the age of cliques, gangs, and "Riot Grrls." Group identity overcomes individual identity. There is safety and security in the group identity as they move from who their parents want them to be and struggle to find out who they are.

Again, this is perfectly normal, but

I've noticed among myself and my female friends, all highly educated and "right thinking," what must be an unconscious belief that there's really only one correct way for a woman to be. We tend to surround ourselves with people who live their lives the same way we do, and we become upset or threatened if someone "steps out of line." In a group of working women, for example, it can be distressing if one member decides to quit her job and have a baby. If that's the "right" thing to do, doesn't it mean that the rest of us are "wrong"? Once you realize what's going on, of course, you can laugh about it, but it still upsets me because I don't think men go through this. Can you imagine a man thinking to himself, Well, if Kent wants to be a doctor, that must be the right thing to do. Maybe I should be a doctor instead of a musician. Maybe men can't be musicians. I mean, it's so obvious. Men just have so many more choices, and maybe that makes them more comfortable with other people's choices, too.

—*Woman, 30*

you don't want your daughter to get stuck there. It's up to you to help her conduct a formal identity search, beginning in childhood. The remainder of this book is meant to aid you in your efforts.

It's time for a change

The old roles no longer fit. Change is difficult, but it is also necessary. Your daughter no longer needs to be socialized for a lifetime of domesticity. She needs to be a competent achiever as well as a loving caretaker. By developing both sides of her personality (achievement/masculine and relationship/feminine) and understanding her unique self rather than trying to conform to a gender stereotype, she will be psychologically healthier, more self-reliant, and economically responsible.

Everybody wins. When all our daughters are raised in this way, we will see a decrease in poverty among women and children. As this happens we will see stronger family units for all types of families. With stronger families will come more security and safety (emotional, economic, and physical), which will develop more stable children. As children become more stable and secure, they will be better prepared to learn when they are in school. With a better-educated population we will have more productive adults and, therefore, a more secure society.

Isn't it worth the effort?

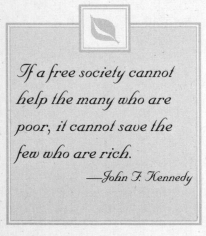

If a free society cannot help the many who are poor, it cannot save the few who are rich.

—John F. Kennedy

Checklist for helping your daughter develop her identity:

☐ Help her learn to appreciate herself as a unique individual based upon her own passions, values, strengths, weaknesses, skills, aptitudes, and talents—not gender roles. Encourage her to seek out new experiences and explore a wide variety of interests.

☐ Provide opportunities for her to conduct formal identity activities so she can learn to articulate and define who she is.

☐ Recognize her achievements and support her identity as an achiever as well as her relationship qualities.

☐ Reinforce, model, and expose your daughter to behaviors and experiences that encourage her to be all she can be.

☐ Expose her to role models and strategies for successfully mixing career and family-related identities.

chapter six

Developing a Hardy Personality

Before she can form a strong identity, become an achiever, and maintain her self-esteem, your daughter has to develop a set of key skills for interacting with the world. These skills are *step one* on the road to self-esteem. When girls master these fundamental traits, they can more easily succeed at the more complicated developmental tasks to come. The earlier a girl learns them, the better, but she can learn them later, too—and, indeed, needs them before she can move on to the next steps.

The eight skills that you must incorporate into your daughter's education are the abilities to

1. *Recognize and tolerate anxiety and act anyway.*
2. *Separate fantasy from reality and tackle reality.*
3. *Set goals and establish priorities.*
4. *Project into the future and understand how today's choices affect the future.*
5. *Discriminate and make choices consistent with her goals and values.*
6. *Set boundaries and limits.*
7. *Ask assertively for what she wants.*
8. *Trust herself and her own perceptions.*

These skills will enable your daughter to be the kind of person who approaches life with enthusiasm and weathers its challenges well. Suzanne Kobasa Ouellette, a professor at the City University of New York, coined the phrase *hardy personality* to define such people: those who feel in control of their lives, are committed to their activities, and look forward to change as a challenge and an opportunity for growth.

The dictionary defines "hardy" as being "capable of surviving unfavorable conditions," and if that's not a plus for any female growing up in America today, we don't know what is.

A key characteristic among people with this personality is the feeling of being responsible for their own actions and in control of their own lives. These people do not say that things happen to them, that their fate is in the hands of some exterior force. Rather, they take the credit or the blame for present circumstances and move on, feeling that they can create something good and lasting from whatever comes their way. In addition, they regard change as a challenge and they remain committed to their own values and what they are doing.

Unfortunately we don't often see these qualities mirrored in our daughters. While people with hardy personalities generally feel in control of what happens to them, girls more often feel controlled by others or by events. While hardy personalities set their own standards, girls learn that pleasing others is of foremost importance. People with hardy personalities are committed to their own lives and careers. We tell our daughters to put others first and to think of their life's work as "something to fall back on." People with hardy personalities embrace change, but girls too often shy away from it or become its victims.

In her initial study, Ouellette found that those with a hardy personality were able to tolerate and manage stressful situations in their lives with a much lower incidence of physical illness, such as hypertension, a heart attack, cancer, or peptic ulcer, than their less hardy colleagues. In subsequent studies, Ouellette and her colleagues demonstrated that those with a hardy personality were less likely than others to manifest symptoms of anxiety or depression.

The individual with a hardy personality interacts with the environment effectively. Ouellette and Mark Puccetti studied the support that families gave to individuals under stress. Families of individuals with hardy personalities apparently encouraged their members to go out and tackle the stressful situations. Supportive families of less hardy individuals provided them with a retreat from the stressful environment. How does this tell us to support our daughters?

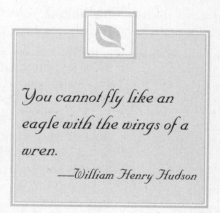

You cannot fly like an eagle with the wings of a wren.
—*William Henry Hudson*

We'll talk about each of the eight skills in some depth, and then, throughout the rest of the book, we will provide examples and activities you may want to use with your daughter. We believe that the skills of a hardy personality will serve as the foundation on which your daughter can build the self-esteem and self-sufficiency that will ultimately lead her toward a happy and successful life.

1. Recognize and tolerate anxiety and act anyway.

"Looking back, I can see that for years of my life I was virtually ruled by fear," says Julie. "I went to try out for the church choir, but when my name was called I ran out of the room and never went back. I registered for a high school speech class, but dropped it after the first session. I can remember walking back and forth in front of a pizza parlor because I was afraid to go in and apply for a job. In college I actually changed my major after reading the catalog descriptions of some required classes that were coming up. My adviser might have talked me out of it, but I never saw him. I was too afraid."

Like Julie, many women grow up believing that if something makes you anxious, you shouldn't do it. As Julie's story illustrates, however, this attitude can put a real crimp in a person's life. Not to try is the ultimate failure.

Anxiety tolerance is the ability to endure the uncomfortable feelings that overwhelm us when we face a task or situation that makes us afraid, nervous, or apprehensive. Think back to a situation that caused you anxiety and try to remember exactly how it felt. Did those uneasy feelings ever stop you from doing something you wanted or needed to do?

Once again, the chief cause for this inability to tolerate anxiety seems to be the way girls are "rescued" from infancy and on. "It seems like my parents should have been more concerned about my older brother," Julie adds. "He was always coming home with a gash in his head or a broken wrist or whatever. But they'd take him to the emergency room, get him stitched up, and he'd be back on his bike or off exploring with his friends. Me, now that was a different story. Every time I did something the least bit venturesome, my mother would get this worried look in her eyes. There'd be a sharp intake of breath, and she'd stand there with her hand at her throat, as though I were about to jump off a fifty-story building. Then she'd rush in to help."

> *Courage is rightly esteemed the first of human qualities because it is the quality which guarantees all others.*
> —Winston Churchill
>
> *Courage is resistance to fear, mastery of fear, not the absence of fear.*
> —Mark Twain

Little wonder that Julie learned to back away from new situations. Anything that could make her mother look so concerned must be very dangerous indeed. At least that is how a small child probably experienced it. And if she was constantly in need of all this "help," Julie thought, she must not be competent or capable enough to act on her own.

Loving parents and other adults often begin early in a child's life to undermine anxiety tolerance in girls. Mindy recently had dinner with a dear friend and his eighteen-month-old grandchildren, Scott and Sara, who are fraternal twins. After dinner her friend decided to give Sara a piggyback ride and hoisted her up on his shoulder. She'd never experienced this before and began to cry and show signs of stress. He put her down immediately, cuddled her, and sympathized with her. A few minutes later, though, he tried the same thing with Scott. Scott, too, was clearly uncomfortable and responded the same way as Sara, but instead of putting him down, his grandfather persisted, told Scott he'd be fine, and encouraged him to be brave. In a few minutes Scott was having the time of his life. Sara didn't get another chance.

Children need to practice tolerating uncomfortable situations. If we tend to rescue them, we will not allow them the opportunity to experience the uncomfortable feelings, then learn to tolerate them and proceed anyway.

Right from the start, parents tend to see their daughters as more fragile than their sons, but studies show that this has little to do with the individual child. In one study, when adults were asked to describe an infant they were told was a boy, they used words like "strong" and "active." Another adult, told that the same child was a girl, saw "delicacy" and "femininity" in her every movement.

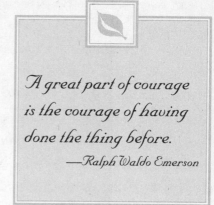

A great part of courage is the courage of having done the thing before.
—*Ralph Waldo Emerson*

It's important to understand, therefore, that your desire to rescue your daughter has more to do with you and imposed gender roles than it does with her. Is it really more dangerous for her to climb that tree than it is for your son? Is he likely to be any less injured if he falls off his bike?

Fathers, especially, seem to want to "help" by rescuing their daughters. Group coordinators of the Mother-Daughter Choices program noticed this tendency often when men were included in the groups. One of the exercises involves putting together a budget, which, of course, requires doing some math. The mothers and daughters would work through the process together, but the fathers almost always jumped in and completed the problems for their "little girls."

If your daughter is still young, vow now to start treating her like the sturdy and capable child she probably is. This means you need to manage your own anxiety! Next time you're tempted to rescue her, stop and ask yourself if you'd do the same thing for a boy. You want to ensure her safety, of course, but don't stifle her urges to explore the world and feel comfortable in it. Keep yourself calm and applaud her efforts. Encourage her to keep trying if she doesn't master new skills immediately. Your own challenge is to keep her going in the face of your anxiety and hers.

There will inevitably be times when she feels afraid: the first day of school, the first swimming lesson, are bound to make her anxious. Though you won't tell her, you may be anxious, too. Instead, tell her that this new situation is a challenge and you are sure she can meet it. If she seems worried, explain that it's okay to be afraid—most people are when they face new challenges. Make sure, though, that she understands the necessity of acting in spite of her fears. If you cancel the swimming lessons or let her stay home from school, she will learn that feeling anxious is a

For twenty-four years I thought my main role as a father was to protect my daughter, even after she became an adult. I wanted to be her hero, the guy who'd rescue her from all those dragons: cash shortages, back rent, overextended credit cards, and cars that wouldn't run. Then I learned that what I was doing wasn't helping her, it was denying her the opportunity to struggle with and solve her own problems.

When I noticed that her inability to tolerate anxiety was keeping her from taking some necessary risks—changing graduate schools, giving up a dead-end job, moving out of her comfort zone—I resolved to change. I knew I had to stop jumping in trying to make her life more comfortable, that I had to step back (tolerating my own anxiety) and allow her the dignity of struggling to find her own solutions.

We had a talk, and I explained that I was doing this not because I didn't love her anymore, but because I did. I still support her emotionally, of course, but I don't leap in to offer my solution to any of her problems. I just wish I'd realized how important this was when she was little. It would have been so much easier for her back then.

—Father of a young woman in her early twenties

sign to stop, turn back, or change plans. Remember, the messages you send are powerful identity clues. By lovingly helping her get through the difficulties, you are teaching your daughter that she is stronger than she thought, that she can live through and even thrive on challenge. If she can tolerate anxiety, she will take more risks and experience more success. With each success she will become more enthusiastic and confident, and her self-esteem will soar.

If your daughter is older and appears unable to tolerate anxiety, some remedial work may need to be done.

Start by explaining how the situation may inadvertently have come about, and that it's important to change in order to address the challenges she faces in life. An adolescent daughter or young adult daughter can understand this. Tell her that you are going to stop rescuing her, not because you don't love her, but because you know how capable she is and you want her to realize this fact for herself.

Be explicit. Tell her that life is full of exciting challenges and meeting those challenges provides some of life's greatest satisfaction. One highly successful businessman we know says that when he is afraid of anything, he makes himself do it. He treats his fear as a challenge, a goad to action. Your daughter can do this, too.

If she is old enough, you may want to use visualization techniques to help her overcome any specific fears. Every day, have her close her eyes, relax, and see herself, step by step, being successful at the activity that makes her anxious. Then, slowly, she can start to act.

If she has a number of anxieties, ask her to list them in order, from least frightening to most frightening. Then encourage her to take them on, one at a time, starting with the easiest to master and moving toward the most difficult. If she is successful in overcoming the first fear on her list, she will have more confidence to deal with the second, and so on. Your goal is to help her identify anxious feelings, understand them, and get through them. Each time she learns she can handle anxiety in a given situation, she becomes ready to move up and take on a more difficult task. Success builds self-esteem.

Long-term fears may need to be confronted one step at a time. If she is afraid of public speaking, for example, she might start by volunteering an answer in class at least once a day. When she becomes comfortable with that, she might register for a speech class that starts the following school year. Meanwhile she can keep speaking up in her other classes, perhaps volunteering to do an oral report. When the speech class begins, she might try visualizing herself doing well in it. After a few "public appearances," the whole idea is likely to be less threatening.

If your daughter appears phobic or has a fear that debilitates her, you will want to seek professional advice.

Many people have found Outward Bound–type experiences empowering. These wilderness camps involve taking on new challenges among a group that's supportive but doesn't rescue. The final challenge is usually spending a couple of days alone in the woods or wherever, with minimal provisions. Graduates of these programs usually come away with an "if I can do that, I can do anything" kind of feeling.

They also know that they can be alone, which is one thing many young women fear. Unless your daughter knows she can get along just fine on her own, she may cling to unsatisfactory relationships—especially with men—simply because "it's better than being alone."

Without an ability to tolerate anxiety, your daughter's control over her life will be severely limited. Without confidence in her capacity to take on the unknown, how can she hope to go away to school? Master science and math classes or learn to use a computer? Take on new job skills? Change jobs or accept a promotion? Start new relationships or bring unsatisfactory old ones to a close?

> *Never grow a wishbone, daughter, where your backbone ought to be.*
> —*Clementine Paddleford, writer*

Successful individuals tell us that anxiety tolerance is one of the most crucial skills a woman can have. If you aren't successful in helping her develop it, get her professional help.

2. Separate fantasy from reality and tackle reality.

Some women are particularly prone to dwell in fantasy, perhaps because they've had so few choices in reality. While boys can fantasize about becoming anything from an

I really identified with the movie
Pollyanna. Everything is wonderful—
or at least that's what I was raised to
believe. Although there were some ob-
vious problems in the family, I was not
allowed to talk about them. Daddy
wasn't drunk, he was "happy." He
didn't pass out at the dinner table, he
simply fell asleep. When I grew up, I
continued to live in a fog of fantasy and
ignored the signs that things weren't
how they appeared. My husband was an
alcoholic philanderer who'd got us
heavily into debt and was about to lose
his job, but I didn't realize any of this
until the morning they came to foreclose
on our house. The recent divorce has left
me almost penniless, because for years I
refused to acknowledge the personal and
financial difficulties we were getting
ourselves into. I put all my stock in
happy endings, yet here I am nearly
fifty and having to start over.

—Woman, late forties

astronaut to a zookeeper, girls' dreams have been channeled more narrowly. If your only choice is to grow up and get married, then that marriage had better be pretty darned wonderful. Enter the prince. Exit clear thinking. Raised on fairy tales, middle-class white girls in particular are likely to believe in the "happily ever after." Unfortunately, things seldom turn out that way.

We can't help but wonder, too, if the way girls are "rescued" by parents and other adults from infancy on reinforces this "knight in shining armor" fantasy, and if the lack of confidence the world shows in their ability to cope might make women doubt themselves. When reality seems too frightening, believing the fantasy brings comfort and relief. On the other hand, facing reality provides the chance to achieve one's dreams.

Fantasy can be a wonderful thing. It's the first step in visualizing an ideal future. We hope you'll encourage your daughter to dream. But don't let blind assumptions or misinformation put her future at risk. Ask her how she plans to meet the challenges presented by her dreams. Provide facts when necessary if she's been misinformed or misinterpreted the messages of peers or society. For example, when a young woman in one of our Mother-Daughter Choices programs said she wanted to be a lifeguard when she grew up, the group leader asked how much she thought a lifeguard earns. "Oh, about a hundred thousand a year," the young woman replied.

It might also be a good idea to consider what messages your own actions in this area are sending your daughter. If you are constantly on the lookout for one more "get rich quick" scheme, or if you invest more money in the lottery than in your savings plan, telling her to quit fantasizing is not likely to be effective.

Begin discussing the concepts of fantasy and reality with your daughter as soon as she's old enough to discern the difference, at about age six or seven. It's not necessary to destroy the fantasy of a book or movie, only to make sure she sees it for what it is. ("No, I'm afraid little girls don't grow up to be mermaids, but wasn't that a lovely story?")

As she gets older you can ask her to judge whether her own plans are practical and help her evaluate the probability of success. Again, the idea is not to pour cold water on her dreams, only to help her see things clearly. Some young women do become Olympic gymnasts, and if your daughter has enough talent and enthusiasm, she may just be one of them. It's important for her to know, however, that a tremendous amount of work is involved, that only about half a dozen American gymnasts will make the team, that there is no guarantee of success.

Being entirely honest with oneself is a good exercise.

— *Sigmund Freud*

Oddly enough, your daughter may have a more realistic view of her chances of becoming an Olympic gymnast than she does of more everyday situations. Some myths are remarkably persistent, even when the facts seem obvious. Millions of teens, for example, believe there is little chance of getting pregnant or of acquiring a disease from unprotected sex. No matter how many broken homes they've seen, and even if their own parents are divorced, young women tend to believe that their own marriages will last forever. Her own mother and the mothers of all her friends may have jobs, but your daughter may still believe she won't have to work after she's married. These powerful myths must be dispelled if your daughter is to maintain control of her life and meet its realistic challenges.

3. Set goals and establish priorities.

As your daughter becomes comfortable with reality, she will learn that there is no magic genie in a bottle waiting to grant her every wish. She will be, in large part, responsible for making her own dreams come true. Learning to set goals and establish priorities will help her do that.

Again, this is something that women in our society tend not to do. Having goals and priorities suggests taking an active role in one's own life. Traditionally, women are more passive. They wait to be chosen rather than choosing for themselves. Activities important to them are "penciled in," and it's understood that plans will be cancelled if "something comes up" (something important to someone else, of course). Burdened with other people's expectations, errands, and chores, they find it easier to let go of their own hopes for achievement. These habits are not empowering.

Setting goals and establishing priorities are. Setting a goal is like setting a desti-

I find it puzzling. My daughter has always been extremely focused on her career goals. She even changed schools in eleventh grade to make sure she'd get the appropriate chemistry and math classes she needed to enter medical studies in college. She moved out of her college apartment and came back home because there was too much partying and her roommates weren't serious about their studies. But now, as a college senior, she's started talking about careers less challenging than medicine. Just the other day she said she'd rather get into a field requiring much less education. It's interesting that this change in goals correlates with her increased interest in a certain young man.

—Professional woman, East Coast

nation for a journey. If your daughter knows where she wants to go and where she is now, figuring out the route she'll have to take is usually not that complicated. If she wants to buy a new bike by next summer, for example, she needs to find out how much the model she wants costs, and then she has to decide how she will earn or save that amount. If she wants to attend a particular college, she needs to learn the admission requirements and then work to meet them.

Make sure she understands that realizing her dream takes both vision and action. The future she wants will not come courting her like a potential suitor. She must pursue it. This requires time, energy, and commitment, and it may be hard work. If she's used to getting what she wants—now—this may take some explanation.

If your daughter is "gifted" and has excelled at everything she's tried so far, you should remember, too, that encountering a difficult subject or task will seem unnatural to her, and she may want to give it up. Help her understand that some things require more work than others, but that doesn't mean she can't master them or that she is in any way deficient. In fact, she has control over just how hard she works.

If your daughter is like most people, she'll have many goals—long-term and short-term, essential and not so important. This is where establishing priorities comes in. Should she take that Saturday night baby-sitting job to earn money for the bike, or should she go to the movies with her friends instead? Short-term goals often seem more compelling at the moment, but achieving those distant dreams usually leads to more lasting satisfaction. For decisions that are appropriate for your daughter to make, it is up to her to set her priorities—and then make decisions that are consistent with them. Her friends and employers offer her choices; she controls her decisions, and she needs to know that.

Even young women who are extremely goal-oriented are likely to have their determination tested when they start forming serious relationships, as in the story quoted in the box on page 86.

No young woman is immune to this syndrome, but the more practiced your daughter is in formalized planning and goal setting, the more natural this process becomes for her, the less likely she will be to scale back her plans or seek out shortcuts to achieving her goals.

You can start teaching your daughter these things as soon as she's old enough to articulate what she wants and understand her own power to go after those things. What is her goal for the day? For the weekend? For the school year? Make sure she knows that a goal doesn't have to be work related. Finishing her science project can be a goal, but so can going to Disney World. Goals can be fun!

What's more, accomplishing a goal successfully builds self-confidence, which leads to higher self-esteem, which encourages a willingness to set new and more challenging goals. As she meets each new challenge, your daughter will feel more in control of her own destiny.

As far as priorities are concerned, make it clear that it's okay for her to put her own needs or desires ahead of other people's expectations. Women have a hard time with this one, and it's an important aspect of controlling her life.

When your daughter is old enough to have long-term goals, suggest that she set aside time each day or every week to work toward them. Long-term goals often get lost in the daily shuffle, so keeping them in sight is important. The older she gets, the more demands she'll have on her time, so this is a good habit to get into. If she learns to control how she uses her time at an early age, she can manage her time more effectively as she gets older.

I never saw a future for myself beyond my wedding day. Why would I? The stories I was told and the movies I saw as a child all ended with a big extravaganza of a wedding. No one ever talked about the difficulties of life when the honeymoon was over.

—Woman married at 19, divorced at 28, with three children

4. Project into the future and understand how today's choices affect the future.

Part of taking control of her life is imagining the future and making good choices now. Wrong choices are made by people who don't consider the effect of today's choices on tomorrow's life. Studies show that young women who have mastered the skill of projecting themselves into the future are less likely to marry too early or become teen parents.

The fact is, most women do get married, at least for a while, and 80 percent eventually have children. If this is the only vision your daughter has of the future, or even the primary one, however, it will likely cause her to give up some power and control of her life. If marriage is seen to be the central event in her life, she may relinquish control and give up her other plans until she finds out who her partner will be. So as she enters the "serious dating" stage (when the young men she dates become candidates for marriage), she may begin putting her life on hold. Today, because of the social pressure to go steady, this can happen at any time from junior high school on.

If, however, she understands the realities of adult life, the challenges and responsibilities as well as the moments of magic, she is far more likely to develop the skills needed to deal with them successfully: impulse control and delay of gratification. If she can project herself into the future, actually visualize herself in a challenging adult role, she is far more likely to plan for life in the real world, not in the fantasy concocted by our culture. Her focus on the future allows her to control the tendency to avoid present discomfort.

Sandy had always wanted to be a journalist. With help from her parents, student loans, and the earnings from a summer job, she made it through the first three years of college. But her parents, who were not well off, had done all they were able to do. She could get another loan, but not one large enough to see her through to graduation. And the summer job market seemed to have disappeared.

Except for a few at the local turkey-processing plant. They were hiring people to debone and devein turkeys. On the night shift. For $1.65 an hour. For Sandy, a life-long vegetarian, the prospect was less than appealing. But the choice was clear: Take the job or relinquish her dream.

She took the job. Every evening at 6 P.M. she'd walk past the recently beheaded birds still hanging on hooks while the last drops of blood dripped out onto the floor, punch in, put on her hair net and set of rubber gloves and apron, and walk through the metal doors into the refrigerated room, where for the next six hours she cut up turkeys as fast as her frozen little fingers could go.

The summer finally ended, and her boyfriend went with her to pick up her last check. As he started to open the door for her, he saw that the knob was covered with blood and, understandably, recoiled. For her, though, it was just another day at the plant. She was, actually, rather pleased with herself. The experience, unpleasant as it had been, reinforced her determination to complete her degree. She was headed back to school. The summer's hard work had kept her dream for the future alive.

The ability to project into the future will help your daughter struggle through dilemmas and situations when she might otherwise be tempted to take the easy way out. Even when she has no control over those dilemmas, she can control how she resolves them.

Studies show that young women with plans for a career outside the home are less likely to become pregnant at an early age. If your daughter has seriously thought through her life and made plans for achievement in the greater world, she will see clearly how an early or unplanned pregnancy could sabotage her goals. Most teens, after all, know what causes pregnancy. The students at San Marcos High School in California already had had sex education, but that didn't keep 150 of the 692 girls from getting pregnant one year. What did help was a mandatory class in planning for their future developed around our Choices series. Only seven girls became pregnant the following year.

It takes experience and practice to be able to project oneself into the future. But, like any other skill, it can be learned. You'll find activities and discussion questions to help you teach it to your daughter throughout the rest of this book. (Also, our books *Choices*, *More Choices*, and *Career Choices* have step-by-step activities she can use to plan her life and career.)

5. Discriminate and make choices consistent with her goals and values.

The suggestion that it's okay to be discriminating may make you uncomfortable—especially if you're a woman. The little "be nice" voice in the back of our heads seems to be a particularly persistent one, and ignoring it usually results in feelings of guilt. Often, though, listening to the voice can be even more damaging.

The word *nice* has taken on too much meaning for too many women. Perhaps it is because we heard the command "Be nice" so often from those we loved and wanted to please, our parents and teachers. One therapist told us that when female clients are asked to describe their strengths, the majority begin their list with some variation of the statement "I'm a nice person." The "nice" woman is described as selfless, pleasing, quiet, unquestioning, behaved, not imposing, and proper.

Keep in mind that making discriminating relationship choices is not the same as discriminating against someone on the basis of prejudicial stereotypes.

I think the word <u>nice</u> should be struck from the English language. My parents said it to me all the time. "Now, come along, be a nice girl. Play nicely. Be nice to the cat. Eat nicely, speak nicely, sew nicely, write nicely": <u>everything</u> was nicely. The boys didn't have to be nicely anything. They just had to be quiet, but they never were.

—*Woman, 35*

I have a very clear recollection of a particular Saturday night when I was twenty. Five minutes before my date for the evening (someone I barely knew and cared even less about) was due to arrive, I got a phone call from an old boyfriend, up till then the love of my life and someone I'd been desperately hoping to hear from. There I was on the phone, my date now at the door, and my mother standing in between with this "I certainly hope you're going to do the right thing" look on her face. I wanted to ask the old boyfriend if I could call him back in five minutes. I wanted to explain to the new guy that something important had come up. But that wouldn't have been "nice." My mother's message received, I said a quick "I gotta go now" into the phone and headed out for a miserable evening with this guy I never saw again. I've always regretted it.

—*Woman, 48*

When I was growing up, my parents expected me to be nice. If I ever said I didn't like someone, I was immediately stopped and reminded that, on the contrary, "We like everyone." So I did.

When I grew up, the inability to discriminate, to pay attention to my own perceptions and feelings about people, led me right into two failed marriages, one to a con artist and another to an alcoholic I thought I could "save." Things weren't much different at work. I didn't consider what was reasonable and take control of what I did on that basis. Instead I'd perform any unreasonable task, asking nothing more than a little reassurance that I was still the "good girl" my parents raised. There was a time I did two full-time jobs at once. It nearly killed me.

I will never forget the day a close friend, who is also a therapist, took me aside and said, "If I do nothing else in this life, I am going to help you learn to discriminate between good relationships and bad relationships."

She soon had me understanding the messages I'd received from my parents (messages never sent to my brother). I learned that as an adult I had a responsibility to myself to evaluate my relationships and walk away from those, both personal and professional, that were not supportive. I took control and chose some relationships while rejecting others.

Three years later, I have a new business, new friends (fewer but better ones), a positive relationship with a man who respects me, and a sense of control I've never known in my life.

—Single mother

Prejudging or making assumptions about others based on their race, sex, class, religion, or appearance is never acceptable. Neither is treating people rudely or badly. Being discriminating, in the sense that we use the term, simply means allowing yourself to follow through on your true feelings and prefer the company of some people to that of others, being more direct and honest in important relationships, and feeling free to walk away from those that are less than satisfying.

Psychologist Sally Archer points out that the "be nice" expectations we place on our daughters can actually lead them to acts of cruelty. When they are not allowed to be honest in their relationships, they can find all sorts of underhanded and nasty ways to let someone know that he or she is no longer in favor. In commonplace stories, females perform some of the cruelest acts to other females, all in the name of wanting to appear "nice."

For many young women the inability to discriminate and be honest in relationships translates into being unable to say "no" to a man. Sometimes this results in regrettable behavior: "I can't believe some of the things I did to perfectly nice young men whose only crime was liking me," says Greta. "Once I answered the phone and, in my own voice, told this guy I wasn't home. He knew it was me, of course. Before hanging up, he said, 'Good-bye, Greta,' in this really sad voice. What's even sadder, now that I think of it, is that I learned this tactic from one of those 'teen girls' magazines. My gosh, why couldn't we just have been honest and direct?"

If your daughter cannot make good choices and be direct in relationships, the results can be more serious when the men she's involved with aren't "perfectly nice." Date rape is such an underreported crime that it's difficult to say how many women have been its victims. Nearly every woman has experienced some sort of unwanted

I've done more harm by the falseness of trying to please than by the honesty of trying to hurt.

—Jessamyn West

I remember when one of "our" group fell out of favor way back in grade school, she was ignored or left out of activities. No one bothered to tell the offender what the problem was so she would have a chance to resolve it. No, we had to be "nice," we could not confront. Heaven forbid we would have any negative feelings. The individual was emotionally banished without a word. Then, in high school, it happened to me. More than a dozen years later, that act of cruelty still impacts my self-confidence in relationships.

—Woman, 32

sexual advance. Even when they are physically attacked, however, many are reluctant to defend themselves.

That's why the willingness and ability to be discriminating is so important to developing a hardy personality. A woman who can't say no to a man—even to defend herself—is not in control of her life. Someone who cannot get out of damaging relationships will lose her self-respect and self-esteem. A person who is forever trying to meet other people's needs, no matter how unreasonable, will not have the energy to meet her own.

We are not saying that in order to have a hardy personality a woman must avoid relationships. On the contrary, she must be free to choose the ones she finds meaningful and stimulating. Healthy relationships are freely chosen.

Help your daughter understand that she should make and keep close relationships only with people who respect her thoughts, feelings, and opinions. You can't choose these relationships for her. But you can help her take control. You can encourage her to decide for herself whom to associate with and help her learn to reject people gently but firmly. You can also encourage her to decide what she wants to do in an age-appropriate way on the basis of her own needs, values, and safety. The freedom you grant her early will provide the experience she needs to make wise choices later. If she has never known this kind of freedom, she may not recognize and turn away from men or women who are controlling or possessive. Their behavior, on the contrary, will seem quite normal to her.

By letting her make her own mistakes and empathetically supporting her when she does, you will help her learn from them. She will figure out how to do better next time and develop confidence in her ability to discriminate. And discriminating will enable her to exert some control over the relationships she has.

Finally, try to eliminate "Be nice" from your vocabulary. Your daughter will get enough of that in the outside world. Be descriptive and help her sort through the characteristics she wants to have. Use the words *kind, poised, thoughtful, courteous, diplomatic, generous, patient,* and *refined* to describe desired behavior. We want our daughters to "have class" rather than "be nice."

6. *Set boundaries and limits.*

As a staff writer for a small daily newspaper in the mid-1970s, Sandy had an opportunity to do a variety of jobs and was happy in her position until she learned that the men in the office (she was the only "girl reporter") earned substantially more than she did. When she told her immediate supervisor that, as she understood it, this was probably illegal, he expressed surprise. So she wrote a letter describing the situation to the state department of human rights and received an answer confirming her suspicions.

She brought the letter to her boss, expecting that with this clarification all would be made well (she admits to being a tad naive). He told her he would have to broach the subject with the publisher, and for several months she waited patiently for a reply.

Right about then two other reporters resigned, and her boss told her he might be able to get her more money if she would "apply" for one of their jobs. (She'd done them both. In fact, she'd trained one of the men.) She agreed, but two days before she expected to assume her new position, she was told that "because she was doing so well where she was," a man with no journalistic experience had been hired to fill the job.

That did it. Trying to maintain her dignity, holding back the tears, she said, "Fine. You do what you have to do, and I'll do what I have to do." She went back to her desk, removed the form for filing a discrimination suit from the top drawer (the state had sent this with its letter), completed it, and dropped it in the mail.

She was subsequently fired, but, looking back, she thinks it was all worthwhile. It was hard, because that job was the only good thing in her life at the time. It didn't exactly earn her any friends, and she needed that meager little salary. But it really clarified things for her—who she was and what really mattered. Ever since then she's known that there is this line she's drawn in the sand, and that she will never allow anyone to step over it. She knows what she will stand for and what she won't stand for. She thinks most people probably don't realize it's there because she's pretty soft-spoken. But she feels that they don't need to know. It's enough that she knows.

Let's use a metaphor of people as protozoans. Think of men as paramecia and women as amoebas. Like the oval-shaped paramecium, a man is likely to have definite boundaries, while a woman tends to take on an amoebalike indefinite and changeable form. To get along, she often tailors her shape and form to match the expectations of others in her environment.

At times it's good for a woman to set her boundaries more flexibly. When their children are infants, for example, the best mothers put aside their own needs and expectations to meet the needs of their infants. The new mother must pay attention to the child she has. If she has a placid baby, it is easy. If she has an active, irritable one, she must learn to respond to that irritability without irritation of her own.

While adapting to the needs of others is appropriate for the parents of young children, it does not mean having no boundaries or limits at all. Insisting on a regular bedtime is an appropriate limit, essential to both the child and the mother. Some children clearly need less sleep than others, and good parents take that into consideration. At the same time, they establish regular bedtimes that the child can count on and the parent can count on, so that the child gets enough rest—and so does the parent.

A parent at home with a baby gears her responses to meet the needs of the baby. She plans her days around feeding schedules and sleeping schedules. This is a temporary situation, however, lasting only a short time in a long life span. In most other adult situations it is not necessary or even desirable. Therefore helping your daughter learn to set boundaries and limits is important.

Without personal boundaries, it's difficult for a woman to remain loyal to who she is or what she stands for. She puts other people's needs ahead of her own, often at great expense to her happiness and self-esteem.

A twice-divorced woman said, "I used to think it was extremely romantic, the notion of giving yourself up for love. It led me into a series of relationships with unstable and manipulative men who treated me poorly. Even so, things had to get awfully bad before I would leave. One of my favorite songs used to be 'As Long as He Needs Me.' Now, I get furious every time I hear it."

This story is not unusual. Women in our society have traditionally been raised to define themselves only by their relationships to others. They become whatever someone else asks or tells them to be. Following in this tradition will not help your daughter take control of her life in a way that is consistent with her own values and meets her own goals. Quite the contrary. If she has no boundaries, she may take drugs if her friends want her to take drugs or have sex if her boyfriend wants her to have sex. If she believes she must bend with the wishes of others, she literally may not believe she has the right to say no.

Every young woman needs to develop as much respect for herself as she has for others. You can help your daughter build character and set strong boundaries by showing that you have respect for her. Encourage her to have her own opinions. Ask her what she thinks about the issues of the day. Allow her to stand up for herself when she's been bullied or mistreated. Let her turn down invitations and decide for herself which activities she wants to pursue. Make sure she knows that her opinion of herself is more important than what anyone else thinks of her.

And understand that the first invitation she will turn down will be yours! A busy woman who set aside a day to spend with her ten-year-old daughter was dismayed when her daughter wanted to spend the day playing with a friend. When this happens to you, tell her how pleased you are that she is coming to her own conclusions. Likewise, when she disagrees with you and expresses her own opinion, even if it is an opinion you detest, tell her you are glad she is brave enough to disagree with you.

7. Ask assertively for what she wants.

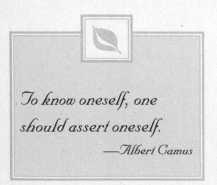

To know oneself, one should assert oneself.
—*Albert Camus*

Ever since Freud, men have been posing the question "What do women want?" For much longer than that, we're afraid, most people have been ignoring the answers. As one cliché goes, men are supposed to get what they want . . . women are supposed to want what they get. While this sounds absurd, doesn't it play itself out in real life?

What's considered "assertive" behavior in a male is "pushy" in a female. Men are "strong," women are "obstinate." Men "persuade," women "nag." Women learn this lesson so well that many eventually have no conscious idea of what they want, much less the will to ask for it.

As children, women are taught not to express their preferences in many small ways. One evening, while eating out, Mindy observed a family—a mother and father and a boy and a girl about the same age. The children wanted hamburgers while mom wanted them to have something more wholesome. The girl started to argue but was quickly rebuffed by her father and told not to talk back to her mother. The boy took another tack; he complained loudly, squirmed on his seat, and started debating the issue. This aggressive behavior was accepted in the son. Mindy noted the girl sat sullen and dejected the rest of the evening, with a vacant look on her face. When the dinners were delivered, the son had a hamburger.

That little girl learned an indelible lesson that evening. Try to avoid this mistake with your daughter. If she abdicates her own choices and doesn't know what she wants, chances are she won't get it.

What can you do? Make it a habit to ask what she wants, starting when she's very young. Even if you can't give it to her, listen carefully and acknowledge her choice. Never contradict her or tell her what she should or does want. Banish from your vocabulary phrases like "You don't want that, you want this" and "You don't really feel that way." As she gets older, encourage your daughter to express her wishes without prodding from you.

Allow her to be assertive. Parents tend to be less comfortable with assertive behavior in their daughters than with similar behavior in their sons. Even educators have this problem. As a high school teacher and then as a professor, Susan listened to the evaluative statements her colleagues made. While the educators called assertive young women "arrogant" and even said "She thinks she's smarter than everyone else," they never said those things about the young men in their classes. And those attitudes came through loud and clear in their responses to assertive young women.

But a person who is unable to act in her own best interests is left with few options. Our friend Penny recalls as a seven-year-old being handed an unwanted ice-cream cone before entering a theater for a holiday pageant. Unable to refuse or get rid of the ice cream, because she wanted to be accommodating and nice, she held it quietly throughout the performance as it melted, soaked her dress, and ran down her legs in sticky streams.

When your daughter can say "yes" or "no" to the opportunities that come her way, she will control her life's direction, and she'll be more successful at home and at work. Being unable to ask for what she wants and needs, on the other hand, can leave her feeling bitter and angry.

Pay attention to your own feelings about her assertiveness. When you encourage your daughter's assertiveness, she will practice it first on you. You need to be ready for that, because it is often an unpleasant surprise. And support her taking a stand. Tell her if you disagree with what she is saying and give her reasons why, but also tell her that you are delighted that she is expressing her own wishes and beliefs. Encourage her to stick to it.

Assertiveness is a positive trait. Even the dictionary says so. When you encourage it, you demonstrate that you value your daughter's individuality, that you want her to explore all her options, and that you support her right to have the life she most values.

Aggression, a more forceful version of assertiveness, also has its place. In small children it encourages exploration and helps teach them to master their environment. For adults, work is often an aggressive act. In his book *Work and Love: The Crucial Balance*, Dr. Jay B. Rohrlich states that "people who fear and suppress their aggressive drives are usually unsuccessful at work."

We'll offer some ideas on helping your daughter develop assertive communication skills in chapter 11, "Ages Six to Ten."

8. *Trust herself and her own perceptions.*

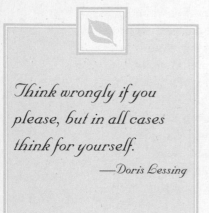

Think wrongly if you please, but in all cases think for yourself.

—Doris Lessing

Sandy's first husband started talking about marriage on their second date. It seemed like a joke at first, so she went along with it. The truth was, she had other ambitions, an unresolved past relationship, and no desire to get married, period. But he was a charming guy with a strong personality and a great deal of persistence. Every time they walked by a jewelry store, she was dragged over to examine the engagement rings in the window. Wouldn't she like to have one of those? When did she think they should announce their engagement? Would a spring wedding be nice, or how about the fall?

She finally agreed to marry him, though not without a great number of misgivings. There was no one she felt she could talk to, so she spent the summer before the event reading books, looking for an authority that would give her permission to call the whole thing off. She did try to cancel once, then allowed her fiancé to talk her out of it. Her first thought when she woke up the day after the wedding was, I guess my life is over now. She was twenty-one.

If there's one thing a person should be able to trust, it is her own feelings, her own judgment. That is basic to her effective pursuit of her own values, beliefs, and goals. Yet we see evidence that women do not. They look for an authority to cite or an outsider to validate what their minds tell them is true. They seek permission to follow their heart. If you think the story above is uncommon, guess again. We heard it many times over while interviewing women for this book.

We need only consider common speech patterns reported by research scientists to see how pervasive this situation is. Women often turn declarative statements into questions, as though needing confirmation from their listeners that what they are saying is true ("I was shopping at the mall?" "I'll have a cup of coffee?" "And then it started to rain?"). Or they tag a question onto sentences that don't require one ("I left my keys on the table, didn't I?" "He's usually not like that, okay?" "This is a pretty sweater, isn't it?").

Women even turn commands into questions ("Will you please leave me alone?" instead of "Leave me alone"). They insert words like "might" and "could" to add an element of doubt to their statements ("I might want to go over that paper again"). And when giving commands, they almost always politely say "please." In other words, women's language is filled with questioning, begging, and doubt. Not exactly the traits to instill trust and confidence, even in yourself.

Using such language is a way of sneaking in your opinion, hoping no one will disagree with it. Worse, it is a way of preventing attack. Everyone knows that when smaller, weaker dogs encounter larger, stronger dogs, they stop the large dog from attacking by lying down in front of it and baring their throats. Tentative speech is a kind of baring the throat that women do all the time—when they don't need to. Sure, if someone with a knife wants your daughter's purse, she should give it to him! But if she wants to state her opinion at a meeting, she should go ahead and do so. She probably won't get stabbed! And mothers, you can help her develop the speech patterns that facilitate her being true to herself by using them in your own speech. Be positive, direct, and clear when talking to the adults around you.

If you succeed with steps one through seven, you shouldn't have any trouble with number eight.

A young woman who can take necessary action, even in the face of great fear, has the best chance of realizing her dreams.

A young woman who can tell fantasy from reality is nobody's fool.

If she has her own goals and priorities, she won't let momentary fancies get in her way, nor will she feel she has to be like everyone else.

A young woman who can do today what she believes is in the best interest of her tomorrow will be less likely to settle for the pleasures of the moment and will have the stuff to persist when others find the going too difficult.

If she's learned to be discriminating, she'll be able to trust her feelings about people and situations. There won't be any "that's not the way you really feel" voices to confuse her. Nor will she feel guilty for asserting her own needs.

If she's learned to set boundaries, she won't be pushed around. She'll have solid beliefs and opinions—and the character to stand up for them, even when it's not popular, even when it means standing up for herself, an act that's too often considered selfish for females.

If she's learned to be assertive and ask for what she wants, your daughter won't confuse her own desires with what everyone else is always telling her she should want. She'll be an individual and proud of it.

Here is a person even your daughter can trust. And who could help but love her?

When you start writing "Your Plan," on page 459, you will be asked to consider what messages you want to give your daughter about each of these points. Think about appropriate messages as you go through the book and record them in "Your Plan."

chapter seven

Where to Start?

Several months after writing about the hardy personality, Mindy was trying to explain its importance to a friend. Grabbing a pencil and paper, she began to sketch a diagram in the shape of a pyramid or triangle. "Look," she said, "the skills of the hardy personality have to be here at the base. They're fundamental. Everything else follows from them. Once they're in place, a young woman can start to form an identity as an achiever."

Mindy added another level to the diagram. "That will allow her to enhance her self-esteem in adolescence, rather than letting it diminish the way it usually does in the teen years. This gives her the strength to become emotionally and financially self-sufficient."

She added two more levels. Finally, at the apex, she affixed the goal: a life of meeting the challenges of work and love in a way that provides satisfaction and continued growth.

Everything suddenly became clear to the friend and, oddly enough, to Mindy as well. Though she had never articulated this theory before, it seemed to explain a lot of things. Why, for example, do programs designed to give adult women job-seeking skills and support often fail? The women can seem ready to conquer the world when they leave the program, then go off on their own and never land that dream job. Perhaps they don't even try. Could it be that, never having developed anxiety tolerance or learned to ask for what they want, they are emotionally incapable of going after a job, even though intellectually they know they must? Is it possible that young women

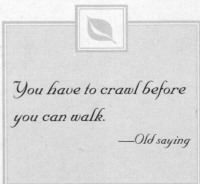

You have to crawl before you can walk.

—*Old saying*

who say they know better continually get into bad relationships or fail to work up to their potential for similar reasons?

We believe that it is. In this chapter we will expand on the theory and show you how to use it for your daughter's benefit, whether she is an infant or a young adult.

Here is the hierarchical model to use as your guide. We believe that it suggests tasks particularly important to women that are consistent with the developmental model proposed by Erikson and described later in the book.

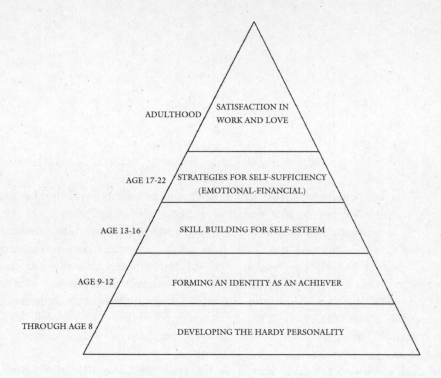

ADULTHOOD — SATISFACTION IN WORK AND LOVE

AGE 17-22 — STRATEGIES FOR SELF-SUFFICIENCY (EMOTIONAL-FINANCIAL)

AGE 13-16 — SKILL BUILDING FOR SELF-ESTEEM

AGE 9-12 — FORMING AN IDENTITY AS AN ACHIEVER

THROUGH AGE 8 — DEVELOPING THE HARDY PERSONALITY

The special developmental stages of girls

You'll note that we've added some approximate ages at which it is appropriate for girls to work on the tasks. Again, don't worry if your daughter is older. We'll get to that in a minute.

Ideally, though, you will begin to teach your daughter the skills of the hardy personality between birth and age eight. This should eliminate the need for remediation later on. If, for example, you have encouraged anxiety tolerance by allowing your daughter to soothe herself and deal with her anxious feelings, she won't need to overcome learned helplessness later in life. If you allow her to be assertive, she won't learn passive or passive/aggressive behaviors that will have to be unlearned. It will be easier to be discriminating and to set boundaries if she hasn't already learned that being pleasing is the highest good for a female.

Between the ages of nine and twelve your daughter can, with your help, form an identity as an achiever. It's important that she start to think of herself that way before she reaches adolescence. If she can appreciate her uniqueness as well, she will be less vulnerable to society's dicta on female limitations.

If she has already developed the skills of the hardy personality, it will be easier for her to form her own identity. For example, if she trusts herself and sets her own boundaries, she will be less susceptible to peer pressure, which encourages her to be just like everybody else.

If she does not succeed in forming her own identity, on the other hand, she is likely to erect a pseudosense of self, designed to please others. Without a genuine sense of self, your daughter may eventually become depressed, irritable, and uncooperative.

A sense of her own identity will also allow her to build on her childhood sense of herself and develop the self-esteem of a woman. This should be your goal for her when she is thirteen to sixteen years old. This is a critical time, when she will make many potentially life-altering decisions. As you've already learned, the odds are against her being able to hold on to her self-esteem during this time. If she knows who she is, however, and if she continues to pile up achievements that reinforce her sense of self, she has a much better chance to successfully weather this developmental stage.

When your daughter is seventeen to twenty-two years of age, your most important task as a parent is to begin letting go. This is the final stage before she becomes an adult, and as you send her off into the world, you should be secure in the knowledge that you have helped her develop the skills to be both emotionally and economically self-sufficient.

You don't want to wait until she's seventeen, though, to begin instilling these skills. You'll find activities and ideas throughout the book that will help you prepare your daughter for an adult life of satisfaction and peace, the ultimate goal.

What if your daughter is older?

Don't be discouraged if your daughter is already a teen or a young adult. It's never too late to change. Be sure, though, to become very familiar with the important tasks discussed here and to read through the entire book, because you will probably still be dealing with issues from her infancy and childhood. For example, if you find yourself rushing in to rescue your young adult daughter because she can't seem to manage her finances, chapter 10, "Infant, Toddler, Preschooler," will help you understand why this is a bad idea. You will also want to begin working with her on setting goals and priorities and projecting into the future—while trying to develop your own anxiety tolerance. It will probably come in handy during the months ahead, when you may, as Mindy did, begin to lose perspective about the way you've parented your daughter to this point.

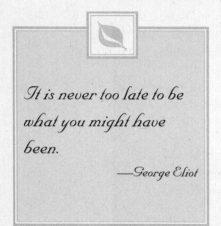

It is never too late to be what you might have been.

—George Eliot

Mindy's daughter, Wendy, turned eighteen while we were writing this book. To Mindy it seemed the research was providing more and more evidence of all the things she'd "done wrong" while raising her. She felt overcome with guilt, and at times it was very painful. Obviously, it seemed at the time, she had inadvertently—perhaps irrevocably—damaged her life.

She managed to overlook the fact that Wendy was actually doing quite well and that they had a better relationship than many other mothers and daughters she knew. Gradually she calmed down and realized that things were not as bad as she'd originally thought. But she felt there was still room for improvement. She began to apply the principles outlined in this book, to discuss them with Wendy, and to watch and listen more closely to what was going on in her life and to what she had to say. All the while, though, she was careful to treat her as the young adult she had become. When Wendy came to her with a problem, for example, Mindy asked if Wendy wanted her advice instead of telling her what to do. Surprisingly, quite often she did want the benefit of her "wisdom" and experience.

It's been a remedial process for both of them, but Mindy believes it's been a real boon to Wendy, to her, and to their relationship.

Analyzing where to begin with your daughter

In order to help your older daughter in any given situation, you both need to be operating at the same developmental level. If she is still at the hardy personality level, appeals to her identity or self-esteem are not likely to be successful.

Say, for example, that your seventeen-year-old daughter has been awarded a scholarship to the school of her dreams, three states away. At first she's thrilled. A few days later, however, she announces that she's decided not to go. This school has one of the best music departments in the country, and your daughter wants to conduct an orchestra someday. She tried so hard to get in. You are puzzled.

Your first impulse may be to tell her that a degree from this school and the contacts she'll make there practically guarantee success at her chosen career. She is not swayed. Perhaps this is because you are addressing the fourth level of development—self-sufficiency—and she isn't there yet.

Okay, you say. Being awarded this scholarship is a tremendous honor. Wouldn't it be a shame to give that up? You have just broached the third tier, self-esteem. And she's still not moved.

But music is her passion, you remind her. With her leadership qualities and willingness to work hard, she has the potential to be a great conductor (identity). She listens a little closer but is still staying home.

You've reached the fundamental level. Which skills of the hardy personality are called for here, and does your daughter have them? You admit that her anxiety tolerance and ability to project into the future need work. And that's where you must begin *your* job. By beginning at the appropriate level, your success ratio should improve dramatically.

Once you've helped your daughter develop a hardy personality, you can move up to work on the other things she might be missing. The rest of the book will provide you with activities, dialogues, and ideas to help you in your efforts.

You will need to discuss the issues with your older daughter, tell her exactly what changes you intend to make, and explain why they are important for her self-esteem and life satisfaction. Because she is old enough to understand, the process may be easier than you think. Just remember that emotionally she needs to move through the lower developmental stages before she can be successful at the higher ones. And don't despair! It can be done!

A case study

As a freshman in college, Wendy was assigned a roommate for her one-bedroom dorm apartment. The roommate had a friend at a college about fifty miles away who began spending a great deal of time in the apartment. By the end of the semester she was there three or four nights a week. The two friends tended to stay up talking most of the night and, on weekends, slept until midday—in the living room. All of this deprived Wendy of sleep, space, and privacy.

According to school rules, it was up to Wendy to confront her roommate and set limits. Until she'd tried this, the authorities would not intervene. And she *did* try—only to reach agreements that were subsequently broken within a week. She didn't want to move, and even if she did, there were no openings in the area.

It was time for Wendy to file a complaint, but she couldn't bring herself to do it.

Mindy was frustrated, too. Why couldn't her strong, competent, focused daughter take a stand? Instead she was talking about dropping out of school.

At last Mindy realized that the skills called for in this situation—being assertive and setting boundaries—were not traits she had encouraged in her daughter. Instead she had rewarded Wendy for being obedient and complacent. But that was about to change.

Over the course of several long-distance phone calls, Mindy apologized to her daughter and explained that she had failed to help her develop the skills called for in this situation. She discussed why it was important to be able to be assertive and set boundaries, not only in the immediate circumstance, but throughout life. Finally she offered to teach Wendy what she needed to know and even to model the appropriate behaviors for her, if necessary.

Wendy accepted the offer, and Mindy proceeded to explain the basics of assertive communication. They even practiced over the phone. Then, the next week, Mindy attended a meeting with Wendy's resident adviser, her purpose being to model assertive communication and boundary setting for her daughter.

Wendy watched carefully as Mindy insisted—firmly, but fairly—that the adviser be present at a meeting with the roommates to assure the desired outcome. Wendy set the boundaries—neither roommate would be allowed more than one overnight guest each month (the college minimum)—and she didn't back down.

Becoming your daughter's teacher or role model

At this point you may not feel competent to help your daughter develop a hardy personality and move successfully through the other developmental stages outlined in this chapter. Don't worry. By the time you reach the end of the book, you'll have learned a lot. If you start now to monitor your own behaviors and work to improve any skills you're deficient in, you'll learn even more.

You might also want to consult other books. We've listed some in the appendix, and your library or bookstore is sure to have more. Perhaps your community education department or a local college offers classes that can help, too. It's generally easy to find one on assertiveness or communication skills, and there may be others as well. Here's a way to empower yourself as you learn how to help your daughter.

There are also books you can give your daughter. For example, our *Career Choices: A Guide for Teens and Young Adults—Who Am I? What Do I Want? How Do I Get It?* includes activities that will help your daughter begin a formal identity search process and learn to project into the future, set goals and objectives, separate fantasy from reality, and develop anxiety tolerance. You might want to read it first yourself, so you can discuss it with her as she works through the book. (We also have an adult version, *Career Choices and Changes,* that you might consider working through together as a parent/daughter activity.)

If you still feel unable to give your daughter the help she needs, we suggest that you contact a counselor, teacher, coach, or other adult who might be better able to assist in the task. Explain the situation and enlist their help and understanding. Community support groups or individual counseling sessions are also an excellent option. Your daughter will probably benefit more from a bit of outside remediation at age sixteen or nineteen than she will at thirty-eight.

Some of you may want to take steps to make sure these kinds of programs are available to other young women in your community. You'll find more information on being an advocate for girls in chapters 27 and 28.

A note to professionals who work with girls

As we mentioned at the beginning of this chapter, our model for the special developmental stages of girls may have implications for any program that deals with girls and women. If you are a teacher, counselor, program director, or community organizer, we hope you will think about the problems you've encountered and consider whether they may have something to do with a difference in the tier of the hierarchy you're addressing and the skill deficits of your clients or students.

For example, if bright young women are dropping out of your math classes, you may need to help them learn anxiety tolerance before you can help them learn calculus. If the graduates from your displaced homemaker program can't seem to find or keep a job, you might want to add some sessions on asking for what you want or separating fantasy from reality to your program. If the battered women from your shelter keep going back to their abusers in spite of your appeals to their self-esteem, maybe they're still at the stage where they need to learn about setting boundaries, being discriminating, and trusting themselves.

Whatever your program, evaluate where it falls within the model. If you run an employability program for low-income youth, let's say, you are probably working on skills for getting and keeping a job. This is fourth-tier stuff, financial self-sufficiency. Have your clients reached this stage? Do they have the skills of the hardy personality, or do you need to address this concern first? Can you supplement your program to provide information and allow practice in these skills?

Are your clients or students secure in their identity as unique individuals? If not, read farther for ideas you can use to help them acquire self-knowledge and value who they are.

It is probably futile to teach employability skills to young women without the self-esteem required to get and keep a job. Perhaps you need to include activities and opportunities to build this essential characteristic within your traditional curriculum. We hope this model is of use to you, and we welcome your ideas, comments, or reports.

chapter eight

Your Role

Today's families come in all sorts of shapes and configurations. When we say "your role," we know that "you" can be a married parent, single parent, stepparent, part-time parent, foster parent, grandparent, or other person significant in a girl's life. It would have been too cumbersome to list all the possibilities over and over again, but we hope that you will edit the following chapter as you read to fit your own circumstance. Whatever your relationship to the girl in your life, this chapter—and this book—is for you.

Your expectations

While you can influence your daughter's life in many important ways, you cannot mold and shape her to meet your own expectations. If you expect her to be a scientist or a professional tennis player or a Supreme Court justice, we hope you will put aside those dreams.

Our mutual goal must be to help her become the person she wants to be. It is her life and her responsibility to live it the way she pleases.

Your expectations, therefore, should concern the process, not the results. You can expect her to put forth her best effort. In the past, many parents expected less of

When our first daughter, Debbie, was born, my wife and I made a conscious decision to raise her to be independent. We were both working then, struggling somewhat financially, so my wife was not able to stay home and be a full-time mother. By the time we had our second daughter, seven years later, I was doing well enough to support the family, so my wife, Dorothy, decided to stay home and be a more traditional mother to Liz. Dorothy felt she had missed out on something with Debbie, so she changed her whole parenting style. Liz was much more sheltered, much more what I called "s-mothered." I was busy with my career and pretty much an absentee father.

They're both grown now, and Deb's still independent—a real go-getter professional. She lives in a distant city, has a top job in her field, while Liz, who's always been more tentative, hasn't quite found herself yet. She lives near home, has a job that is below her educational level, and her self-esteem is quite low.

—Engineer, 50

their daughters than they did of their sons, leaving countless young women feeling incapable and unvalued. When your expectations are high, you are telling your daughter that you have faith in her and her abilities.

You must also have faith in her judgment. It is important that you not view her life as a second chance for you. Perhaps you regret a road not taken, but your aspirations may not be hers. If she becomes the self-sufficient young woman we all hope she does, she will have her own dreams to pursue. Give her your blessing and let her fly.

Parenting rules of thumb

It is not our intent to deal with general parenting techniques in this book. You'll find many excellent sources for these materials at your bookstore or library. Before you choose one, check the copyright date—newer books are more likely to be in line with your own thinking. Then turn to the index and look under "gender identification," "sex roles," "sex-role stereotyping," and "girls." Reading portions of these sections should tell you whether the author shares your feelings about raising daughters in the 1990s. If you're comfortable with what the author has to say about these topics, you're likely to find the rest of the book acceptable as well.

Before we begin with specific parenting suggestions as they relate to girls, we want to review what we feel to be the most important things you can give your children, whatever their age or gender. As you begin your own plan for your daughter, you may want to build these ideas into it. In any case, you will not want to design a strategy that goes against these parenting basics.

1. Unconditional love.

Every child deserves to know that she is loved, even when she misbehaves. Make sure you criticize the behavior, not the person. Find new ways to tell her how important she is to you. Child care author and columnist Vicki Lansky recalls how delighted her young daughter was when Lansky told her, "I really enjoyed you today." For days afterward, she reports, her daughter asked repeatedly, "Did you enjoy me today?" Take joy in your child and let her see it.

2. A physically and emotionally safe and secure environment.

It goes without saying that every child needs a safe and warm place to live, a healthy diet, and regular medical care.

Just as vital, though, is a home where she feels emotionally secure, one without a great deal of stress, where family members cooperate and conflicts are solved as quickly as possible. Whoever provides it, her care should be consistent, and there should be some structure to her days.

You can also nurture her emotional security by helping her develop at a steady pace. For example, toys should be stimulating but not beyond her capacity

I can't recall my parents ever making a decision for me when I was growing up. The message was—you're a very smart girl, very sensible, and we trust you to make up your own mind about things. I used to think that they didn't "do enough parenting"— imagining that other kids were getting more help from their parents. We were the kind of family that never talked about problems, or even faced conflicts head on, choosing instead to kind of wait until they went away, so I've had to learn how to handle conflict and disagreement. But the basic approach worked for me, because I have always had confidence in my ability to make the right decisions. And I heard so many times that I was smart and sensible, that I truly believe I am.

—Entrepreneur and mother, 37

Character building begins in our infancy and continues until death.

—Eleanor Roosevelt

to handle. If they are too advanced, she will experience frustration and failure. If they are not stimulating enough, she will not learn from them. The best toys—usually those marked as being appropriate for her age—provide a challenge that she can handle without undue difficulty, thus allowing her to feel successful.

3. Respect for her individuality.

Each child has her own strengths, needs, and vulnerabilities, and the best kind of parenting recognizes this fact and encourages her to celebrate her individuality. This can be difficult. If you're laid-back and she's hyperactive, or vice versa, it may often seem that she's trying to irritate you when all she's really doing is being herself. If you've always wanted a child who's a musician and she is determined to be an athlete, it may be hard to give your blessing. But you must.

It's important, too, to change the rules as she grows older and let her grow up. A ten-year-old should not be treated like a three-year-old. Although it may be difficult for you to see her become more independent, it is absolutely essential that she do so. In fact, the way that you react to change will provide a model for her. Accept it and adjust as quickly as possible.

4. Time and attention.

What's time and attention? The fact that you and your child are under the same roof or sitting in front of the same TV set is not enough. She needs your undivided attention on a regular basis. It's impossible to say how much time is the right amount, but we can say that quality is more important than quantity—and even quantity is important. Knowing that you have time just for her gives her confidence and assurance of your love.

The time you spend together will also help her get to know you and get to know herself. Tell her about the family history and its traditions. Share your own beliefs and values. She may not agree with everything you say, but she will have a better foundation on which to build her own identity.

You can also use your time together as a learning experience for your daughter. Let her work beside you as you prepare a meal or putter around in the garage. Passing on your own skills and abilities and helping her discover the joy of learning are gifts she'll always treasure.

5. Open and honest communication.

A child needs to know what's going on in her family. Be open about your own feelings, and encourage your daughter to tell you what's on her mind as well. If you sense there's something wrong, ask questions and listen carefully to her replies. We'll give you strategies for this later in the chapter.

Think before you speak. A thoughtless comment can be devastating to her self-esteem. But do speak to her, beginning at birth. Talking to a child is an important way of showing her attention and making her feel part of the family.

A parent's voice is one of the most comforting sounds a child can hear. Try not to let tensions or time constraints place limits on your conversation.

Good communication is also a vital part of teaching your daughter to cope with anger, grief, or disappointment. She needs to know that, while it's normal to feel these emotions, there are acceptable and unacceptable ways to deal with them. Contrary to what she may see on TV, violence is not acceptable. Make sure your daughter knows she can come to you with her concerns, assured that you will understand and try to help.

Some problems—a serious illness or major financial or marital problems, for example—are simply too big for families to deal with on their own. Do you have a support network in place, friends or family members you can turn to when things get out of hand? If not, consider other places to find the help you need. Neighbors, other parents, or community organizations or hot lines may be able to offer informal advice, or your daughter's teacher may prove helpful. Professional guidance is available from your pediatrician or family doctor, members of the clergy, and family or marriage counselors. Today no stigma is attached to asking for help. Everyone needs it from time to time. Most problems are solved more easily early on, so act quickly, before the situation escalates.

Neither of my parents was a big talker, and I didn't know how to start a conversation. I remember when I was about four I'd sit on one of the basement steps right outside the kitchen while my mother made dinner, just hoping she'd say something. She usually didn't, so I'd make an attempt. "Mom?" I'd say, and she'd say, "What is it?" I'd say, "Nothing," and sit awhile longer, then try again. "Mom?" "What?" "Nothing." I'd wait a few more minutes. "Mom?" "What do you want, Lil?" "Are we going to the store tonight, Mom?" "No, not tonight." "Oh."

—Woman, 43

6. *Good role models.*

You, her parents, are your daughter's earliest and most significant role models. We've already discussed this and will continue to do so in later chapters. There will be lots of other people in her life, too, of course, and they will—for better or worse—also be potential sources of emulaton. Your control is limited, but try to expose your daughter to people you admire from a variety of backgrounds. If her mother, aunts, and grandmothers are mostly full-time homemakers, make an effort to find women mechanics, electricians, plumbers, housepainters, and so on. Try to find baby-sitters who are athletes, scholars, or student leaders in addition to the ones who are cheerleaders and beauty queens. Let your daughter spend time with your friend, the pilot; your mentor, the attorney; or your favorite aunt who picketed for nuclear disarmament in 1960.

The mother's role

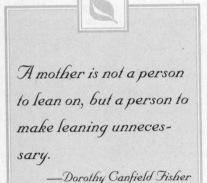

A mother is not a person to lean on, but a person to make leaning unnecessary.

—*Dorothy Canfield Fisher*

The earliest attachment for children of both sexes is with the mother. This is one area in which girls may have an advantage over boys. They need only identify with and imitate the person they probably already spend the most time with. Boys, on the other hand, must somehow figure out what it means to be male, even though their fathers may be absent much of the time. Much of their information comes from being told what is not appropriate for them. Not surprisingly, then, fewer problems in sex identity are reported among girls, who are more comfortable within their sex role. The relative freedom girls have to assume some of the "masculine" behaviors tends also to make girls less hostile to boys and male activities than boys are to girls and "feminine" behavior.

When it comes to her relationship with her mother, however, things get a bit more complicated for girls. A mother bonds quickly with infants of either sex, but she is more likely to see a daughter as an extension of herself and may, therefore, come to identify with the child just as the child is learning to identify with her. During this stage, known as *symbiosis*, their mutual dependency can become quite intense.

According to developmental theorist Nancy Chodorow, daughters maintain these strong ties with their mothers longer than do sons. At some point, however, a daughter needs to separate from the relationship, and this stage, known as *separation*, can be difficult for a mother who may be living vicariously through her child.

Perhaps this is why mothers and daughters often have such volatile feelings for each other. No other attachment is as important for the daughter, yet for her own survival, she needs to loosen the tie and become her own person.

It seems likely, then, that your daughter's adolescence will be a time of change. As we have said, this is the time when she will struggle to arrive at her own identity.

Mothers, who may have always been more protective of their daughters than their sons, are often reluctant to let go. A mother who hangs on too tightly or too long, however, is doing her daughter a disservice. If your daughter does not complete this identity process, the consequences for her self-esteem will be severe and long-lasting.

You can make this stage easier by allowing her increased freedom and privacy and by considering your relationship to her. If you're jealous of your daughter, or trying to compete with her, you'll make her situation more difficult. Why not use the time you'll gain from your decreasing maternal duties more profitably and pursue a goal of your own instead?

Whatever behavior you want your daughter to adopt, modeling it yourself will give you the highest probability of success. A mother who reads books, discusses the issues of the day, takes classes, solves her own problems, welcomes change and adventure, and never shrinks from a challenge cannot help but be a powerful model.

The best thing a mother can do to help her daughter become an achiever is to encourage her independence and competence right from the start. Young women who are raised to be emotionally dependent instead of autonomous are less likely to achieve and more likely to suffer from fear of success. They are simply unable to make the commitments or take the risks necessary in order to succeed.

This does not mean that mothers should be cold or emotionally unavailable to their daughters. On the contrary, a mother's unconditional love provides the security her daughter needs in order to explore, experiment, accomplish, and come to know herself as a competent individual. If you support and encourage your daughter to meet challenges in the world, she has a good chance of developing a hardy personality. In addition, according to Debold, Wilson, and Malave in their book *Mother Daughter Revolution*, you can avoid "*unnecessary* separations" between yourself and your daughter "that come from forcing a girl to choose between her mother and her peers, her own exploration of the world and her mother's politics, or her self-esteem and her mother's esteem for her."

Then, when your daughter is fully grown—when she reaches the final, *individuation*, stage of your relationship—you are more likely to settle into a comfortable, mature friendship with her.

Problems between you and your daughter are to be expected when she reaches adolescence, no matter how good your previous relationship has been. You can ease the pain somewhat, though, by monitoring your own behavior. Are you being overprotective? Are you in any way jealous of your daughter? Are you trying to compete with her, to live vicariously through her, or to push your own unfulfilled ambitions on to her? Any of these actions will make it more difficult for her to find her own identity.

She will need her privacy at this time. Respect it. Don't insist that she spend more time with the family. Don't enter her room without knocking. And don't be surprised or offended if she becomes less communicative with you and turns to a friend or another adult woman for support and advice. Your daughter is not rejecting you; she is simply trying to establish her own identity and find her own place in the world.

It is normal for individuals from different generations to have frequent disagreements. And it is inevitable that your daughter will pull away from you at this time as she struggles to let go of her childhood and define herself as a woman.

The father's role

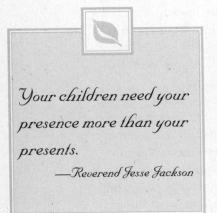

Your children need your presence more than your presents.

—Reverend Jesse Jackson

Perhaps the most important thing a father can do for his daughter is to be there, actively involved in her life. Traditionally, fathers have been the absentee parents, spending most of their time at work and, even when home, tending to be less available to their children. Not sure how to relate to girls, particularly when they entered puberty, fathers were apt to devote most of their parenting time to their sons, if they had them.

Today fathers are likely to be more involved in parenting— if the family is intact. But in 1991, one in six families in the United States was headed by a woman, and 87 percent of single parents were women. In many cases this is no cause for alarm. "Weekend dads" may actually spend more "quality time" with their daughters than some full-time parents. When there is no woman around, these fathers have an opportunity to exhibit their nurturing and caretaking skills as well.

But many children from single-parent homes, unfortunately, have little contact with their fathers. If you are one of these men, we urge you to try to establish a better relationship with your daughter. It's likely to be a rewarding experience for you, and it could make all the difference for her.

If you are a single mother and your daughter's father is not willing or able to be part of her life, is there another man who could serve as a surrogate? He should be someone who shares your beliefs about child rearing, someone who genuinely cares for your daughter, someone who will continue the relationship with your daughter regardless of his feelings about you, and, of course, someone who will not abuse or exploit her in any way.

You may wonder why, if most daughters have not had significant relationships with their fathers in the past, it is so important for your daughter to have one now. A quick look at studies of women who have been close to their fathers makes the reason apparent: In their groundbreaking book, *The Managerial Woman,* Margaret

Hennig and Anne Jardim reported that among the women in the M.B.A. program at Harvard Business School during the 1963–64 academic year, "all had had extremely close relationships with their fathers and had been involved in an unusually wide range of traditionally masculine activities in the company of their fathers, beginning when they were very young." In *Reinventing Womanhood*, Carolyn Heilbrun reports, "Except during periods of high feminist activity, there has been one positive role model for achieving women: the father. . . . Woman in her search for 'identity,' or a self not ultimately defined by a relationship, follows the only model available: the male one." While mothers tend to be the predominant role model for nurturing or expressive behaviors, fathers serve most often as their daughter's role model for achievement.

Certain behaviors or attitudes on a father's part can also hold a daughter back. As we noted earlier, men tend to have more stereotyped beliefs about gender roles than women do, for example. Many fathers also have a conscious or subconscious wish to hang on to "Daddy's little girl." If either of these sound like you, be careful. You're likely to reward your daughter more for looking good than for doing well, more for playing it safe than for taking risks—in general, you may inadvertently encourage your daughter to adopt or hang on to the behaviors that in the long run will diminish her self-esteem and her capacity for self-reliance.

Finally, next to the way their fathers treat their mothers, few things do more for a daughter's self-esteem than knowing she is loved and admired by her father. Tell her and show her that she is at every opportunity.

My mother is an extremely bright woman, but my father has always loved to tease her. Whenever she said something, he would have a quick rejoinder. One day at dinner, everyone was uncharacteristically silent. My little sister, who was then about four, wanted to liven things up, I guess. She said, "Talk, Mom, so Dad can make a joke."

—Woman, 30

The parenting team

In the two-parent family, the gender roles assumed by each person and the way your daughter's father treats her mother are extremely important. The more traditional the roles within the family, the more likely your daughter is to assume the traditional feminine roles and attitudes that will limit her aspirations and her chances for success.

My grandparents had a very traditional relationship, but I always thought of Grandma as a strong, competent woman. When Grandfather died, though, she went to pieces. She couldn't balance a checkbook and rarely drove a car. She had no idea how to manage the family finances. It was sad to see her like that, so childlike and helpless.

—Woman, 33

As she observes the relationship between her parents, your daughter will learn how women are valued and what their expectations should be. If her father expresses support for her achievements, yet treats her mother's dismissively, she will come to doubt his sincerity. If he doesn't respect his wife's intelligence, it will be difficult for her to have faith in her own capabilities. She will see, instead, that intelligence in women is not valued, and their contributions are taken lightly.

Young women need to see their mothers taking an equal part in family decision making. In fact, why not form a family council to discuss any issues that come up, with mom and dad taking turns as the chair? Both parents should give orders, make decisions, and solve problems. The language you use, too, should reflect the sharing of family responsibilities. Avoid statements like "Wait until your father gets home." Instead try something like "Your mother and I will discuss this and see if we can reach a solution."

Does mom ever drive the car when dad is along on the trip? If she is the family caretaker, does she get as much respect as her spouse, or are her contributions taken for granted? Is dad obviously in control? Is mom overprotected?

The single parent

When Wendy's father and Mindy were divorced, a counselor said it was important that each not bad-mouth the other to their daughter. "Wendy sees herself as half of each of her parents," he said, "and if she's told that one of them is bad, she'll feel that she must be half bad, too."

As a divorced couple, you're sure to have personal conflicts, but if you can settle them with some measure of mutual respect, you'll be doing your daughter a favor. If you are a single mother, you can be a powerful role model for your daughter simply by taking responsibility for your life and becoming self-sufficient.

Your daughter will still benefit from having a man in her life, however, so if her father is absent, try to enlist someone else for the job. The appropriate candidate is probably a relative or someone else who is likely to be around until she is grown. Make your request formally, perhaps over lunch or dinner. Explain exactly what you are looking for, but don't press too hard. It's a big responsibility, and some men will naturally be reluctant to take it on. The right candidate won't need to be pressured.

Once he's accepted the job, give him some training: share the message section of this book with him, and discuss your goals for raising your daughter. Let him read the entire book, as well as a copy of *How to Father a Successful Daughter* by Nicky Marone.

If you are a single father, you'll want to recruit female assistance in much the same way as outlined above. Marone's book will serve as a valuable guide for you as well.

Siblings

If your daughter is not an only child, you must also consider the often overlooked influence her brothers and/or sisters will have on her identity and her self-esteem. You, of course, will make every effort to treat your children equitably. Don't undermine this by allowing other family members to tease, denigrate, or humiliate anyone else. (Older brothers in particular can do great damage to a fragile female psyche.)

Instead, enlist older children to be mentors and role models for their younger siblings. If, for example, you tell your son, "Johnny, you are such a good mechanic, why don't you teach your sister how to fix the chain on her bicycle?" you are not only building *his* self-confidence, you are also letting your daughter know that it is appropriate for her to work with tools and get her hands dirty.

If your daughter has younger siblings, let her be the teacher. Like most busy parents, you will probably need her help in caring for the younger children, but be careful not to do this so often or in such a way that it tells her you value her relationship skills more than her other achievements. Don't, for example, ask her to skip her karate class in order to baby-sit, or to take her younger brother to his swimming class when she's supposed to be studying for a test.

Recruiting support

Whatever your situation, it will be difficult for you to make things better for your daughter unless all of the significant adults in her life work together to make it happen. This needs to be a team effort. Explain what you are doing and why, and ask for their cooperation. Sharing this book with them might be helpful.

The more people you can get actively involved, the better. Don't assume that your daughter's uncle, the jock, is a sexist who should only be allowed in the house on holidays when he'll be too busy watching football to do any damage. He might be thrilled to teach her how to do a lay-up or execute a double play. Explain what you are trying to accomplish and see if he'd like to get involved.

Even if her grandparents made some mistakes in your upbringing, it probably wasn't for lack of love or trying. If they are like most grandparents, they adore your daughter and can lavish her with the kind of acceptance and attention that will help her thrive. They may have more time and patience than younger adults and need only to be asked to teach her all about gardening or fishing, playing chess or ballroom dancing, listening to opera or playing a mean country fiddle. Tell them of your plan and ask for their assistance.

Good role models are essential. If you know other adults you'd like your daughter to emulate, try to bring them into her life. Establishing an ongoing relationship isn't always necessary (though it can be extremely rewarding). Having lunch with cousin Lucy, the radio personality, could make a lasting impression, as could watching your friend Monica, the lawyer, take a case to trial. If the woman next door likes to tinker with cars, she might be enlisted to explain the workings of the internal combustion engine. Or perhaps your daughter can spend a day or two working alongside a woman on a family farm. The essential point is that your daughter observe women doing things she's been told are possible for her.

A girl's mother is likely to be the most influential woman in her life. If your daughter sees her mother as strong, independent, courageous, assertive, and intelligent, she will believe those traits are acceptable in a woman, even if society tells her otherwise. Similarly, her father can be a powerful influence by demonstrating and encouraging achievement, supporting assertiveness, and making her feel accepted as a feminine person. Your daughter needs to see adults of both sexes using all of their talents and abilities, showing sensitivity in their relationships, acting as fully functioning human beings. We think you'll find it's worth the effort for you as well as for your daughter.

This is likely to take lots of practice, as well as constant vigilance, so be gentle with yourself. You will make mistakes; everyone does. But few mistakes are irreversible. Make it your goal to keep getting better, and give yourself credit for the strides you've made.

Parenting styles

These parenting practices will go a long way toward building your daughter's self-esteem, but how you parent is also important. Experts say that, basically, there are four parenting styles. Briefly, they are as follows:

> 1. *The authoritative style.*

This parent sets rules and limits, but will tell a child why, and is willing to discuss the situation and sometimes compromise, recognizing the child's need for growth and independence.

> 2. *The authoritarian style.*

There's no arguing with these parents. They expect obedience and hand out punishment if they don't get it.

> 3. *The permissive style.*

Permissive parents have no rules beyond protecting their child's safety. They feel their daughter should make her own decisions, though they are ready to support whatever she chooses to do.

> 4. *The harmonious style.*

Children of these parents seem to know what is expected of them almost intuitively. The parents have control but do not need to exercise it.

These styles relate directly to the development of competence in your daughter. The authoritative and harmonious styles (which are so similar that the latter often evolves from the former) are conducive to helping girls build self-esteem and achieve their goals. The authoritarian and permissive styles are not. The former does not allow her to make decisions for herself, and the latter does not hold her accountable for the choices she makes.

We've said it before, but it bears repeating: In parenting, actions speak louder than words. What you say will not be effective unless it is reinforced by what you do. When you must use words, it is often better to ask questions than to make statements or demands. Read on.

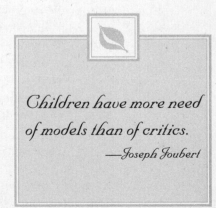

Children have more need of models than of critics.

—Joseph Joubert

Parent/daughter
communication

If you think back to your own adolescence, you may recall that there's only one good thing about having your parents tell you what to do: it eliminates one of your options. If they wanted you to play the violin, you had to take up the electric guitar instead. The more they disapproved of your hairstyle, the more you had to defend it. Going along with their recommendations was impossible. And so, your parents may have thought, were you.

Actually, it's all just a part of growing up. As you did, your daughter needs to assert her independence, her own personhood, by making her own decisions. Even if you could make her do what you say, it wouldn't be a good idea.

This is not to say, however, that you should not provide her with a certain amount of guidance. There's an easy way to do this: by asking questions. By asking the right questions, you can help your daughter make her own best decisions, decisions based on logic and clear thinking rather than blind rebellion.

It may sound sneaky, but it's quite the opposite. Asking questions has always been the best way to get to the core of an issue, to help a person find the truth. Socrates used this approach, and although it didn't do him much good with the establishment, it won him a loyal following among the youth of Athens.

It matters, of course, what kinds of questions you ask. "Are you out of your mind?" or "Do you have any idea what this will do to your father?" and the ever-popular "Is this what we've sacrificed our lives for?" have not been shown to be particularly effective.

Here are some questions that work and what they do:

- What do you think? (Teaches her to be discriminating.)
- Where do you draw the line? (Helps her learn to set boundaries.)
- What do you want? (Helps her make decisions, gives permission to ask.)
- How will you get it? (Helps her set goals and priorities.)
- How realistic is it? (Separates fantasy from reality.)
- What will be the consequences? (Teaches her to project into the future.)
- How would you handle that? (Teaches her to trust herself.)

If this isn't your communication style, you might want to copy these short questions onto a three-by-five card and tape them to the lower corner of your bathroom mirror. Practice them each morning as you get dressed. You'll be surprised how valuable they will be in building communication, not only with adolescents, but also with anyone you care about.

If she's going to come to the same conclusion as you, wouldn't it be simpler just to impose your will? No. The process makes all the difference. You won't solve her problems for her, but

- you will reinforce her autonomy instead of your own authority.
- you will support her self-sufficiency instead of making her feel that she needs to be rescued.
- you will help her feel competent instead of making her feel inadequate.
- you will help her build character and willpower instead of encouraging her to be dependent.
- you will encourage her to be her authentic self instead of molding her to fit your own image.
- you will help her know that she is valued as an individual instead of making her feel like a second-class citizen.

What's more, you'll keep the lines of communication open. She'll be able to come to you with all of the large and small crises she's sure to encounter, and she may even ask your advice from time to time. If she does, go ahead and tell her what you think. This is the time to share your wisdom and show your concern. But let the final decision be hers.

Mindy had to think quickly when Wendy, while a senior at a prep school three thousand miles away, called to say she was thinking of getting a Mohawk haircut. Trying to calm her racing pulse, she decided to put this question-asking business to test. Here's how it went:

("What do you think?" Teaches her to be discriminating.)
MOM: Wendy, how do you think that will look?
WENDY: Really awesome, Mom. All my friends think I should do it.

("Where do you draw the line?" Helps her learn to set boundaries.)
MOM: What if you don't like it? Who's going to have to live with the results?
WENDY: It's going to be great. I'm a senior, and I'm ready to do something radical!
(Strike one. Keep trying, Mindy.)

("What do you want?" Helps her make decisions.)
MOM: So you want to look different? Have you considered something less permanent?

WENDY: Permanent? What do you mean?
(If your daughter replies with a question, don't answer directly. Ask another question.)

("How will you get it?" Helps her set goals and priorities.)
MOM: You have a lot of important events coming up in the next few months. What will a half-grown-out Mohawk look like?
WENDY: (Pausing) It'll be back to normal by prom and graduation.

("How realistic is it?" Separates fantasy from reality.)
MOM: How long do you think it will take to grow out?
WENDY: Well, uh . . . a couple months.
MOM: (Sensing she's making some progress.) Really?
WENDY: Well, maybe six or eight months.

("What will be the consequences?" Teaches her to project into the future.)
MOM: The end of the school year's coming up. How will you look for prom and graduation? And what about your college interviews? Do you think you'll make a good impression?
WENDY: (Hesitating noticeably now) Well, I haven't thought about that. . . .

("How would you handle that?" Teaches her to trust herself.)
MOM: Well, I know you'll make the right decision for yourself. Let me know what you decide. Good night, sweetheart.

Mindy hung up quickly, before she could say the wrong thing, and spent a restless night. Two days later Wendy called to inform her she'd decided not to get the haircut.

For Mindy, it was a lesson in anxiety tolerance—she calmed herself, resisted the impulse to give directives, and waited for Wendy to call instead of phoning the next day. The wrong words or tone of voice could push her daughter in the wrong direction, she thought. For Wendy it was a clear message that her mother felt she was a mature and capable young woman who could be trusted to make her own decisions. That had to make her feel pretty good about herself. And—just possibly—she may have decided that a Mohawk would promote the wrong image for such a responsible young adult.

Whenever you're unsure of how to proceed in a conversation with your daughter, one question will almost always clarify the issue and set you moving in the right direction: "How do you feel about that?" Use it often!

The other side of the coin:
learn to listen!

There's little point in asking questions of your daughter unless you're willing to listen—really listen—to her answers. She'll realize it if you don't, and sooner or later she'll stop talking.

Here are some points to keep in mind if you want to communicate effectively:

1. Make your daughter feel that she has your attention.

It may be possible to have a good conversation while the two of you are doing dishes or driving to school, but if you are racing around trying to find your keys or carrying on another conversation with a third person, your daughter is sure to feel slighted.

2. It's not just what you say, but how you say it.

Your tone of voice should be serious and concerned, not sarcastic, flippant, or threatening.

3. When your daughter tells you something, be aware that she may be looking for approval or recognition.

Never pass up an opportunity to praise her intelligence, integrity, or whatever. If she tells you she got an A on her math test and you respond by asking how she did in history, she's likely to feel unappreciated. Give her the recognition she deserves, and then you can move on to other topics. Be careful about telling your daughter you're *proud* of her as if her accomplishment is yours. Choose the same words you'd use with an adult friend.

4. Don't interrupt or tune your daughter out because you think you know what she's going to say.

Making assumptions can lead to misunderstandings.

Children require guidance and sympathy far more than instruction.
—*Anne Sullivan,*
Helen Keller's teacher

5. When you're doing the talking, be as clear and precise as you can be.

Don't assume that your daughter understands everything you say or that she can read your mind.

6. One question to use sparingly is "Why?"

This one tends to make people defensive. You're likely to get a more satisfactory response if you ask "What were you working on last night?" rather than "Why didn't you finish your English paper?"

7. Respect your daughter's right to have her own thoughts and opinions or to disagree with you.

Acknowledge her feelings, even if you can't endorse them. If she comes in from playing with a friend and proclaims, "I hate her," for example, don't respond by saying, "Oh, you don't really feel that way." Instead ask questions that acknowledge her statement: "How does that feel?" "What happened to make you feel that way?"

Help her explore her feelings rather than deny them. If you tell her she doesn't really know what she thinks or how she feels, you instill a sense of self-doubt, which often leads to the "I don't know" syndrome among girls and young women. If your daughter begins to use this phrase often, it's a sign that somehow her feelings have been invalidated. Unable to trust her own thoughts or emotions, she may develop the passive personality that bears little resemblance to the confident, decisive, problem-solving young woman you want her to be.

8. Use "I" messages instead of "you" messages.

This allows you to express your feelings without sounding accusatory. Say "I worry when you're not home on time" instead of "You make me worry when you're not home on time"; "I get upset when you don't clean your room," not "You upset me when you don't clean your room."

9. If you're a male, don't let your wife do all of the communications work with your daughter.

You may feel left out because the two of them seem to be able to talk more freely about "girl stuff" (feelings, relationships, and so on). While it's true that women usually find it easier to talk to each other about some of these topics and that men are reluctant to broach them, don't give up your responsibilities in this area. You'll regret it, and so will your daughter. You may feel uneasy at first, but with practice you can become the kind of parent she'll feel comfortable coming to with her personal problems. And, just as important, you'll be showing her that men are willing to talk with her about feelings.

Forming a mother-daughter group

Many of the activities in this book can be group activities. We strongly recommend that while your daughter is in fourth, fifth, sixth, and seventh grades, you form small groups of girls and their mothers to address many of the issues in this book. Some groups have included fathers, and this might work for your particular gathering, although some girls are more comfortable discussing these issues in the company of women and girls, and there is also great value in the sharing of experiences from one generation of women to the next.

Chapter 28, "Forming Mother-Daughter Groups," gives specific advice on organizing a small group of girls and their mothers, or other significant females in their lives, for a series of meetings and activities. There are also many other opportunities for girls to gather, through organizations such as Girls Incorporated and the Girl Scouts, through religious communities, through school activities, and, more informally, just as friends.

We realize that people are busy and time is short, and not everyone will be able to participate in these gatherings, and for those mothers and daughters, the activities can be done as a twosome. They will still work to help preadolescents and adolescents avoid that nasty dip in self-esteem that too often takes place at this age. We do urge you to consider forming a group, however, for the following reasons:

1. Girls learn better in groups.

Males and females seem to have different learning styles. While most boys perform better in lecture-style individualistic settings, girls tend to learn more from group discussions and cooperative learning. Perhaps this is because they place more value on relationships and find this atmosphere more congenial, or perhaps it's because they enjoy exploring the what-ifs and the gray areas of an issue. Since most schools don't accommodate girls in their preferred learning style, we've found that most young women become enthusiastically involved when someone takes the time to create a setting where they can thrive.

2. There's safety in numbers.

Among adolescents, peer pressure can be strong enough to wear down the resolve of even the most committed and mature individuals. Because relationships are so central to the lives of young women, they are particularly at risk. Being part of the group now can seem much more important than working toward some faraway goal. A young woman with a number of like-thinking friends, however, can feel that she belongs, can get the support she needs, can turn away from the negative influences she is sure to encounter.

3. Girls need practice in building good relationships.

Relationships are a central part of women's lives, yet few of us are ever taught how to build them or even how to recognize a good one when we see it. The young women in these groups will have a rare opportunity to develop the skills necessary for making and keeping good friends.

4. Moms need support, too.

No one said raising a teenage daughter would be easy. Even in the closest of mother-daughter relationships, these years are almost certain to include some tense and difficult times. When they arrive, it's nice to have the support of other women who truly understand what you're going through.

Consider starting a mother-daughter group, or explore other ways for your daughter to experience the benefits of working through important issues with her peers.

Another group that can be very helpful is a mothers *for* daughters group. Consider starting a group just for the mothers, to discuss raising daughters and share support and ideas. Mothers often use these groups to talk also about their own experiences being female and ways they can become better role models for their daughters.

✎ In this section we've given you an overview of the problems and the theories of bringing up girls with high self-esteem. Now it's time to get practical. Roll up your sleeves and prepare to start writing the plan and making the changes that will make all the difference for you and your daughter.

11.

Self-esteem at every age

chapter nine

Your Plan

In chapter 2 ("What Attitudes, Experiences, and Feelings Do You Bring to Parenting?") you had an opportunity to review the way you were raised and the messages you received from important adults in your life while you were growing up. Perhaps the preceding chapters have provided some insight into how these messages have helped or hindered you in your own life. Now it's time to start considering the messages you'd like your daughter to receive.

In a special section at the back of the book (starting on page 455) we've listed some topics that directly affect a young woman's self-esteem, including the eight characteristics of a hardy personality. What messages would you like to give your daughter about them? Since actions speak louder than words, we've asked you to record both a verbal message and one you can send by example. Remember, the verbal and nonverbal messages children get from their parents form the nucleus of their sense of self.

Just to get you started, a verbal message about sex-role stereotypes might be "It's okay for a girl to wear dungarees, climb trees, and get dirty." If, at least once in a while, the women in the family do the yard work or tinker with the car while the men make dinner and care for the baby, your actions will send an even more powerful nonverbal message.

There are lots of pages to fill in, and some are about issues that you may feel you don't know enough about yet. Or perhaps you may feel that you don't know yet

> *Tell me and I forget.*
> *Show me and I remember.*
> *Involve me and I understand.*
>
> —Old Chinese saying

what's appropriate for each age. Help is coming! The rest of the book will help you answer these questions. As you read, you'll want to turn to these pages and complete them in more detail. (Boxes at the ends of many chapters suggest times that you probably will want to return to your plan.)

We'll get you started by providing examples for the topics on career planning and sports and physical fitness. If our sample statements are in line with your thinking, feel free to adopt them. Adapt them to fit your situation or family values more closely, if you like, or use your own ideas entirely.

If your daughter is beyond the preschool or elementary age level, we suggest you fill in the blanks for the earlier stages anyway, as if she is an infant. Ask yourself what you would do differently if you knew then what you know now about self-esteem, identity, a hardy personality, and so on. Complete these sections of the exercise accordingly.

Perhaps, when your daughter was three years old, you often told her that she was pretty, nice, or sweet. Today you might change that message, saying instead that she is smart, strong, and ambitious. Would you also send an action message by taking pride in your own intelligence and letting your daughter see you as a problem solver? Would you demonstrate your strength (emotional as well as physical) and let your daughter see you as capable? Would you take credit for your achievements and celebrate them with your daughter?

Call it remediation parenting or reparenting. Even if your daughter is sixteen years old, if you change your message and—most important—your actions, your daughter will notice and begin to change herself in light of these new, less limiting, and more empowering options. But watch out! If you change only your verbal messages and not your actions, your daughter might consider you an "unreliable source" and begin to discredit anything you say.

We suggest that you keep this book with your other family albums and records and consult your plan periodically to judge your progress and adjust your strategies, if necessary. Someday—perhaps when she has a child of her own—you might want to pass this book on to your daughter as a memento of her own youth and a possible guide for the next generation.

Career planning

INFANT TO FOUR-YEAR-OLD

Verbal message: Work is fun.

Action message: Provide "work" toys like building blocks and tool bench in addition to dolls and stuffed animals.

FIVE- TO EIGHT-YEAR-OLD

Verbal message: You are a good worker.

Action message: Use the term *work* to describe chores like picking up toys and activities like painting a picture. Praise her with phrases like "Good job!" and "Good work!"

NINE- TO TWELVE-YEAR-OLD

Verbal message: You can be anything you want to be.

Action message: Expose her to women doing all kinds of different jobs. Explain what the work entails. Ask if she thinks she would be interested in a job like that. Take her to work with you.

THIRTEEN- TO SIXTEEN-YEAR-OLD

Verbal message: A woman must be able to support herself financially.

Action message: Form a mother-daughter group to discuss career and life planning issues. Take part in a mother-daughter computer class or some other activity that builds work skills for both.

SEVENTEEN YEARS AND UP

Verbal message: You can do it!

Action message: Encourage her to take math and science throughout high school. Petition school to provide comprehensive career planning classes. Answer questions and provide information on careers in which she has expressed interest, post–high school education, and so on. Express expectations for her that are as high as those for your son.

Sports and physical fitness

INFANT TO FOUR-YEAR-OLD

Verbal message: Sports are fun.

Action message: Give her balls and other "athletic gear" appropriate for her age. "Race" her to the car or the corner. Dress her in clothing that allows her to move freely.

FIVE- TO EIGHT-YEAR-OLD

Verbal message: You are a good athlete.

Action message: Play catch with her. Teach her basic athletic skills in a low-key manner. Keep it fun. Praise her for being strong and fast. Don't rescue her when she doesn't require rescuing.

NINE- TO TWELVE-YEAR-OLD

Verbal message: Athletics are as important for girls as they are for boys.

Action message: Provide experience or instruction in sports that interest her. Take her to athletic events and explain what's going on. Include her in discussions about sports with your son or other males. Let her participate in the sport of her choice. Attend her games or meets. Cheer for her.

THIRTEEN- TO SIXTEEN-YEAR-OLD

Verbal message: It is not unfeminine to be an athlete.

Action message: Tell her she looks great when she's sweaty from exertion. Show support for other female athletes or teams. Attend her games or meets. Cheer for her.

SEVENTEEN YEARS AND UP

Verbal message: Physical fitness is a lifelong priority.

Action message: Stay active and fit yourself. Play tennis or golf with her, or shoot baskets together in the neighborhood park.

Get the idea? Turn now to page 455 and at least familiarize yourself with the topics and start *thinking* about a plan for your daughter. If there are issues you feel strongly about or very familiar with, you may be ready to begin writing. Don't feel pressured, though. Jot your ideas down when they come to you. And, trust us, they will.

chapter ten

Infant, Toddler, Preschooler

Sugar and Spice and everything nice . . . that's what little girls are made of.
Snakes and snails and puppy dogs' tails . . . that's what little boys are made of.

—Anonymous

The words we often use to describe a baby girl—"fragile," "delicate," "dainty"—suggest she might break and should be handled with care. All children, of course, should be cared for and protected. But is your daughter truly more prone to injury or hurt than her brother?

Quite the contrary.

Baby girls are generally tougher than their male counterparts. Developmentally they are ahead of boys at birth (even though their average gestation period is shorter), with stronger bones and, some say, a more developed central nervous system. Fewer females are miscarried, and there are also fewer birth defects and deaths among newborn girls. In addition, your baby daughter is likely to have a significantly higher IQ than her brother at the same age.

She will probably hang on to these biological advantages throughout her life. Women, on average, live longer than men. Most experts agree that all of this has something to do with the X-chromosome. She gets two—one from each parent—while males have one X-chromosome and one Y. The X is larger than the Y, carries more genes, and therefore gives females more genetic material to work with. Sex-linked disorders are also less likely to appear in females since they are carried on an X-chromosome and can be offset by the other, healthy, X. Males have no such backup system.

Ironically, though, many adults treat little girls as though they will disintegrate in the faintest breeze unless they are constantly watched, protected, and rescued. Cultural conditioning has trained us to see our daughters as frail, delicate, and vulnerable, so we treat them that way—even though, if we look at the evidence, we would be more justified in being protective of our sons.

Another cultural myth is that fathers are, by nature, less nurturing than mothers. When parents of newborns were observed, together and alone, with their infants in the hospital, the men were at least as nurturing as the women (except they didn't smile as much). This was true of men of varying classes, races, and educational levels and whether or not they had taken childbirth classes or had been present when their child was born.

There seems to be no biological reason, therefore, why you fathers shouldn't be thoroughly involved with your children right from the beginning. We know you want to be. Just like new mothers, you may feel a bit clumsy at first, but within days you can be diapering and burping like a pro.

A note to mothers: Sharing child care duties with your spouse may leave you feeling ambivalent at the beginning, sort of like sharing housework. You want the help, you need the help, but giving up the power associated with being the person in charge isn't always easy. Allowing your husband to assume major child care responsibilities is important to all of you, though, so let him do it. Don't insist that he do things exactly as you would.

Susan remembers feeling uncomfortable when her husband dressed their tiny daughter to go out in company. Her clothes didn't match the way she thought they should, and her diapers weren't tucked neatly inside her rubber pants. She thought, There is no way anyone is going to look at that kid and think, Her *father* dresses her funny! But she kept her mouth shut. She didn't want him to lose interest just because she was afraid of criticism.

Back to the baby. We will not presume to tell you who your daughter is. She is quite capable of doing that for herself. Even if she hasn't been around very long, you may have noticed that she has a distinct personality. As she develops, though, she will learn a great deal from you.

Children's differences in shyness and in activity level appear to be inherited, according to researchers at a recent conference sponsored by the American Psychological Association's Science Directorate. How the child's personality develops, however, is influenced by the reactions of her parents and others to her individual characteristics.

You may like cuddly, snuggly babies and want one, or you may prefer a more independent, active baby. Susan remembers talking with a colleague when she was pregnant. "What if I have one of those babies that doesn't like being held?" she asked, because she loved to snuggle. "Don't worry," he said. "If she's like that, she'll grow up more independent and leave home sooner." While she was startled at his matter-of-factness, she realized that he was right; there are advantages and disadvantages to every childhood characteristic.

As Bernice Weissbourd recently wrote in *Parents* magazine, "The infant's sense of herself and her sense of others are the same; therefore the beginning of her self-worth is inescapably tied to how well her caregivers care for her." Is she important? Are her needs met? Is she okay just as she is?

The first stages of forming an identity

In *Childhood and Society*, psychoanalyst Erik Erikson presented his influential theory of development and described how, as a child moves through the eight different stages of the life cycle, she must resolve certain crises or conflicts in order to achieve her identity.

Erikson believed the most basic element of a healthy personality is a sense of trust toward herself and toward others. At first a child feels conflict: should she trust others in the strange world in which she finds herself? She needs, for instance, to believe it is safe to put her mouth around that nipple she finds in front of her face; when she does and obtains the nourishment she needs, she feels secure and comfortable. To the degree that her needs are met, reliably and predictably, her sense of trust develops and her mistrust recedes in the first stage.

By the end of the first year of life, Erikson said, a healthy child has a well-established sense of trust. She is then free to initiate actions that please her and explore her environment. While she develops her sense of trust and mistrust in the first stage by reacting to her environment, she develops her sense of autonomy in the second stage by acting. The wise parent encourages her child to experiment with behaviors she enjoys.

When a thirty-five-year-old woman came to a hypnotherapist, she reported that whenever she was happy in a new situation, she became frightened that something bad would happen. In a hypnotic trance she retrieved the following memory. "I am in my crib, bouncing. The door opens, and I can see the light on the floor through the bars of the crib, and I know something bad is going to happen." Out of trance, the woman reported hearing from her mother that whenever she bounced in her crib, her father had come in and spanked her.

It is easy for parents, like that woman's father, to believe that bouncing in cribs, eating dirt, defecating on the rug, or saying "no" are just bad behavior. In fact, they are completely natural explorations. While the sensible father teaches the child to defecate in the toilet, he allows his daughter to say the word *no* without punishing her. He encourages her new endeavors as long as she is safe, because he knows that if she fails to explore, if she retreats to the comfort and security of the first stage of life, she will develop more shame and doubt than autonomy.

By the age of four or five, a child has discovered she is an autonomous person. In the third stage, according to Erikson, a child's principal task is to learn to take the initiative. She can move faster and farther and talk more. It is at this stage that the questions surface: Why, why, and why? A parent who encourages her child to roam and to question facilitates her development. On the other hand, the parent who shames her diminishes her initiative and encourages the development of guilt.

In addition to questioning her environment, a young girl is questioning herself. "Who am I?" she asks. At four or five she begins to answer that question by imitating her parents, especially her mother, and other adults. By introducing her to many different female models in books, on television, in person, the parent increases the possibilities her child can imagine for herself. Susan remembers planning to be a queen, like Ozma of Oz, when a friend of her father's told her, "You can't be a queen in this country." Just as she began to feel foolish and retreat into guilt for even thinking such a thing, the friend said, "But you could be the first woman president!" It was an image she held on to until adolescence.

Before she starts kindergarten, your daughter will have, for better or worse, worked through these first three stages. If her parents' care is reliable, consistent, and predictable, she will develop trust. If her parents encourage her explorations

When I was about four, I was wild for anything "cowboy": western movies and TV shows, horses, hats, boots, six-shooters— you name it. I'd put the hat, boots, and guns on every morning and wear them till bedtime. Then one Saturday my mother appeared with "the" dress: I can still vividly see it. It had a pink and itchy dotted Swiss skirt and a black velvet top that laced up the front. No self-respecting cowboy would have been caught dead in it. But we were going somewhere "special," and if I wanted to come along, I had to wear the dress.

I wanted to go, but there was quite a battle over what I would wear. Tears and threats were traded, and I finally came up with a compromise: I appeared in the dress, wearing my hat and boots. My mother remained firm in her position, a baby-sitter was called, and I stood sobbing on the front lawn as the rest of the family drove away.

—Woman, 40

with enthusiasm, she will develop autonomy. And if her parents support her initiative, including times full of wild ideas or days spent with imaginary friends, her initiative will blossom. Her future drive, hope, self-control, willpower, direction, and sense of purpose also depend, in part, on what happens to her in these important years.

Unfortunately, cultural conditioning can get in the way of a girl's ability to resolve the conflicts of these stages satisfactorily. How is she supposed to feel that she is "all right," for example, if

- *her parents act as if feeding her and holding her is a tremendous bother?*
- *her parents make it clear that they would rather have had a son?*
- *she is expected to conform to preconceived notions of "femininity" rather than allowed the autonomy to be herself?*
- *someone always steps in to "help" her, never allowing her to feel competent or to succeed on her own?*
- *she is gently persuaded to play with dolls rather than blocks, or she is punished for clinging to an "inappropriate" toy or article of clothing?*

Rescuing

We've said it before: Don't rescue your daughter when she's not in danger. Do, however, try to provide a safe environment where she can exercise the emerging autonomy that will be the basis of her self-esteem in later life. It is far easier to support her explorations if you have removed your best crystal vases from the bottom bookshelf. Mindy recalls taking her young daughter, Wendy, to the beach, where she could explore at will under the careful—but unnoticed—surveillance of her mother. Sometimes she'd get as far as fifty yards away from Mindy, picking up interesting objects or stopping to visit with other youngsters. As long as Mindy kept her in sight and knew she could get to her in a few seconds, she let her go. She couldn't help but notice that there were plenty of boys Wendy's age engaged in similar activities, but most of the other girls stayed very close to their mothers. Maybe it was their choice, but given her experience with Wendy, she has to assume they'd received some kind of message from their mothers. Some years later, the day Wendy calmly left home to fly across the country to attend high school all by herself, Mindy thought back to those days at the beach, where she got that first taste of independence.

If you stop to think about it, you are giving your daughter several damaging messages when you step in to rescue her unnecessarily. First, you are casting a vote of no confidence. You are telling her that you don't think she is capable of doing things for herself. Second, she is learning that she will not be held accountable for her actions. If she never has to pay the price for making a bad decision, she can hardly be expected to become a responsible adult, and she will never develop the internal confidence that comes from knowing she can struggle through the bad times and come out stronger on the other end. Finally, your often-rescued daughter may become a victim of learned helplessness. According to this concept, once a person becomes convinced that any action on her part is futile, she will simply stop trying to act. Instead she will passively accept whatever happens to her. Clearly this is not a good way to get through the trials of modern life.

Other points to keep in mind as you care for your infant, toddler, or preschooler

1. Don't worry about "spoiling" your infant daughter with too much love and attention.

The more the better! The care she receives now will affect her ability to trust and her future self-esteem and happiness.

2. Be a good mirror to your child.

Tell her what you see in her. This helps her to see herself more clearly. And tell her the truth about herself, without evaluation. Say, "I see that you like playing with those blocks." The more your statements about your daughter match her perceptions about herself, the more you will facilitate her growing sense of self-esteem. Most people would rather be seen accurately than praised.

3. On the other hand, praise your daughter lavishly as she acquires new skills.

Smile. Squeal with delight. Applaud. Applause and admiration at this stage are essential in the development of a person's secure sense of self.

4. Don't give in to unreasonable wishes.

Respect your daughter's right to ask to keep playing when she needs to take a nap, but put her down, even when she screams. Part of developing self-esteem is learning to tolerate appropriate frustration.

5. What characteristics do you most want to encourage in your daughter?

Look back to the exercise at the end of chapter 3 ("Redefining Femininity") and choose five or six. Post your list somewhere where you'll see it often, and use these words to compliment your daughter. (Aren't you smart to put your toys away so they won't get stepped on! What a brave girl to climb the stairs alone!)

6. Build your toddler's sense of competency by choosing clothes she can put on herself from an early age.

Think elastic and Velcro, not tiny rows of buttons or elaborate sashes. Stimulate her with toys and games that offer a challenge but are not beyond her capabilities.

7. When you are teaching her words, don't use sexist language or labels.

It's "police officer," not "policeman"; "flight attendant," not "stewardess." When referring to individuals in nontraditional jobs, don't include their gender. Say "doctor," not "lady doctor"; "pilot," not "woman pilot"; "secretary," not "male secretary"; and so on. Gently correct your daughter whenever she makes similar misstatements.

8. Think about the behaviors you praise in children of different sexes and the language you use to do so.

Many adults never think of complimenting a child for characteristics or achievements usually associated with the other sex (John can be praised for running fast, but not for being thoughtful; with Judy, it's the other way around).

Similarly, parents and teachers often find different reasons to commend boys and girls for the same action. For example, a girl might be congratulated for not getting paint on her dress or hands, while a boy would be praised for his skill as a painter. Give your daughter credit for the positive things she does, not for passive behaviors like staying clean or being quiet or for things beyond her control, like the color of her hair.

9. *"Treat girls and boys differently to achieve equity for both,"* suggests Girls Inc.'s booklet *Facts and Reflections on Careers for Today's Girls.*

"Differential treatment of girls and boys begins so early and is so pervasive, that by the time they reach preschool, children need corrective action from adults. Offer girls special encouragement to be exploring and adventuresome. Offer boys special permission to be interested in dolls or to want a hug along with a Band-Aid."

10. *Be aware of outside influences on your daughter's worldview.*

One mother who was making a conscious effort to raise her daughter in a nonsexist manner was disconcerted when the child insisted that only a man could own a family's home. "Where does she get these notions?" her mother wondered. It turned out that the nursery school her daughter attended had a regular time when everyone "played house," and that during this activity, the boys were always acknowledged as the home owners. When you choose a nursery or preschool for your daughter, be sure to ask about the instructors' philosophies on gender roles and the differences between the sexes. Observe your baby-sitters' attitudes and assumptions. Get to know the parents of your daughter's friends, if you can. We don't mean to say that you can or should keep her from hearing sexist messages, but if you know what's going on, you can often reverse or limit the damage.

Are girls and boys born different?

It's not an easy matter to determine whether the differences we attribute to males and females are based in biology or socialization, although countless studies have been made. Newborn babies have a limited range of behaviors to observe, and they are incapable of direct communication with the researcher. Is Bobby crying because he's angry and Barbie because she's afraid? Bobby and Barbie aren't talking.

But because cultural conditioning begins so early in life, studies of only slightly older children are suspect, too. Is there a physiological reason why girls are more verbal, or is it just that mothers tend to talk to them more?

The one undeniable fact is that there are physical differ-

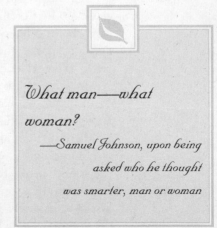

What man—what woman?
—*Samuel Johnson, upon being asked who he thought was smarter, man or woman*

ences between the sexes. Besides the obvious ones, it seems to be true after puberty that males are faster runners while females have more endurance, and males have greater upper-body strength while female strength is more likely to be concentrated in the lower body. Again, however, this is true of the genders as a whole, not necessarily of individuals. Joan Benoit, the first Olympic women's marathon champion, clearly could run faster than a great many men.

In addition, it seems quite likely that male and female hormones contribute to some behavioral dissimilarities. Researchers have also been studying the human brain and finding some variations between those of men and women.

There isn't a great deal of information we can report as fact, but what follows is a summary of the latest and/or most widely accepted studies. Making yourself familiar with them is important, because we all carry around with us a "culturized critic," a little voice looking for opportunities to point out that "girls can't," "girls don't," or "girls aren't interested" in the topic at hand. From now on, when you hear from your critic, use this material to help decide how much credence you want to give what he or she has to say.

There is little clear evidence of behavioral differences between the sexes before age two. It is commonly believed that girl infants are more vocal and boys more active, but the studies do not seem to bear this out. They do indicate a possible difference in the way male and female infants react to vocal stimulation: the boys' responses seem to indicate general restlessness, while the girls appear to be trying to assimilate or understand the event.

It's difficult to say, though, that these reactions prove any kind of basic difference between the sexes. It's quite possible that girls are more attentive because they are born with a more fully developed central nervous system than boys and so are somewhat developmentally advanced. It's possible, too, that the variations could be the result of the ways parents react to their infants: mothers have been shown to spend more time talking with their daughters, while it is suspected that parents are more likely to engage in physical kinds of play with their sons.

Parental social class relates more to the development of girls than of boys. Because mothers of all classes believe that their sons will grow up to be providers, they raise them to be independent, self-sufficient achievers. The belief that girls should develop similar traits is less universal. Upper-middle-class mothers are the most likely to see wider choices in their daughters' future and to raise them accordingly.

In other words, the way you feel about your infant daughter's potential for success in later life may be a self-fulfilling prophecy. When you believe in her abilities, and treat her as an achiever, you are increasing her potential to thrive.

By the time infants are three months old, mothers react differently to the cries of boys and girls. At three weeks, infants of both sexes get prompt attention from their mother. At three months, daughters are more likely to receive responses to their cries than sons. Males seem to cry more and sleep less than females during the first months of life, so perhaps these mothers are more exhausted and frustrated than the parents of daughters. It's also possible that parents believe their sons require less comforting or should learn to be tough, while they feel more need to coddle their daughters.

Baby girls do not seem to be more fearful or irritable than baby boys. There does seem to be a difference, however, in the way those who exhibit these traits develop. Irritable boys, by age two, scored lower on vocabulary tests and had less well developed speech, while irritable girls had become active and restless by the same age.

Fearful boys remained inhibited and apprehensive at age two, while fearful girls became more verbal, outgoing, and precocious than average. The most likely explanation for these disparities is that parents react differently to fearfulness and irritability in boys and girls, but there is no proof that this is so.

Studies of dependency in infants show little or no difference between the sexes. By the time children are thirteen months old, however, boys will wander a greater distance from their mothers, and maintain that distance for a longer period of time. Girls are more vocal and touch their mothers more frequently.

Although, during the first six months of life, mothers tend to have more physical contact with their sons (perhaps because boys sleep less), they spend more time talking to, smiling, and looking at their daughters from birth on. After age six months, daughters also receive more physical contact. Researchers interpret all this to mean that mothers are more likely to encourage independence in their sons and to bond more closely with their daughters.

As children grow up, dependent boys often become less so, while dependent girls are likely to become dependent women. Many experts believe this is the result of societal pressure: dependency in women is more acceptable than dependency in men. It seems reasonable to believe, then, that you can foster independence in your daughter by loosening the parental strings and demonstrating your belief in her and your regard for self-sufficiency.

From about age two on, males are more aggressive than females. This is one of the few areas in which the evidence is persuasive, and the difference is probably biologically based. Males are more aggressive across all cultural lines and even in nonhuman species. Studies on female rhesus monkeys treated with the male hormone testosterone demonstrated that aggression can be induced: the monkeys became more aggressive when they received the hormone.

It should be noted that all females naturally produce some testosterone and also that cultural conditioning has an influence on aggressive behavior. Girls do have aggressive tendencies, though it is less socially acceptable for them to behave aggressively.

At the risk of sounding militant, we would like to suggest that you actually encourage a certain level of aggressiveness in your daughter. It's okay for her to defend herself or stand up for her rights. Among other benefits, children who are more aggressive and outgoing make friends more easily when they start school. Interestingly, society seems less tolerant of aggression in women than in men, even though in females the trait is seldom related to violence. Rather, girls who score as more aggressive in studies tend to be more interested in "masculine" activities, such as athletics. Though the most aggressive boys have fantasies about violence, the most aggressive girls daydream about winning and achieving.

Beginning in mid- to late childhood, boys and girls seem to excel at different types of mental skills. We'll discuss this more thoroughly later in the book, but briefly, girls seem to have better verbal skills, while boys excel in mathematics and have better spatial skills. It is important to remember that there are individual differences. A woman who is chief city planner for a northern California city was tested and told that her spatial skills were better than 85 percent of all adults. Don't make assumptions that limit your daughter's career options.

Gender is not destiny. Making assumptions about your daughter's temperament, intelligence, or ambition based on her sex is doing her a great disservice. Instead it is essential to focus on the individual traits and abilities that are uniquely her own.

Now that you've seen how stereotyping behavior as "feminine" or "masculine" can place limits on your daughter, turn to "Your Plan" on page 457 and consider the messages you want to give your young daughter on this topic.

chapter eleven

Ages Six to Ten

The elementary school years are magical for many girls. They are learning, doing, mastering skills, and exploring the world, which seems to offer boundless opportunities. They aren't yet aware of the limitations faced by adults and especially by women. Treasure this time with your daughter.

At this age, children need to develop a sense of competence. They want to learn to do everything, partly because by doing things they gain a sense of importance.

Increasingly, they spend time with their peers, and they assess their competence by comparing themselves to others. To find themselves wanting in too many areas leads to a sense of inferiority. The wise parent encourages the development of skills in a realistic way. Now is your chance to frame each new task, each change in your daughter's life, as a challenge.

Formerly interested primarily in play, children of both sexes now become learners and workers. They take pride in their achievements, which are made possible, in part, by their increased attention span and ability to follow a project through to completion. If you have endowed your daughter with a sense of confidence and competence, she should relish this challenge.

When she goes off to school, she enters a world in which your role is diminished. School is a completely different culture. Here she must earn the approval of the teacher, a strange adult who may not offer the kind of unconditional love your daughter gets at home. And she must compete for attention with a room full of other children her age, who may be brighter, louder, or more popular than she. If she is not successful, she may begin to feel inadequate or inferior.

Your ongoing love and encouragement, as well as the preparation you've done, are essential at this point. If your daughter starts school with a high level of self-esteem, she will feel capable of completing the tasks of learning. Her achievements will, in turn, reinforce that sense of competence. If, however, she starts out feeling incompetent, she is less likely to do well at school, and the experience will make her feel even worse about herself. Ideally, from a developmental standpoint, she should be prepared for the coming challenges when she enters school, and the school should do its part by providing her with learning tasks at an appropriate level of difficulty.

Emergence of the authentic self

In her book *The Girl Within*, author Emily Hancock paints the world of an eight- to ten-year-old girl as an idyllic time when she feels capable and valued. Anything seems possible for her. According to Hancock, this is the time when a female's "root identity" or "authentic self" emerges, only to be quickly submerged with the onset of adolescence.

Hancock demonstrates this "vital self" by quoting one of her interview subjects: "At nine, I can remember walking on a fence, all around a park, thinking I really liked being nine years old and I wouldn't mind being nine forever. . . . I remember having a real sense of joy, of confidence about negotiating the world on my own. . . . I felt secure and self-contained. I had a sense that 'I can get by in the world, even if it means I am alone.'"

Describe yourself at that age, in "You at Nine" on the following page.

Most women will find that they are different now. What happened? Hancock's theory, one that seems to be upheld by Lyn Mikel Brown and Carol Gilligan in *Meeting at the Crossroads: Women's Psychology and Girls' Development*, is that as they enter adolescence, girls are instructed to leave that "root identity" behind.

Adolescence is a time of such major psychic upheaval that few young women will get through it with their previous identity intact. By encouraging your preadolescent daughter, however, and applauding her efforts and achievements, you can help solidify this "authentic self," assuring that it will be hers later on, when she wants to reclaim it. Better yet, if you can make her believe that it is okay to be "different" from other girls, she may be able to hold on to the conviction throughout her life.

The adult women Emily Hancock interviewed had only their memories to help them find "the girl within." You can provide more substantive materials for your daughter by maintaining a journal of her ninth year (feel free to start earlier if it

You at nine

Women readers, do you remember your ninth year? Think back to that time for a few minutes. You were probably in the fourth grade.

What school did you go to?

Who was your teacher?

What were your favorite subjects?

What did you do after school?

Who were your best friends?

What did you feel passionate about?

What were you like? How would you describe yourself at that time?

Can you see yourself at a family gathering during that year? What were you doing? How did you feel?

What were your dreams?

What was the most memorable event of that year?

How are you the same or different today?

seems appropriate). Try to be more of a reporter than a parent while carrying out this exercise: be objective, don't insert your own feelings or assume that you know what your daughter is thinking or feeling ("Cindy has now filled fourteen shoeboxes with her rock collection," not "Cindy seems very fond of rocks, but I'm sure she's only imitating her older brother").

Quote your daughter directly when you can. Include photos, schoolwork, letters from camp, and other primary sources.

Write about her passions, her dreams, her energy, her self-assurance. Tell the stories of her life, and remember to use language that is empowering. Recognize her skills and strengths, celebrate her successes and failures, acknowledge her courage and her fears.

Here are some things to watch for and include: Where and with whom does she spend most of her time? What are her favorite outdoor activities? Indoor activities? What does she like to wear? Does she collect things? What? What are her favorite subjects at school? Her best subjects? Her hobbies? Her ambitions? How does she like to wear her hair? What opinions does she voice? Is she good at sports? Which ones? What books is she reading? Who are her heroes (male and/or female)? What gifts does she request? What does she spend her allowance on? Describe her activities on a typical day when she's free to do whatever she pleases. Put positives in the journal, not negatives.

When your adolescent daughter has a self-esteem-threatening crisis, get out the journal and share it with her. You'll know the right time. Later on, perhaps to celebrate a milestone such as graduation, marriage, or motherhood, wrap it up and give it to her to keep. It will be a continual reminder, helping her stay true to her unique identity.

If your daughter is older than nine, make a scrapbook of all the photos, school papers, and so on that you have from that time. They should help you write about your memories of her at that age. Record your recollections in as much detail as you can.

Career awareness begins in childhood

As we've noted before, children tend to have sex-stereotyped views concerning work. Categorizing who can do what by gender may be the easiest way for youngsters to make sense of the world. Unfortunately, their perceptions have not kept pace with changing times. Even though more women are working at a wider variety of jobs, children are still likely to think that females can be mommies, teachers, secretaries, or nurses. Perhaps these messages come from the media, or maybe we are still passing on the same messages we received from our parents.

Some children assign gender to task according to what they see. If mom's job is to stay home and take care of the family, your daughter is more likely to see that as the "correct" role for women, and she will probably spend more time playing house than the daughters of mothers who work outside the home as well. This tendency to consider jobs appropriate based on the sex of the people who occupy those positions can work the other way, too. A child whose mother is an airline pilot and whose father is a nurse is likely to believe that most pilots are women and most nurses are men.

As they get older, children tend to modify their views, but it is still a good idea to let your daughter see women working at as many kinds of jobs as you can find, and men also nurturing children.

Take a girl to work

Talk to your daughter about your work (too often, children have little or no idea what their parents do every day when they leave the house), and take her along with you for a day, if you can. Better yet, make it one day a year—during the summer so as not to interfere with her school schedule. She doesn't have to do anything except observe you and your co-workers (and not get in anyone's way). This is called "shadowing." We will discuss it in more detail in chapter 24, "Helping Girls Realize Their Career Potential." This can be an enlightening and rewarding experience for girls, as hundreds of thousands of parents discovered in April 1993 when the Ms. Foundation sponsored its first national "Take Your Daughter to Work Day."

As your daughter gets older, you might arrange for her to spend the day with people who do jobs different from your own. Then, when she starts expressing interest in various careers, try to find someone working in that field who is willing to be shadowed. A school career specialist or counselor might be able to help you find the right individual, if you don't know anyone personally. But take the lead in this effort. Don't wait for your daughter's school to do it. This requires coordination and some detective work. Teachers and counselors rarely have the time to perform this important function even though they would like to.

In the past, when many jobs fell into the "hard labor" category, some good arguments could be made for keeping women out of them. Most (but not all) men are bigger and stronger than most (but not all) women, particularly in upper body strength. Today, physical stamina is less often a requirement. Why, then, do so many people still feel that particular careers are best suited for one sex or the other? Have your daughter and her friends fill in the "Job Descriptions" activity on page 151.

Defining and valuing work

People generally think of work as something physical and/or something you get paid for doing. Make sure your daughter understands that work encompasses a much wider variety of activities, and that it is valuable in and of itself. Performing all kinds of tasks, including mental tasks and volunteer activities, is working. Be sure that you refer to mothers as "employed outside the house" or "working at home" instead of "working" or "not working."

Mindy's daughter, Wendy, attended Montessori school. One of Maria Montessori's key goals was to help children value work, and the instructors at Wendy's school made it very clear that "work is good" and asked parents of new students to reinforce that notion. They applied the label to everything from cutting bananas to picking up toys. When Mindy would visit on parent days, Wendy would come and talk to her for a while, then say, "I'm going to work now," and toddle off to complete the tasks that she loved and valued.

You can impress your daughter with the same message by using a phrase like "Let's go to work" when you ask her to do her chores. At the dinner table let everyone take turns announcing what "work" he or she accomplished during the day. Try not to say that you are "going to work" when you leave the house in the morning, as it implies that your other tasks are not work. And, again, don't assign household chores based on gender.

Perhaps this is a good time to examine your own feelings. Do you often complain about your job, or say things like "Work isn't meant to be fun"? Or are you one of those terminally responsible types who works long hours without seeming enjoyment and then has little time or energy left for anything else? Perhaps you like what you do. If so, do you ever tell your daughter? "Once I told my daughter," Ebony said, "that I was really lucky because I can use all of my talents and ideas in my job. 'That's great, Mom!' she said, and then she went on to discuss what jobs might fit her own talents and ideas."

We like the Maria Montessori approach, which encourages children to develop

Job descriptions

Next time your grade-school-age daughter has a group of friends over, ask them to write down the key tasks performed by people working at the following jobs. Give them ten minutes to come up with their list.

Crane operator on a construction site
TV news anchor
Instructor at a nursery school
Surgeon
President of the United States
Parent

Award the teams one point for each reasonable task they can list. Then ask them to underline any task that could not be completed by a male and circle the tasks that a female could not do.

If a team can convince the rest of the group that any of its perceived limitations are valid, award five points for each. This should lead to some interesting discussions. The team with the most points is declared the winner.

initiative by emphasizing that work is valued. With or without the help of Montessori schools, you can make it clear to your daughter that the term embraces both housework and homework. Mental exertion is just as valid as physical toil.

You can help her start to develop a positive attitude at an early age by allowing her to take part in household chores as soon as she's marginally able to perform. True, you could make the bed faster, but keep in mind that getting the bed made is of secondary importance here. What you're really doing is building your daughter's self-esteem and preparing her for a successful future.

Use the words *work* and *job* often to deepen her awareness. ("You did a good job!" "Do you enjoy this kind of work?") As she gets older, expect a higher level of performance. Give her more responsibility, too. Some experts suggest that older children receive "promotions," along with an informal job description outlining the chores for which they will be held accountable.

And consider "Who Does the Grocery Shopping?" in your house.

Who does the grocery shopping?

Consider which chores you assign to your daughter. For that matter, think about all the jobs that are done around your house and whether they are usually completed by a male or female. We've listed some common chores below. Put an "F" in front of those items usually done in your home by a female, an "M" in front of the chores usually performed by males, and an "FM" in front of jobs shared by both sexes.

__ Grocery shopping	__ Cleaning the bathroom
__ Setting the table	__ Fixing appliances
__ Preparing food	__ Lighting the fireplace/furnace
__ Clearing the table	__ Yardwork/gardening
__ Making bag lunches	__ Watering plants
__ Taking out the trash	__ Feeding pets
__ Making beds	__ Caring for pets
__ "Picking up" the house	__ Paying bills
__ Getting the mail and/or newspaper	__ Auto maintenance
__ Dusting	__ Recycling
__ Vacuuming	__ Scheduling repairs
__ Laundry	__ Taking deliveries
__ Ironing	__ Changing the baby
__ Mending clothes	__ Feeding the baby
__ Going to the cleaners	__ Playing with the baby
__ Washing floors	

Take another look at your list of chores in "Who Does the Grocery Shopping?" If most chores in your house are divided along traditional lines (men mow the lawn and take out the trash, women cook and clean and care for the baby), your daughter may be getting the wrong message (and the women in your house are probably over-worked!).

Why not make some changes? Try listing all the chores on pieces of paper and then have family members draw their "jobs of the week" out of a hat. Or just make a switch. For a day or a week or a month, let the males do the jobs usually done by females, and vice versa. No one in your family should feel that by virtue of her sex, she is either totally responsible for or totally incapable of completing any task.

Many girls spend most of their time in the company of women and thus become familiar only with traditional female activities. Allow your daughter to tag along with you, Dad, when you do your weekend errands. Take her to the hardware store or to get the oil changed in the car. Explain to her how you're repairing the faucet or the roof. But don't feel you have to be uncharacteristically "macho." If you are the primary grocery shopper and cook in the family, your daughter will still learn that these tasks are not gender related.

Present being female as an expanding experience, not a limiting one

In the fall of 1992, when the Minneapolis *Star Tribune* asked its young readers to respond to the question "Would you rather be a man or a woman?" a ten-year-old girl wrote: "I want to be a woman because I can do or be whatever I want. I can be president or a mom, mow the lawn, shovel driveways and rake the lawn. I can have a greenhouse. I can write books; I can read books. I can wear a skirt or a dress. I can get my ears pierced and have long hair. I can be an inventor. I can be a scientist or I can be a doctor. I can cry. I can cut firewood. I can work at a store. I can be rich. I can have a mansion. I can be an art teacher or music teacher or a diver. I can be a clock maker. I can make clothes. I can go to the North Pole."

This young woman may soon lose her "can do" spirit, but we hope it doesn't happen. We hope, too, that you will do everything you can to foster the same kind of confidence and expansive hopes in your own daughter.

Girls who foresee limitless opportunities for themselves are likely to have mothers and other female role models who do not view life in either/or terms. Sometimes they put up tents and build campfires; sometimes they wear high heels and go dancing. Sometimes they work at the computer; sometimes they make brownies. They do what they can and what they want, and they clearly enjoy it.

If a girl could have a mother like that and a father who also felt comfortable in a variety of traditional and nontraditional roles, and if he voiced respect for his wife and encouragement for his daughter, chances are that girl would feel good about being female. It would look like fun to be an adult woman.

What else can you do? Show your encouragement in actions as well as words. If your daughter expresses an interest in collecting butterflies, get her a butterfly net. Take her to the library and check out books on the subject. If she likes cars, take her to a museum. Buy her some model kits. Check out some more books. And so on. Never, ever say, "You can't do that because you're a girl."

"Introduce your daughters to the bigger world," suggests Jan Fritzen, professor in the Department of Women's Studies at Saddleback College in Irvine, California. Exposure to different places, people, and experiences allows for a broader vision, she says. Even if you can't afford frequent trips to distant destinations, take advantage of all your own region has to offer—museums, zoos, theaters, concerts, athletic events, ethnic festivals, and so on. Tour the state capital, sit in on a court proceeding or an orchestral rehearsal. Watch someone paint a picture or build a wall. Introduce your daughter to women working at "untraditional" jobs. If possible, take her to a woman doctor and dentist, use a female mechanic or handyperson, and so on.

Provide experiences for your daughter. Dreaming about being an astronomer or reading about it is great, but getting a telescope to study the night sky or visiting the local observatory is even more meaningful. Girls need as many opportunities to do things as they can get.

When Mindy was a child, she spent almost as much time with the next-door neighbors, Dick and Frances Taylor, as she did with her own family. Their children were grown, with families of their own, and for whatever reason, Dick decided to adopt her as his "son." She'd spend weekends with them at their desert cabin, where he taught her to shoot a rifle. They'd go on long hikes and he'd teach her about nature. At night they'd play poker. They spent hours and hours throwing a baseball back and forth, and he let her work beside him in his workshop as he built lamps and fixed household items.

One summer, when she was nine, she spent three weeks with the Taylors in the wilds of northern Montana. There was a neighbor girl her age, and many mornings they'd pack a lunch and ride horses—bareback—out into the foothills of the mountains, where they'd spend the entire day exploring. It was a wonderful adventure. Mindy has always loved the Taylors, but it's only in retrospect she can see how truly lucky she was to have them in her life. Their expectations of what she was capable of doing helped her become a leader, decision maker, and risk taker.

Acquiring skills is a definite boon to self-esteem. Try to see that your daughter can boast of achievements in each of the following areas:

1. Sports.

Participation, especially in team sports, builds strength and courage, teaches assertiveness and leadership skills, and much more. See chapter 18, "Lessons Learned on the Playing Field."

2. Conquering the outdoors.

Hiking, biking, camping, swimming, climbing, and so on are not only important skills, but they build self-confidence and allow ample opportunities for relatively safe risk taking.

3. Games of skill.

Chess, video games, poker, and the like encourage decisiveness and creative thinking.

4. Activities that build manual and technical dexterity.

Working at a computer, building model cars and airplanes, and similar activities are valuable for teaching these important skills.

You can also make it a point to pay attention to women in the news and discuss their accomplishments with your daughter. Give her biographies of accomplished women, and books with strong female characters. When you choose videos, look for those with positive role models for women.

Encourage your daughter to become a leader

When girls are asked what they want from a career, "helping others" is the response at the top of most lists. It's an admirable goal, but unfortunately girls tend to think of giving help at only the most direct levels. Thus, they take supportive positions like secretaries and nurses' aides or go into traditional female careers like teaching. Many of these jobs don't pay well enough to support a family.

"How do you become a leader?" asked Sally.

"Well, first, you have to be pretty clever," responded Hattie. "Then you have to study, practice and work hard to gain the respect and confidence of those who must follow you. But once you are the leader, you usually make the rules."

—*from My Way Sally by Mindy Bingham and Penelope Colville Paine*

Even more important for society, this attitude deprives us of half our leadership capability. Girls need to begin seeing at an early age that in positions of authority, they can help more people in more ways. The nurse can be a doctor or a nursing supervisor, the teacher can be a principal, and she can affect the treatment of more people than she did before.

Try to provide opportunities for your daughter to act as a leader. Give her tasks and challenges that require her to give orders, supervise others, be decisive, and take control.

Start, too, to discuss politics and world events with your children. What would they do if they were in charge? As a group, try to come up with win/win solutions for social, political, or environmental problems. When your daughter begins to consider future careers for herself, suggest that she think about a life in politics, or becoming a responsible business leader, religious leader, or humanitarian. Encourage and support her when she runs for class or club office.

Many people find this difficult to think about for two reasons:

1. *Nurses, secretaries, and teachers are valuable contributors to our society, and the society needs them. However, the society doesn't value them enough at this point to pay them what they need to support a family.*

2. *Some of our daughters, like our sons, are natural introverts. They don't want to stand up and tell others what to do. However, you can point out that they had no difficulty telling their "children" what to do when they were playing house and go from there.*

There are many ways to obtain power and influence others; one path, for example, is developing valuable skills, such as those needed for scientific research. Help your daughter develop talents that people will admire and pay for. Having more women working at the decision-making level in many occupations could be key to making the future better for everyone's daughter.

You might want to get a copy of *My Way Sally* from the library, read it as a family, and use the questions at the end for a discussion. The book, winner of the 1989 Ben Franklin Award, is the story of a young female foxhound who works hard to become the leader of the pack so she can make more compassionate and creative rules.

Begin your daughter's financial training early

Like sex, money is an emotionally charged subject. Historically it has been linked to power, identity, control, and sexual prowess, all characteristics considered masculine or, at least, unladylike. For these reasons, many women have either refused or been denied the opportunity to deal with it, and this failure has created much hardship.

The ability to handle money responsibly contributes to high self-esteem in adults of both sexes. The inverse is also true. People who don't know how to deal prudently with their finances feel incompetent and not in control of their lives.

For all its symbolic attachments, money is only a tool. If your daughter is to use it wisely, she needs instruction and practice. If she can master this subject, she is likely to become a financially self-sufficient adult and to acquire the feelings of competence and autonomy that go along with that status. Learning to live within her means will build her character. As a prudent money manager, she will be valued by society. Being economically secure will help her maintain high self-esteem.

We don't mean to imply that making money should be the central joy and purpose of anyone's life. It is important, though, to be self-sufficient and able to live within a budget, whatever its size. In a recent national poll, women said that lack of money was the major cause of stress in their lives. If you want to spare your daughter from this fate, begin now with a solid education in finance. Those who learn early, learn best.

Your daughter is ready for an allowance as soon as she is able to add and subtract. Negotiate the amount with her, and make it clear what the money is for and what she must do to earn it. Depending on her age, the weekly amount might cover a snack or treat each week, her favorite monthly magazine, savings for a larger purchase (an audiotape or hair ornament), some kind of entertainment (a movie or a round of miniature golf), a specified amount for a charity or religious organization, and an amount to be saved each week and deposited in the bank each month.

When she enters fourth or fifth grade, expand her allowance to cover the cost of school lunches and bus fare. If she wants to make her own lunch and save that money, allow her to purchase the groceries she needs (monitoring for nutritional value) and allocate the money left over as she sees fit.

One of Mindy's earliest memories is of the day her mother took her to open her first savings account at the bank. She had just learned to write and felt very proud as the bank officer helped her fill out the account information. Afterward her mother took her out to lunch to celebrate this momentous occasion. Mindy saved a part of her income throughout childhood and her first twenty years in the workforce. This

I had no clue about how to be responsible for myself financially when I left home. I guess my parents thought the ability to handle money prudently came naturally (just like they thought everyone knew about sex). The topic of money in my house was just as hush-hush as the topic of sex. My first year on my own, I ran up a lot of bills on my credit card. I finally had to get a night job to pay those bills off. When my dad offered me a loan to get me through, I felt terrible. I felt like a failure. I wanted to be able to stand on my own two feet.

I've just completed a money management class through our adult education unit. Hey, this isn't rocket science. I wish I had known what I know now when I was younger. I probably would have made different choices in a number of areas in my life.

—Woman, 24

money allowed her to quit working for someone else at age forty and invest in herself. She started a publishing company specializing in educational textbooks. Saving money is a value and skill she wants her daughter to have, too.

Help your daughter open a savings account as soon as she can write her name. Choose a bank that's conveniently located so she can deposit her savings every month. Make it a ritual. Let her do as much of the work as her skills allow.

If you belong to a credit union or some other formal savings plan, take your daughter along when you deposit money or attend to business affairs. Explain early what a pension is and how compounding interest tax free works over thirty or forty years. Perhaps your banker has a chart that illustrates the difference in retirement income between those who began saving at age twenty-five and those who waited until they were forty-five or fifty. For a ten-year-old girl, this is a startling revelation.

One day when Mindy's daughter was ten she proudly showed her mother how she'd learned to write checks at school and asked if Mindy needed any checks written. Mindy looked at Wendy's eager face and thought, Why not? She spent an evening showing Wendy a system that would allow her to pay the family bills and maintain the checkbook balance.

Once a month Mindy would go through all the bills and circle the amount of each check, underlining whom it should be made out to. Wendy would then write the checks, enter them in the checkbook, address the envelopes if necessary, stamp them, and leave each check and return receipt tucked under the envelope flap. Mindy would review and sign each check before sealing the envelopes and putting them all in the mail. Wendy soon became familiar with the household expenses and the cost of living. She developed a sense of how far a paycheck went. To this day she is a conscientious shopper and has no illusions concerning financial matters.

Many ten-year-olds are capable of performing this task, but you might choose to wait until your daughter's a bit older. We recommend the "old-fashioned" handwritten method instead of the computer program many people have adopted. She'll learn more from the "hands on" experience.

Don't use this activity with your daughter if your family is experiencing financial difficulties. Seeing that there isn't enough money to go around and not being able to do anything about it is an extremely stressful situation for a child.

By age ten, your daughter is probably ready for more long-term planning and spending activities. Sit down with her and negotiate an average annual clothing allowance that's acceptable to both of you. The chart "The Clothing Allowance" should help. Mindy's father began using this activity with her when she was in the seventh grade, and Mindy started using it with her daughter when Wendy was a sixth grader.

By the second or third year of doing "The Clothing Allowance," your daughter is likely to have improved her negotiation skills.

For two years Wendy tried to get Mindy to increase her clothing allowance substantially. One day, just before she left to go back east for school, she walked in with a copy of *Choices,* turned to the page with a chart abbreviated from the original one above, and said, "Mom, let's use this to determine my clothing allowance."

What could Mindy say? She had coauthored the book. Wendy went through the chart item by item, and her projections did not seem unreasonable to Mindy. Wendy quoted department store and discount house averages, not boutique prices. And yes, she was growing like a weed. Mindy was shocked and Wendy was delighted when the total came to nearly $1,100. She nearly doubled her clothing allowance that day.

Clothing allowances, or any kind of allowance structure that gives the child responsibility for planning and saving, are excellent for building self-reliance and a feeling of being in control of her world. There will probably be times, however, when your daughter will encounter a problem. What if, for example, her allowance runs out right before the big dance? You may be tempted to rescue her, but try not to. Perhaps this story will give you strength.

Wendy's clothing allowance year was July 1 to June 30. Because she went to high school on the East Coast, she had to have a winter wardrobe, something the family was not quite as concerned about in Southern California. One year, following a sudden growth spurt, Mindy got a plaintive call from Wendy saying she'd spent her clothing allowance, but she needed warm clothes. Wendy had been particularly frivolous the previous summer in her clothing purchases, even though her mom had reminded her about the budget. Mindy fought the urge to rescue her, struggled with the little voice inside her that was whispering what a horrible mother she was, and said, "No, Wendy, you are just going to have to work something out."

The clothing allowance

With your daughter, decide how many blouses, sweaters, and so on your daughter is likely to need in the coming year and a reasonable cost for each item. Total your figures to determine the allowance. Make sure your daughter is an active participant in this process. Encourage her input. She should feel satisfied with the amount she receives. Negotiate, too, whether and how much of this figure she should earn. You might compromise, deciding that she will have to pay for all her accessories, for example.

	NUMBER/YEAR		AVERAGE PRICE		TOTAL COST/YEAR
Dresses		×	$	=	$
Blouses		×	$	=	$
Skirts		×	$	=	$
Sweaters		×	$	=	$
Jackets		×	$	=	$
Pants		×	$	=	$
Shorts		×	$	=	$
Tops		×	$	=	$
Panties		×	$	=	$
Bras		×	$	=	$
Panty hose		×	$	=	$
Socks		×	$	=	$
Shoes		×	$	=	$
Bedclothes		×	$	=	$
Coats		×	$	=	$
Swimsuit or sportswear		×	$	=	$
Jewelry		×	$	=	$
Hair ornaments		×	$	=	$
Miscellaneous		×	$	=	$
					Total:

Mindy felt terrible! Twice she went to her desk with the intention of writing a check. She tossed and turned all night. Late the next day she got a call from an excited, exuberant young woman: "Mom, guess what I just discovered? The XYZ thrift store in the village! I got two pair of wool pants—and they're lined, Mom—and one great wool parka. The pants were three dollars each and the coat was five." She bubbled on about her purchases, and you would have thought from the excitement that she had just walked out of Saks with an armful of designer wear.

The exitement wasn't over the clothes, it was over the realization that she could take care of herself. She could be self-reliant. Her self-esteem soared that day.

Give your daughter the gift of dignity. Let her learn to take care of herself.

Encourage entrepreneurial endeavors

Earning money is exciting for young people. Can you remember how you earned your first dollar? Sooner or later your daughter will probably want an opportunity to augment her allowance. But there are few opportunities for elementary-age children. Why not encourage your daughter to go into business for herself?

Some children can be quite successful with the traditional lemonade stand if they live in the right place. Mindy's daughter, for example, ran a lucrative business because they lived across the street from a nature preserve that was also the entrance to a beach a mile farther on, at the bottom of a steep cliff. The trip back was arduous, and people were thirsty by the time they reached their cars parked along Mindy's street. At age nine Wendy borrowed a large cooler from a neighbor, got her mom to put venture capital into the first cans of frozen lemonade, outfitted her wagon to carry the cooler, and hand-lettered some signs. Soon her business grew to the point where she needed to hire other neighborhood children to help her. Everyone's self-esteem grew with the success of the little business.

Mindy remembers one day walking out to check on the kids. She saw Ronnie, the self-proclaimed vice president, riding his bike down the street. "Ronnie," she said, "why aren't you working?" He looked her straight in the eye and said in all seriousness, "I'm on my break."

This kind of activity will offer your daughter a positive work experience before she holds her first "real" job. Help where you're needed, but allow her to take charge of everything she's capable of doing.

The jobs available for most teens today are usually of the dead-end, low-skill variety. While they can teach important work ethics and attitudes, they aren't particularly satisfying, especially for talented, energetic young women. If she's had an experience like Wendy's, your daughter will realize that work doesn't have to be that way, that it can be creative and exciting—particularly if she's the boss!

Another entrepreneurial activity your daughter might enjoy is one Wendy started at age ten and continues to do when she's home from college. When Mindy was working full-time, grocery shopping was one of her least favorite things. The thought of struggling through crowded aisles and standing in long lines after an exhausting day on the job made her crazy. But Wendy loved to shop. She'd locate the needed items, look for the best deals and right sizes, and check them off the list.

The market offered "double coupon discounts," a great idea but one Mindy seldom had time to take advantage of. Wendy, however, loved coupon hunts and one day made her mom an offer she couldn't refuse: She would do the shopping and put away the groceries if she could keep all the money they saved by using coupons. Sounded win/win to Mindy.

It worked better than she expected. Wendy got an old accordion-type folder, combed the newspapers for coupons, and filed them by category (cleaning supplies, paper goods, frozen foods, beverages, and so on). Then, after Mindy gave Wendy her list, she would go to her folder and pick out all the appropriate coupons. (There was no room for brand loyalty in this arrangement. They used whatever soap or peanut butter she had coupons for. But they did get to try a lot of new products!)

Mindy would drop her off at the market with a signed check made out to the store. (She always added a note on the lower left corner of the check saying it was not to exceed a certain amount, just in case Wendy lost it. She never did.)

Wendy was the hit of the store. Small for her age, she could barely see over the handle of the grocery cart. The management was aware of the arrangement and let her check out, filling in the correct amount for her purchases. She would be waiting for Mindy at a prescribed time in front of the store with the bagged groceries.

Once they arrived home, she would put everything away and then sit down with her calculator to figure her "cut." Usually it would be between $25 and $35 for a major shopping trip and at least $14 to $18 for weekly groceries.

Before long Mindy was getting calls from the mothers of her classmates. They wanted to know all about this. Wendy also started taking on other clients, doing their shopping, too.

This kind of activity is beneficial in many ways. It involves both math and reading. Your daughter must develop a system for organizing the job. She has an opportunity to practice her negotiating skills (particularly with those highly regarded "$1 off" coupons). And she gets to enter the world of commerce as an adult. She gets to see just how far a dollar goes at a grocery store today. It's a good reality check for a youngster who is used to paying only for her own snack foods. (And it shows parents what their daughter can accomplish, if allowed.)

Preparing for the next years

To recap, your daughter's elementary years are the time to instill the attitudes that will carry her through more difficult periods. To quote one of the women Emily Hancock interviewed for *The Girl Within*, "I was good at absolutely everything. I was interested in almost everything I knew about. I was a kind of Renaissance eight-year-old, if you will. That, for me, was equated with happiness. The seeds of self-ownership were there."

What messages would you give your daughter about economic self-sufficiency? Add them to "Your Plan," page 474.

chapter twelve

Adolescent

dolescence is a much more traumatic experience for girls than for boys. While boys become larger and stronger versions of their younger selves, girls suddenly find themselves living in transformed, unrecognizable bodies. Used to being individuals, they are confronted by an entire culture that defines them only by gender. Once they could be bold; now they must be careful. Once they could "do"; now they must "be."

For girls, adolescence is largely a time of loss: loss of voice; loss of innocence; loss of freedom; loss of individuality; loss of confidence and assurance.

In retrospect, the AAUW survey's finding that 71 percent of adolescent girls have low self-esteem is not surprising. (You may want to review the discussion of this report in chapter 1, "Self-Esteem: A Key to Unlocking Your Daughter's Future.")

Can your daughter get through this period with her self-esteem intact? Can she hang on to her authentic self? Let's look at some issues you'll have to deal with. If you've raised your daughter to have a hardy personality, and if she knows

What I saw happen to the girls between sixth grade and eighth grade was almost eerie. In sixth grade they were confident, adventurous, and full of themselves. By eighth grade they'd become conformists— constrained and unsure of themselves. What happened?

—Mother of two boys and three girls

who she is (knows her identity), they should be less troublesome. If, as you first read this, your daughter is nearing or has already entered adolescence, some remedial work will likely be required.

As we stated before, according to Erik Erikson, the key task of adolescence is the formation of identity: Who am I and how do I fit in this world? You may want to review chapter 5, "Forming an Identity as an Achiever," for the issues surrounding identity and females. This chapter focuses on activities that assist your daughter in retaining and strengthening her identity in the face of pressure to give it up. Adolescence has too many critical issues to address in one chapter. In following chapters you will find more detailed assistance on such topics as dating, eating disorders, career preparation, sexuality, and peer pressure.

You will notice that many of the activities in this chapter are group activities. We strongly recommend that you form small groups of girls and their mothers or fathers to address many of the issues in this book. Chapter 28, "Forming Mother-Daughter Groups," presents a complete plan of how to form a group and how to facilitate it. This blueprint will help you get started.

Going from a unique identity to a female identity

There aren't many rules for being a child, especially a female child. Girls can be as rough-and-tumble as their brothers without being considered aberrant. They can excel at school, play piano and first base, dream of greatness, and speak their mind.

Then, suddenly, it all changes. Rules abound, and they seem to have nothing to do with being Itoko or Angela or Diane. There are things they have to do, things they may not do, things they cannot do, all because "you're a girl."

What does it mean to be a girl or a woman? The female identity seems to center mostly around the way she looks, since women aren't expected to do very much. Just when a girl is feeling most awkward about her body, she learns that, for women, appearance is one of the few things that count. She opens a magazine and sees emaciated fashion models; she looks at her developing body and sees it as fat. She turns on MTV and sees Whitney Houston; she looks in the mirror and sees acne and braces. Her self-esteem plummets.

While it used to be okay just to be herself, she now wants to be everybody else. What can you do?

Don't criticize or tease her about her changing body or her appearance, and don't make your own or anyone else's appearance a matter of concern, ridicule, or envy. (See chapter 19, "Mirror, Mirror, on the Wall," for more advice on this topic.)

Encourage her (in word and deed) to stick with some of her old interests and passions. Don't suggest that she give up the soccer she loves for a course in ballroom dancing. Attend her games and cheer her on!

If she insists that all of her former activities are now "boring" or "for kids," try to help her discover and develop other talents or interests—things she's good at—so she can feel both capable and somewhat differentiated from the other girls her age.

Going from knowing to not knowing

Although it takes them a while to learn all the rules, two that most girls grasp immediately are that 1) girls should not flaunt their intelligence—and certainly not appear smarter than boys, and 2) girls should never disagree with or offend anyone else, no matter what. These rules, combined with girls' uncertainty about their new role and the fact that their opinions are questioned more than boys', lead them to question themselves. Ask them anything, and they "don't know." Their former assertiveness—a trait required for success in the greater world—is traded in for passivity and subordination.

Adolescent girls develop patterns of speech that may stick with them throughout their lives. It is mostly women, for example, who state declarative sentences as if they are questions ("I was watching TV?" "I bought this new pair of shoes?"). We discussed these habits earlier in the book, but it bears repeating that they seem to express doubt about the validity or importance of what is being said or to ask for confirmation from the listener.

In women, the culture values sympathy, unselfishness, loyalty, purity, and muffled voices. Girls insert doubt into their words and silence their own thoughts to avoid hurting others or giving offense. They become withdrawn and unreachable. What can you do?

Monitor yourself. Are you in the habit of questioning your daughter? Do you make remarks like "Are you sure?" when she tells you something? If you have a son, do you question him as much?

When your daughter says she "doesn't know" something, express your confidence that she does. Encourage her to trust herself and say what she thinks—and accept it without showing hurt or anger.

Never make statements like "You don't really believe that" or "That's not what you really think."

From expansive dreams to limited hopes

At younger ages a girl may feel she can do anything, be anything, cope with multiple and contradictory roles. She can be a brain surgeon and a rock star, Supreme Court justice and fashion designer. Then, at adolescence, reality sets in. Looking around, she sees that, for women, the limits are less than sky-high. The majority seem to be working at dull, dead-end jobs. What's more, they are also doing most of the child care and housework. How can they hold a responsible career and be the primary parent at the same time? (We deal extensively with this issue in chapter 25, "Strategies for Mixing Career and Family.")

From same-sex to male-female relationships

As girls' hormones kick in, they get interested in boys and start practicing for their future relationships with them. They learn quickly that if they are too bold, males become threatened and reject their advances. Socialized to base their self-worth on male approval, young women retreat. If the boys want them to be compliant, selfless, supportive, and silent, so be it. For much more on this topic, see chapters 20 ("I'm Nobody Till Somebody Loves Me"), 21 ("Sex and the Teenage Girl"), 22 ("Developing Healthy Sexual Attitudes"), and 26 ("Out into the World").

Setting an example

On the following pages you'll find a number of exercises and activities designed to help your daughter get through this difficult period. Before we start, though, a reminder: You are your daughter's most important role models. She will be watching you and molding her behavior accordingly. If your actions don't reflect the traits you're trying to help her develop, your efforts are not likely to succeed. Do you practice what you're about to start preaching? Ask yourself the following questions:

1. *Do you give precedence to your own needs, or do you usually make other people's desires a priority, no matter how trivial they may be?*
2. *Does it seem like others often take advantage of your willingness to be helpful or supportive?*
3. *Do you make it clear to friends and family members that your feelings deserve as much consideration as theirs?*
4. *Are you uncomfortable voicing your own opinions when they differ from those of someone close to you?*
5. *Is it easier for you openly to discuss your faults than it is to admit your strengths and accomplishments?*
6. *Do you feel uneasy when people begin discussing their feelings or ask you to share yours?*
7. *Do you say what you mean and ask for what you want, or do you often rely on less direct means of communication (tears, tantrums, "the silent treatment," inducing guilt or fear, and so on)?*
8. *Is is easier for you to take criticism or to accept a compliment?*
9. *How would you describe your behavior most of the time—selfless, selfish, or self-full? (The dictionary doesn't offer a word with precisely the right meaning. We're using "self-full" here to mean knowing and owning one's self and acting in a way that respects both self and others.)*

Your daughter is most likely to model her behavior after that of her mother (or another significant adult woman in her life), but her father's actions (or those of another significant male) will also tell her what it means to be a man or a woman.

You can teach her the skills of assertive communication, but if Mom gets her way by sulking and Dad is prone to making threats, she will learn that it's not acceptable to ask for what she wants. It will do no good to teach her how to accept criticism if Mom gets hurt and Dad gets angered when their actions are questioned. If one parent is selfless, while the other is selfish, it will be difficult for your daughter to become self-full (sure of her identity and boundaries and comfortable as an individual).

As you read through the following activities and suggested strategies, consider your own adult relationships and how you might work to improve them. Doing so should be beneficial for you, and it will also have an impact on your daughter's attitudes and behaviors.

Help your daughter develop good friendships

For most young women, developing and maintaining relationships is vital to happiness and self-esteem. Few things are worse than being rejected. This attitude, unfortunately, often leads to behaviors that in themselves are damaging to self-esteem as well as conducive to forming superficial rather than authentic relationships.

As women, we believe that we must always be pleasing, whether or not what others do is pleasing to us. We must not ask for what we want, but we must anticipate the desires of our friends. We can be hurt, but we must not hurt others. We must not be angry or critical or demanding. We must never accept the credit for doing something good, but we are always responsible when something goes wrong.

This can be carried to absurd levels. In her book *The Girl I Left Behind,* for example, author Jane O'Reilly notes, "I once saw my best friend apologize to a dining room chair when she kicked it by mistake. When my dog trips me up in hallways, I become overly abject and I apologize to him. My sainted mother has not written me a letter in twenty years without apologizing for the weather, whatever it has been, wherever I have been. . . . I have never heard a man make a personal apology for the weather."

Girls who grow into women like these are not likely to be terribly discriminating in choosing their friends or demanding in maintaining their relationships. And, ironically, all this effort to be "nice" often leads to acts of cruelty: girls who can't resolve their differences assertively form cliques, from which anyone can be arbitrarily excluded, particularly those who do not follow the "rules." This is a uniquely female form of aggression. Strength and individuality are denigrated rather than encouraged. Since it is never acknowledged that someone has been banished from the group, and the transgressor is not told what she has done to deserve this fate, she is left feeling bewildered as well as rejected.

One is taught by experience to put a premium on those few people who can appreciate you for what you are.

—*Gail Godwin*

Remember, too, that your daughter will employ the same tactics she develops in her relationships with other girls when she begins having relationships with boys. "I remember being at a party when I was about nineteen," says Maggie, "where one of the couples got into a fight. The guy hit his girlfriend across the face with a beer bottle, among other things, and finally had to be pulled off of her. I was trying to take care of the woman, putting ice on her swollen face and everything. She was hysterical, couldn't stop crying, but she kept insisting she had to go apologize to this jerk. I couldn't believe it!"

Girls who feel they have to "be nice" are also more likely to give in to a boy's desire to have sex or to ride in a car with friends they know have had too much to drink. Some women have actually married men because they didn't want to hurt their feelings by saying no.

What does your daughter need to know in order to avoid a similar fate? Carol Gilligan, author of *In a Different Voice*, recommends (among other things) the following: Girls need to learn

> *I was angry with my friend;*
> *I told my wrath, my wrath did end.*
> *I was angry with my foe;*
> *I told it not, my wrath did grow.*
> —*William Blake*

- *to take risks in relationships*
- *to face fears in displeasing others*
- *to sustain disagreements*

Dr. Karen Johnson, author of *Trusting Ourselves*, has identified the following additional needs. Your daughter should

- *be able to express feelings to others as she chooses*
- *establish and maintain friendships only with people who respect her and her feelings*
- *know what she likes, wants, and needs, and be willing to ask for it*
- *feel comfortable making positive statements about herself, to herself and others*
- *be able to recognize her shortcomings, accept them, and take criticism without it impacting her self-worth*

To these, we would add that girls must learn

- *to establish boundaries, set limits, and say no*
- *to tolerate anxiety*
- *to discern the difference between being selfish, selfless, and self-full*

- *to take credit for their accomplishments*
- *to talk about the internal struggle between what they value and what they feel society wants them to value*

"Liking Herself," "Appreciating Her Uniqueness," "Learning to Give and Take Criticism," and "Learning to Discern Between Friendly Criticism and Abuse Behavior" are activities to help your daughter develop these important traits.

Liking herself

Next time you have a group of girls together, ask them to form two circles, one inside the other, with an equal number of participants in each. Have the girls in the inner circle turn to face the outer circle so that each girl is directly in front of someone else. Instruct each of these pairs to take turns completing these sentences:

I like you because _____

I like myself because _____

Allow two or three minutes for each girl to make her statements, then have the inner circle move one step to the right and repeat the process with these new partners. With each turn, the girl must think of a new way to complete the statement concerning what she likes about herself. Continue in this manner until the girls have made a full circle, or at least for five turns.

Then pass out a piece of paper and pencil and ask the girls to try to remember and write what was said with each partner. If you feel you need to make this into a game, the girl who could remember the most statements could be declared the winner.

Follow the activity with a discussion. Which was easier, saying something nice about someone else or saying something nice about themselves? Most girls will find it more difficult to articulate what they like about themselves. Remind them that it is important to recognize their own strengths. Their written record from the activity could be posted on a mirror.

Appreciating her uniqueness

This is a particularly good icebreaker for introducing a group of girls who don't know each other well. Have the girls sit in a circle and ask one to introduce herself and then make a statement about why she is unique ("My name's Debbie, and I'm unique because I'm the only girl I know who plays the saxophone"). Instruct the next person to introduce herself, make a similar statement, and also repeat the names and unique characteristic of the girl who preceded her. Continue around the circle in this manner, each time having the next girl repeat the unique characteristics of all who went before her.

Ask a group of younger girls to design a label that incorporates their own name and replace the labels on their jeans, book bags, or whatever with these "personalized designer" labels. There is no reason to encourage our cultural obsession with attaching our identity to the manufacturer of the clothes we wear or the purse we carry.

I didn't belong as a kid, and that always bothered me. If only I'd known that one day my differences would be an asset, then my early life would have been much easier.

—Bette Midler

Learning to give and take criticism

If you have a very mature group of girls, girls who know each other and have built a certain level of trust, you might want to do the following exercise. Explain to the girls that they are going to practice giving and receiving criticism. Tell them that the focus is not on the criticism itself, but on how well they deliver it and receive it. (This activity is not as much pure "fun" as many of the others, but we have found that girls like and value self-discovery activities—all depends on the attitude of the leader, you.)

Divide the group into threes. For each round the girls will take turns being the critic, the recipient, and the observer. The observer will pay careful attention to the way the criticism is delivered and received; she will especially attend to the language of the participants.

The critic says: "I find it difficult [making a statement about her feelings first] when you _____." Ask her to fill in the blank with a specific behavior of the other girl, such as "when you say you'll be there and then you don't come" or "When you call me up but don't have anything to talk about."

The recipient takes thirty seconds (timed by the observer) and then says: "I would like to change, and I will do _____ next time." Ask her to fill in the blank with a specific behavior or, if she prefers, to say, "I would like to make you more comfortable, but this is something I don't want to change."

The observer follows up by commenting on how well each player followed the guidelines in giving and receiving criticism. Then each takes a new role and the cycle is repeated until all the girls in the triad have had a chance in each role.

Again, discuss. How did it feel to have someone make critical statements about them? Did they feel angry or hurt? Or were they able to stay calm, consider the information, and respond to it honestly?

Emphasize that everyone has shortcomings, everyone gets criticized, but it is important to be able to handle the criticism well and feel good about oneself in spite of these failings.

How difficult was it for them to criticize others? Did the language rules make it easier to say what they wanted? Did the other person fall apart or lash out in return? Does the group feel that this exchange has strengthened, weakened, or maintained the relationships among its members?

Learning to discern between friendly criticism and abusive behavior

What is the difference between friendly criticism and abuse? Most girls will recognize physical violence as abuse, but beyond that, things get a little murky. Where is it appropriate to draw the line? Discuss the matter with your daughter or with a group of girls. Do the following situations constitute abuse? Why?

One person inflicts physical pain on the other.

One person forces another to have sex against her will.

One person yells obscenities at another.

One person routinely yells, threatens, and throws things.

One person repeatedly tells the other that she is stupid or ugly.

One person makes demands on another but gives nothing in return.

One person threatens to harm the other if she doesn't do what she is told.

One person threatens to harm himself if the other doesn't do what she is told.

One person uses his own weaknesses (emotional problems, drugs, or alcohol) to excuse his bad behavior toward another.

One person repeatedly puts down the other's goals, values, interests, abilities, and so on.

One person routinely finds fault with the other's appearance.

One person seems to take pleasure in humiliating the other.

In your discussion, emphasize again the fact that friendly criticism is aimed at something a person does, not at who she is. Nor is it delivered in an angry, threatening, or condescending way. Any action that frightens the other person, coerces her to act against her will, degrades her, or makes her feel less than equal to the other constitutes abuse.

Discuss which of the following pairs of statements is criticism and which is abuse.

One person says the soup the other has just prepared could use more salt.
One person throws the bowl of soup the other has just prepared across the room.

One person says he thinks the other looks better with less makeup.
One person smears the other's makeup off with a dirty rag and calls her a slut.

One person says he wishes the other would try harder to be ready on time.
One person tells the other if she ever keeps him waiting again, he will punch her out, and he's not kidding.

One person tells the other he doesn't like her favorite kind of music.
One person tells the other he doesn't like her friends, family, or opinions, the way she walks, the way she talks, the way she eats, the way she dresses, or the way she talks back.

One person says he doesn't like the other's best friend.
One person says if the other doesn't give up all her other friends, he won't see her anymore.

Does your daughter know of relationships she believes are abusive?

Learning that you can't please everyone all the time

Woe unto you, when all men shall speak well of you.

—*Luke 6:26*

Remember when Sally Field accepted her Academy Award by proclaiming: "You like me"? Can you imagine Clint Eastwood saying that, or Al Pacino? There's a great deal of truth in the cliché that men want to be respected and women want to be liked. During adolescence, girls especially want to be liked. The problem is, no one is ever liked by everyone. Achieving women, particularly, are targets of abuse.

The more successful your daughter becomes, the more she opens herself up to criticism and dislike from less successful people. If she needs to have everyone like her, she is likely to sabotage her own career. Furthermore, she is unlikely to have others' respect, no matter how much people may "like" her. It is important, therefore, for her to come to terms with the fact that there will always be those who don't like her as well as those who do. More important, she needs to seek out and find friends who support her and value her ideas, strengths, goals, and ambitions—those who, as Nathaniel Branden says, are friends of her enthusiasms. This takes effort. You can help a group of girls or your own daughter by doing "You Like Me!" on the next page.

Learning to reach her own conclusions

Review the concepts on parent/daughter communication in chapter 8, "Your Role." How are you doing? Are you asking enough questions, or have you fallen back into a pattern of trying to tell your daughter what to do? If so, is it working? Why do you think it's not working?

Try to phrase at least half of your comments to your daughter as questions.

You like me!

Ask a group of girls to list on one piece of paper all the people they can think of who like them for who they are. Then have them list on another those they know don't like them. Ask them to read over their lists of those who like them for their strengths and ideals, taking time to think about each of these people. Then have them tear up the list of those who dislike them or would want them to be different people.

Did anyone list herself as someone who likes her?

At the end of the exercise, ask each girl to think of somone else she knows who has similar values and goals, someone who would say "yes" to the same things and "no" to the same things, someone she doesn't know very well. Ask each girl to think of ways to become better friends with that girl who is like her. One friend who shares her values helps her hold out against contrary peer pressure.

To encourage the group to "get into" this activity, explain that this is different from just a game. It's about self-discovery and a chance to learn a skill that will help them as they grow up.

("What do you think about Mary's decision to take an after-school job?" "How much studying would you have to do to get an A in biology?") You'll be surprised how this develops a dialogue between you and gets her thinking for herself. With practice, you can say as much by asking leading questions as by lecturing. Letting her come to her own conclusions will also help her become her own authority. Remember, too, that critical thinkers are highly valued in today's workforce.

Eliminating the Pollyanna posture

It may be tempting to shield your daughter from the unpleasant side of life, but don't. Maintaining that everything is wonderful, perfect in every way, will only harm her. If she sees that there clearly are problems, your denials will cause her to question her own ability to perceive the truth. And she will think of problems as something so terrible that they can't be talked about—or faced. On the other hand, if she believes you have no difficulties in life, you are setting her up for disappointment and failure when she encounters her own.

Refuse to idealize life, and don't gloss over your own problems. Let her see that everyone has challenges in life, but that solving or coming to terms with them is a rewarding life experience. We reiterate: Refer to your problems as challenges.

Life is easier than you'd think; all that is necessary is to accept the impossible, do without the indispensable, and bear the intolerable.

—Katherine Norris, writer

Learning to be assertive

If only we could retain the assertiveness of girlhood. A friend recently told us this story about her granddaughter's first day of kindergarten:

"How was school today, Annie?"
"Not so good, Grandma."
"Why not?"
"I got in trouble and had to sit in the hot seat."
"Why was that?"
"The teacher told me to pick up the toys and I said no. I told her I did not come to school to learn that. I already know how to pick up toys!"

Assertive communication and behavior is something the whole family needs to practice. Consider formal training for yourself and/or your daughter, or at least pick up one of the many books available on the topic and share what you learn with the rest of the family.

Very briefly, behavior is categorized as passive, assertive, or aggressive. Passive behavior, often linked with women, involves giving in to someone else's wishes when you don't want to or getting out of an unpleasant situation by lying or some other devious action. It is passive to accept an invitation you don't want or to decline it by saying you're going to be out of town that week even though you're not.

Aggressive behavior, associated more with men, involves making your own wishes known, but in a way that offends or does not take into account the feelings of others. When a child waits outside a stadium in hopes of getting her favorite baseball player's autograph and the star appears, only to tell her to "get lost" as he slams his car door in her face—that is aggressive behavior.

Assertiveness takes the middle road. An assertive person says what she wants, or what she means, but in a way that doesn't attack or insult the other person. An assertive response to an unwanted invitation might be, "Thanks for asking, but I'm not interested in hiking. How about a movie instead?" (if it's the event you're turning down) or "I'm flattered that you asked, but I think it's best if I don't socialize with my co-workers" (if it's the person—and if that really is your policy). The baseball star could have made his young fan feel a little better if he'd said, "Thanks a lot for coming, but I don't have time to stop now."

Generally, while using passive or aggressive behavior makes a person feel like a doormat or a jerk, asserting herself makes her feel powerful. She stood up for herself without showing any disrespect for others. It is particularly valuable for a girl to learn that she can ask for what she wants and the world will not come crashing down around her head. People may not like what she says, and they may argue with her. But if she speaks calmly and assertively, she will be able to stand her ground. She won't spend the rest of her day thinking about "what I should have said." When you teach your daughter to be polite, teach her to defend her own rights as well. It is important that she understand the difference between being flexible and being submissive, between compromising and giving in.

It should be noted, however, that all three styles may be used from time to time. The important thing is making a choice, not blindly following an old pattern of behavior. Sometimes she may choose to give in to another person's wishes. Or she may run across people for whom anything less than an aggressive response is too subtle. Most of the time, though, assertiveness is the best tactic. "Passive, Assertive, or Aggressive?" (pages 180–181) will help her recognize the different styles.

Assertive communication skills will help give her the confidence to say "no" without attacking her friends. They may even keep her from succumbing to peer pressure in situations involving premature sex, drugs, or alcohol.

It is important to help your daughter find ways to disagree

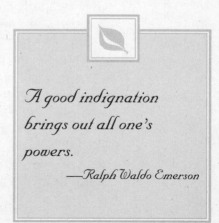

A good indignation brings out all one's powers.

—Ralph Waldo Emerson

Passive, assertive, or aggressive?

Explain to your daughter what assertiveness is, then read the following statements to her and ask her to identify the passive, assertive, and aggressive responses.

1. *Your mother wants you to wear a sweater to school because she thinks it's cold. You aren't cold at all.*
   __ You say, "Nag, nag, nag! I'm sick of you always wanting me to wear a sweater!"
   __ You say, "Mom, I'm not cold, so I don't plan to wear a sweater today."
   __ You say nothing and wear the sweater.

2. *Your best friend, Sandra, wants to borrow your new outfit. You haven't even worn it yet, and you really don't want to lend it to her.*
   __ You say, "Sandra, I don't want to lend you my new outfit. Let's go through your closet and see what we can find."
   __ You lie and tell her it's at the cleaners.
   __ You say, "Sandra, why don't you get your own outfit? No way am I going to give you mine!"

3. *Your father wants you to help him wash the car, but you have an important test tomorrow.*
   __ You ask your mother to tell him you can't help.
   __ You say, "Dad, I'd like to help, but I have too much homework tonight. Give me a little more notice, and I'll make time to help."
   __ You say, "Dad, I am not your slave. Don't you know I have work to do?"

4. *The most popular girl in class wants to copy your homework because she didn't have time to complete hers.*
   __ You let her copy the paper.
   __ You say, "Mary, don't you know that's cheating? I'm sorry, but you'll have to get it done on time next time."
   __ You say, "Copying homework is against the rules of the class and I do not want to break the rules. We have a few minutes before class, let me help you get started."

5. *Your teacher asks you to stay and help tutor another student after class, but you have arranged an outing with your best friend.*
__ You say, "I have better things to do. No way!"
__ You say, "I'd like to help, but I have other plans today. I'm free tomorrow, or maybe David or Lee could help."
__ You stay after school and cancel your plans.

Now ask her to come up with an assertive, aggressive, and passive response for each of the following situations.

1. *Your mother wants you to eat your spinach. You don't like spinach.*
Passive:
Assertive:
Aggressive:

2. *Your best friend makes plans to go to the movies with you, then asks if she can bring along someone you really don't want to spend time with.*
Passive:
Assertive:
Aggressive:

3. *Your father's golfing buddy is coming to dinner, along with his five-year-old son, whom you had to care for last time. The child was a terror, and you don't want to sit with him again.*
Passive:
Assertive:
Aggressive:

4. *The most popular girl in class, who is chairing the booth at the school carnival, asks you to be on the cleanup committee. You'd rather be on the decoration committee, and you know there's still room.*
Passive:
Assertive:
Aggressive:

5. *Your teacher gives you a C on a paper you think deserves at least a B.*
Passive:
Assertive:
Aggressive:

Go over your daughter's responses with her and ask how she would feel about herself if she had actually made each of them.

with her friends without attacking what they are doing. One twelve-year-old expressed respect for a friend who smiled and said, "No, thank you; I'm not having any," when the other girls were passing around glasses of beer. While this assertive young woman expressed her own choice, she did not say "You girls shouldn't be doing this" or "You're stupid."

Learning to disagree

Sandy recalls that when she started sixth grade in the fall of 1960, her wonderful teacher, Mrs. Harberts, decided that the presidental election of that year should be an ongoing topic of discussion. Normally Sandy was extremely shy, but as one of the few Kennedy supporters in the group, she felt obligated to speak up on his behalf. It was one of the best educational experiences of her life. Everyone got very involved, watching the debates and reading the newspapers to gather ammunition for the classroom discussions, as well as the arguments that were constantly going on in the halls and the cloakroom. After the election, she says, she reverted to her quiet former self, but ever since she's been quite comfortable expressing her opinions, even when others strongly disagree. She's noticed, though, that it's almost always men who enjoy a good argument as much as she does.

It's difficult for people who can't handle conflict to be effective. We've been in meetings, for example, where one strong woman proposes a course of action that every other woman in the room privately opposes, yet because none of them is willing to stand up to her, she gets her way. Those other women may just as well have stayed home, and many times they end up dropping off the committee.

You can help your daughter learn to feel comfortable with disagreements through your own behavior. Make it a habit to have family discussions on political issues or other controversial topics. If there's an issue you feel strongly about, take some action: write a letter, form a committee, or whatever. And, fathers especially, don't expect your daughter to "be a good girl" and please or agree with you all the time.

Encourage your daughter to write letters to the editor or to public officials with whom she disagrees. If she notes that a particular TV show is sexist or offensive in some other way, suggest that she write to the network. Similarly, she might express her displeasure in a letter to a manufacturer whose commercials reflect gender stereotypes and so on.

Suggest forming a committee that will voice a grievance to a governing body. If boys' athletics at your daughter's school gets more funding than girls' sports, for example, the committee could gather evidence to this effect and present it at a meeting of the school board.

Or a group of girls could form their own debate teams and, periodically, stage an event to discuss a topic on which they strongly disagree.

Does your family take the position that for every argument there has to be a winner and a loser? If so, try to change. Instead of endlessly rehashing the same argument until someone gives in and admits that he or she was "wrong," let the disagreement stand. Agree to disagree. Use that phrase, in fact. By demonstrating that two people can have different opinions and still respect and care for each other, you can lessen your daughter's anxiety about saying what she thinks: she'll see that a disagreement does not necessarily mean the end of a relationship.

Perhaps this chapter has brought to mind some messages you'd like to give your daughter about relationships. Add them to "Your Plan."

iii.

What's a parent to do?

chapter thirteen

Games Girls Play

The mother of a four-year-old girl was distressed when her daughter came home crying because her male playmates insisted that she couldn't be a Ninja Turtle. She could only be the girlfriend, April.

A four-year-old boy's mother was surprised when, as she struggled to keep the roughhousing of the male guests at her son's birthday party from getting out of hand, one of the little girls in attendance approached timidly and asked permission to remove her party hat.

A father determined to raise his young daughter in a nonsexist manner didn't know what to think when, upon receiving a toy steam shovel, she pointed to the serrated edge of the shovel and said, "Comb!"

Where do kids get this stuff? Is it good or bad, and is there anything to do about it?

Studies indicate there are few biological reasons for the very different behaviors usually exhibited by boys and girls. "Yet most children still learn that 'boys do; and girls are,'" according to *Facts and Reflections on Careers for Today's Girls*, a research review published in 1985 by Girls Clubs of America (now known as Girls Incorporated). This synthesis of nearly two hundred published reports sheds some light on why we see such disparities in the ways children play and the toys they choose, as well as on how these early choices relate to career selection in later life.

The research shows that by the time they are three or four years old, most girls will choose to play with dolls rather than

Play is children's work, and its importance cannot be overemphasized. For in playing, children are doing.

—Doris McNeely Johnson, *Children's Toys and Books*

cars and trucks, and most boys will make the opposite selection. "As children are learning to distinguish 'me' from 'not me' and learning whether they are girls or boys, they incorporate social definitions along with the facts of anatomy and become rigid enforcers of sex stereotypes," the report states. Influenced by toy catalogs, TV images, and what they see and hear from the adults around them, little girls are already being conditioned to see themselves as future mothers and homemakers. Family roles and relationships are central to girls' play even in preschool and kindergarten, and these youngsters already see fewer options for their futures than do boys. It is through play that children begin to form their identities.

As they get older, girls' play and work continue to emphasize social skills and domestic abilities. Games like jump rope and hopscotch stress taking turns more than competing or excelling. Girls, more often than boys, are likely to be assigned such chores as dishwashing, cleaning, cooking, and caring for younger childen, which again reinforces the image of woman as caretaker. And even though adults in their own families may have taken on nontraditional occupations or roles, children persist in stereotyping jobs by sex.

The news isn't all bad, though. Young girls are often willing to play with boys' toys, while the reverse is almost never true. Older girls are much more likely to participate in competitive sporting events than they were in the past.

And parents can make a real difference in their daughters' perceptions. If you indicate that it's okay for your daughter to play with nontraditional toys, she is likely to accept your judgment. The activities you encourage her to pursue and the chores you assign her at home can make a big difference in the way she sees herself. Your daughter may still prefer playing house to playing soldier, but she is less likely to see a domestic role as the only option for her future if you do.

Encourage her to play with toys and play at activities that are both traditionally male and female. Look for those that require "doing" rather than "being." The more time your daughter spends exploring, singing, building, creating, pretending, running, dancing, imitating, painting, swimming, cooking, climbing, testing, making music, making noise, making sand castles, solving problems, or putting on shows, the more possibilities she'll see for herself.

Answer the questions in the activity "What Messages About Play Are You Sending Your Daughter?"

What messages about play are you sending your daughter?

Answer the following questions to get a better idea.

When your daughter is (was) an infant and up until her third birthday:

1. *Which would you be more likely to buy her?*
   a) a rocking horse, toddler truck, or building blocks
   b) a play telephone, stuffed animals, or toy vacuum cleaner

2. *Which would you choose as her Halloween disguise?*
   a) a pirate costume
   b) a witch costume

3. *What would you be most likely to do if your toddler daughter ran off by herself at the beach?*
   a) Race after her and bring her back
   b) Make sure she's safe, then let her return when she decides

Would you choose differently for a son?

When your daughter is (was) three to six years old:

1. *What would you be most likely to buy for her birthday gift?*
   a) toy trucks, Lincoln logs, or action figures
   b) dolls, a china set, or a mock kitchen

2. *At Halloween, which costume would you select for her?*
   a) a cowgirl
   b) a princess

3. *What would you do if your daughter asked to remove the training wheels from her bike?*
   a) Agree reluctantly to remove them, then hover over her as she takes her first trip without them
   b) Show her how to remove the wheels herself

Would you choose differently for a son?

When your daughter is (was) seven to ten years old:

1. *What would you be more likely to give her for her birthday?*
   a) Legos, a basketball, or toy walkie-talkie
   b) a dollhouse, jump rope and jacks, or children's cosmetics
2. *At Halloween, which costume would you be most likely to choose?*
   a) a firefighter
   b) a ballerina
3. *Which chores would you be most likely to assign her?*
   a) Taking out the trash
   b) Setting the table

Would you choose differently for a son?

When your daughter is (was) eleven to fourteen years old:

1. *What would you be more likely to give her for her birthday?*
   a) a chemistry set, Nintendo, or model kits
   b) makeup, a diary, or an embroidery kit
2. *What Halloween costume would you select if she asked your advice?*
   a) a rock star
   b) a model
3. *Which chores would you be more likely to assign?*
   a) Mowing the lawn
   b) Dusting and vacuuming
4. *How would you respond when she decides to try the high dive at the city pool?*
   a) Forbid it, because she might get hurt
   b) Congratulate her on her courage

Would you choose differently for a son?

When your daughter is fifteen to nineteen years old:

1. *What gifts would you be more likely to give her?*
   a) a computer, athletic gear, or electronic equipment
   b) jewelry, clothes, or tapes or CDs
2. *Which costume would you rather see her in as she leaves for the high school masquerade ball?*
   a) a monster
   b) a vamp
3. *Which would you be more likely to assign your daughter?*
   a) kitchen detail
   b) car care
4. *If your daughter decides to run for a class office at school, which would you encourage her to try for?*
   a) class president
   b) class vice president

Would you choose differently for a son?

The importance of play

The importance of play should not be underestimated. As she plays, your daughter is developing her intellect, her powers of concentration, her physical abilities, and her social skills. Play also affords opportunities for self-discovery, testing different personality traits and defining who she is. As she plays, your daughter is working at the job of becoming a healthy, functioning adult.

But the kind of play girls engage in is usually quite different from the play of boys. When psychologist Erik Erikson asked individual ten- to twelve-year-old boys and girls to construct an exciting scene from a fantasy movie script, the girls tended to set up peaceful interiors, sometimes with the threat of an intruder (always male or animal) causing the residents of the scene to hide. The boys, on the other hand, built exterior sets—buildings and towers that were often knocked down again, elaborate walls, streets populated with automobiles and animals.

Erikson attributed the disparity to biology and anatomy. As future childbearers, he said, girls are naturally passive, protective, and concerned with interior matters, while boys are more active and attracted to external objects and activities.

Erikson never considered the role of socialization in the play of these children, though in studies of other cultures he clearly shows how a society can and does mold its youngsters for particular occupations in the adult world. The Sioux cultural system, he says, is designed for "specializing the individual child for one main career, here the buffalo hunter," while "the Yurok child . . . is to be trained to be a fisherman." The "children" he speaks of, of course, are all male. The females are mentioned in passing (as being prepared for their roles of wife and mother) or not at all.

While it is undeniably true that women are capable of bearing children, it is obviously inaccurate to assume they will do nothing else. Your daughter's play, therefore, while it may prepare her to be a nurturing adult, must also prepare her to go out into the world and participate on an equal basis with other men and women.

Barbie and Ken may make a handsome couple, but for your daughter they simply aren't enough. She needs toys and activities that stimulate her imagination, build her confidence, and expand her horizons. For the most part, these forms of play are likely to be those traditionally assigned to boys.

Think about it. Will your daughter learn more from ironing her doll's clothes or from building a model airplane? Is it more creative to practice wearing high heels and lipstick or to design a space station? Will her powers of concentration improve more by playing dolls or by playing chess? Encourage activities that place an emphasis on creativity and constructive problem solving—active, stimulating games rather than passive, stifling ones.

The monster in the box

There are many things you can do to help your daughter, but you should know that you'll be up against some powerful opposition. Among the most damaging and most pervasive opponents are the toy manufacturers who sponsor children's TV shows. If your daughter is like most children, she watches more than three hours of programming a day, and during that time she is at the mercy of advertisers who can undermine all your best efforts to build her self-esteem.

Young children are especially at risk, because they are not able to distinguish ads from programming, much less to dismiss their messages as the marketing tools they are. In fact, things have deteriorated to the point where there really is no difference in many cases. Since it became legal to market toys that are affiliated with TV shows in the 1980s, many children's programs are little more than thirty-minute commercials. According to Nancy Carlsson-Paige and Diane E. Levin, authors of *Who's Calling the Shots?: How to Respond Effectively to Children's Fascination with War Play and War Toys* (New Society Publishers, 1990): "By December 1985, all of the ten best-selling toys had television shows connected to them; and in the fall of 1987, 80 percent of all children's television programming was produced—literally paid for—by toy companies."

This is a bad situation for children of both sexes—and for parents! The fadlike nature of these toys make them almost required equipment for any child sensitive to peer pressure. But the enchantment seldom lasts, and the toy is soon abandoned for something still more up-to-the-minute. As you may have already noticed, these toys are often expensive, and they tend to come with multiple figures and accessories, each of which must be purchased separately.

Possibly the most damaging aspect of this dismal situation is that toy manufacturers have diminished a child's ability to entertain herself. It's the manufacturers who tell children what they should play and what they should play with. But the toys themselves usually have just one function and are soon discarded. Though children have more toys, they often have less fun and are certainly less stimulated by their play.

There are steps you can take, however. We encourage you to limit the amount of TV your daughter watches, though we realize making a change like this is difficult. You need to explain to your daughter that too much television stops her from doing other interesting things. (Susan's daughter, on hearing that many children watch more than forty hours of television a week, said in scorn, "Get a life!") Tell her that you are going to watch less television also, unless you are already watching very little. You can increase your success with limiting television viewing if you provide other sources of entertainment, such as books, puzzles, games, occasional carefully selected videos, and the like. If you spend time reading or playing games with your daughter, she will soon prefer that time to television.

You might also spend some time watching your daughter's favorite shows with her, pointing out the problems with the ads ("It's too bad they only show boys playing with that toy. I guess they don't realize that girls can do it just as well." "It seems like all the girls in these commercials only have dolls to play with. Aren't you glad you have so many other toys to choose from?").

Become a critic and "Write Your Reviews of the Commercials on Kids' Programs."

Write your reviews of the commercials on kids' programs

Spend a Saturday morning watching the commercials on children's shows or videotape the programs so you can fast-forward to the commercials. Are more girls or boys featured in the ads? What do they show boys doing? How are the girls portrayed? Who is more active? Who is sickeningly sweet? Who can get dirty? Who is in control? Are boys shown in nurturing roles? Are girls shown in leadership or action roles? What possible careers does this commercial suggest for girls?

Had enough? Okay. Call the manufacturers (many have toll-free numbers), ask for their public relations department, and complain about the messages their commercials are sending to girls. If they receive enough complaints, they may pass them on to their advertising agency, which created the ads in the first place. Once everyone is educated on this topic, things are likely to change.

What girl games are all about

Remember the movie *Big*, in which Tom Hanks portrays a child who wakes up one day to find he has literally grown up? Much of the film's charm comes from the play involved. Hanks and his best friend play computer games, make up stories, communicate through walkie-talkies, ride bikes, play baseball, and in general have enough fun to make anyone nostalgic for childhood. Hanks's experience with computers allows him to get a job with a toy manufacturer, where his playfulness and creativity soon earn him a vice presidency. Could this movie have been made with a female in the central role?

Sure, but producers would be afraid that viewers wouldn't buy the idea. While the games boys traditionally play allow them to fantasize and use their imaginations, girls seem more concerned about proper behavior, even at play. Dr. Lillian Carson, a psychoanalyst in Montecito, California, tells a story that illustrates this point. A local Sunday School teacher, she says, made a painting of the inside of the church and asked her kindergartners to draw themselves into the scene. The boys put themselves in the pulpit, in the stained-glass windows, even swinging from the chandelier. The girls—every one of them—placed themselves sitting quietly in the pews.

Girls' games are about practicing. They practice taking turns at hopscotch, jump rope, and jacks; they practice changing diapers; and they practice setting the table for tea. This is usually not the stuff of great comedy or drama, nor does it prepare girls for success in corporate America.

Girls do love to play house, and there's nothing wrong with that. Boys should be encouraged to play house, too. It's the segregated nature of this activity that causes problems. What does your daughter learn about the value society places on nurturing and caretaking tasks when boys are laughed at or steered gently to another activity if they try to take part? Whom do children of both sexes come to see as totally responsible for all domestic and familial chores? Ask your daughter's teacher to encourage girls to engage in a wider range of activities: kickball, foursquare, computer games.

If your daughter has a coed play group, try to see that some time is set aside for girls and boys to play house, or encourage her preschool or kindergarten teacher to make this a required activity. Boys will become more nurturing and helpful, and girls will perceive that the caretaking roles they cherish do have value in the larger world.

"Does Your Daughter Play This Game?" will help you look at the kinds of play experiences she is having.

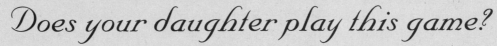

Does your daughter play this game?

Below is a list of a number of games and activities that girls often participate in between the ages of about six and eleven. Which of these activities does your daughter take part in? Place a "Y" in the first column beside each of these games. Leave the space in this column blank beside any activity she does not play. There's room for you to add any of your daughter's favorites we've missed at the bottom.

THE GAME	YES?	WHERE? (S OR L)	LEARNING? (I OR H)

Games and Activities

Hopscotch

Jump rope

Kickball

Softball

Soccer

Foursquare

Swings

Sandbox

Sewing

Modeling with clay

Dolls

Coloring

Skating

Swimming

Hide and seek

Collecting things

Riding bike

Card games

Board games

Computer games

Hangman

Other:

(continued on next page)

Now consider the environment for each of your daughter's favorite pastimes. Place an "S" in the second column beside each activity that occurs in a small, secure space. Place an "L" in that column beside activities that have large, expansive environments.

What is your daughter learning from her play? In the third column place an "I" beside pastimes that encourage independence and exploration, an "H" beside those that foster group harmony and interdependence.

As you consider this chart again, does it seem that your daughter is enjoying a good mix of activities, or are they too much alike? If it seems she could benefit from some variety, think of alternatives you might suggest to her and list them below.

Alternatives

_____   _____
_____   _____
_____   _____
_____   _____
_____   _____

Girls and dolls

We'll keep this brief. Most dolls are fine. Girls enjoy cuddling them and caring for them, and they are also a source of comfort. A favorite doll can become almost a best friend—someone to tell secrets, someone to hug all night long.

And then there's Barbie. By the time she is five or six, your daughter will have developed long-lived, if not permanent, body image ideals. For millions of American women over the last thirty years or so, that ideal has been Barbie. Barbie's measurements, if she were a real woman, would be 36-18-33. Few of us know anyone who looks like that, but the huge amounts of time and money spent on diets and exercise regimens, the alarming number of women who suffer from anorexia or bulimia, indicate how difficult it is to give up on an ideal, even when it causes pain and suffering.

Now, even more alarming, there is My Size Barbie, three feet tall and promoted as "girl's best friend" and "the first Barbie little girls can actually share clothes with!" Yes, this hundred-dollar nightmare comes with a glittery skirt that will stretch to fit your three-foot daughter, allowing her not only to idolize a mannequin, but to become one.

Fortunately, more reasonable voices are beginning to be heard. High Self-Esteem Toys Corporation produces the Happy to Be Me doll, a more realistic version of Barbie (36-27-38 in real woman numbers) that wears flats instead of stiletto heels.

Your daughter may still want a Barbie if all her friends have one, but you may be able to dilute the effect if she has a variety of dolls in as many shapes and sizes as possible. Also, if you encourage her to use her imagination and come up with more entertaining things to do, she might soon become bored with dressing and undressing Barbie.

The most inspirational example of this we've found comes from an article Laurie Colwin wrote about her daughter for *Allure* magazine. More interested in pretending to be a cat or dressing up like her hero, Pippi Longstocking, this delightful child had her first Barbie encounter at age four, when a same-age houseguest arrived with seventeen dolls. "Soon she was clamoring for a Barbie of her own," Colwin reported.

"Her daddy brought her the least-horrible-looking Barbie doll he could find, and for a few days she played with this loathsome object by tying a string around its slender neck and hanging it from the banister. But as soon as her friend left, the Barbie doll disappeared."

There are other kinds of dolls—especially the pricey ones doting grandparents like to buy—that are lovely to look at but not really appropriate for play. If your daughter has any of these, make sure she understands that while there are *dolls* meant only to be admired for their beauty, this same standard does not apply to *girls*. You don't want her to identify too closely with these icons of female passivity.

Selecting toys for girls

In general, toys of all kinds are suitable for children of both sexes. The adults who buy the toys, however, don't see it that way. When they set out to find a gift for their daughters, their first inclination is to choose "something pink," according to Linda Brown, their toddler/preschool toy buyer for Creative Kidstuff in Minneapolis. She's even had parents ask if there are pink Legos for girls.

Brown points out that manufacturers often promote the idea of sex-specific toys by showing only boys or only girls on the packaging, although some European companies, in particular, are beginning to change this practice.

Then there are the manufacturers who make different versions of similar toys for boys and girls. Brown mentions one company that offers two push toys: a fire engine and a vacuum cleaner (guess which one is pink!).

When choosing toys for your daughter, look beyond the obvious. Little girls get as much physical gratification as boys do from pounding toys, for example, but parents are more likely to focus on toys that build small-motor skills for their daughters instead.

Building toys—blocks, Legos, Duplos, and the like—are excellent selections for girls, according to Brown. They are educational and imaginative, and they provide instant gratification as well as a boost to your daughter's self-esteem by helping her master new skills and use her own creative powers.

Butterfly nets, tape measures, and bug sets are other unconventional choices loved by many girls. Next time you go to the toy store, venture beyond that sea of pink, ignore the packaging, and see what other treasures you can find. Since more toys are perceived to be for boys than for girls, you'll more than double your selection, and these new choices are likely to be the ones to expand your daughter's mind and her horizons.

Seeing me be

Page through old magazines to find pictures of workers in as many kinds of occupations as you can, particularly people wearing uniforms or holding some object that makes it easy to identify his or her job (a hammer or gavel, for instance). Cut out the bodies and paste them on sheets of heavy poster board or cardboard. Replace the workers' heads with photos of your daughter pasted into place. (You can bring a favorite photo to your local photocopy center and have it reproduced in various sizes to fit the different bodies.) Cut out the figures and let your daughter play with them, or post them around her room, adding to the collection whenever you come across a figure representing a new occupation.

Your daughter's nursery school teacher might use this activity with the entire class by simply adding a thin piece of Velcro to the figures' heads and the backs of the children's photos. That way the youngsters can change roles as often as they like.

Lights, camera, action

Let your daughter star in the movies of her imagination. Once a week or so, perhaps at bedtime, introduce a fantasy situation and ask her to complete the story. The imaginary scripts should allow her to assume many different roles, to have adventures, solve problems, take on leadership roles, be the hero.

You might start things off something like this: "Good evening, ladies and gentlemen, and welcome to our movie of the week. Tonight's film stars Susie Jones as the president of the United States. As our story begins, Susie is about to make an important announcement to the American public. Let's listen. Lights, camera, action!"

We've listed some other ideas you might find appealing below, or make up your own.

- *Working to save endangered species in Africa, your daughter encounters a group of poachers intent on killing the animals (gorillas, elephants, or whatever) she is trying to protect.*
- *Mountain climbing in the Alps, your daughter learns that one member of her team has been separated from the group by a minor avalanche.*
- *Alone in a castle, your daughter must find a way to defeat the evil dragon approaching through the woods.*

Some of these toys may be challenging for her at first, which is part of their value. As you watch your daughter struggle to solve a problem or master a new skill, resist the temptation to "rescue" her.

"Seeing Me Be" and "Lights, Camera, Action" are activities that can help your daughter see infinite possibilities for herself—and they don't include any toys at all.

chapter fourteen

Once upon a Time

I t's just a story." That's what many of us were told by parents or teachers when we needed comfort or reassurance. Old Yeller wasn't really dead: "It's just a story." The Wicked Witch of the West would not make a surprise appearance in our room at night: "It's just a story."

But, true or not, stories do more than entertain. They instruct. Subtly or not so subtly they teach your daughter what it is to be a girl and the proper way for her to become a woman. The heroes and heroines she finds in books will strongly influence her identity. We are sad to report that, overall, her interests are being badly served by the books she is most likely to find at the library or in the bookstore.

In recent years very little monitoring of the situation seems to have occurred, but a 1984 study found that only 28 percent of the characters in children's books were female. When cleverness, bravery, problem solving, or adventure were part of the plot, the characters were three to four times as likely to be male. Females were portrayed more often than males as being incompetent, passive, and domestic. If anyone was victimized or humiliated in the story, that character was female more than 90 percent of the time.

A study of gender portrayal in children's picture books was done back in 1973 (at the height of interest in nonsexist books for children—the fact that there is nothing more recent is in itself telling). Eighty-three percent of those portraying women at all showed them in domestic situations, while just 17 percent showed women working outside the home. More than half of these professional women were teachers, maids, or nuns. Other

What the mother sings to the cradle goes all the way down to the coffin.
—*Henry Ward Beecher*

occupations women can hold, according to these books, include nurse, flower vendor, store clerk, flight attendant, cook, and fat lady in a circus. Men, on the other hand, were portrayed working in more than seventy different jobs, including fisherman, farmer, horseman, musician, carpenter, cowboy, king, thief, hunter, athlete, doctor, and matador.

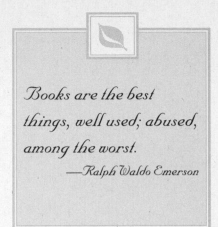

Books are the best things, well used; abused, among the worst.
—*Ralph Waldo Emerson*

Interestingly enough, the same study found more female characters cooking than performing any other task, while the most favored recreational activity for male characters was eating. Men could also be found driving, flying, and playing sports, while walking the dog was about as active as women were allowed to get.

What is your daughter likely to learn at the library? Well, if she goes to the classic nursery rhymes and fairy tales, she'll learn what we did: that boys have adventures and girls have nasty stepmothers; that boys act and girls cry; that boys are heroes and girls are victims; that boys are valued for their brains and courage and girls are valued for their beauty and obedience.

Contemporary picture books are often confusing. They may say that girls are smart or brave, but the underlying message may be quite different. The female "hero" is still often rescued by a male, for example, or the illustrations show female characters standing idly by as the males work, act, or make decisions.

If she goes to the biography section, it will be difficult for her not to notice that most of the people considered important enough to be written about are men. If your daughter is Latino, African American, or Native American, she will find a very limited number of books about women who look like her.

As she gets older and moves into young adult fiction, she will have row upon row of books to choose from. Nearly all of the titles, though, are romances that reinforce the message that, for girls, identity and esteem come from male approval.

As we mentioned above, there was a time during the mid-1970s when nonsexist books were being published and received with great enthusiasm. This was the age of *Free to Be You and Me; He Bear, She Bear;* and a few other classics that are still in print. In the past ten years or so, however, interest in nonsexist literature has waned with publishers, if not with readers.

What happened? We can't say for sure, but "the times" probably had something to do with it. The 1980s was a decade when people seemed to believe either that women had already achieved equality and no further efforts were required or that women had gained too much in the previous decade and their progress should be halted.

We also suspect that the publishers' profit motive was involved to some degree. While girls are willing to read books about boys, it's been shown that the opposite is not true. Boys overwhelmingly reject any book or toy that is the least bit girlish. It is more profitable, therefore, to keep pumping out male-centered books.

Whatever the reason, the result is damaging to your daughter's self-image and confidence. Let's take a closer look.

Nursery rhymes

Say something often enough and you'll start to believe it. That's common knowledge among adults, but we don't always think about the ways in which constant repetition of any phrase, verse, or story affects young children. According to some pediatric psychologists, however, they strongly affect a young child's personality and her perceptions of the world, especially when they come from parents or other important people in her life.

The concept is called *linguistic programming,* and we encounter it in many facets of our lives. Politicians and public speakers repeat the same phrases again and again to stir up a crowd. Repetition is involved in the rituals of most of the world's religions. Advertisers spend billions of dollars hoping to imbed their slogans or jingles indelibly in our minds. People successfully reprogram their own minds through the use of daily affirmations. And young children often get their first impressions of what the world is like through the nursery rhymes they hear hundreds of times from parents, grandparents, caretakers, and siblings.

Some of the rhymes are delightful, and others are probably harmless. But a disturbing number are frightening, violent, or insensitive. That's not really surprising. Most of Mother Goose is hundreds of years old. The rhymes originated in a world where hardship and cruelty were taken for granted, and by the way, most were composed for adults, not children. At a time when books were rare and few people could read, verses and rhymes offered a way to pass on an oral history. New ones were composed or old ones changed as events warranted. Then, early in the nineteenth century, they were first printed, and they haven't changed since.

In 1985 Dr. Doug Larche's book *Father Gander Nursery Rhymes* proposed an alternative. Dr. Larche, head of the Department of Speech and Theater at Grandview College in Iowa, rewrote many of the Mother Goose rhymes to make them nonsexist, nonracist, and nonviolent.

Reaction to the book was mixed—some people loved it, while others found the whole idea of changing the classics shocking. But no one, it seems, could ignore it. Newspapers and magazines from San Francisco to New York to London, from Newport News to San Diego, argued all sides of the question. Johnny Carson read it more than once. Even *Saturday Night Live* produced a skit based on the book. Larche received thousands of letters—and a death threat. All the attention and the intensity of people's reactions lead us to believe that the rhymes—whatever version—do have a profound and lasting impact on us. It seems to take hold early: one mother reported that when she tried to read *Father Gander* rhymes to her young son, he corrected her, replacing the modern lines with the old ones he had learned in the nursery.

You may want to take a look at *Father Gander* or at some of the other books of rhymes that have been published recently. Or you might simply choose to edit out some of the most negative of the traditional verses. Keep in mind, though, that you are doing more than entertaining your daughter when you recite a rhyme. You are teaching her some of her earliest lessons.

And they lived happily ever after

What comes to your mind when you hear that phrase? Write down your impressions and associations:

One adult male, asked to do the same, replied, "Isn't that part of the marriage ceremony?"

Although we seldom realize it, many of us have so internalized the messages of the fairy tales we heard as children that we no longer recall their source. Girls, especially, seem to fall prey to the "happily ever after" scenario, complete with prince and fairy godmother. They may deny it, but far too many young women believe that someday, some way, they will be rescued and taken care of for the rest of their lives. This belief is not exactly compatible with one that encourages them to become emotionally and economically self-sufficient. Which one do you suppose they would rather cling to? It would be wonderful if believing in fairy tales could make them come true, but as a press release for our book *Choices* stated so well, "For the girl growing up today, a pumpkin, six mice, and a pair of glass slippers just won't do it!" Dispelling this myth is one of the most important things you can do for your daughter.

"Fairy-Tale Messages" may help you recognize some common themes.

Fortunately, there are some little-known fairy tales that deliver more positive messages for girls. Author Alison Lurie has rewritten fifteen of them in a book called

Fairy-tale messages

Below, list as many fairy tales as you can remember. Star those that were your favorites.

	a	b	c	d	e	f	g	h	i	j	k	female villain
1.												
2.												
3.												
4.												
5.												
6.												
7.												
8.												
9.												
10.												

Do any of the following themes appear in these fairy tales? Put a check mark after the appropriate story in the box that matches the letter of each statement below.

a. A woman's life story ends when she gets married.
b. "Good" girls live for or through others.
c. Men are active, women are passive.
d. Only evil women go after what they want.
e. Women are not capable of solving their own problems without help from men or supernatural beings.
f. Magic plays a major role in most women's lives.
g. Men are often transformed by the love of a good woman.
h. Women who venture too far from home generally get into trouble.
i. Beauty is a woman's most important asset.
j. Smart or active women are not beautiful.
k. Women are most appealing when they are sleeping or dead.

Do any of the stories have a villain who is female?

Clever Gretchen and Other Forgotten Folktales (Thomas Y. Crowell). In her introduction Lurie explains that there are thousands of folktales, most of which were told originally by working women. "They lived active, interesting lives," she says, "and the stories they told show it."

However, the first stories were collected and published in Victorian times, when girls and women were idealized for their innocence and passivity. Thus, the mostly male editors chose "Sleeping Beauty" instead of "The Sleeping Prince," "Cinderella" instead of "Clever Gretchen," and "Snow White" instead of "Kate Crackernuts."

Somehow, the stories that were selected because they fit a certain need at a particular time have been enshrined as "classics" that must not be criticized, let alone changed or abandoned.

Publishers also like fairy tales. Because they are not copyrighted, they can be rewritten and reissued at will. There is no author to deal with, no royalties to be paid. It seems likely, then, that new editions will continue to be published—as long as people keep buying them.

We realize that many parents look forward to sharing the books they loved with their children. Before you do, though, see if you can't recall some stories that were more empowering for girls. Consider some of the newly collected folktales instead. If your daughter is old enough, discuss the story with her. Make sure she understands that no one expects her to fall asleep for a hundred years or to find fulfillment taking care of a house full of vertically challenged men.

If you think sharing a familiar story with your child is a special experience, wait until you try telling her your own version or having her help you write it! Reading to your daughter is great (please don't give that up!), but you might find that this brings the two of you even closer together.

It's not necessary to change the stories completely. You might try something as simple as role reversal: suddenly Cinderella is a poor but obedient young man (Well, you might have to change the names. Remember *Cinderfella*?), and it's the Princess determined to find her one true love, the lad whose slender foot will fit the glass sneaker he lost as he fled from the ball at the stroke of midnight.

The essential thing is to change the messages. Maybe Snow White leaves the palace because she is bored, not because of the evil Queen. Perhaps she moves in with the dwarfs because she's heard housekeeping is an exciting thing to do. But maybe she's still bored, and when Sneezy is denied medical benefits for his persistent allergies, she decides to unionize the mine workers instead.

Have fun with this! You might come up with an inventive version of one of the traditional tales, or you might even create a story or a character of your own. Encourage your daughter to make her own creative contributions. If she's just learning to write, reinforce the positive messages by having her copy the text to practice her penmanship. This activity can provide ongoing delight for the whole family. You might even submit your idea to a publisher.

Children's picture books

There seems to be a lot of confusion, even among teachers and librarians, about what makes a children's book positive and empowering for girls. It is difficult. As we said earlier, the messages and images are so ingrained, the reactions so automatic, that unless you make a deliberate decision to seek them out, they can get right by you. It is important to make that decision, because the messages will not get by your daughter.

We thought it might be helpful for you if we did a quick comparison of some books that are supposed to contain positive messages for girls and some that actually do. As you hone your own critical reading skills, you too will notice subtle negative messages and will be able to make better reading choices for your daughter. We'll compare Mindy Bingham's *Minou* to Kevin Henkes's *Chrysanthemum* and Sandy Stryker's *Tonia the Tree* to Shel Silverstein's *The Giving Tree*. Please forgive us for using our own children's books as the "good" ones. We do so simply because we know them so well—why they were written, how they developed, even the slipups we almost made.

We chose *Chrysanthemum* because it is relatively new (copyright 1991) and because several children's librarians mentioned it to us as a book with positive messages for girls. *The Giving Tree* was selected because it is so popular (just about every bookstore we've been in has multiple copies on its shelves, even though the book is nearly twenty years old) in spite of what appear to us to be horrible messages about gender roles and about the environment.

Chrysanthemum is a female mouse. Her loving parents tell her they chose that name because it is "absolutely perfect," just like her. Chrysanthemum is very pleased with herself and her name until she goes off to school, where she is teased by the other "children," especially a classmate named Victoria. Crushed by their reaction, "Chrysanthemum wilts." Back at home, her parents are able to restore her self-esteem, but when she encounters the same situation at school the next day, she is once again convinced that she is totally worthless. It is only when the well-loved and pregnant music teacher, Mrs. Twinkle, announces that her name is Delphineum and that she might name her baby Chrysanthemum if it is a girl that the poor little mouse can finally take pride in who she is.

Minou offers quite a different story line. Minou is a pampered Siamese cat who lives in Paris with her mistress, Madame Violette. But when her owner dies, Minou finds herself out on the streets, hungry and alone. She has no idea how to take care of herself, but her efforts to entice a new master or mistress are in vain. Minou meets Celeste, a wise street cat, just in time to avert starvation. Celeste teaches Minou how to take care of herself. The story ends with Minou taking a job as the mouser for Notre Dame Cathedral, proud to be "a cat of independent means."

Let's compare the two stories. Both are warmly written and charmingly illustrated. *Chrysanthemum* features a loving and supportive family as well as a pregnant working woman (this is one of the things the librarians liked best), and these are certainly qualities we would like to see in more books. But the problem with Chrysanthemum is that she has absolutely no sense of her own identity. If Mom and Dad say she's great, then she is. If the kids at school say she's weird, she's weird. In the end, Chrysanthemum lets Mrs. Twinkle define her once and for all. She is not the kind of role model you want for your daughter.

Minou, on the other hand, learns exactly who she is, what she wants, and how to get it—on her own. She experiences the anxiety of being responsible for herself but comes to enjoy her sense of accomplishment so much that she rejects offers from would-be caretakers. This is an important point. A more traditional ending would let Minou find out she could take care of herself and, secure in that knowledge, allow her to accept being rescued by a new mistress.

Note, too, the difference in the way the two authors present other female characters. Chrysanthemum's classmate, Victoria, is nasty and obnoxious and the real villain of the piece. In *Minou*, however, Celeste is portrayed as a friend and a mentor. Too many children's books feature a "good" girl and a "bad" girl pitted against each other. This encourages girls to see others of their sex as rivals or enemies, and it also promotes a black-and-white perception of the world: something or someone not totally good must be totally bad.

Okay, let's move on. *The Giving Tree* is supposed to be about unconditional love, but is it? The tree character is a female. The only other character is a boy who grows into old age by the end of the story. The boy comes to play under the tree, and the tree grows to love him. He goes away, however—for years! When he returns, the tree is delighted to see him, but he hasn't come to play. He wants money. She offers him her apples to sell. He takes them and goes off again, leaving her to wait still more years. The next time he comes, he wants a house so she lets him cut off all her branches. This goes on. The "boy" eventually cuts the tree down altogether, and when he returns as an old man, she graciously offers him her stump, the only thing she has left.

Tonia is a different kind of tree. She lives in a forest surrounded by friends who become alarmed when Tonia stops growing. The friends try to help, and then call in the tree doctor, who tells Tonia that she must move—she can no longer grow where she is. At first Tonia is reluctant to make such a drastic change, but, encouraged by the doctor and her many friends, she decides to take a deep breath and do it. The experience exhilarates the tree. She finds that change and growth are adventures to be pursued, not terrifying events to be avoided. Inspired by her move, Tonia becomes a role model for others in the forest.

Which tree would you rather have your daughter emulate? Maybe we're off base here, but it seems to us that most women do not need any more instruction in how to be a doormat or in how to spend their lives waiting for men who never give them a second thought. Nor do most men need encouragement to see themselves and their own needs as the only ones worthy of consideration. (This might be a good book to try the role reversal exercise on.)

Tonia the Tree, on the other hand, portrays a society in which there is mutual give and take. Characters care for each other, cheer for each other, teach each other, and serve as role models. Sandy almost got into trouble with one of those ingrained images we spoke of, however. In her first draft of the story, the tree doctor was a man. She was embarrassed when more astute friends pointed this out, but her blunder illustrates how difficult it is to eradicate the stereotypes in your mind even when you're trying to. Moral: Don't expect perfection from yourself when it comes to this kind of thing. Just keep trying to improve.

You *and* your daughter need to work at becoming critical readers. Here and later in the chapter we've provided some points to keep in mind. If you want more "guided" practice, you might take a look at some of our children's books: each of them includes a page at the back with questions, suggestions, and activities to facilitate discussion between you and your daughter. The most important thing, though, is to keep reading—the good and the bad—and keep talking. The more exposure your daughter has to a variety of publications, the better critic she'll eventually become.

Biographies

As we stated earlier in the chapter, there are many more biographies of men than of women. Do include stories about outstanding women in your story hour, though, and encourage your daughter to read their biographies and autobiographies on her own when she's older. Buy them for her, if you can. Dozens of strong and admirable women are now having their stories told for the first time. If she starts to put limits on her own ambitions, a collection of these books can be a visible reminder that women have lived lives of adventure and achievement.

As a rule, newer books will be more inspiring than older ones. In her perceptive book *Writing a Woman's Life*, Carolyn G. Heilbrun points out that until recently women were often not even portrayed as the heroes of their own stories. Biographers seemed to take the position that their subjects, because of their extraordinary achievements, were somehow aberrations. In their autobiographies the women themselves usually attribute their successes to luck or fate, while taking full responsibility for any perceived failings. They could not allow themselves to be seen as ambitious, either. Heilbrun states, "Each woman set out to find her life's work, but the only script insisted that work discover and pursue her, like the conventional romantic lover."

The lives of these women are still worth reading about, of course, but in most cases you should be able to find more recent biographies.

Does your library have at least a fairly good selection of books about women? If not, ask why. Encourage the librarian to give this section a higher priority. If funding is a problem, suggest to a women's service organization that purchasing books for the library would be a valuable way to serve the community.

Classic novels and young adult fiction

Have you ever wondered why, if most children's books are geared toward the male market, there is such a proliferation of books obviously written for female preteens and teenagers? As a librarian explained it to us, it's really quite simple: "Boys stop reading at about age twelve." Enter the romance novel!

If all of her friends are reading romances, your daughter will probably read them as well. Forbidding her to do so will only make them more appealing. Instead make a habit of discussing the books she reads with her. Ask questions to help her draw her own conclusions about the books' messages. Again, you're helping her become a critical reader. Don't be sarcastic or condescending; show a real interest. What was the basic plot of the story? Did she enjoy the book? What were the main characters like? Which one did she like best? Why? How did the story end? Did she think it was a good ending? A realistic one? Can she imagine what happened to the characters in later years?

This is not to say that there aren't other, better solutions. If it's true that publishers can't depend on male readership in this age group, it might be possible to convince them to offer a wider selection of books for young women, books that do not make courtship and romance the only worthwhile events in a woman's life. (The girls seem willing to give other topics a try. Librarians tell us that in addition to romances, horror stories are very popular. An interesting pairing!) Why not share your thoughts on this topic with publishers of the books your daughter reads?

As your daughter enters this age, she will probably also begin to read classic literature at school and, we hope, on her own as well. Encourage her in this, but remind her, too, that books are a product of the time when they were written. Many otherwise worthy novels are sexist or racist, and in nearly all of them the hero is a male.

In reading these books, your daughter needs to make some mental adjustments if she wants to gain what they have to offer. The first step is to recognize the sexist or racist aspects for what they are and, while not excusing them, set them aside. The second step is to appropriate the role of the male hero for herself—without giving up her own identity as a female. This is the central thesis of Carolyn Heilbrun's book *Reinventing Womanhood*. "The possibilities for action which seem inevitably male . . . must now be seen as human, possible for women also. Woman must learn to contrive plots in which she is the actor, in which she struggles for control of her own destiny, slays her own dragons. She must learn to look at the male protagonists who have, until now, stood as models for human action, and say: that action includes me."

You can help, once again, by discussing the books with your daughter in a way that lets her imagine herself as the central character. What would it be like to be Huck Finn or David Copperfield? Would she have made the same decisions they did? What does she like best about them? What does she like least?

While you may not have much to say about the books that are assigned at school, you do have some influence on your child's outside reading. We hope you'll use it to promote books by women. Contemporary women writers, as a rule, do provide female role models who are strong and smart and independent, while many men are still writing about women as objects or victims.

Women writing in the nineteenth century produced books featuring some of the most memorable female heroines ever conceived. Jo in Louisa May Alcott's *Little Women* has been a role model for generations of achieving women, even though the author loses her courage at the end and forces her character to marry. Charlotte Brontë's *Jane Eyre* is likewise beloved. Jane Austen's female heroines are unfailingly blessed with intelligence and strength of character. George Eliot sometimes created male heroes, but her feminine sensibility comes across nonetheless.

Perhaps you have favorites of your own to introduce, or you might want to start a list of titles that are favorably reviewed or recommended by people you trust and respect.

Identifying nonsexist books

Here are some general guidelines to help you choose nonsexist children's books for your daughter. Some of the points are adapted from the Council on Interracial Books for Children's "10 Quick Ways to Analyze Children's Books for Racism and Sexism."

1. Check the copyright date.

Pay close attention to books published before the mid-1970s. Because there was so little awareness of the problem before this date, even well-intentioned authors were likely to portray and promote stereotypes and sexist attitudes.

2. Consider the story line.

Are girls and women successful because they are smart, creative, and/or courageous, or do females only win by being pretty and obedient or through their relationships?

How would the story be different if the genders of the central characters were reversed?

3. Examine the characters and the relationships between them.

Are female characters related only to roles or careers traditionally held by women? Are the females rescued by the males?

Do the females initiate action, make decisions, or solve problems? Or are only male characters portrayed as leaders, decision makers, and powerful in their own right? Do female characters display the characteristics of the hardy personality?

Are some of the central characters female, or are the girls only incidental to the story? Are females allowed to function effectively in a wide variety of activities and occupations, or are they portrayed as helpless or only good at "traditional" female tasks?

Are male characters supportive of strong female characters, or do they ridicule or humiliate them? Are similarly strong women shown favorably, or does the author portray them as shrews and witches? Are girls allowed to be friends, or are they pitted against each other as rivals for some kind of prize? Are mothers seen as either the wicked stepmother or the helpless housewife?

Are only females allowed to be nurturing or to cry or show fear? Are all males seen as strong, serious, and unemotional?

4. Look at the illustrations.

Do the girls stand by idly while the boys take charge of the action?

If there is a strong female character, is she seen to be less attractive than other females in the story? Are girls allowed to wear play clothes and get dirty, or are they seen only as flawlessly groomed "dolls" in party dresses?

Do the male characters seem to take up more room than the females? Are they shown as bigger-than-life kings and heroes who seem to loom over the females? And are those females seen to be pampered, passive, and of value mainly because of their beauty?

5. Check the language.

Is the male pronoun used to refer to both sexes? Have occupational titles been updated (firefighter, not fireman; mail carrier, not mailman; flight attendant, not stewardess; police officer, not policeman; and so on)? Are girls who like to climb trees and play baseball called "tomboys" or boys with nurturing tendencies called "sissies"?

6. Look for books from small or alternative presses.

Many of these specialize in multicultural, nonsexist books, and their titles are turning up more often in bookstores and libraries.

Let them know what you think

Like all businesses, publishers need to keep their customers satisfied if they want to succeed. If you have a complaint about one of their books, why not drop them a note? (Be fair, though. Check to see that the book is still in print before you make your complaint—your librarian or a clerk at your favorite bookstore will be able to furnish you with this information. Publishers should not be taken to task for past mistakes—unless you find a continuing pattern of sexism on their part.) Have you found a book you really like? Send your compliments! Encourage them to keep up the good work! (Addresses are usually found on the copyright page of the book.)

Offer suggestions, too. We think it would be great if more publishers made a real commitment to race and gender equity in their books—not just adding females and minorities as window dressing, but addressing the real issues and psychological issues of an underrepresented population. This would involve setting up guidelines and making sure that the editorial staff is made familiar with them.

Or, what if, before a manuscript was accepted, it was read by a specialist in the psychology of girls in order to pick up any sexist nuances that may not be apparent to the regular staff?

By taking steps like these, publishers could rightfully claim with a statement on all their covers that "we are a race- and gender-equity publisher." It would be good for their image, and it would certainly make your job easier. With enough input from the parents of American girls, publishers just may find that it's possible to do the right thing and still make a profit.

Making things better

There isn't much you can do to remove offensive books from your library's shelves. We don't believe in censorship or book burning or in harassing librarians. The American Library Association has a "right to read" policy endorsing freedom of access to all but the most egregiously offensive materials.

Most librarians are sympathetic to our cause, but they are under a great deal of pressure from many interest groups, and they have limited power to make sweeping changes. See your librarian as a friend, not an adversary.

You might encourage her to recognize Women's History Month each March by displaying biographies and autobiographies and other women's books, perhaps along with relevant posters, photographs, news clippings, and the like. There should be a good selection for preschoolers and young readers as well as for older children and adults. The librarian might also be willing to ask a local history teacher to talk about some aspect of women's history on a Saturday morning or even to have a series of these talks. Possible topics include the first suffragist movement, women and labor, women inventors, women aviators, women in math and science, Rosie the Riveter and the role of women in World War II, and so on.

Another project might be asking a local service organization to sponsor an annual awards program for the best new books for girls. Your librarian's cooperation will be needed for this as well. Her job is to nominate five to ten books in each category you select (children's picture books, young adult fiction, and so on), based on the criteria you provide for her.

A committee from the service organization then chooses the winning books. Winners might be announced at a news conference, or you could have a ceremony at the library. You might even invite one of the winning authors to speak at a luncheon.

If library officials approve, you might want to make up an award sticker for your winners so that other parents can immediately identify them as "safe" reading for their daughters. At the very least, see that the list is published in your local paper. It's also a nice gesture for the service organization to purchase extra copies of the award-winning books for the library's collection.

If you have any connections with a national service organization or a national women's magazine, you might propose that it set up a project for evaluating children's books and listing the ones that are most empowering for girls each year. National distribution of such a list would be beneficial to millions of parents and children.

If your daughter is at an advanced reading level, suggest forming a book club with a few of her friends. This can be very informal. The girls just agree to read the same book and then discuss it over sodas at their next meeting. It's a good way to encourage reading, build support among girls, and learn to question and debate.

Book list

Just to get you started, here are a few children's books we can recommend without reservations. All are usually available or may be ordered by children's bookstores or general bookstores with large children's sections; addresses for the smaller presses are included in "Ordering Information" at the back of this book.

I Like Me by Nancy Carlson (Viking, 1988)
Amazing Grace by Mary Hoffman (Dial, 1991)
The Paper Bag Princess by Robert Munsch (Annick Press, 1980)
Father Gander Nursery Rhymes by Father Gander (Advocacy Press, 1986)
Brave Irene by William Steig (Farrar, Strauss & Giroux, 1986)
Kate Shelley and the Midnight Express by Margaret Wetterer (Carolrhoda Books, 1990)
Dove Isabeau by Jane Yolen (Harcourt, Brace, Jovanovich, 1989)
Hannah the Hippo by Linda Schwartz (Learning Works, 1991)
The Country Bunny and the Little Golden Shoes by DuBose Heyward (Houghton Mifflin Company, 1939)

Naturally we'd like to recommend our picture books (available in bookstores or from Academic Innovations; see "Ordering Information"):

Minou by Mindy Bingham (Advocacy Press, 1987)
Tonia the Tree by Sandy Stryker (Advocacy Press, 1988)
My Way Sally by Mindy Bingham and Penelope Paine (Advocacy Press, 1988)
Berta Benz and the Motor Wagen by Mindy Bingham (Advocacy Press, 1989)
Mother Nature Nursery Rhymes by Mother Nature (Sandy Stryker and Mindy Bingham) (Advocacy Press, 1990)

Midgrade and Up:

The True Confessions of Charlotte Doyle by Avi (Orchard Books, 1990)
M. C. Higgins, The Great by Virginia Hamilton (Macmillan, 1974)
From the Mixed-up Files of Mrs. Basil E. Frankweiler by E. L. Konigsburg (Dell, 1967)
Pippi Longstocking by Astrid Lindgren (Viking, 1950)
Ronia, the Robber's Daughter by Astrid Lindgren (Puffin Books, 1985)
Sarah, Plain and Tall by Patricia MacLachlan (Harper & Row, 1985)
Island of the Blue Dolphins by Scott O'Dell (Houghton-Mifflin, 1960)
Lyddie by Katherine Paterson (Lodestar Books, 1991)
Saving Lenny by Margaret Willey (Bantam Books, 1990)

Sexism in textbooks

Although Title IX (the 1971 federal legislation mandating gender equity in schools receiving federal funds) does not apply to sexism in textbooks (that would violate the First Amendment guarantee of freedom of speech), these publishers seem to have made a much greater effort to eliminate racism and sexism than have publishers of fiction. For them it makes good business sense. Textbooks are heavily screened and must be approved by at least one board before they can be adopted by a school. Some states have specific guidelines for any books used within their borders, and publishers are careful to abide by these rules. After all, they are spending a lot of money to produce the books, and it makes no sense to deliberately forgo selling them in a state the size of Texas (a state with some of the most stringent guidelines).

Rewrite the classics

Suggest that junior high or high school English teachers organize a debate. The topic: Should the classics be rewritten to eliminate sexist language? (Again, we aren't saying they should be. We just want to deepen awareness.)

Coed teams are suggested. One team should argue for rewriting the texts, the other should make the case for leaving them as they are. Following the debate, the class could vote on the question.

It seems, though, that there is still more sensitivity to racist statements or photos than there is to sexism in a textbook. And sometimes a bad book inexplicably makes it through the screening process. If your school uses texts that are ten or more years old, you might also have a problem.

Do you know what the guidelines are or what the process is for adopting books in your schools? Do you know anyone on your school board, or are you aware of its position on sexism? Keep your eyes open, but this is probably not a major area of concern.

Sexism in fiction is another matter, however. As we pointed out earlier, our most revered literature includes many titles with limiting messages for girls. It is important not to ban these books, but to raise the consciousness of students so that they can recognize and dismiss the outdated materials and still appreciate all that is valuable within the text. Talk to your daughter's teacher about organizing a debate on whether we should "Rewrite the Classics."

Most elementary schools are now teaching reading through the whole-language approach, which uses regular fiction and nonfiction books instead of textbooks. If your daughter's school has adopted this method, you may want to take a look at the kinds of books that are being used.

Why reading is worth the effort

If books can be damaging as we've implied, you may be wondering, Why not just forget the whole thing? Is reading really that important? We know the answer to that question, and so do you. People who don't read don't get very far in our society, and the situation is bad enough already. Today only 34.9 percent of Hispanics, 39.2 percent of African Americans, and 63.3 percent of white Americans can read proficiently by age thirteen. Young people with poor reading comprehension most often become our high school dropouts, and it's all downhill from there.

Read to your daughter when she is young. It's one of the best ways to insure that she will read well in later years. Talk about the stories you read with her, too. Ask questions. Be *active* readers. Encourage her to think.

As she gets older, encourage your daughter to read on her own. By then she should be questioning the stories herself. Keep discussing her current reading matter with her. Follow our suggestions to help her find books that are not sexist, that do not put limits on her aspirations. Further, help her to identify sexist elements in books, and make sure she understands these messages do not apply to her or to any girls and women. And always do what you can to promote her love of books and of lifelong learning. It will prove to be a source of solace and pleasure, and it will help her weather the many and varied changes that lie ahead.

Besides, if she doesn't read, she'll probably just watch more TV. And if you think the book situation is bad . . .

chapter fifteen

Lessons Learned from the Media

There's no escaping it. No young woman today can grow up unaffected by the pervasive influence of media: TV shows, movies, music, advertisements, magazines, and even the news and newspapers will tell her what is expected of her, what is valued, how she should look, and how she can be. The only solution is to teach your daughter, whatever her age, to become a savvy critic who can spot the offending materials and messages, disregard them, and, better yet, take steps to improve matters.

Children's television is, most network programmers say, a boy's world. And they aren't fighting it anymore.
— *Bill Carter, The New York Times News Service*

You grew up with TV, too

"It's very strange," says Sylvia, a landscape architect, "but some of the most vivid memories from my childhood never really happened: they were on TV. My memories of Beaver Cleaver's best friend, Larry Mondello, are much clearer to me than those of my own best friend, Connie, who lived two houses down from mine. . . . And it's not just that I was a *Leave it to Beaver* freak.

There were lots of shows I felt that way about. What did I learn from them? On some level, I guess, I thought that they were real, or at least that they showed things the way they were supposed to be."

What TV generation were you a part of? Did you grow up with the Andersons and the Nelsons? The Cleavers and the Petries? The Partridges? The Bunkers and the Jeffersons? The Keatons and the Huxtables? The Conners and the Simpsons? Do you remember the names of the children and the dogs and the neighbors? Can you hum the theme song?

How has TV altered your psyche? Parents who grew up without the ubiquitous box had no way of knowing how it would affect their children. We don't have that excuse.

How do you think TV affected your childhood? How did it relate to your vision of the world, your family, and yourself? Did it limit your aspirations or fuel your ambitions? Did it affect your schoolwork? Your social life? Your health? If you had it to do over again, would you watch as much TV? More? Less? These are all factors to consider when you set up your family's guidelines for viewing.

TV and the toddler

Children's programs scheduled to be broadcast on a recent Saturday morning included the following: *Sesame Street, G. I. Joe, Fievel's American Tails, The Little Mermaid, Garfield and Friends, Teenage Mutant Ninja Turtles, Back to the Future, Raw Toonage, WWF Wrestling, Goof Troop, Addams Family, Winnie, Land of the Lost, Wild West, Bugs Bunny, Scooby Doo, T-Rex, Davey and Goliath, Richie Rich, Fantastic Max, Wacky Racers, Dastardly and Muttley, Little Rock, Superboy, Captain Planet, Dog City, Bobby's World, Tom and Jerry, Tazmania, Plucky Duck, Eek the Cat, Super Dave,* and *X-Men.* The same mix can be found in the cartoons that are now run after school in the late afternoon.

Where are the girls? They are largely absent, and purposely so. TV executives are well aware of the fact that girls will watch shows with male leads but the reverse is not true.

Nothing personal, the network programmers say. It's purely business. They do claim to be making some concessions to their female audience: there's April O'Neil, who gets to watch the Mutant Ninja Turtles do their superhero thing, and Kanga, the mother in *Winnie-the-Pooh.* As a special treat, writers (80 to 85 percent of whom are men) have been asked to "include female attributes in the male characters," Jennis Trias, ABC vice president for children's programming, told *The New York Times.*

My funny, clever, bold, adventurous daughter is forming her gender ideas right now. I do what I can to counteract the messages she gets from her entertainment, and so does her father. . . . It sure would help if the bunnies took off their hair ribbons and if half of the monsters were fuzzy, blue—and female.

—Katha Pollitt,
The New York Times Magazine

A character might actually hug someone, she speculates or, "maybe he can look at the scenery around him and say, 'Oh, isn't that beautiful.'"

There's really nothing to be concerned about, says David Poltrack, CBS senior vice president for research, in the same article. "Girls are more likely to find something else to do on Saturday morning: go out, go shopping with their mothers to the mall."

The message is clear. Boys count. Girls don't.

The situation doesn't improve greatly on public TV, though some changes have been recently made. *Sesame Street* has been lauded as the educational, egalitarian, self-esteem-building children's program of the past quarter century. Only in the last year or two have people begun to wonder out loud why all the major Muppet characters (except Miss Piggy) were male, as were all the adult puppets, while the females have been portrayed mostly as babies and little girls.

Some parents try to get around the problems of television programming by substituting videos of movies. Unfortunately even Walt Disney, every child's best friend, has a clear preference for boys. The Disney studios have tried to make amends in recent years, but with only partial success. In *The Little Mermaid*, Ariel gives up her voice in exchange for marriage. Belle of *Beauty and the Beast* is smarter and more independent than the animated heroines who came earlier, but why, when the Disney people released the book, did they put a stereotypical "beauty" on the cover instead of the more ordinary-looking character who appears in the film and inside the book? For the most part, Disney females are still either princess types or villains.

In May of 1992, while Mindy was attending the American Booksellers' Association's national convention in Anaheim, she and her husband, Jim, spent an evening at Disneyland. There was a spectacular show around the lake surrounding Tom Sawyer's Island that night—Mickey Mouse was battling evil. During the course of the show, images were projected onto a towering screen of water shot up from the lake. At one point villains from many past Disney movies were featured: the witches and evil stepmothers from *Sleeping Beauty*, *Snow White*, and *Cinderella*; Cruella deVil from *One Hundred and One Dalmatians*; and so on. When it was over, Jim turned to her and said, "Did you notice all the villains they featured were female?"

What is the cumulative effect of all these messages? Even before they start kindergarten, many of our daughters have learned some lessons very well: that their options are limited; that they exist mainly to watch, serve, and someday be chosen by a male; that girls don't matter much. And, of course, our sons are learning exactly the same thing. Help alleviate this situation by watching along with your daughter and encouraging her to become a critical viewer. Is it true that only boys can have adventures? Did that little girl really need a boy's help to get down from the tree? Before long she'll begin to ask herself the same kinds of questions.

Prime time: getting better, but . . .

Things do change. Back in the 1950s, when Betty Anderson of *Father Knows Best* considered becoming an engineer, she decided instead that "it's more important for the engineers of the world to have a pretty wife to come home to." What would Murphy Brown say to that?

Most of the women on TV then were mothers or daughters, teachers, or secretaries, though a few nontraditional jobs were represented: *The Flying Nun* and *My Mother the Car* come immediately to mind. Today women on TV can be doctors, lawyers, judges, broadcast journalists, interior designers, pilots, photographers, city planners, police officers, bartenders, truck drivers, mystery writers, and, as they say, much, much more. There have even been sightings of women over forty (*The Golden Girls*) and overweight women (*Roseanne*).

The problems are more subtle, but don't let them go by without comment. Again, we strongly suggest that you watch TV with your daughter (unless—praise be—she doesn't watch it herself) and discuss these situations when they arise:

1. The absent mother.

In TV land, the overwhelming majority of single parents are, and have always been, men. From *Bonanza*, *My Three Sons*, *Bachelor Father*, *Gidget*, *A Family Affair*, and *The Andy Griffith Show* to *A Year in the Life*, *Full House*, *My Two Dads*, *Davis Rules*, *Valerie's Family*, *L.A. Law*, and *I'll Fly Away*, Mom's dead and Dad's in charge. Make sure your daughter understands that 87 percent of single parents are women.

2. The either/or woman.

TV writers seem to have a problem creating women characters who are successful in both their personal and professional lives. Murphy Brown is great at her job but lousy at relationships. Maggie on *Northern Exposure* is a pilot who can shoot ducks and fix plumbing, but every time she gets involved with a man, he dies in some bizarre accident. Roxanne on *L.A. Law* made great strides professionally, but not personally. It's difficult for young women to make a commitment to a career if they think it means they'll spend their lives alone and miserable.

3. Who's the boss?

Murphy Brown may be brilliant, rich, and famous, but she still needs her house-painter to put her in her place. On *Cheers* Rebecca started out as the manager but was subsequently demoted and generally got no respect from anyone. In *Who's the Boss?* Judith was supposed to be the successful career woman, but it was Tony, the male housekeeper, who really ran the show. Your daughter needs to know that women can take charge, can be their own authorities.

4. How do they look?

Young, thin, and beautiful, probably. Remind your daughter that in the real world, people come in many different kinds of packages, and they don't fall off the edge of the world on their fortieth birthday.

5. What is it that they do?

Although female characters now come with many kinds of job titles, we seldom actually see them working, unless they are lawyers or police officers. It would be great if this changed, but even the way things are now, you can use TV time to discuss the various careers with your daughter. Does she know what a city planner or an architect does? What kind of training is necessary? (If you don't know, make it a point to find out, or take her to the library and learn about it together.) How much math and/or science is required for entry into the program?

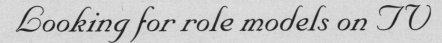

Looking for role models on TV

Are any of the women portrayed on TV role model material? We would like to suggest that you take a look at both male and female characters in your daughter's favorite shows and, together, evaluate them according to the traits required for high self-esteem.

1. Are the characters autonomous, in control of what happens in their lives, or do others control them?
2. Are the characters self-sufficient or are they needy, dependent, or powerless?
3. Are the characters competent, or are they inept, bungling, or unprofessional?
4. Do the characters have willpower, or are they weak in their convictions, easily swayed, unable to follow through at the first sign of problems?
5. Are the characters true to their authentic selves, or are they trying to fit into some existing role or pattern?
6. Are the characters valued by others, or do they have second-class status?
7. Do you see any pattern of differences between the traits exhibited by males and those exhibited by females?

The news

Just as there has been some progress in prime-time TV shows, news reporting is also getting better. Sexism still exists, however, both in who presents the news and the way that news about women is reported.

The perception that TV newswomen need to be young and attractive came to our attention, if we hadn't already noticed, when Christine Craft, a Kansas City anchorwoman, was fired for being "too old [she was thirty-six], too unattractive, and not deferential to men" in 1983. Craft brought a sex discrimination suit against her ex-employers, but, although two juries found in her favor, the rulings were overturned by a male judge.

Since that time, a number of women over forty (Barbara Walters, Diane Sawyer,

Geraldine Ferraro . . . the first woman to be nominated for vice president and . . . a size six.
—*Tom Brokaw, NBC News, July 19, 1984*

Connie Chung, and Leslie Stahl, for example) have managed to keep their jobs, and some have even been promoted.

But there are other problems. Meredith Vieira was forced to quit her job as a correspondent for *60 Minutes* when she asked to cut her hours in order to have more time for her family. Connie Chung was widely ridiculed for wanting time off to try to have a child. Jane Pauley was replaced as a host of *Today* by the younger Deborah Norville, who was herself let go soon after she allowed herself to be photographed nursing her infant. When Diane Sawyer signed a hefty contract, *Time* put her on its cover under the headline IS SHE WORTH IT? As much-traveled newswoman Linda Ellerbee might say, "And so it goes."

What can you do about all this? You and/or your daughter can always call or write to complain. You can also monitor both the national and local newscasts and elect to watch the ones that include more women, women whose looks are more representative of the general population, and women doing less traditional jobs. Many local stations now have female meteorologists (not "weather girls"), for example, and women doing the sports. Ratings are one thing all broadcasters pay attention to.

Another problem with TV news is the way it portrays women newsmakers. Again, too often their appearance is made a central part of the story, as in the quote from Tom Brokaw above. Did anyone ever mention what size suit George Bush, Ferraro's opponent in that election, wore? There is also a tendency to be condescending. During live coverage of the 1992 New York City marathon, for example, a network male sportscaster repeatedly said in tones of outright amazement that Lisa Ondieki, who set a new women's course record, actually ran the race faster than a lot of men! Those guys she was passing weren't just allowing her to win, he said, they were running as fast as they could! Watch and listen for sexist incidents wherever they occur—on TV shows or the radio, in the movies or commercials, whatever. Discuss them with your daughter. Help make her a discriminating viewer.

And now a word from . . .

It's possible to lessen the impact of advertising on older children. Younger children, however, cannot discriminate between programming and commercials. In light of what we already know of how girls are devalued and ignored by the Saturday morning shows, therefore, we suggest that you keep your daughter away from them as much as possible.

Let her watch her favorite nonsexist videos instead, or insist that she tune in to noncommercial stations only. Make it a family tradition to do chores together on Saturday morning or to go out for breakfast. Get her involved in a Saturday play group. It's not necessary to be fanatical about this. Periodic viewing won't do much harm, and she's sure to learn all about the toys that are advertised from her friends anyway. It's the constantly repeated messages that will burrow into her brain.

In 1985 *The Wall Street Journal* interviewed a group of five- to seven-year-olds to determine what they had learned from ads on radio and TV: "The kids easily supplied the missing words in these slogans: 'Go tell your mother what the big boys eat: Wheaties'; 'Trix are for kids'; 'Coke is it'; 'Soup is good food'; 'Nothing beats a great pair of L'eggs'; and 'Red Lobster for the seafood lover in you' (this one they usually sang, as they also did with 'There's more for your life at Sears')."

The article also noted that these children watched an average of twenty-seven to twenty-eight hours of TV a week and that they were "remarkably traditional when it comes to sex roles. Among the all-girl group, two want to be nurses, two teachers, one a dancer, and one an artist when they grow up. . . . Among the all-boy group, one wants to be a doctor, one a welder, one a policeman, and one won't tell. Two are undecided." Here, it seems to us, is another good reason for limiting your young daughter's TV time.

As far as older girls are concerned, advertising can be damaging because of the images it promotes and because of its limiting messages. Commercials still tend to portray women as either housewives or sex objects.

A final thought on commercials—with the remote control most TV sets now feature, it's easy to skip the ads altogether. Don't discourage your children from flipping around from station to station. It may unnerve you at first, but, in the long run, it could be beneficial for them.

Make a family project of a "Commercial Watch" (see page 226).

Teens want their MTV

A Minneapolis "classic" rock radio station encourages listeners to "play it loud and embarrass your kids." Every generation, it seems, needs to reject what came before and have its own music. In MTV and music videos, however, today's teens have something more powerful: the visual images.

While a good percentage of popular song lyrics have always been sexist or

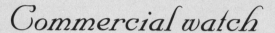

Commercial watch

Make a week-long project of monitoring the ads that appear while any member of the family is watching TV. Keep a notebook and pen near the set and instruct anyone who turns it on to jot down the product's name and the activity or job of the woman in the ad, if any woman is shown. At the end of the week discuss the results as a family.

> What is the advertiser trying to sell?
> What emotions does the ad appeal to?
> What is the image of women in the ad?
> Is it reasonable to expect that by buying the product, a person would also achieve that image?
> Is the ad directed primarily to men, primarily to women, or to both sexes?
> Is there a difference between the images of women in ads primarily directed toward men and in those primarily directed toward women? What is the difference?
> What do most of the women in the ads look like?
> How intelligent do they seem? How independent? How active?
> What kinds of problems do they have?
> How do they solve their problems?

Make it an ongoing habit to watch commercials with these questions in mind and to discuss them with your children when they are present. Encourage your daughter to do the same on her own. Praise her insights.

You might also have family members act out the commercials, reversing the male and female roles. Do the words or actions of the women sound silly when a man says or does them? What does this tell you about the advertiser's view of women? (If anyone in the family is a budding filmmaker, videotape your efforts and send the tape to one of those home video TV shows. A great advocacy effort—and it should get a lot of laughs!)

stereotyped, the images that now accompany the words demonstrate graphically what young women are supposed to look like, how they are supposed to dress and act, and what men can be allowed to do to them. Many of the scenarios are highly erotic—some would say pornographic—and a disturbing number seem to advocate violence against women as well.

Because popular music tends to define the culture for American youth, MTV is extremely powerful. Young men and women alike take their cues for appropriate appearance and behavior from the videos. The fashions, makeup, and hairstyles shown as desirable for women may appall you, but even more disturbing is the role females are assigned. Almost exclusively, women are seen as sex objects and treated as something less than human.

This is true not only in videos by male stars, but also in those starring female vocalists or groups. Consider Madonna, for example. Her decision continually to exploit her own sexuality is tragic, because she is not just another disrobed, exploited, or abused body like the hundreds of others that populate MTV videos: she is a role model for at least one generation of young women, most of whom are more likely to emulate her "dumb blonde" image rather than her less obvious business acumen.

The young men who watch MTV are not likely to be critical of the way women are portrayed, either. After all, this situation is not so different from that of the Saturday cartoons they grew up with. Once again, males are dominant, females subservient. Men act, women are acted upon. There is no single "ideal" for male beauty, but females must reflect the current, extremely constricting, image.

Clearly, the videos can be harmful to young women and men alike. Trying to prevent your daughter from seeing them at all is probably hopeless, but it is reasonable to set some restrictions. Try to help her analyze the films, too. Writing in a quarterly publication produced for the Center for Media and Values, Myra Junyk, an English instructor in Toronto, recommends making this a topic for class or group discussion. She suggests that teens watch the videos carefully at home as part of the assignment, perhaps taking notes, and then come to class ready to talk about what they've observed. "Reports by individuals or small groups can focus discussions centering around how people in each video are dressed and what they are doing," she suggests, "whether the images of women and men are presented positively or negatively, how they relate to each other and what role violence plays." Why not suggest a similar activity to one of your daughter's teachers? Or do it at home, as a family.

Analyze lyrics, too, to lessen their impact. Like commercials and nursery rhymes, they can take hold of the unconscious when heard over and over again. You might also try exposing your daughter to a wide variety of music in the hope that she'll latch on to something more positive. This might at least dilute the negative messages by decreasing how often they're heard.

Movies: some thumbs up, some thumbs down

The movies can be a great instructional medium, providing inspiration, advice, and wonderful role models. Or they can perpetuate destructive myths and stereotypes. Teach your daughter how to tell the difference, use what's good, and disregard the limiting messages, by watching the videos listed below together and then discussing them.

Videos can also be used effectively to teach problem solving. Ask your daughter what she would have done at a crucial point in the story. If she was the writer or director, would she have changed the plot? The ending?

We suggest that you wait until your daughter is at least thirteen to do this activity, as most of these films were made for adults. Let her maturity level be your guide. You can start immediately, however, to discuss and ask questions about any movie or video you see together.

A few of the films we've selected have "R" ratings, and those are so indicated. If you're concerned about this, view the films alone first so that you can fast-forward through any objectionable scenes when you watch with your daughter. There shouldn't be more than one or two per movie, and missing them won't have any effect on following the rest of the film.

We have provided summaries and discussion questions for a selection of films with positive, negative, and mixed messages, as well as a brief list of other videos we believe are empowering for girls and young women. The movies come from a variety of genres. Some are old and some are new.

SOME GOOD ONES

His Girl Friday

Disregard the patronizing title. This classic comedy from 1940 stars Rosalind Russell as star reporter Hildy Johnson; Cary Grant as her editor and ex-husband, Walter Burns; and Ralph Bellamy as Bruce Baldwin, the dull insurance agent Hildy plans to quit her job to marry. Walter wants to prevent the marriage, not only because he still cares for Hildy, but because she is the best reporter (and only woman) on his staff.

Why does Hildy want to marry Bruce?
How does she feel about her job?

What qualities does Bruce admire in Hildy?
What qualities does Walter admire in Hildy?
What qualities make Hildy a better reporter than her male counterparts?
If Hildy had married Bruce, what do you think would have happened
    to her?

Fried Green Tomatoes (PG-13)

This 1991 comedy/drama blends two stories, one from the past and one from the present. Jessica Tandy stars as Ninny Threadgoode, a nursing home resident who tells the story of Idgie Threadgoode (Mary Stuart Masterson) and Ruth Jamison (Mary-Louise Parker) to Evelyn Couch (Kathy Bates), an unhappy, overweight housewife. Idgie was a strong, nonconforming woman during the 1930s who did what she liked, stood up to authority, and saved her friend's life. Evelyn is inspired by the story to make changes in her own life.

What "rules" did Idgie break?
What risks did she take?
Was she considered to be "nice"?
How would the story have been different if she had been "nice"?
Which people in the movie admired Idgie?
Which people didn't like her?
What did Evelyn Couch learn from Idgie's story?

Norma Rae (PG)

Sally Field stars as Norma Rae in this 1979 drama, based on a true story, about unionizing the workers in a cotton mill. An uneducated single mother, Norma Rae decides to help Reuben (Ron Leibman), a labor organizer from New York, and in so doing becomes a truly "hardy personality," sometimes to the regret of her second husband, Sonny (Beau Bridges).

What future seems likely for Norma Rae at the beginning of the film?
What hopes do you think she has for herself? Is she ambitious?
How and why does she become more assertive?
What is her goal?
In light of that goal, what priorities does she set?
Who is displeased by the "new" Norma Rae?
Who admires her?
Do you think she was afraid when she held up the sign?
How do you think she felt about herself afterward?
Do you think Norma Rae had a better or worse chance for a satisfying fu-
    ture at the end of the film?

Private Benjamin (R)

This 1980 comedy stars Goldie Hawn as Judy Benjamin, a privileged young widow who decides to join the army and gets quite an education.

How realistic was Judy's idea of what the army would be like?

Were her attitudes early in the movie more traditionally "feminine" or "masculine"?

What about her attitudes later on?

Which Judy did you like better?

Which Judy do you think she liked better?

In what ways was Judy better able to take care of herself after she left Henri than she was after Yale died?

Whom, in the end, did Judy decide to trust?

SOME BAD ONES

An Officer and a Gentleman (R)

Many women love this film, perhaps because it is a classic "waiting to be rescued" story. Made in 1982, it features Debra Winger as Paula Pokrifki, a millworker who falls in love with Zack Mayo (Richard Gere), a young flyer at a Naval Aviation Officer Candidate School in her area. Paula finds happiness when Zack marches into her mill and carries her away as her co-workers cheer and applaud.

What is appealing about the story?

How realistic is it?

Who is in control of Paula's life?

What do you think she would do to support herself if Zack was killed in a plane crash?

Compare the character of Paula with that of Norma Rae from the movie discussed above.

Which one do you like better?

Which one do you think likes herself better?

Woman of the Year

As usual, Katharine Hepburn plays a smart, self-assured, and successful woman in this 1942 comedy/drama. But this is one of those "either/or" films that assumes a competent professional woman has to be a bad wife and mother. Hepburn is Tess Harding, an international affairs writer who marries Sam Craig (Spencer Tracy), a sportswriter on the same newspaper. Her dedication to her career jeopardizes the marriage, and she finally vows to make domestic life a priority.

How realistic is it that a woman as smart as Tess would be unable to prepare
   a simple breakfast, as the movie shows?

Does the movie provide any good reason why a woman cannot be successful
   both at home and on the job?

How supportive was Sam of Tess's career?

Compare the character of Sam to that of Walter in *His Girl Friday*.

Which do you think makes a better husband for a working woman?

Pretty Woman (R)

Here it is again, the fairy tale girls are brought up to hope for and believe in. Julia
Roberts stars as Vivian Ward and Richard Gere as Edward Lewis in this romance
from 1990. Vivian is a prostitute who meets Edward, a wealthy corporate takeover
specialist. He buys her services for a week in Los Angeles, takes her on a fabulous
shopping spree, falls in love with her, and, of course, hauls her off into happily-ever-
after land.

How realistic is this story?

Who controls Vivian's life?

What kind of future do you suppose this couple will have?

If the relationship ends, how will Vivian be prepared to support herself?

Compare the changes Vivian undergoes with the ways in which Judy Benjamin changes in *Private Benjamin*.

Which one is better prepared to maintain a relationship on her own terms?

Pollyanna

Hayley Mills stars in this 1960 comedy as the girl whose name has come to mean a
blindly optimistic person.

If Idgie in *Fried Green Tomatoes* had shared Pollyanna's attitude, do you
   think she would still have given food to the poor people?

Would she have noticed the poor people?

Would she have noticed that Ruth's husband was abusing her?

How would the movie *Norma Rae* be different if Norma Rae were like
   Pollyanna?

Would Judy Benjamin in *Private Benjamin* be able to admit that Henri was
   not the kind of man she wanted to marry if she thought like Pollyanna?

Before making a decision, setting a goal, or choosing a mate, is it better to
   be realistic or to assume that everything will work out for the best?

TWO MIXED BAGS

Baby Boom (PG)

This comedy from 1987 stars Diane Keaton as J. C. Wiatt, a successful business-woman who inherits an infant from distant relatives. Unable to cope with her job and the baby, she moves to the country and eventually starts her own company. The film has been criticized for implying that women must choose between job and family, but we think J. C. is admirable for taking matters into her own hands and coming up with a solution that allows her to be a good parent and a self-sufficient woman—on her own terms.

> How supportive is Steven when J. C. inherits the baby?
> How supportive are her employers?
> Can you think of things they might have done that would have allowed
>   J. C. to keep her old job?

Working Girl (R)

Another bad title, but this 1988 romance illustrates many of the traits a woman needs to succeed in the world. Melanie Griffith stars as Tess McGill, a secretary who is trying to better herself. She goes to night school, takes speech lessons, studies the newspapers, asks for new assignments, and deals assertively with sexist male co-workers. When she learns that her new female boss (Sigourney Weaver) has stolen one of her ideas, she decides to go after the deal herself, with help from an outside deal maker (Harrison Ford as Jack Trainer). In *Backlash*, Susan Faludi complains that "only the woman who buries her intelligence under a baby-doll exterior is granted a measure of professional success without having to forsake companionship" and that "she achieves both goals by playing the daffy and dependent girl," but we feel Tess is a much stronger character than Faludi claims. We do agree, however, that it is unfortunate that the makers of this film set up another woman to be the villain. As Faldui says, "In '80s cinema, as in America's real boardrooms, there's only room for one woman at a time." How does Tess demonstrate these characteristics of a hardy personality?

> Being discriminating:
> Establishing boundaries and setting limits:
> Being assertive:
> Setting goals and priorities:
> Separating fantasy from reality and acting on the reality:
> Tolerating anxiety and acting anyway:
> Projecting herself into the future:
> Trusting herself:

ALSO RECOMMENDED

Almost any film starring Katharine Hepburn, with the exception noted above. We particularly recommend *Pat and Mike*, *Desk Set*, *Adam's Rib*, *Alice Adams*, *Little Women*, *Holiday*, and *The African Queen*.

A Bunny's Tale   This made-for-TV movie stars Kirstie Alley as the young Gloria Steinem working undercover at a Playboy Club in order to write an article about the experience. It illustrates the many kinds of inequalities that existed at the time and that led to the women's movement and increased solidarity among women.

Julia (PG)   Vanessa Redgrave as Julia is an extremely strong and appealing character who, among many other things, gives wonderful advice to her friend, Lillian, played by Jane Fonda. ("Work hard. Be very bold. Take lots of chances.")

Say Anything (PG-13)   This teen romance starring John Cusack as Lloyd Dobler and Ione Skye as Diane Court does a complete turn on the standard story line. Here the young woman is the bright and ambitious one, courted by a sensitive and loving young man.

My Brilliant Career (G)   Judy Davis stars as Sybylla Melvyn in this Australian film about a strong, sensible young woman in the late 1800s who, against the wishes of her friends and family, wants to have a career.

Born Yesterday   A hilarious comedy starring Judy Holliday as Billie Dawn (not the remake with Melanie Griffith), the "dumb blond" mistress of a crooked businessman who comes to realize her own strength, intelligence, and courage. (Okay, so she has a male tutor. We still think it's great.)

Coal Miner's Daughter (PG)   Sissy Spacek as country music star Loretta Lynn and Beverly D'Angelo as Patsy Cline portray two very strong and appealing women.

The Turning Point (PG)   Anne Bancroft and Shirley MacLaine are ballet dancers who made different choices for their lives as young adults and now, years later, meet again and wonder if they did the right thing. A good lesson in making the best decisions possible and then trusting in them and in oneself.

Steel Magnolias (PG)   The story of half a dozen southern women who make their own decisions concerning how to live their lives but support each other unconditionally in those choices.

The Way We Were (PG)   Barbra Streisand stars as Katie Morosky in this tearjerker romance that also stars Robert Redford as Hubbell Gardiner. Katie is a passionate, committed, and idealistic woman who remains true to herself and eventually wins the respect of Hubbell's more socially correct circle of friends.

AN UNMARRIED WOMAN (R)   The story of a woman (Jill Clayburgh as Erica) who learns to take control of her own life when her husband leaves her.

Magazines and newspapers

The print media is often blamed for discovering and perpetuating "issues" that are either much exaggerated or totally false. Remember when *Newsweek* proclaimed that a single woman over forty was "more likely to be killed by a terrorist" than to get married? It wasn't true, of course, but it did get everyone's attention, and it did sell magazines. The media may or may not have ulterior motives for printing such falsehoods, but no one denies that they are trying to make a profit, and if sensationalizing the news is what it takes to do that, so be it.

In *Backlash* Susan Faludi gives evidence that the magazines largely created such "news" as, first, the success of the women's movement and, later, the death of feminism; the "man shortage"; the "biological clock"; the "mommy track"; and the "new traditionalism." Your daughter may be too young to read these articles, but they may affect the way you think, so be wary. Does the article use terms like "some women may feel that" or "women are likely to" instead of providing hard data and real-life examples? Are the authorities quoted men, or women known to be hostile to equal rights? Do the claims of the article fit in with what you know to be true about yourself, your family, and your friends?

What's on the cover? This is a good way to gauge what publishers think is newsworthy. For example, from February 1993 through February 1994, *Sports Illustrated* featured photos of women on five out of fifty-two issues. You might think that's an improvement over the bad old days when women's sports were completely ignored, but take a closer look. Who, exactly, was pictured, and why? Champions and record setters, right? Not quite. The featured women included one model (on the "bathing suit issue") and five victims: Monica Seles with a knife in her back; Nancy Kerrigan after the attack on her knee; the widows of two baseball players; and Mary Pierce, a tennis player abused by her father. What message does this send to young women athletes?

Your preteen or teenage daughter is also likely to page through adult women's magazines like *Vogue, Elle,* or *Cosmopolitan.* Many publications of this sort have made big improvements in the types of articles they run. For example, it's no longer uncommon to come across articles with titles like "Why Diets Don't Work." Unfortunately for your daughter, however, this philosophy is not reflected in the fashion and beauty pieces or in the advertisements, and she is more likely to be affected by the photos of emaciated models who still glare out at her accusingly from every page than by the more reasonable editorial claims.

Many young women clip these photographs and pin them to their bulletin boards to remind themselves that they are unattractive, or they stick them to the refrigerator door in case they should be tempted to eat. Obviously, this is an unhealthy situation. We'll offer some hints on helping your daughter feel comfortable with her appearance in chapter 19, "Mirror, Mirror, on the Wall."

Newspapers can also influence people's perceptions by the photographs they choose to run. The one time it seems acceptable to feature the least attractive woman in a group, for example, is when it is a group of feminists. (From our admittedly unscientific poll, she should also be grossly overweight, have her mouth wide open, and be wearing a T-shirt or carrying a sign that says something derogatory about men.) Call and complain if your newspaper succumbs to these tactics.

Monitor the papers, too, for their general coverage of women's news, and write or call if you have complaints. How much space is allotted to women's sports? Do female athletes get their picture on the front page of the sports section a reasonable percentage of the time? Are stories about successful businesswomen printed in the "life-styles" section or with other business news? What percentage of the bylined editorials are by women?

Take a look at the ads in your magazines and newspapers. Are women portrayed as victims or sex objects? Are girls represented? Kodak recently ran a lovely full-color ad featuring a group of children surrounding a baseball player. They had obviously made an effort to select children from every race—but they were all boys. When you come across similar ads, or offensive ones, drop a note to the advertiser.

What kinds of magazines do you have in your house? Don't expose your daughter to any that exploit or demean women.

What kinds of magazines does she read? Take a look at them from time to time and talk to her about them. Articles in recent *Teen* and *YM* magazines, for example, emphasize attracting males, with titles such as "Can You Ever Get That Guy?," "Real Guys Tell All: Stuff You Do That Gets on Their Nerves," and "How to Make Him Want You Bad," or demean teens' bodies with titles such as "Body Fix-its," "Intimate Advice: How to Get Rid of Your Most Embarrassing Body Problems," and "Shape Your Body Like Hollywood's Hottest." First, discuss the emphasis on "being" rather than "doing" and the ways in which the articles tend to diminish girls' self-esteem. Then show your daughter who advertises in this magazine and how the advertisers influence the content of the articles. If you can, compare the articles in some teen magazines with those in *Sassy*, a nonsexist magazine for adolescent girls.

When a group of girls and parents in Duluth, Minnesota, couldn't find the empowering magazines they wanted, they developed their own. *New Moon: The Magazine for Girls and Their Dreams* first appeared in March 1993. About twenty-five girls between the ages of eight and fourteen are completely responsible for its content and production. Its message: "You can be whoever you want to be."

Parents Joe Kelly and Nancy Gruver thought other parents could use some advice about parenting girls, too, and developed a companion publication, *New Moon Parenting*.

Both magazines are bimonthly and available by subscription. Consider placing an order, or suggest that your daughter and her friends start their own magazine. What a terrific way to empower girls!

Media guidelines for parents

1. Monitor the TV shows and movies your daughter watches.
2. Watch along with her and discuss any sexism you see on the screen.
3. Help your daughter develop the skills to be a conscious consumer of programming and advertising alike.
4. Encourage your daughter's school to develop lessons and conduct projects on the issue of media consciousness.
5. Subscribe only to magazines that support women's equality, options, and ambitions.
6. Try to find nonsexist children's and teen magazines that actively promote developing hardy personalities in both boys and girls. When your daughter finds objectionable materials in them, have her write letters to the editor.
7. Complain about advertising that is demeaning or limiting to women by calling or writing the offending company. You can locate toll-free 800 numbers by calling your 800 information operator or by obtaining a copy of the AT&T Toll Free 800 Directory.
8. Listen to the lyrics of popular songs with your six- to eight-year-old daughter and discuss their messages.
9. Help or encourage her to rewrite songs with more empowering messages. This is a good party game for fifth- and sixth-graders.

chapter sixteen

Lessons Learned in School

s you read this chapter, in public and private classrooms across America, boys are learning to think, question, speak their minds, demand attention, make their own rules, and feel good about themselves, their intelligence, and their prospects for future success.

In those same classrooms, from the same teachers, girls are learning to watch the boys' performance—at great cost to their own education and self-esteem.

The country's attention was directed to sex discrimination in public schools when, early in 1992, the AAUW (American Association of University Women) released "How Schools Shortchange Girls." A summary of 1,331 studies of girls in elementary, middle, and high school, this was by far the most comprehensive report ever issued on "sexism in the schoolhouse."

Researchers Myra and David Sadker, often considered the leading experts on educational equity, have also made a major contribution by videotaping and studying the interaction in classrooms over the past twenty years. Their 1994 book, *Failing at Fairness: How America's Schools Cheat Girls*, spells out their findings in fascinating and horrifying detail.

From kindergarten through graduate school, girls are ignored, harassed, stereotyped, and demeaned—all the while receiving an inferior education.

Most teachers, of course, do not intend to and are not even aware that they do mistreat girls. But, in their book *Meeting at the Crossroads: Women's Psychology and Girls' Development*, Lyn Mikel Brown and Carol Gilligan confirm, too, that teachers

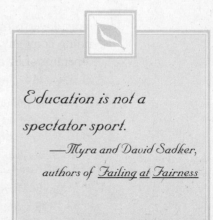

Education is not a spectator sport.
—*Myra and David Sadker, authors of* <u>Failing at Fairness</u>

play a role in causing most adolescent girls to become more fearful of taking risks or giving offense and less enthusiastic about their education.

Some of the most important findings of these studies and others:

- *Teachers call on boys more often and encourage them to work through problems and finish projects when they need help. When girls need help, teachers are likely to tell them the answer or complete the project for them, depriving them of active learning.*
- *The most neglected group of students is usually made up of the brightest girls, who tend to be quiet and undemanding.*
- *Boys are allowed to call out answers. Girls are required to raise their hands before speaking.*
- *Teachers thought girls had talked more than boys in a film of a classroom discussion, though the boys actually talked three times as much as their female classmates.*
- *While boys tend to be praised for intellectual achievement, girls are more likely to be praised for the neatness and form of their work.*
- *Most classrooms are structured around boys' needs. For example, since boys often need help with reading, remedial reading classes have become a standard part of the curriculum. Girls often need help with math, but no comparable remediation is available to them. Furthermore, most schools offer a competitive setting—that which works best for boys—even though it's been shown that girls learn better when students work together cooperatively.*
- *Though the gender gap in math scores is closing, it's getting wider in science achievement. Girls are doing worse than they were in 1978, and boys are doing better.*
- *Girls are often discouraged from taking the advanced math and science courses required for careers in technology, as well as for entry into more than half of all college majors.*
- *By high school, girls tend to stick to areas where they have been most encouraged, usually English and the arts. These areas also offer lower risks, since half answers can often be given—and girls have learned that taking risks is frowned on.*
- *Verbal and physical sexual harassment is increasing and largely being tolerated by school authorities. In a 1993 survey commissioned by the AAUW, two-thirds of all students in grades eight to eleven said they have experienced unwelcome sexual behavior at school. The survey also revealed that the negative impact was far greater on girls than boys, with many reporting that it affected their ability to study and a third saying it made them not want to go to school at all. Forty-three percent of girls said it makes them feel less confident.*
- *Even when girls have strong backgrounds in math or science, they are much less likely than boys to consider technological careers. A Rhode Island study*

found that of all high school seniors taking physics and calculus, 64 percent of the boys and 19 percent of the girls planned college majors in science or engineering.

- *Among the brightest high school students who do not go on to college, 75 to 90 percent are women.*
- *Girls tend to underplay academic achievement or attribute it to "luck." Boys take credit for their abilities.*
- *Teachers are often not aware of their bias but tend subconsciously to think that "boys will be boys, and girls should be ladylike."*
- *Girls become almost as assertive as boys in class when teachers get re-training.*
- *Girls spend four times as long watching and listening and 25 percent less time handling science equipment when the sexes work together on projects.*
- *The group most likely to have professional ambitions is that of girls who like math and science.*
- *More boys than girls drop out of high school, but a much higher rate of poverty exists among women who do not have a diploma.*
- *Women's achievements are largely ignored in school curricula.*
- *According to Myra and David Sadker, discrimination takes place in the counseling office as well as the classroom. "Boys get more of everything," Myra Sadker told Guideposts. "More praise, more criticism, more help, more probing questions, more time in general."*

The truly insidious thing about all of this is that the discrimination is not obvious. Most teachers honestly try to, and believe they do, treat their students equally. The girls themselves are unlikely to be able to point out blatant examples of male preference. Still, over the years the accumulated slights and disparities leave girls and young women feeling less intelligent and less valued than their brothers. It leaves them with a lesser education. And they can't think of anyone to blame but themselves.

Writing in *Fortune* magazine in March of 1992, Daniel Seligman protests that "How Schools Shortchange Girls" "blames the schools rather than nature for girls' persistent tendency to behave like girls in the classroom (e.g., to be less aggressive than boys about wanting to speak). Ignoring the hundreds of studies demonstrating that teachers give girls better grades than boys, it complains bitterly that teachers favor the boys."

As an advocate for girls, you're likely to be challenged by similar arguments. We hope you took immediate exception to Seligman's notions concerning girls' "nature" and boys' inborn tendency to talk a lot (we'd always heard that's what women do—isn't the male cliché the "strong, silent type"?). And, of course, there's quite a difference between achieving and getting good grades.

Factually, the article didn't teach us much. Its tone, though, speaks volumes: every paragraph drips with contempt for women. It is in ways like this—sometimes subtle, sometimes not so subtle—that girls' enthusiasm for school is worn down, along with their self-esteem. This is a matter of utmost concern, not only because it makes young women feel less valued and less intelligent than their brothers, but because it diminishes their motivation to get a good education and, in fact, deprives them of that education.

The state of education today

How did we get to this point? Basically, our educational system has not kept pace with the changing world. Much of the curriculum used today was developed in the late nineteenth century, when a group of educators from an Ivy League university decided that students needed to be competent in math, science, history, geography, writing, and grammar. At that time, of course, many people believed that no education was required for women, minorities, and lower-class white males, so their needs were hardly considered. Nor was the technological revolution that would soon burst forth and change the way Americans work forever.

Today it is widely acknowledged that our schools are failing a high percentage of students from all backgrounds and both sexes. Curriculum reform has been widely debated and discussed in recent years, but "little of the national discussion on improving education has centered on erasing gender discrimination that affects half the children in schools," according to the AAUW study on gender equity in the schools.

The movement to restructure schools could, however, be extremely beneficial to girls and young women. This is an ideal time for you to get involved and to speak out in favor of a curriculum that encourages critical thinking, problem solving, and creativity, as well as equity.

In May of 1990 the National Coalition on Women and Girls in Education—of which the AAUW is a leader—submitted recommendations to the National Governors' Association and the Bush administration, pointing out the ways in which achieving the National Education Goals depends on meeting the needs of girls and women. The AAUW's brief on restructuring education summarized the coalition's report as follows (the National Education Goals—proposed by the National Governors' Association and the Bush administration and signed into law in 1994 by President Bill Clinton—are printed in bold, the coalition's recommendations follow):

1. **By the year 2000, all children in America will start school ready to learn.**

Requires enhancing the ability of female-headed households to prepare children for school, including achievement of adequate living standards and access to parental leave, child care, Head Start funding, and adult female literacy programs.

2. By the year 2000, we will increase the percentage of students graduating from high school to at least 90 percent.

Requires addressing factors that have a particular impact on keeping girls in school, including provision of gender-fair curricula and instruction, pregnancy prevention programs, and assistance to pregnant and parenting teens.

3. By the year 2000, American students will leave grades four, eight, and twelve having demonstrated competency over challenging subject matter, including English, mathematics, science, history, and geography, and every school in America will ensure that all students learn to use their minds well, so they may be prepared for responsible citizenship, further learning, and productive employment in our modern economy.

Requires gender-fair curricula, teaching methods attentive to the learning styles of individual students, and methods of assessing competency that do not rely on standardized tests, which can contain race and sex biases.

4. By the year 2000, U.S. students will be the first in the world in mathematics and science achievement.

Requires developing interventions at key junctures in girls' academic lives to increase their participation and success in these subjects.

5. By the year 2000, every adult American will be literate and will possess the knowledge and skills necessary to compete in a global economy and exercise the rights and responsibilities of citizenship.

Requires gender-fair programs in vocational education and encouragement of the participation of women in employment and training programs including post-secondary training for technical and professional careers.

6. By the year 2000, every school in America will be free of drugs and violence and will offer a disciplined environment conducive to learning.

Requires ensuring safety from sexual and racial harassment and assault in the schools.

If these gender-equity goals are to be met, it is imperative that parents and other advocates for girls and women get involved with the schools in their community. At the very least, write a letter to your local school board, encouraging efforts to meet the goals listed above.

What you can do

Your daughter may be able to give you some sense of what's going on in her class. Is she enthusiastic about school? Does she like her teacher? Have you noticed any changes in her actions or statements indicating that her view of herself and her visions for her future are either expanding or contracting? Try to engage her in an ongoing dialogue, so that when you ask about her day in school, she will say more than that it was "fine."

If you've praised her for substance rather than image, it should be natural to praise her for her intellectual accomplishments rather than the correctness or neatness of her work. If she learns to trust herself, she will become more comfortable with taking credit for her accomplishments and therefore more willing to strive to higher accomplishments.

Encourage decision making, problem solving, and critical thinking within the family unit. Use cooperative learning situations in the home. Problem solve as a family or in small groups of family members.

Review her homework. Look at her textbooks. Do they seem to be equitable? Does she study women of achievement? Make it a point to recognize the accomplishments of women, both in today's society and in history.

Get to know your daughter's teacher. Consider observing a classroom discussion from time to time. Listen carefully to her teacher's comments during parent-teacher conferences. Does she seem more interested in your daughter's behavior than in her academic achievement? If a specific issue comes up that smacks of unequal expectations of your daughter, ask if that is also an issue with the boys in the class.

If, as we said earlier, it is true that the brightest girls often receive the least attention from their teachers, it is not unreasonable to believe that half of our gifted population is not being recognized and nurtured. Girls who have not been identified as potential high achievers by the time they are in fifth grade

Parents have become so convinced that educators know what is best for children that they forget that they themselves are really experts.

—Marian Wright Edelman

may be lost forever: as they reach adolescence, it becomes more and more likely that they will hide their talents for the remainder of their academic careers.

What efforts does your daughter's school make to recognize gifted girls early and help them reach their potential? This is something parents need to be concerned about, particularly if they believe their daughters may be among the intellectual elite.

Find out how your school chooses students to enter the special programs. If you think your daughter is gifted, be sure to bring that to the attention of the school. Do not be shy about this. Your daughter's future depends on it.

Attend school activities, plays, parents' meetings, and sporting events. Take mental note of any discrimination and discuss this with your daughter.

While the day-to-day contact between student and teacher has the most immediate impact on your daughter, it's the school's overall educational policies that will follow and affect her as she moves from grade to grade. If you have questions about these policies, schedule a meeting with a school board member or the school principal or take her or him to lunch and raise your concerns. What is the school or the district doing or planning to do about teacher training and evaluation to ensure gender fairness? Is a cooperative learning style encouraged in the classroom? Is showing women and minorities as doers, leaders, and decision makers one of the criteria textbooks must meet before they are adopted for classroom use? Are both boys and girls being educated as future workers *and* parents? If you are not satisfied with the answers to your questions, consider organizing a committee to formally raise community concerns, or think about running for a post on the school board yourself.

Mindy remembers Wendy coming home one day quite indignant about a sexist comment made in jest by the principal of her school. "Our whole group of girls got upset and we told him what we thought of it—right there in class." This group of girls had completed a mother-daughter group the year before (see chapter 28, "Forming Mother-Daughter Groups").

You can talk to your preadolescent daughter about the studies of the inequities in the classroom. Help her learn to be discriminating and to be able to identify unequal treatment and sexist attitudes. Teach her what verbal and sexual harassment is, even in its most subtle forms. If you have taught her the skills of assertive communication, she'll be more likely to stand up for herself and ask for equal time, attention, and respect in the classroom. If you've helped her develop anxiety tolerance, she will be much more likely to take the risks required to acquire a first-rate education and not feel compelled to follow the crowd.

A girl with a hardy personality is going to be better prepared to weather whatever discrimination she may face, in the schools and in society.

Host a presentation to get other parents involved

Talk to a representative of your parent-teacher organization and offer to facilitate a one-and-a-half- to two-hour meeting around the topic of gender equity in the schools. If there is no active organization at your daughter's school, recruit a sympathetic teacher to help you and approach the principal for permission to organize a meeting on your own.

The information you'll need to do that is included below. To make a success of your efforts, hand out fliers announcing the meeting in classrooms, or organize a phone tree to notify all parents. Remember to order videos well ahead of your target date, and don't forget to bring along copies of the agenda and "The Startling Statement Quiz" on pages 366–369, notepads and pencils, and so on.

You may want to plan a coffee hour after the presentation to create a friendly but determined atmosphere. This is the kind of event that gets people involved with the subject and committed to working toward the agreed-upon goals.

AGENDA FOR PARENTS MEETING

1. Begin by showing the video *Making Points* (eight minutes). It features a TV reporter asking a group of boys on a basketball court about their plans for the future and their sex-role identities. Their responses generally provoke laughter in the crowd, but at the end of the video viewers learn that all the statements they just heard were actually made by a group of girls. This is an extremely effective way to get a discussion going. The video is available from Direct Cinema Ltd. (see "Ordering Information," page 482).

2. Break the audience into small groups of three to six people and allow seven to ten minutes to discuss what they learned from and their reactions to the video. Were the attitudes portrayed prevalent when group members were growing up? Do they know any girls or young women with similar limiting attitudes?

3. Hand out copies of "The Startling Statement Quiz" in chapter 23, "Getting Girls Ready for Career Education," and ask each group to complete it or, for a more lively activity, break into groups of three people and ask each group to get consensus on their answers. Offer a prize to the group with the most correct answers. This should take about fifteen minutes.

4. Show the AAUW video *Shortchanging Girls, Shortchanging America* (fifteen minutes). It dramatically addresses the issue of gender inequity in American education. A video discussion guide and sample speech accompany the video. (See "Ordering Information.")

5. Ask the principal or head school counselor to give an overview of the school's equity efforts to date (make arrangements with this person ahead of time, of course). Allow ten to fifteen minutes for the presentation and questions from the audience.

6. Break up into groups of five to seven people and ask each group to brainstorm a list of suggestions for improving the gender fairness in the school. Use large sheets of paper so the suggestions can be hung around the room. Have each group share its suggestions (fifteen minutes).

7. Now is the time in the meeting to plan for action. Invite participants to join a special equity committee to help facilitate an equity agenda for the school. Ask for volunteers to sign up for the committee.

The committee might be involved in such things as making presentations to the school board, supplying speakers for any group that requests them, setting up shadow opportunities and locating role models for students, holding fund-raising events to help pay for resources and special teacher training sessions on equity issues, or conducting a school survey of equitable opportunities. Sample surveys can be found in the *Women Helping Girls with Choices* handbook (Advocacy Press) or through the AAUW National Office. Phone (see "Ordering Information") and ask for the Gender Equity Assessment Guide.

The surveys help you assess the present state of services for girls in your community. It is important to compare girls' services with those serving boys: What do they do? How many are there? How much money do they receive? How many children do they serve? In organizations serving both sexes, what is the ratio between boys and girls? With information like this, you'll be better able to direct your efforts. If you find, for example, that your community's United Way is giving twice as much money to boys' groups, one goal becomes clear immediately: changing that situation.

8. Invite mothers to indicate their interest in forming mother-daughter groups (see chapter 28, "Forming Mother-Daughter Groups"). Take about five minutes to explain the purposes of these groups.

9. Close by showing the video *One Fine Day* (seven minutes). This inspiring film provides an upbeat ending for the meeting. It is available from Ishtar Films (see "Ordering Information").

Note: Ask your principal or superintendent of schools if funds are available to purchase the recommended videos, or check with your public library. It may already have the videos, or it might be interested in adding them to its collection.

Teacher training

As we said earlier, most teachers are not overtly sexist, but like most of us, they have some ingrained ideas about sex roles, and they are also faced with the challenge of keeping order in a class full of boisterous, attention-demanding males. They may need only to have the problems that develop because of these factors brought to their attention and then be provided with some better solutions in order to change. Why not talk with a guidance counselor at the school about arranging a meeting or a series of meetings to do just that?

A first step might include using the survey at the beginning of chapter 3, "Redefining Femininity," to assess how teachers feel about women's equality and building a discussion around their responses. Some of the exercises in chapter 2 ("What Attitudes, Experiences, and Feelings Do You Bring to Parenting?") could also be helpful in bringing about a realization of how damaging sex-role stereotypes are for girls and young women

When researchers have asked teachers to remember their favorite students, it always ends up being kids who conformed to gender stereotypes. The ones they like best are assertive males, and the ones they like least are assertive females.

—*David Sadker, as quoted by* Newsweek, *February 24, 1992*

today. Teachers should be urged to start thinking of personality traits in terms of in-strumental and expressive instead of masculine and feminine.

There are also ways to deal with those disruptive boys. Since they tend to raise their hands immediately, for example (whether they know the answer to the ques-tion or not), the counselor might suggest that teachers wait a few seconds for other hands to go up. Since boys often jump around and wave their hands because they want the attention they get from being called on, teachers can make a rule that no one engaging in that type of activity will be asked to answer the questions. (And *follow* it! The Sadkers found that teachers did sometimes make such a rule, then al-lowed the boys completely to disregard it. If a girl spoke without raising her hand, however, she was likely to be reprimanded and reminded of the necessity to follow orders.) They can also request an answer from a certain part of the room, thereby giving the quiet students a chance.

Girls learn best in cooperative settings, not the competitive style that straight rows of desks encourage. Teachers should be instructed to assign more team projects and to conduct some classes with everyone sitting around a table, preferably round. The AAUW report "How Schools Shortchange Girls" suggests "limiting lectures and recitations and replacing them with interactive learning methods that develop critical thinking skills. 'Coaching'—assisted performance through modeling, ques-tioning, and dialogue—helps to develop problem-solving skills, as does collaborative learning. Interdisciplinary teaching that tackles real-world problems, especially when combined with hands-on projects, demonstrates the use and value of knowl-edge far better than the typical ingestion and regurgitation of 'facts.' " These teach-ing styles go hand in hand with the styles recommended in the recent SCANS report from the U.S. Department of Labor. Problem solvers and critical thinkers are required for today's workforce. We can no longer compete with workers who need implicit directions and an elaborate hierarchy of supervisors.

There are professionals who conduct workshops on correcting gender inequity in schools, Myra and David Sadker among them. You can contact the Sadkers at the School of Education, American University, Washington, DC, 20016.

A wonderful book to help raise awareness of the issues is *School Girls: Young Women, Self-esteem and the Confidence Gap* by Peggy Orenstein in association with the American Association of University Women. We recommend that this be your next gift to your daughter's teacher or the school's teacher resource library.

Some people may be thinking, The problem is the old-timer teachers, right? So won't the problems go away as new teachers enter the system? Unfortunately col-leges aren't doing their parts to change things. The college curriculum for education majors needs to be adjusted so that new teachers enter the classroom prepared to conduct their jobs free of gender bias. Many schools are forming parent committees that, among other responsibilities, make recommendations on the hiring of new teachers. If you don't choose to sit on that committee, at least make them aware of the skills to look for in new hires.

Are single-sex schools the answer?

When you go back and reread the list of ways schools shortchange girls, one thing becomes obvious: Remove the boys, and many of the problems are solved. Suddenly the girls are answering questions, getting attention, being academically challenged. All the math and science classes are filled with girls. All the school leaders are girls. The entire athletic budget goes to girls' teams. Everything is given to girls, and in return, everything is expected of them.

Is single-sex education the answer or your daughter? There are many good reasons to consider it, at least for a few years. "We learned to compete for excellence, not for either male attention or approval," Senator Barbara Mikulski, a graduate of St. Agnes College, told *USA Today.*

Indeed, studies show graduates of women's colleges are more likely than graduates of coed schools to choose nontraditional careers and to be very successful in them. The biggest drawback, at this time, appears to be that the schools are disappearing. In 1993 there were only two public girls' high schools, Western High in Baltimore and Girls' High in Philadelphia. Among private high schools, 38 percent of Catholic and 24 percent of independent schools are single-sex.

Adolescence is a time when individuals, both male and female, begin developing their sexual identity. A great deal of energy and time goes into attracting the opposite sex. If the same amount of en-

When girls go to single-sex schools, they stop being the audience and become players.

—Myra Sadker

It's called the "Hillary" factor.
—USA Today, commenting on the upswing in interest in all-female colleges because Hillary Rodham Clinton attended Wellesley College

I remember being more interested in the guy sitting behind me in my geometry class than anything the teacher could be saying or demonstrating at the front of the class. I nearly flunked the class because my mind was elsewhere.

—Mother of teenage girl

ergy and time went into classwork and learning, it stands to reason students would be better educated. This is another important consideration for single-sex high schools, and this point deserves study within the educational community.

The 1960s and 1970s saw a rash of mergers among private single-sex high schools and colleges and, while it seemed like a good idea at the time, many people have come to question the decision. When Mills College, a private women's school in California, announced that it would go coed beginning in 1991, students and alumni raised such a chorus of disapproval that the administration decided to recant. The girls and women, it seems, are very much aware of the value of attending a school of their own.

Without boys around, girls don't feel the need to "play dumb." At Girls' High, 50 percent of the students take honors or advanced-placement classes. In 1991 more than 90 percent of the graduates from both Girls' High and Western went on to college. And these are not upper-middle-class, suburban schools. Both serve inner-city populations. Girls' High has a 64 percent minority enrollment; at Western, 77 percent of the girls are African American.

If these schools are so good, why aren't there more of them? There soon may be. One benefit that's come out of the failure of the old educational system is that desperate officials are willing to consider all sorts of alternatives.

The concept of single-sex or single-race public schools raises some constitutional questions, but the debate goes on. Magnet schools, which meet the needs of particular populations by focusing their programs on languages, science, or whatever, have been successful in many parts of the country. Perhaps the idea of schools that cater specifically to girls is also valid. Sandra Wighton, principal at Western High, told *USA Today* that ten years ago "my thought was we'd better hold on because we're the last of a breed, a special jewel in public education." But now "I tend to think this is the beginning of another era as people begin to look at new ways to solve the problems of education."

Single-sex education is hardly new, but it does seem to offer solutions to many of the problems facing girls and young women. When the TV show *20/20* did a report on the topic, one young woman at Western told the reporter, "Now I think I've gotten to the point in my life where I'm ready to go on and show myself off to the rest of the world, and show myself off to all those boys who think they can do the best. I'm going to show them what I've learned here; what I've learned in self-esteem and self-confidence."

Any new messages you'd like to give your daughter about the importance of education? Add them to "Your Plan."

chapter seventeen

Math, Science, and Computers

There seems to be a general feeling among parents that 1) boys are more interested in and naturally better at math and science than girls, and 2) it doesn't matter. Both are false, and both are potentially damaging to your daughter's future and her self-esteem.

Boys' superior performance in these subjects, beginning in junior high (throughout elementary school there is almost no difference in performance between the sexes), seems to have more to do with attitude and expectations than with innate ability.

And according to the AAUW report "Shortchanging Girls, Shortchanging America," girls who like math and science have higher self-esteem, aspire to more ambitious careers, cling more tenaciously to those career goals, and even feel better about their appearance than girls who do not like these subjects.

What's more, a solid education in these fields is required for entry into a great majority of careers paying a living wage. Math has become the language of business, government, and social science. And as technology changes the way almost everyone works, being able to work with it is absolutely essential. As we move into the twenty-first century, that trend will only become stronger. Without a strong background in comput-

The bad news is at tender ages, girls are under-encouraged and under-exposed to science, math, and technology. The good news is when they're encouraged, they respond with enthusiasm.
—*Heather Johnston Nicholson, Ph.D., Girls Incorporated*

ers and technology, your daughter will be ineligible for most high-paying jobs. Whether she goes to college, attends vocational school, or enters the job market after high school graduation, she will do better and go farther with a good working knowledge of math and technology. But if she doesn't get the prerequisites she needs for college-level work while still in high school, serious study of mathematics, science, engineering, or economics will be off limits.

What is the root of this problem? Study after study has failed to establish a gender-linked "math gene." Differences in performance can be accounted for by the fact that parents and teachers still tend to expect boys to do better; most science and math teachers are still male; there are still too few women role models visibly working in the fields most obviously identified with math and science; and boys, probably as a result, have higher expectations for themselves in these subjects than girls do.

There are some very good reasons why you should work to see that your daughter is not deterred by these negative circumstances. With a solid education in math and science, she will have

1. More choices.

If she does not take math and science courses throughout high school, she greatly decreases her options for future careers. She needs these courses just to qualify for entry into a more than half of all college major programs. A math and science background will also get her into training programs for high-paying jobs that don't require college.

2. More money.

Jobs requiring math pay more, on average, than jobs requiring verbal skills. Nearly all high-paying jobs require advanced math.

3. More flexibility and control.

The low-paying jobs, the ones that don't require math or science, the ones held traditionally by women, tend to be the most rigid in terms of setting schedules, negotiating time off, parental leave, and so on.

4. More time.

Women in low-paying jobs often need to work extra-long hours just to get by financially. Those who excel at math and science often have their pick of jobs, and some earn enough so that they can work only part-time if they choose.

5. More problem-solving ability.

This is extremely helpful in school, on the job, and in just about every other facet of life.

It isn't clear why girls who like math and science feel better about themselves, but the important point is they do! Studying these subjects also leads to higher level jobs, calling for more responsibility and awarding greater respect.

At each stage in the educational process, from junior high to graduate school, girls and women become a smaller percentage of the students in math, science, and technology. In 1988, for example, only 17 percent of the doctorate degrees awarded in math went to women. With your help, your daughter can beat odds like these.

What it takes

More so than boys, girls tend to feel that if they have any talent for a subject, success in that area should come easily for them. As math and science classes move beyond the elementary level, however, they require a certain amount of effort from all students. Girls who do not understand this are likely to back away from the challenge, into more "comfortable" subjects like English. And because parents and teachers are accustomed to believing that it's not really necessary for girls to have a solid math and science background, they often go along with a young woman's request to scale back her efforts.

Success at math and science also requires problem-solving skills. Girls need to develop the confidence to delve into problems even when the solutions are not readily apparent. They get less practice at this than boys, however, since teachers and parents are more likely to jump in and provide the answers for females instead of allowing them to reason them out for themselves.

Anxiety tolerance is also called for: in math and science, things are black and white, right or wrong. Occasional failure is almost inevitable. Individuals who like to take risks and are willing to put their reputations on the line are more likely to thrive in these classes. And, still, those individuals are likely to be male.

In order for girls to be successful and to seek careers in these fields:

1. *They must see themselves as successful in math.*
2. *They must have support and high expectations from family, teachers, and peers.*
3. *They must understand what's in it for them. Why is math important to their future success and satisfaction in life?*

Seeing herself as successful at math

Attitude is extremely important. The AAUW survey on self-esteem found that girls are more likely than boys to believe they are not good at math. That is undoubtedly one reason they take fewer classes than boys, but when girls do sign up for math, other studies indicate, they perform as well, or nearly as well, as their male class-mates. The more positive attitude you can instill, therefore, and the earlier you can instill it, the better.

Any phrase, if it is repeated often enough, will have an impact on those who hear it. When Mindy's daughter, Wendy, was a preschooler, Mindy started repeating the following statements at every appropriate opportunity from then on:

Math is fun.
Mommy's best subject was math.
I like math.

Mindy continued to repeat these when Wendy was doing her math homework, when Mindy balanced her checkbook, at the grocery store when they figured out which size of detergent was the better value, and so on.

We suggest that you use these phrases, or similar statements, to help your daughter develop a healthy attitude.

If she's already expressing doubts about her abilities, you might help her use af-firmations to stop the negative inner voices. As we said earlier, affirmations are sim-ply brief, positive statements like the ones above, except they are things you say to yourself. Affirmations should always be in the present tense, as if they are already true, and they should include the person's name. Two of the statements above can quite easily become affirmations: "I, Lizzie, like math" (not "I, Lizzie, will try harder not to hate math") and "I, Mary, think math is fun" (not "I have to start thinking that math is fun"). Other possible math-related affirmations:

> I, (your daughter's name), am good at math.
> I, (your daughter's name), like to be challenged.
> I, (your daughter's name), am a problem solver.

These should be repeated several times a day, especially before tackling an assignment or taking a test.

When she's a bit older, you can also help her to counter her own ideas about "being good at math." Americans believe that people are born with capability and that those who get ahead are naturally smart. That's why we select students for gifted programs through test scores. Japanese, on the other hand, believe that those who get ahead are those who work harder. Passing national examinations with a high score is attributed to harder work rather than higher intelligence.

American children learn in grade school that the smart kid is the one who finishes the test first; if it takes someone a long time to finish, she must be dumb. This works for children with good memories as long as memory is all that is required to do well in school. But when a subject, like math, requires slower reading and a problem-solving approach, things fall apart.

It's also a good idea to help your daughter stay slightly ahead of the rest of the class, particularly during the elementary years, when she's learning her rote computations.

With Wendy, Mindy used quiet moments in the car, waiting in lines, eating out, and so on to work with her on math. On a vacation to Jackson Hole and Yellowstone the summer before Wendy started fourth grade, for example, they made it a habit to use the restaurants' paper placemats as "worksheets" and—breakfast, lunch and dinner—they did multiplication tables. By the end of their ten-day trip Wendy could recite the tables through nine, and she began the school year with an advantage. The payoff? Halfway through her first semester at college, Wendy called Mindy

I thought I was no good at math. I could never get it in that quick way I was used to. When I was in seventh grade, however, I made a discovery. It was just before daylight savings time began, and I was waking up early every morning. Since there wasn't much to do, I started fiddling around with my math homework. All of a sudden I understood the concepts, and I did better that spring than I ever had done before. I realized that I was good in math, that I just hadn't spent enough time on it! After that, I never got less than an A in a math or statistics course.

—Woman, college professor, scientist

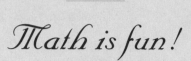

Math is fun!

1. Games with two or more dice offer practice with addition. If your daughter's games come with only one die, add another to "make it more fun."

2. In card games like twenty-one, the players have to add up the scores quickly and decide based on probability whether they want to risk drawing more cards. This kind of game can help your daughter feel more comfortable with numbers.

3. An important part of mathematical thinking is grasping spatial relationships. Building toys like Tinker Toys, Erector sets, and Lincoln Logs are great. So is sewing—it takes good spatial thinking to put a sleeve in right.

4. Another way to develop spatial thinking is puzzles—from simple toddler ones to that thousand-piece number that takes the whole family weeks to complete.

5. It's helpful to use physical objects when teaching basic math to young children. It doesn't matter if you use marbles or apples or paper cutouts, it's simply easier for a child to understand something she can see. Telling her that three minus two is one is not nearly as effective as putting three apples in front of her, asking her to take two of them away, and then having her report how many apples she has left.

6. If your community has a store for teachers, pay a visit. You'll find a wealth of games and books that make math fun. Or ask your daughter's teacher to share with you the many supplemental educational catalogs received through the mail.

7. Make it a habit to purchase at least one new math game or book for each birthday and Christmas. Give math games to your daughter's friends at their birthday parties, too.

8. Use the language of physical fitness to help your daughter visualize her math development as an exciting and challenging workout. Talk about "exercising her mind." Schedule "brain workouts" with the help of special problems found in math activity books. Encourage her to "stretch her mind" as she grapples with new concepts, to "go for the burn" as she takes on problems that require perseverance. Teach her how to "compete with herself" as she tries to reach new plateaus of learning.

Math baseball

This is an ideal activity for the classroom, a church or club event, or your daughter's next birthday party. It is important, though, to know ahead of time something about each player's level of proficiency in math. Your daughter may be able to help you with this information, or you might need to call teachers or parents.

The only required equipment is a set of math flashcards appropriate for the age level of the players. Divide them into three piles: one for the easiest problems, one for problems of medium difficulty, and one for the most difficult. Your job, as the pitcher, is to draw cards (inconspicuously) from the pile that best reflect each player's ability.

Decide on four spots around the room to serve as first, second, and third bases and home plate. Divide the group into two teams of from five to fifteen girls, and have both teams form lines behind home plate. Designate one team as "at bat"—the players on that team can advance to a base if they are the first to supply the correct answer. Members of the other team will start the game as "catchers" there in the "field."

Have one girl from each team come to the plate. Draw a flashcard. If the "batter" is the first to give the right answer, she advances to first base. If the "catcher" is first, the batter is out. After three outs the teams change roles. If another "batter" answers correctly, she goes to first base and the previous runner advances to second, and so on. Points are earned when a player moves around the bases and crosses home plate.

Keep score on a blackboard or large piece of paper. Decide ahead of time how many innings are to be played. You might also want to appoint yourself "coach" and line the girls up according to their abilities so that, for example, the two strongest math students will compete against each other at homeplate.

Kids love this game! It shows that math can be fun.

in distress because she'd received her first bad grade: a C- on a paper she'd written for a class in political science, her major. "Mom, maybe this is too hard," she told Mindy. Uh-oh, Mindy thought, here it comes. "Maybe I should change my major to something easy," she continued. Mindy drew in her breath. "Like math," she concluded. Mindy had to laugh.

Show your daughter that math can be fun. "Math Is Fun!" lists some activities to do with young girls, and "Math Baseball" is always a hit with groups.

The University of California at Berkeley's EQUALS program is designed to interest girls in math. Their book, *Family Math,* has games and activities that families can do together. (See "Ordering Information" at the back of this book.)

Finally, if your daughter is to see herself as successful in math, she must be successful in math. It's easy to fall behind or get lost in this subject, and once that happens, lost ground is hard to regain. Ask your daughter's teacher to alert you immediately if her work is not keeping pace with the class. If you can't coach her yourself, find a tutor who can provide the remedial work she needs. This might be an older sibling or a patient teen from down the block if the problem is relatively mild. If your daughter needs serious help, get a professional tutor. Ask her school to recommend someone—preferably a woman—for the job.

Showing support

If you haven't seen it, we recommend you rent the video *Stand and Deliver,* an inspirational dramatization of Jaime Escalante's fabulous success as a math teacher in a Los Angeles barrio. A great believer in the importance of parental support and high expectations, he has often stated, "If you expect kids to be losers, they will be losers. If you expect kids to be winners, they will be winners." But, he says, "School alone cannot educate. We need the help of the parents."

There is evidence to suggest that about the time girls enter junior high, we start expecting them to be losers—at least as far as math is concerned. Mothers, especially, can pass on the message that math is too difficult for women. As comedian Paula Poundstone said during the PBS broadcast *Math: Who Needs It?:* "I remember my mother repeating that she wasn't good at math over and over, and I suppose I thought it was like going bald—it was in the mother's genes." If you suffer from math anxiety, try to overcome it by taking a basic math class or joining a support group. Be the right kind of role model for your daughter.

Monitor your statements about math and science. Do you grimace or make sympathetic noises when your daughter announces it's time to do her math, or do you show enthusiasm? Escalante recommends that you spend time doing some of the homework with (not for) her, and that you frequently use phrases like "I believe in you. You can do it." And, of course, when she does well, praise her lavishly.

It's been shown that parents' attitudes have more impact on a child's confidence than her grades do. Children are also more likely to spend more time on subjects that are valued by their parents. Never make statements like "I always hated math" or "I was never any good at math." Even if they're true, your daughter doesn't need to know.

Watch the gender issue, too. Mothers, when your daughter comes to you for help with math, do you tell her to ask her father? Quite commonly, mothers help younger children, but fathers take over as the kids enter junior high, in effect saying that higher math is for men only. In many ways it's better, if no female in the house can serve as a tutor and role model, to get outside help from a woman instead of turning the job over to Dad or big brother. It's also been shown that parents are more likely to go along with a daughter's request to drop out of math, while they expect their sons to "tough it out." Have high expectations for all your children.

Monitor your daughter's teachers. Ask their opinions about the importance of math for girls. If you don't get a satisfactory response, explain—firmly but politely—why you want your daughter to be encouraged in this all-important field.

Most schools offer remedial reading classes—something boys need more than girls—but fewer have remedial math classes, which girls often require. Encourage your school to start a program if it hasn't already done so. And while you're there, find out what percentage of the math and science teachers are women. If it's not close to half, request that your school board start moving toward that goal with new hires.

I'd always done very well in math, including trig in my junior year. I liked it, too. But when it came time to sign up for calculus for my senior year, my mom mentioned that she thought I might take shorthand instead, her thinking being that a girl could always support herself if she had secretarial skills. I don't recall thinking much about it one way or the other. So my class's valedictorian went off to college without higher-level math—and with a skill that no employer has wanted in years. I could have caught up there by taking calculus, but somehow a shift had happened in my thinking about math and science. I gravitated to the English and history courses instead. Interestingly, when I did take my science requirement, choosing physics, I loved the class and did better than the mostly premeds in it—but I never considered switching my emphasis.

—Publishing entrepreneur, 35

Seeing the
relevance

The program *Math: Who Needs It?* offers the best explanation we've seen of why math and science are so important. It goes a long way toward dispelling the "nerd" image sometimes associated with these subjects by talking about how they are used in such "nonnerdy" jobs as designing athletic shoes, bicycles, automobiles, and roller coasters; composing music; working in robotics or as an aqua culture researcher finding new ways to grow food; being an architect or an engineer; and much more. Interspersed with these interviews is footage of Jaime Escalante working with his math students, along with statements from celebrities like Bill Cosby. It is a highly motivating program, even for diehard math and science dodgers, and it is available on video from its producers, the Foundation for Advancement in Science and Education (see FASE Productions, "Ordering Information," page 483).

For schools, the same production team has put together over twenty fifteen-minute programs called *Futures*, in which Jaime Escalante and a guest discuss different job possibilities within various fields and how math and science are used in each of them. If your daughter's math or science teachers haven't heard about these *Futures* programs, suggest that they call PBS-ESS at (800) 344-3337 for more information.

Make sure your daughter understands that if she doesn't take higher-level math classes in high school, she is seriously limiting her options for the future. No matter what her plans are after graduation—employment, vocational school, on-the-job training, or college—she will be better qualified to train for or enter more jobs, higher-paying jobs, with this credential. Math is often called the "critical filter" because students who graduate without it shut themselves off from entry into more than half of all college majors. Many vocational programs, especially those leading to higher-paying jobs, require high school math as well. In most businesses employees without a solid math education cannot be promoted beyond a certain level, as managers and executives must deal with numbers in almost every aspect of their jobs. Finally, careers requiring math generally pay more than those that don't, even when the level of education demanded (such as a college degree) is the same.

Just as important, students believe that those who are good in math are the smart ones. Those good in English and social studies but not math are not considered as smart. So your children's feelings about themselves as competent achievers are affected by their math performance; and their feelings of competence influence their career choices.

In our book *More Choices,* to help young women grasp the importance of math we took readers through a lengthy word problem to illustrate how the effort they put into the subject now will pay off throughout their working lives. We ask them to estimate how many hours a week they need to spend on math homework and, from that number, calculate the number of hours they would work at math over four years of high school. Readers next determine how many hours they are likely to spend in the workforce in their lifetime, then divide that number by the number of hours spent studying math. Girls are then asked to pick two careers they have some interest in from a list provided, one requiring math and one not. They calculate the average hourly pay for both of these jobs, determine the difference, and multiply that difference by the number of hours they expect to work to arrive at the additional amount of money they can expect to earn during their working lives if they learn to do math. As a final step, we ask students to divide this amount by the number of hours they would have to spend on homework to determine how many dollars' worth of future income they can expect to earn for each hour spent studying math. It is not unusual for this amount to be several hundred dollars, which, for most teens, is highly motivating! (You will need to cover the information on precareer awareness with your daughter before she will be able to understand this concept. See chapter 23, "Getting Girls Ready for Career Education.")

Since most young women (about 90 percent) say they want to have children someday, showing your daughter how a math education leads to higher-paying jobs, which allow a woman more freedom to be a mother, is also effective. Again, this concept is explained in detail in chapter 25, "Strategies for Mixing Career and Family."

Take every opportunity to make math relevant to everyday living. Besides the check-writing and shopping activities described in chapter 11, "Ages Six to Ten," try the activities in "Using Math Day to Day," page 263.

Math and future earnings

To help your daughter see the importance of math in a very graphic way, try this activity from Mindy Bingham's book *Lifestyle Math* (Academic Innovations). Ask her to list ten careers she would like to have if she could choose from the entire spectrum of possible occupations. Then help her divide those careers into three categories:

Those requiring only basic high school math
Those requiring advanced high school math (algebra 1 and 2, geometry)
Those requiring college-level math (calculus and statistics)

Together, look up the average annual salaries for each of the jobs. *The American Almanac of Jobs and Salaries* by John W. Wright (Avon Books) is an excellent and easy-to-use source for these figures.

Finally, make a bar graph showing the salaries for each career. Use different color ink to differentiate careers from each of the three categories.

If your daughter's list doesn't include any jobs requiring college math, ask her to add one or two that do. The point to illustrate here is that the more math she takes, the greater her future earnings potential.

The following example may be helpful.

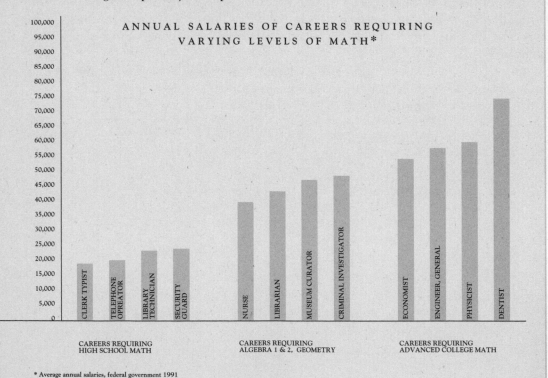

ANNUAL SALARIES OF CAREERS REQUIRING
VARYING LEVELS OF MATH*

CAREERS REQUIRING
HIGH SCHOOL MATH

CAREERS REQUIRING
ALGEBRA 1 & 2, GEOMETRY

CAREERS REQUIRING
ADVANCED COLLEGE MATH

* Average annual salaries, federal government 1991

Using math day to day

1. When eating out, ask your daughter to check the bill and then figure the tip. Once she gets proficient with figuring a tip of, say, 15 percent, vary the percentage.

2. Speaking of 15 percent, teach her mathematical shortcuts. For instance, say that restaurant bill came to approximately $22.00 (a good chance to teach rounding to the nearest whole number). Teach her to quickly figure 10 percent by moving the decimal one plate to the left ($2.20). Then, to find the extra 5 percent, she divides that number in half ($1.10). By adding those two numbers together, she gets the 15 percent tip of $3.30.

3. In the name of energy conservation, teach your elementary-age child to read the electric meter and figure the amount of electricity used in the household each month. As she learns to divide, ask her to figure the daily consumption each month. Later, when she is working on ratios in school, ask her to compare consumption in the summer with consumption in the winter. In a family discussion, let her take the lead in presenting her findings and then leading a brainstorming session on how to conserve electricity.

4. Cooking is an outstanding way to learn fractions. If she's learning fractions in school, ask her to double a recipe and prepare it. Later, have her take a recipe for four people and plan for six.

5. If your daughter is fortunate enough to have her own car once she starts driving, have her keep track of her mileage costs by recording her odometer readings each time she fills up her tank. She can then add her maintenance costs such as oil changes, tires, service costs and repairs. Twice a year, help her figure her costs of transportation and come up with a per mile cost. As motivation, tell her you'll reimburse her per mile for all errands she runs for the family (as long as she keeps good records).

6. If your daughter wants to purchase a particular item that requires long-range saving, suggest that she present you with a written plan of how she plans to finance this item through savings, gifts, work, and savings interest. If she is asking for assistance from you, set aside time for her to make a formal presentation of her plan and request. You might model this activity around one you have experienced when approaching a bank for credit.

7. Allow your daughter to become an integral part of your savings plan for her educational needs beyond high school. Share the monthly statements with her. Show her how the interest compounds and what that will mean over the years. Increase her allowance, let's say 10 percent from what you might normally give her, with the understanding that each month 10 percent is deposited by her in her savings account. You might also agree to match any amount she puts of her own money she has earned by working into her college account.

Science and technology

Much of what we've said about girls and math is equally true when it comes to science and technology: these are the areas in which students must excel in order to qualify for the best jobs in the twenty-first century, but, subtly and not so subtly, girls are made to feel that science and technology are not for them.

This is a tragedy for our country as well as for the girls themselves. Results of the International Assessment of Educational Progress test in 1992 showed U.S. students ranking well below those from many other nations: On the science exam for thirteen-year-olds, for example, South Korea, Taiwan, Switzerland, Hungary, the former Soviet Union, Slovenia, Italy, Israel, Canada, France, Scotland, and Spain all reported higher average scores than ours. Japan and Germany did not participate in the study. Clearly we can no longer afford to let half of our collective brainpower go untapped.

The differences in test results did not relate to the length of time students spend in school or to the amount of money spent on education. There was a correlation, however, between student performance and use of spare time. Not surprisingly, the best students spent their evenings reading and doing homework, while those with lower scores were apt to watch TV instead. (Our children watch more TV than students in any other country.)

The other important factor: attitude. While Asian countries, for example, respect intellectual achievement, "In the U.S., we call our best students nerd or dweeb," Educational Testing Service president Gregory Anrig told *Newsweek*. "As a nation, I think we have conflicting feelings about people who are smart, and as parents, we send conflicting messages to our children about being smart." This is likely to be especially true for girls.

A two-year study conducted by Girls Incorporated found that "girls need more opportunities and encouragement from adults and society to explore mathematics, science and technology." When they get that support, the 1991 report states, girls respond: "In communities that encourage science and math, girls tend to have positive attitudes towards these activities." But, "Adults' ideas about what is appropriate behavior for girls play a major role in determining the atmosphere in which girls learn, and 'traditional' behavioral expectations may be girls' biggest roadblock to pursuing technical studies."

Girls Incorporated recommends the following as steps

I was a little shocked when my daughter asked me for a subscription to Road & Track, *and my first reaction was to ask if she wouldn't rather have* Seventeen *or* Sassy. *But I quickly realized what a mistake that would be, and I bit my tongue.*

—*Mom, professional*

parents and educators can take to get girls more interested and involved with science:

1. Give girls many opportunities to experience science, math, and technology.

You will find that girls are ready, willing, and eager. Too often they just haven't had enough opportunities. Any family or organization that can provide basic household materials such as straws, toothpicks, and inexpensive tools can enhance girls' experience in science. For example, girls can try putting different objects in water to see which ones float, attempt simple household experiments such as making vegetable dyes, or learn to repair their own bicycles. Take your daughter to science museums, planetariums—anywhere she can observe, learn, and get excited about science.

2. Give your daughter a subscription to magazines about science and technology.

3. Help girls get beyond "yuk."

Insist calmly that girls touch a snake, dissect a worm, get their hands dirty.

4. Examine the rules you set for girls—then examine the assumptions underlying them.

Are the rules intended to ensure the safety of girls and staff? To teach girls to take responsibility for their actions? To establish enough order so that learning goals can be met? On examination, rules for girls often seem to be conveniences for adults. Reduce rules to give girls room to explore and take responsibility.

5. Give girls more opportunities to be leaders.

Let them try choosing the activities, making the rules, settling the disputes. Girls who have learned to lead are better prepared to take charge of their own education and career.

6. Create an environment that is safe for mistakes, not safe from mistakes.

Girls need to be encouraged to make mistakes—big, interesting mistakes. They need practice in making mistakes in an environment in which people recognize that mistakes are part of learning and part of scientific inquiry.

7. Give girls more opportunities to be outdoors and involved in physical activity.

Challenge courses and Outward Bound–type programs encourage physical risktaking—and that can translate into the confidence and skills to consider firefighting, flight navigation, and deep-sea exploration. More time spent in nature also piques scientific interest. Girls get beyond "It's pretty" and display curiosity about the stars, rocks, and plants. That's science.

8. Examine your definitions of risk for girls.

Is it the same for boys? Don't rescue girls when you would allow boys to engage in the same activities. Instead teach girls how to assess risks for themselves to insure their own safety. Offer girls more exposure to machinery and equipment, more outdoor and overnight experiences, and more chances to get dirty in the process of exploration.

9. Convey to girls that they are capable of mastering math and science, encouraged to choose these courses through high school, and expected to pursue higher education.

Every girl should anticipate earning a living throughout her adult life. Adults need to show surprise and a willingness to discuss these issues with a girl who says this is not her intention.

✎ The Girls Incorporated Program Operation SMART (Science, Math, And Relevant Technology) was designed to help accomplish these goals. It allows girls to experience such activities as visiting a space center, taking apart a computer, building a model city, going on a worm hunt, blowing a giant bubble, dissecting a fungus, or designing a circuit. Girls are encouraged to get dirty, make messes, use tools, and question the question as well as the answer.

Many Girls Incorporated centers are participating in the project, but other organizations, parents, or teachers are invited to start their own programs, as well. A planning guide, an activities guide, research reports, videotapes, and more are available. For more information, contact Girls Incorporated, National Resource Center, 441 West Michigan Street, Indianapolis, Indiana 46202; (312) 634-7546.

Computers

One day in 1986 while Mindy was executive director of what is now Girls Incorporated of Greater Santa Barbara, she was showing a major donor around the center. The center was very proud of its computer classroom, which was equipped with ten Apple computers. (It had converted a space that previously served as the "beauty salon.") Every afternoon twenty to thirty girls between the ages of six and twelve came in to learn about the computers and use them for their various projects. Mindy was particularly astonished by a girl of about eight who was expertly manipulating the machine to produce an article for the club newspaper. "Where did you learn to do that?" Mindy asked, surprised. The girl gave Mindy a sort of "I'll give you three guesses" look, apparently thought better of it, calmly replied, "Here," and went back to work.

When personal computers first came out, it seemed likely that girls and boys would have an equal opportunity to learn about them, since there was no history— gender linked or otherwise—associated with the new machines. It didn't take long, though, for boys to gain the upper hand. By 1982 there were twice as many boys as girls enrolled in programming classes. Parents bought more computers for their sons than for their daughters. At computer camps, three-fourths of the students were boys. "And the more expensive the computers used at the camp, the greater likelihood that an even larger percentage of boys were enrolled," wrote Charlotte Beyers in *Family Computing*.

As software manufacturers came out with programs involving violence or the mindless mounting up of points, boys went wild and girls lost interest. When boys started taking over computer labs and video arcades, even many of the girls who maintained an interest were too intimidated to intrude.

Unless she can use a computer, your daughter will be locked out of all but the most menial jobs. If that's not the fate you want for her, here are a few strategies to keep in mind.

1. Once more, be a role model.

Girls particularly need to see their mothers working at a computer. No computer in the home? If you use one at work, take your daughter in on a Saturday and show her what you do. Play educational video games with her.

Even without training, you can make use of the "user-friendly" computers commonly found in your community. Let your daughter see you look up a book on the library's computerized card catalog. Perhaps a local department store has its bridal registry on computer. Many museums have computers in their lobbies to help patrons learn more about their exhibits, locate an item of special interest, check calendars, and so on. You can also rent computers by the hour at places like Kinko's. There's no escaping them—and no excuse for trying to!

Fathers can also be role models, of course, and their encouragement is particularly needed.

2. If you possibly can, have a computer in your home.

There's no better way for your daughter to become comfortable with technology, and it will benefit her at school as well as later on the job. Wendy Bingham, for example, was involved with computers from an early age and had her own laptop all through high school. When she started college, her English instructor took the class down to the computer lab, explained how it worked, and gave students three hours to complete an assignment there. He was startled when Wendy turned in her paper twenty minutes later.

3. Get the right software.

Girls tend not to be as interested in war games and monsters as boys are. They are also more likely to want to use the computer to accomplish some other goal, like writing a paper or composing music. Boys, on the other hand, seem to get pleasure simply from manipulating the machine itself, and much of the software is designed for them.

Think about your daughter's interests before you choose. Whether she likes art, music, sports, adventures, puzzles, games, poetry, or whatever, there is likely to be a program that she will find enjoyable.

4. Get her started at an early age.

Many six-year-olds are capable of using a computer. The advantage is not only the extensive experience, but also that she is less likely to have picked up the message that computers are for boys or to be intimidated by the machine. Don't pressure her to get involved, but give her the opportunity and support her interest. Simple low-cost computerlike toys are available for primary-age children. If interest doesn't develop, let it go for a while. Forcing the issue might cause your daughter to form a long-lasting aversion to technology.

Susan's daughter, Carla, wasn't very interested in the computer until they got *Where in the World Is Carmen San Diego?* But her interest really picked up when they bought a modem and subscribed to Prodigy. She found a kids' bulletin board and a penpal list. Soon she was writing to kids all over the country. Every time she walked into the house after that, she'd go first to the computer to see if anyone had answered her mail. Writing all those letters on the computer helped her writing skills, too, and then she got out the atlas to see if she could figure out just where her penpals lived.

5. Start a computer club for girls, or organize a mother-daughter computer class.

Check to see if your local Girls Incorporated center, YWCA, Scouting organization, or the like has such a club and, if not, suggest that they form one. You might volunteer to help raise funds for the equipment or recruit trainers for the classes.

We like the idea of mother-daughter classes, too. If you're interested, start by talking with the computer instructor at your daughter's school. Perhaps together you

Three ways to work with your school on math, science, and computer issues

- Develop a speakers bureau of women scientists, engineers, mathematicians, computer specialists, and so on to talk with students from elementary age and up.
- Sponsor a math and science fair in your school district. Detailed information on setting up a project like this is available in the handbook *Women Helping Girls with Choices* (Advocacy Press; see "Ordering Information").
- The University of California at Berkeley's EQUALS Project also provides training for teachers to help them make their classes more relevant for girls. For more information, write the University of California at Berkeley (see "Ordering Information").

can arrange a series of lessons to be offered weekly for an hour or so in the early evening. This activity was very popular at the Girls Club when Mindy was the director. Mothers and daughters worked together on one machine. This provides a supportive learning environment for girls and women alike.

6. Work with her school.

What is the state of computer education at her school? Are all the instructors male? Do boys dominate the lab so that many girls are reluctant to use it? What kinds of software are available? These types of frequently occurring problems are easy to solve. Almost certainly there are women staff members who are computer literate, even though they may be teaching English or physical education. Administrators often assume that only math or science teachers are suited to offer computer training, but with some prodding from you, they may find that this is not true. If the boys have taken over the lab, suggest that certain times each week be designated for girls only and for boys only, with the lab open to all students the rest of the time. If most of the software caters to boys' interests, raise funds for or ask someone to donate software that is more female-friendly.

By working with your daughter's school, you can help create the kind of atmosphere that is both nurturing and stimulating for girls.

The hardy mathematician and scientist

Two characteristics of a hardy personality will be particularly valuable in helping your daughter get the math and science education she needs:

If she learns to tolerate anxiety and act anyway, she will be more likely to persist when she gets her first really tough assignment or fails her first test.

If she can project herself into the future, set goals, and establish priorities, she will be more likely to choose the trigonometry class over chorus, knowing that the eventual payoff (a career with more autonomy, higher pay, and greater flexibility) is more important than the immediate gratification.

Keeping your daughter in math and science classes is an important part of assuring her future success. Any new messages you'd like to add on these topics? Consult "Your Plan."

chapter eighteen

Lessons Learned on the Playing Field

"I never gave much thought to the importance of competitive sports for girls until last winter," admits Julia, an avowed feminist and baseball fan. "The girls' basketball team from a small town I know well was playing in the state tournament, so I turned on the TV to watch—just for a few minutes, I thought. But there they were—these glorious young women, ponytails flying, so strong and confident and poised, it blew me away. I thought back to my own high school experience, when there was no athletic program for girls, and I know that no one in my class felt as comfortable with her body as these young women obviously did. As if that weren't enough, the cameras panned to the spectators: men and boys were standing and cheering for girls! I can still get choked up just thinking about it. Wouldn't it be great if every young woman could have an experience like that?"

More of them can, and more of them are. In 1971, the year before Title IX legislation mandated gender equity in school programs, 293,345 high school girls were actively involved in athletics. By 1978 that number had jumped to two million. Although equity has still not been achieved and the rate of growth has slowed, competitive sports for girls are here to stay, and your daughter can benefit from taking part in them.

Athletics help build self-esteem in a number of important ways. First, they give a young woman the strength and body confidence that let her stride through the world with assurance. Athletes are not victims. Sports also build her endurance and allow her to get in touch with her body in a way that has nothing to do with appearance. Second, a girl learns skills by partic-

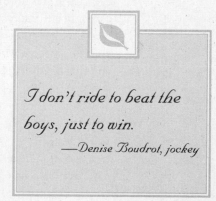

I don't ride to beat the boys, just to win.

—*Denise Boudrot, jockey*

ipating in a sport and, thus, comes to think of herself as more competent. Feeling competent is an important issue in self-esteem. Athletics teach a young woman strategic thinking, how to compete, how to lead, and how to work with others to accomplish goals, skills she will certainly need in her future occupation.

When your daughter takes part in competitive sports, she also learns how to take risks, how to win, and how to lose. She comes to see that she can give something her all, fail, and yet survive. She lives to fight another day, and armed with the attitudes and skills she's picked up along the way, she will try again. This is one of the most important lessons in life, and until recently, too many women have been shielded from it, much to their own detriment.

In 1963–64, when researchers Margaret Hennig and Barbara Hackman Franklin did a study of the women enrolled in the Harvard Business School's M.B.A. program, they found that "team games were important to all of them." This was during a time when team sports for girls hardly existed!

It is probably no coincidence that for years many of the country's top boys' prep schools have made participation in competitive sports a graduation requirement. These students, after all, are expected to move into leadership positions in business and politics, and the lessons learned in athletics transfer into adult life as few others do. Let's take a closer look at some of these lessons.

Team building

It takes teamwork to accomplish most tasks in the work world, but traditional girls' games and activities give no experience in building a team or in playing on one. Playing with dolls, jumping rope, and the like are cooperative activities that encourage girls to be nurturing and cooperative, not to make decisions or to take charge in a crucial situation.

A point guard on a basketball team, however, learns to assess a situation quickly and then decide where to throw the ball. In baseball the pitcher weighs her own skills and those of her defense against what she knows of the batter and then makes her best pitch. If it's hit over the fence, she starts again with the next person in the lineup.

Not everyone can be the captain or the team leader, of course. Athletes learn that they may not be the fastest or the strongest player, but that they have other valuable skills to offer. When Margaret Hennig and Anne Jardim, authors of *The Managerial Woman,* asked men what they learned from playing football, one standard response was, "you learned fast that some people were better than others—but you had to have eleven." In athletics, girls are allowed to see that it takes many different talents to make up a winning team, and they come to appreciate what each of their teammates brings to the game.

All of this will prove beneficial in adult life.

Leadership skills

Ellen, a marketing representative for a large corporation, learned something about girls and leadership when she became involved with her company's Junior Achievement project. "By and large," she says, "the girls were brighter and more competent than the boys, but when it came time to elect officers, a young man volunteered to be president. He wasn't really qualified, but that didn't seem to bother him. Almost any of the young women would probably have done a better job, but they all wanted to be the secretary."

The young man in question had athletic experience. Maybe it's the constant pep talks from the coach; maybe it's the cheerleaders and the approving crowd; the skills and attitudes developed by the game certainly have something to do with it. Give the credit wherever you see fit, but there's no denying that athletics breeds leadership attitudes.

Obviously, sports develops the confidence players need to take on new tasks. That's important, especially for women, who tend to shy away from jobs they haven't done before. But leaders must also be able to anticipate problems, avoid them when possible, and solve them when they occur.

In other words, a leader needs to have a game plan.

Taking risks

There's a second difference in the way men and women view risk: while women see only immediate consequences, men tend to concentrate on future goals. Thus a woman may remain silent during a business meeting for fear of looking foolish if she

Men see risk as loss or gain; winning or losing; danger or opportunity. . . . Women see risk as entirely negative. It is loss, danger, injury, ruin, hurt. One avoids it as best one can.

—Margaret Hennig and
Anne Jardim,
The Managerial Woman

If you can react the same way to winning and losing, that's a big accomplishment.

—Chris Evert

says the wrong thing. A man is more likely to take that risk, believing that in the long run it is important to be recognized as a person with thoughts and ideas, even if they aren't always on target.

Again, these are lessons learned from athletics. It's winning the game that's important, not making every single shot. "You can't win 'em all," but if you never try, losing them all is a certainty.

In sports a young woman takes dozens of risks in every game she plays. With all those chances, the ones that don't work seem less ominous, and with all that practice, risk taking itself becomes second nature.

Learning to win and to lose

A person who learns, as many girls do, that losing is disastrous but winning isn't really nice has several options for acting in the world: don't try too hard, quit if things aren't going well, or perhaps best of all, don't even make the attempt. Practice at winning and losing, on the other hand, imparts lessons of a different kind: you win some and you lose some, give it your best shot, nobody's perfect.

Girls are often praised for things beyond their control (their dimples or the color of their eyes) or for accomplishments they know are not valued by society (being "nice" or helpful around the house). They may even be praised for what they know to be a less than remarkable performance (getting a C in math, something for which their brothers would be admonished). Taking part in a sport allows a girl to view herself honestly. Either she performs well or she doesn't.

Girls and boys alike need a safe place to learn how to fail, and organized sports can provide that opportunity. We may chuckle when Liz Masakayan, one of the first girls to play Little League baseball, recalls, "When I hit my first home run, they had to take the pitcher out because he was crying." By the time he got his first job, however, that young man had probably learned to deal with failure in a more professional manner. Women who have had no comparable experience are at a disadvantage when they start working.

Girls need to know, too, that failing at something is not the same as being a failure. In athletics, problems can be clearly stated: "You need to work on your defense" or "Your fastball's not going over the plate." An athlete may know that her skills need improving, but she is not likely to confuse her weakness with her worth as an individual. The lines become much murkier, however, if she must learn to deal with failure in her relationships or other, more "feminine" pursuits. What "skill" can she work to improve if her best friend abandons her for no apparent reason? A failure of this type is likely to be more devastating and more damaging to her self-esteem.

Athletics also give young women valuable experience in accepting constructive criticism, something parents and teachers may try to spare them but a trait they are sure to need as adults. And it introduces the concept of "fourth-quarter effort," the kind of persistence that's needed to reach a goal or meet a deadline when an exhausted body and mind want to quit. This is a quality that serves an individual well in all areas of life.

And then there's anxiety tolerance. Today, anxiety seems to invade almost every aspect of adult life, and those who cannot deal with it are in trouble. Most of us are lucky if we learn to tolerate the queasy stomachs and the lumps in the throat that come with uncertainty. But athletes seem to thrive on it. For them, pregame anxiety is a way of life, something they have to get through before they can play the game, each one of which is a heart-thumping opportunity to measure themselves against friends, foes, and their own exacting standards. What better preparation can there be for life in the twenty-first century?

Too masculine, you say?

All of this may be shocking to those whose image of proper womanhood encompasses only the roles of helpmate and nurturer. (Can you imagine your mother driving in for the lay-up?) Wives and moms are not meant to be cutthroat competitors, sweating freely and perhaps even—God forbid—spitting onto the outfield grass.

We agree. These behaviors are not always appropriate at

I mentioned to my tennis coach that I tend to sweat a lot and he replied, "Men sweat, women glisten." Good grief, I thought, now we even have to be pretty when we work out.

—*Recreational tennis player, 41*

home—from men or women. If you'll look back to chapter 3, "Redefining Feminin-ity," you'll recall our earlier discussion of androgyny and what has been learned about the characteristics of the most successful and happiest people—that they ex-hibit a wide range of traits, using whichever seems most appropriate in a particular situation. We trust that by now you are convinced that your daughter will need to work and so will have ample opportunity to benefit from the lessons she'll learn in athletics.

And one more thing: it's good for her health!

It goes without saying that exercise is a key element in any good health plan. Women today lead busy and often complicated lives, and exercise helps them deal with the accompanying stress in a positive way. It also helps them maintain proper weight and keep down their blood pressure and serum cholesterol level. Working out improves bone strength, which helps prevent osteoporosis in later life, and aerobic activity keeps the heart fit. Those who were raised to be physically ac-tive are more likely to make room in their schedules for some kind of regular exer-cise.

Although we hear less about the health problems of girls and young women, they, too, require and benefit from physical activity. Perhaps they don't have to worry about their blood pressure, but they do have stress in their lives, and exercise is the best way for them to reduce it. And the long-term health benefits are well worth the effort.

What is Title IX, and how does it relate to your daughter's self-esteem?

Title IX of the Educational Amendments Act is the federal legislation passed in 1972 that prohibits sex discrimination in any education program or activity receiving federal funds. It is supposed to ensure equity in athletic programs, among other things, and it has made some important inroads in that regard. But in most high schools and colleges, boys' sports still get most of the attention and most of the money.

Girls are very much aware of this fact, according to Lynn Jaffee, program coordinator for the Melpomene Institute for Women's Health Research in St. Paul, and it disappoints them. Even preteen girls, Jaffee says, "understand that they do not have the same opportunities as boys" for participation in sports, for earning athletic scholarships, or for using their physical abilities in future careers as athletes, coaches, or instructors.

"There are more rewards for the boys who excel," Jaffee says, and this knowledge is a disincentive for girls to get involved. They see that however well they play, their abilities are not valued by society in the same way that boys' athletic talent is. As a man recently wrote in a letter to the editor of a Minneapolis–St. Paul newspaper, "Most men aren't really interested in women's sports unless their daughters are participating." In other words, even fathers of female athletes believe that male sports are intrinsically better, more interesting, more "worth watching."

These messages are not lost on the young women. Valued less by their families and their culture, they come to think of themselves as less worthy. Since they already have less incentive than boys to take part in athletics, they are more likely than boys to drop out of sports altogether, thus losing out on the valuable lessons of play.

The Melpomene Institute recently completed a survey of seventy-six nine- to twelve-year-old girls concerning their physical activity and self-esteem. Since organized sports are still rare in most elementary schools, the focus groups dealt mostly with gym class and individual athletic pursuits. Still, some of the same old gender equity bugaboos were much in evidence, according to Jaffee. "There is an assumption by boys and by gym instructors that girls are not good athletes," she says. The girls reported that boys took control of the playing field, automatically placing girls at the bottom of the batting order, refusing to pass them the ball, yelling at them for making mistakes, and so on. Put down by the boys, "girls come to doubt themselves," Jaffee reports.

The behavior of gym instructors was also destructive of girls' self-esteem. They tended to favor the boys, the young women said, encouraging and instructing them but rushing in to rescue the girls. When a team of girls plays a team of boys, the instructor almost always steps in to play with the girls, assuming automatically that the boys' team is superior. While this angers the girls, Jaffee says, it also makes them feel less sure of themselves and their abilities.

Asked who encouraged them to take part in physical activities, 84 percent of the girls said "Myself." Seventy-six percent said their mothers encouraged them, 57 percent received encouragement from their fathers.

Overwhelmingly they reported that they disliked playing on coed teams. Jaffee agrees that it's one thing for girls to be allowed to play on Little League and other formerly boys' teams, but quite another for them to actually join. Usually they won't get the same amount of instruction or playing time, and most are not comfortable performing in front of the boys. It's also a fact that as they enter adolescence, most boys pass girls in physiological development. They are bigger and stronger than the girls, and the level of competition is not really comparable. Many parents are opting for same-sex teams for their daughters, putting their efforts into obtaining equitable facilities, coaching, and equipment instead of fighting for the young women's rights to play with the boys.

The girls' gymnastic team was automatically given the worst practice time in the school gym— early, early morning. And even then, if the boys' basketball team decided to show up for an extra workout, we would be forced to leave.

—Gymnastics coach

Jaffee feels that all-girl teams are best, even for younger children. "By the age of six or eight," she says, "girls are often two years behind boys in their level of skill development."

That may help explain the boys' derisive comments about playing with girls, according to Judy Cobbs, western regional director of Girls Incorporated. If she hasn't been instructed in sports, Cobbs says, a girl may come to bat for the first time, hit the ball, and run to third base, "and she'll never live that down." Cobbs sees this situation changing, however. In recent years Girls Incorporated has implemented Sporting Chance, a three-part program for girls age six to fifteen, as part of the solution.

Stepping Stones, the first level, teaches six- to eight-year-old girls how to throw a ball, catch, jump, kick, run—all the basic skills they need if they're to play confidently with the boys. "We get them used to sweating, too," says Cobbs. "They learn that sometimes you have to push yourself."

The program seems to work. Pre- and posttesting, Cobbs says, showed a nearly 93 percent improvement in skill level. The seven- and eight-year-olds, she reports, became so confident, "they were almost obnoxious." In response to their enthusiasm, Girls Incorporated of Greater Santa Barbara formed an all-girl T-ball team and joined the city recreation department's league. The girls played boys' teams as well as coed teams and did so very successfully, according to Cobbs.

If you suspect inequities in your schools

It seems, then, that the choice of all-girl or coed teams is an individual one. Your daughter's abilities and preferences will determine which route is best for her. Here's an opportunity for her to practice her decision-making skills. What you can do is make sure that wherever they play, girls are not treated as second-class citizens in your community. It's up to the adults who fund and support the leagues to make sure that allocations of monies, facilities, and equipment are equitable.

Do girls' teams get a fair share of practice time in the gym? Are the boys equipped with all the latest gear while the girls make do with uniforms that were, apparently, last worn by Babe Ruth's sister? Is the coaching adequate, and are the coaches supportive of women athletes? How much money is spent on the different teams? If the answers to the questions seem to indicate that there is inequity in your schools, you can do a number of things to help redress the problem. First, though, make sure you've gathered as much information as you can and that it shows a pattern of discrimination. The fact that one young woman was refused a particular ice time in the local arena because that's when the boys' hockey team practices may not indicate inequity. But if the boys' basketball team is clearly receiving preference over the girls' basketball program, you may well have a case. And if others agree with you, band together. The more support you can garner for your position, the better.

Does the school district have a Title IX officer? Find out, and raise the problem with him or her. Has a grievance procedure been outlined? Follow it to file your complaint.

If you cannot get a satisfactory response from the school, go to your local Office for Civil Rights and file a complaint there. This is an informal procedure and requires only that you specify in writing the victim of the inequity (person or team), the school, and how and when the perceived wrong took place. Your letter must be signed and your address provided. The school will be notified of your complaint within fifteen days, and an investigator will be assigned to the case if the school is covered by Title IX.

The most drastic procedure is filing a formal lawsuit. This involves legal fees and court costs, however, and should probably be a last resort. Don't automatically rule it out, though. The other party may have to pay all costs if you win.

Assistance may also be available from some of these sources:

National Association of Girls and Women in Sports, 1900 Association Dr.,
Reston, VA 22091-1599; (703) 476-3400.

National Women's Law Center, 1616 P St. N.W., Suite 100, Washington,
DC 20036; (202) 328-5160.

Trial Lawyers for Public Justice, 1625 Massachusetts Ave. N.W., Suite 100,
Washington, DC 20036; (202) 797-8600.

The Women's Sports Foundation, 342 Madison Ave., Suite 728, New York,
NY 10173; (212) 972-9170.

Getting started in sports—and keeping going

If you want your daughter to get involved with athletics, the rule to remember, according to Lynn Jaffee, is this: "If they're not having fun, they're not going to do it."

This suggests several subrules:

1. Make sure your daughter learns basic skills.

Jaffee recommends that you "don't just send the kids out to play. Go out with them and kick, throw, jump, dribble, catch, and so on. Work with your daughter as you'd work with your son." Without those skills a child can't hope to do well in athletics, and forcing her to partake anyway will only make her feel like a failure. She may also acquire an intense, lifelong dislike for sports.

2. Keep in mind that the ability to accomplish various athletic tasks depends on the child's age and physical development.

Pushing her to do something her body is not yet capable of doing is demoralizing and, perhaps, physically dangerous. She may be labeled—by you, by her coaches, or by herself—as "no good at sports" when in fact she simply needed a little more time to develop. Pediatricians say that, as a rule, children are incapable of team participation before age five, and many recommend waiting until they're nine or ten before they attempt to play "real" games on full-size courts or fields.

Some other developmental considerations: The hand-eye coordination required to play tennis usually doesn't develop until about age ten. Young children's eyes are not fully developed, which makes it difficult for most to track and catch a ball until about age six or seven. Pitching a baseball should not be taught before a child is about nine. Infant swimming programs are popular, but children can't be expected to learn strokes until they're at least five. Coordination is a problem through age six or seven, and children younger than this should not be expected to perform such tasks as batting at a pitched ball. Finally, the ability to concentrate may lag behind the ability to perform at athletics. Prolonged games or practice sessions (more than, say, half an hour) are not recommended for children ten and under.

3. Treat sports as a game.

Too much emphasis on winning or criticism of your daughter's performance takes the fun out of athletics. Admire her progress or improvement instead. For younger children, don't make things too organized. They may learn more from informal activities than they do from playing rigidly within the rules or from games in which competition is more of a factor than acquiring skills. Some pediatricians also recommend that children play on smaller than regulation courts or fields.

4. Help your daughter find the sports that are best for her.

Not everyone is cut out to play soccer or softball. The more activities she is exposed to, the more likely she is to find one that she's good at, one that may hold her interest for life. Girls Incorporated's Sporting Chance program set up another part of its agenda to address this issue. Sports Unlimited, for girls eleven to fourteen, allows young women to experience ten different activities, especially some of the less familiar ones, according to Judy Cobbs. If you have access to an organized program like Sporting Chance, take advantage of it. If you don't, set up something similar on your own. What sports do you have knowledge of or experience in? Share these with your daughter. If you've thought about trying other sports, this is the perfect opportunity. Or you might be able to enlist friends who take part in activities you know less about. Watching a variety of athletic events, in person or on TV, might at least uncover some areas of interest. If so, pursue them further. Books about sports, or sporting magazines, are also worth exploring.

Remember that even running and swimming, which adults tend to think of as individual sports, are also team sports in most schools.

If your daughter expresses a strong interest in a particular activity, do all you can to encourage her. Is there someone in the community who could give her lessons? Is there a summer camp she could attend?

Making this effort will help build her self-esteem in several ways. First, this is a "right fit" issue. Your daughter will be out there shooting baskets or hitting golf balls not because Mom and Dad said she had to, but because she feels doing so is a valued part of who she is. It's possible for a young woman to be a terrific runner or swimmer

282 WHAT'S A PARENT TO DO?

or what have you, but if the activity feels alien to her, it won't be very satisfying, and it won't do much for her self-esteem.

Second, the fact that you put some effort into helping her find the right sport tells her that she is a valuable person and allows her to feel like one. Since she is likely to perform at a higher level in a sport that is suited to her, she will also feel more valued by her teammates and coaches and by the wider community. And finding a sport that she likes and can do well in will give her an opportunity to benefit from all of those other esteem builders we talked about earlier in the chapter.

Finally, consider taking up the same sport yourself. Athletics present an ideal opportunity for fathers and daughters or mothers and daughters to enjoy each other's company. Wendy helped Mindy learn how to play tennis; it was a wonderful reversal of roles—because of Wendy's taskmaster coaching style, Mindy developed a mean backhand.

5. Make sure she is competing on the appropriate level.

Athletes benefit most from playing with and against players of approximately the same ability. The challenge is greatest and the game most exciting if there is an almost equal chance of winning or losing. This pushes players to do their best, allows them to take pride in winning, and, in defeat, only encourages them to keep on trying.

To give girls of differing abilities a chance to share in the glory of competitive sports, Girls Incorporated of Greater Santa Barbara developed a program called Novice Gymnastics. (Gymnastics, by the way, is an excellent beginner's sport for many girls. It's one of the few athletic activities in which being smaller and lighter is an advantage, and female gymnasts tend to get at least as much attention as their male counterparts.)

As Judy Cobbs explains it, gymnastics has always been very popular among girls six to eight. Santa Barbara has had as many as five hundred participants a year. As they get older, though, opportunities lessen. A few of the girls are talented and interested enough to join teams that compete under the rules of the United States Gymnastics Federation, but the majority could not perform at this level and so were effectively forced to give up the sport altogether.

Novice Gymnastics lets these young women join teams where they can compete at their own level, continue to develop their skills (which can be used in other sports later on), and benefit from all the other lessons of athletics. Many sports in your community probably already allow for this kind of multitrack competition. If the one your daughter is most interested in does not, you might want to look into setting up a program. As Cobbs says, competition of this type is a real confidence builder. "The message is that every girl's a winner."

What if she doesn't want to play?

No matter how convinced you are that athletics is important, your daughter might disagree. What do you do then? Keeping in mind Lynn Jaffee's maxim about having fun, there's no point in forcing her. Jaffee recommends, instead, that you sit down and think about your daughter. Why doesn't she want to play? The problem might be something as simple as feeling clumsy or incapable of performing athletic skills. If that's the case, find her a tutor, get her some lessons, or spend some time working with her yourself. Has anyone explained to her exactly how to catch or throw? In writing this book, we've talked to many adult women who grew up hating sports because teachers and coaches assumed these things.

Jaffee suggests, too, that you consider your daughter's interests and abilities, and try to come up with activities that suit her. "There's something she's going to like." It may end up being hiking rather than swimming, and there may not be much opportunity for competition. But the activity is good for her health, her confidence, and her self-esteem, and it may be something she'll stay with for life.

Remember that while athletics may offer the best opportunities to learn from competition, there are other paths. Activities like debate, drama, music, dance, chess, and so on also involve competition, building skills, working as a team, leadership, and/or taking risks. If your daughter is, for any reason, unable or unwilling to participate in athletics, provide opportunities and encouragement for her to get involved with another activity that may offer many of the same benefits.

Finally, one last piece of information from Lynn Jaffee: "Parents who are active are going to have active kids." Okay, everyone out for badminton!

I felt like a total klutz until I was about twenty. Then, one day, my boyfriend took me out in the yard and said, "Here, this is how to throw a ball. This is how to catch. This is how to bat. This is how to run." It was a revelation to me. Suddenly, all those clouds just lifted!

—Former couch potato

Are there messages about sports you'd like to record in "Your Plan" at this time? (Remember, actions speak louder than words. When was the last time your daughter saw you out on the courts?)

chapter nineteen

Mirror, Mirror, on the Wall

When it comes to liking the way we look, most women can do little but imagine how it would feel. Every time we turn around, we are hit over the head with the message that appearance is everything—and we don't measure up. Cosmetic companies spend $650 million a year on magazine ads that tell us we're aging and ugly—and we spend $20 billion a year on their products in an effort to "improve" ourselves. Fashion models who are 23 percent thinner than the average woman make us feel fat—and we spend $33 billion a year on diets that usually don't work, thus making us feel even worse about ourselves. Cosmetic surgeons tell us small breasts are a "deformity" and a "disease," and young women receive nose jobs and liposuction as graduation gifts. No wonder most of us are dissatisfied with our appearance.

All of this is bound to affect your daughter. There's no way around it. Your job is to make her feel beautiful, just the way she is, starting right now. There's no proof that a young woman who grows up with a feeling of total acceptance will be immune to the messages of the mass media. There is, however, powerful evidence that those who are raised to believe they are not attractive will never feel comfortable with the way they look.

So tell her she's beautiful, and don't qualify your praise with statements like "if only you'd do something with that hair." The trick is to do this without putting undue importance on the topic. Praise her achievements at least as much as her appearance, and tell her she's pretty in her baseball uniform or dirty jeans, not just when she's "all dolled up." Making her feel pretty is not at all the same thing as pressuring her to be pretty.

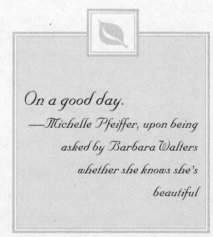

On a good day.
—*Michelle Pfeiffer, upon being asked by Barbara Walters whether she knows she's beautiful*

Remember that song Joe Cocker sang back in the mid-seventies "You Are So Beautiful"? There wasn't much more to it; he must have repeated that phrase about a zillion times. My boyfriend thought it was stupid, but I still love it. Can you imagine how wonderful it would feel to have that kind of overwhelming approval?

—*Woman, 43*

(If she is exceptionally attractive, put more emphasis on her other accomplishments. She may feel that her appearance is all anyone is interested in.)

Giving her this solid base of approval should help, but as she nears adolescence, society's preoccupation with women's appearance won't escape her notice, and it could threaten her self-esteem. It's important for you to be aware of the possible problems so that you can work to lessen their impact.

The main problem, as we see it, is that by trying to meet the cultural standard of proper appearance, a young woman is giving strangers the right to tell her whether or not she is "okay." By doing so, as Naomi Wolf, author of *The Beauty Myth*, puts it, "we will remain vulnerable to outside approval, carrying the vital sensitive organ of self-esteem exposed to the air."

Second, there seems now to be a perceived dichotomy about the connection between a woman's body and her mind: society tells your daughter that she can either be intelligent and achieving—but considered unattractive—or attractive but not taken seriously. In *The Beauty Myth* Wolf tells a poignant story about her graduation from Yale, at which Dick Cavett was the commencement speaker.

"Confronted by two thousand young female Yale graduates in mortarboards and academic gowns," she says, Cavett told them: "When he was at Yale there were no women. The women went to Vassar. There, they had nude photographs taken in gym class to check their posture. Some of the photos ended up in the pornography black market in New Haven. The punch line: The photos found no buyers. Whether or not the slur was deliberate, it was still effective: . . . Waiting for the parchment that honored our minds, we were returned with reluctant confusion to our bodies, which we had just been told were worthless."

The reverse side of this story is also sad. "When I first got involved with the women's movement," says Sunny, an attorney, "one of the other women in my group told me I couldn't be a real feminist until I stopped wearing high heels and makeup. I think I succeeded in changing her mind after a while, but it upset me at the time. She didn't even know me, and yet she felt she could read my character by looking at my shoes."

Which brings us to a third point. High self-esteem is more likely to be found in women who please themselves rather than trying to please others. The question is not so much how your daughter dresses or wears her hair, but why she chooses to do so. "It is easy for little girls to look to their mothers for the final word on how they look," author Laurie Colwin wrote in *Allure* magazine. "It is hard to resist that deference, but I do not want to be the authority on this subject. I want her to be the authority." If you can work toward this same end with your daughter, there's no telling what she'll do. She may go in for elaborate hats, mismatched socks, oversize glasses, or combat boots. She may be a bohemian on Monday, a country-western star on Wednesday, and a debutante on Saturday night. You may be tempted to tell her she's sporting too much hair, too much mascara, or too much perfume, but bite your tongue. If she's doing this for herself, she's trying on different images, living out her fantasies, and probably having a ball.

Our final concern about females and beauty is that it can put women in competition against each other. This is not like athletic competition, where there are rules to play by, objective winners, and always the chance that tomorrow the results will be different. In this kind of game, everyone loses.

"You can wake up in a good mood, get dressed, and leave the house feeling terrific," says Karen, an interior designer. "But then you turn the corner and see this fabulous-looking woman, and all of a sudden you're completely deflated. Who are you trying to kid? you ask yourself. You don't measure up, and you never will." Because there will always be someone who's younger, thinner, better dressed, this kind of competitive attitude is self-defeating. Karen decided to change. "Now I can appreciate the way other women look," she says. "There are so many kinds of feminine beauty, it makes me feel better about myself just to be the same sex."

How parents can help

Your daughter will inevitably be exposed to cultural values and peer pressure regarding her appearance, but as her parents you still wield a great deal of influence. Your words and actions can go far to build her self-esteem—or tear it down. Here are some additional dos and don't to keep in mind when dealing with fragile young egos.

By showing an interest in your daughter's general self-esteem, you've already taken an important step. The better she feels about herself overall, the less vulnerable she'll be to peer pressure or media-imposed images of what constitutes female beauty.

1. Never criticize or make jokes about her face or body or any portion thereof.

One thoughtless comment on your part can lead to years of insecurity for your daughter. An ongoing commentary about the size of her nose or feet can make her hate that part of herself for life.

There was a period in my childhood when, every time I left the house, my mother cheerfully reminded me to "tuck in your tummy." Not "Have a good day" or "Study hard." "Tuck in your tummy." I don't think a day has gone by since that I haven't taken a few moments to check out my profile in the mirror. I always expect to see this huge, protruding belly.

—*Woman*

I once told my mother I thought I had nice hands. She told me that vanity is a sin. That might have been okay if I was some lovely young thing who was always lounging around admiring herself, but I'd already been told that just about every other part of my body was unacceptable. I was left with nothing.

—*Woman*

2. Take every opportunity to give honest praise.

Saying she has beautiful skin when she can see for herself that she has acne will only make her mistrust you. But reminding her that she has graceful hands, a wonderful smile, or a lovely mane of hair will mean a lot. If she says something positive about her appearance, agree with her.

If your daughter expresses concern about acne or wearing glasses, or if her dentist says she needs braces, get her the help she needs if you can afford it. Today doctors can do a lot to clear up adolescent skin, and millions of kids wear contact lenses and/or braces. These relatively minor adjustments can measurably build self-esteem.

Except in extreme cases, cosmetic surgery is another matter, however. Although some procedures are becoming increasingly popular among young women, the possibility of complications or even death should put a damper on most people's enthusiasm. Besides, what does it tell your daughter about the importance of appearance and her own worth as a person if you, her parents, are willing to risk her life rather than let her go on looking the way she does?

3. Mothers, don't obsess about your own appearance.

Your daughter is likely to follow your example. It is particularly important not to express dissatisfaction with your weight. If you find you need to slim down, just say you've decided to eat in a more healthy way.

4. Fathers, don't treat women like objects.

Your daughter will notice, and see it as her fate.

5. Don't criticize other women's appearance or disparage them because of the way they look.

Doing so reinforces the message that women count only if they live up to society's standard of "beauty." If a woman is attractive, comment on other aspects of her personality. Too often we find it impossible to say anything about a woman without mentioning the way she looks. We don't have the same problem when talking about men.

6. Compliment other women on their talents and achievements.

Look for attractive qualities in those who aren't obviously beautiful, and point them out to your daughter: "She has such a terrific laugh! I bet people just love being around her." "She looks so dramatic! I wonder if she's an actress." "Look at those expressive hands!" "What a flair she has for dressing!"

7. Don't compare your daughter's appearance with that of other girls or young women.

Don't put labels on any of your children. No one should limit her self-image to that of "the good one," "the smart one," or "the pretty one." Why can't she be all of those and more?

8. Expose your daughter to women of various ages and appearances who are comfortable with the way they look.

9. Mothers, don't "compete" with other women.

Be accepting of them, and of yourself, no matter where you think you rank on the beauty scale.

10. Point out how the beauty industry profits by making all women feel insecure about their looks.

"I thought I'd treat myself to a facial and makeover at a local department store," says Arlene, an attractive woman in her mid-thirties. "So they get me in this chair, remove my makeup, and shine this bright light right into my face. Then they start the interrogation. What sort of cleanser do I use? Oh, dear, that's too bad, but—yes—they can see it now: the clogged pores, the dead skin. With luck, they might just be able to save me—providing I repent of my evil ways and promise to buy their products, and so on. The makeup part was even worse: I should watch so

I'd know how to make my face look more angular, my nose less broad, my lips fuller. What had I done to my eyebrows? Well, they could fix them. They could cover up those shadows under my eyes, too, and use a special powder to make all those lines less noticeable. It was a nightmare!"

Following this experience, Arlene looked more closely at the ads for beauty products and the way magazine articles instruct women in their appearance. "Everything is a problem with these folks," she reports. "There is no such category as 'just right.' Your skin is either dry, oily, or combination. Eyes are either too close together or too far apart. If they're deep-set, you have to use makeup to 'bring them out.' Otherwise, you have to use the same products to make them look deep-set! Noses are never right, either. They can be too short, too long, too broad, too narrow, or just plain too big. Would you like me to go on?"

11. Start when your daughter is young to emphasize the fun and fanciful aspects of appearance.

Encourage her to think of clothes as a means to help her express her many-sided personality rather than camouflage for her figure "flaws" or portable prisons to restrict her movement. Get her face painted at community fairs and revel in her multiple images. Create elaborate "hairdos" out of shampoo at bath time. Be imaginative and enthusiastic about Halloween costumes. The "beauty police" lose much of their power when you turn their own weapons against them.

12. Show your pride in your daughter's appearance in concrete ways.

Take photos of her often, and display them around your house and office. Send them to relatives. Show them to friends and co-workers.

13. Don't use the clichéd statements about appearance that we all grew up with.

Does a four-year-old really need her "beauty sleep"? Phrases like "age before beauty" reinforce the cultural standard that appearance is valued more highly than wisdom or experience. And do we really want another generation of women to grow up thinking that "in order to be beautiful, you must suffer"?

Mindy remembers being frightened the first time a baby-sitter read her the story of *The Little Mermaid.* The Little Mermaid's mother clamped lobsters onto her tail (very fashionable for mermaids), and when her daughter cried out in pain, her mother reminded her that it was necessary to suffer in order to be beautiful. It seemed like a silly argument at the time, but years later in the 1960s, trying to get to sleep wearing those enormous rollers we all used to put in our hair, Mindy found herself repeating the statement in the dark.

14. Choose your battles carefully.

You and your daughter are sure to disagree about some aspect of her appearance from time to time, but try to keep things in perspective. Is the haircut or the eye makeup so bad that you'd risk damaging your relationship to get your way?

You can, however, teach your daughter that there is such a thing as appropriate dress for specific occasions, and that certain types of attire will probably elicit certain—often undesirable—responses from others. One does not, for example, wear a cocktail dress to a funeral. A young woman hoping to get a job does herself a disservice by wearing tight jeans and combat boots to her interview. If she dresses in a fashion that could be dangerous, such as provoking unwanted advances from strangers, you may need to discuss this reality with her.

It will usually be more effective to ask questions (see chapter 8), set an example, or provide alternatives, however, than to lecture or criticize. If you are seriously concerned about the way your daughter dresses, you might try some of the following:

- *Next time she needs a special outfit, use one of those shopping services most department stores now offer free of charge. Having a professional buyer or "image consultant" select clothes and accessories that are stylish and flattering may provide your daughter with a whole new image of herself, one she'll want to uphold. (Perhaps you could have put together the same outfit, but it's likely to be better received if it comes from an outsider.)*
- *Take her to a fashion show featuring career clothes for women, and talk to her—casually, conversationally—about professional women and how they care about their personal style as an expression of how they feel about themselves.*
- *Go shopping with her. Share information about fabrics, styles, quality of construction, and so on. "When I got my first professional job," says Casey, an office manager in a large corporation, "my wardrobe consisted mainly of polyester pant suits and platform shoes. I knew they were all wrong, but I didn't know why. Fortunately, about that time I became friends with some women who really knew about stuff like that, and they began explaining things to me. It opened up a whole new world."*
- *Let her get her colors done, or do it with her. Find a professional who doesn't just tell you what your best colors are, but shows you. This is a terrific activity, because unlike most makeovers, it promotes individuality ("what's right for me") rather than one "ideal" (what's right according to society) image. Once she sees what certain colors can do for her skin tone or the color of her eyes, she may begin to take more interest and pride in her appearance. This could also end up saving money (she'll be less likely to end up with a closet full of clothes she won't wear because they look awful on her) and making her less susceptible to the whims of fashion.*

15. For a young woman with a disability, adolescence can be especially trying.

She probably already feels "different" in all the worst ways, and she may believe, often with good reason, that others see not *her*, but only her disability. Reassure her as much as you can, but don't dismiss her fears. They are quite real. Don't assume, either, that she is not interested in looking her best or that the styles and fashions adopted by other teens are off limits to her. Is there any real reason she can't have that wild hairdo or the outrageous earrings she's been wanting?

Body image and eating disorders

When Karen Carpenter died in 1983, comedian Joan Rivers reportedly said, "It's hard to feel sorry for anyone who died thin enough to be buried in pleats." That statement roughly reflects the degree of seriousness with which our society treats eating disorders, but it's time for the jokes to stop.

One million American women are afflicted with anorexia and bulimia each year, and about 5 to 15 percent of them eventually die as a result. Another 40 to 50 percent of anorexics never fully regain their health. The organs, muscles, and tissues of the body do not completely recover from the ravages of starvation, and therefore its victims may be weakened the rest of their lives.

This is a disorder of young women. Anorexia often comes on around puberty, while bulimia usually strikes a bit later in adolescence. And it is an illness of achieving women.

It is impossible to know exactly how many victims there are, but some experts estimate that on our top college campuses, up to 20 percent of the women students are anorectic, and up to 60 percent are bulimic.

Anorexia nervosa is a disorder in which (usually) adolescent girls starve themselves, sometimes to death. Victims of anorexia may suffer from hypothermia (dangerously low body temperature), edema (high levels of fluids in the body), hypotension (low blood pressure), and infertility. There are hormonal aberrations. Muscles of the heart weaken, and the chambers get smaller. There are abnormalities of the immune function and

The supreme happiness of life is the conviction that we are loved; loved for ourselves.

—Victor Hugo

the gastrointestinal system, and the lining of the digestive track atrophies. The brain functions less effectively, and sleep disturbances and nightmares are common.

Anorexia's sister disorder, bulimia, is characterized by the binge-and-purge syndrome. Terrified of becoming fat, these young women periodically give in to binge eating—eating large amounts of food in a short time. These binges are followed by self-induced vomiting, using laxatives or diuretics, fasting, or exercising vigorously in order to avoid gaining weight. More common than anorexia nervosa, bulimia is also extremely serious. It can lead to heart and/or kidney failure, as well as a ruptured esophagus or stomach; infections of the bladder, kidneys, pharynx, and esophagus; tooth erosion; and more.

There doesn't appear to be any single reason that young women become anorectic or bulimic, but society's preoccupation with thinness certainly has something to do with it. Most women, in fact, are unhappy with their bodies.

Here are some of the startling numbers: A study by the National Association of Anorexia Nervosa and Associated Disorders found that among nine-year-old girls, 31 percent thought they were overweight, while 81 percent of ten-year-olds were dieters. A 1984 survey of college women by Robin Lakoff and Raquel Scherr discovered that "they all wanted to lose five to twenty-five pounds." In 1985 90 percent of those responding to a survey said they thought they were overweight. A 1984 survey by *Glamour* had 75 percent of the women reporting they thought they were fat—including 45 percent of those who were underweight. In that same survey women said it would mean more to them to lose ten to fifteen pounds than it would to have success at work or in a romantic relationship.

Which leads us to another question: Why are so many women so unhappy with their bodies? Naomi Wolf believes it's because we are barraged every day by images of what we are supposed to look like, even though the media ideal is virtually out of reach for 95 percent of American women. And the culture keeps upping the ante. While the average fashion model used to weigh 8 percent less than the average woman, today she is 23 percent thinner than her real-world counterpart. Dancers and actresses, too, are thinner than 95 percent of American women. Winning contestants in the Miss America contest have steadily become thinner, as have Playboy Playmates.

Since women have traditionally been valued for their bodies rather than their minds, millions of us become chronic dieters, feeling that our other achievements are worthless unless we can also meet the latest beauty standards.

Some of the latest research indicates that dieting itself may be a major cause of eating disorders. Researchers believe that ongoing restrictive eating patterns lead to so much stress on the body and emotions that anorexia or bulimia may quite easily develop.

Eating disorders may also arise when adolescents are troubled by the suffering they see as adult women struggle. By stopping the development of a woman's body, the victims of eating disorders are often trying to stave off this unappealing future. Finally, and most important for the purposes of this book, eating disorders are most likely to arise in young women who have low self-esteem, coupled with perfectionist tendencies and, very often, the wish to gain approval of a distant or emotionally unavailable father.

Anorexics and bulimics are, basically, people pleasers who expect nothing less than perfection from themselves. They are extremely sensitive to rejection and, at the same time, keenly aware of other people's expectations. They know that society expects them to be thin, and many feel that if they can just become thin enough, they might be able to win the attention and approval of the fathers who have abandoned them. Anorexics often feel they don't control much in their lives; they find that they can, however, control their food. Bulimics, on the other hand, often struggle with issues of separation and independence; bulimia is a way of taking on comfort and then throwing it off.

If you suspect your daughter may have an eating disorder, it's imperative to intervene at once. Treatment in the early stages is quite successful, but recovery becomes more troublesome as time goes on. The conditions are difficult to diagnose, but if your daughter is found to be anorectic or bulimic, she will need a combination of physical and psychological treatment. Residential treatment centers are often suggested, but some individual therapists also specialize in treating these patients. Make sure that your caregiver has solid experience in this field and is well acquainted with the latest methods of treatment.

Ways to prevent eating disorders from developing in the first place

Again, building your daughter's self-esteem from an early age and helping her develop a hardy personality is the best defense against eating disorders of all kinds. If she learns to be discriminating, she won't have that terrible need to please everyone that is so evident among anorexics. If she learns to set boundaries, she won't put society's dictates ahead of her own best interests. A young woman who can separate fantasy from reality is likely to realize that no one really looks like the images in the magazines. She is also less likely to have a distorted image of herself, something that most women, in fact, do. When asked to estimate their weight or measurements, for example, women consistently guess that they are bigger than they really are. In addition, they tend to pick that portion of their bodies they like the least and see that body part as far and away their most dominating feature. Anorexics, no matter how thin they become, continue to see themselves as fat.

1. Starting early, teach your daughter about healthy eating habits and demonstrate them in your home.

Explain that food is the fuel her body needs in order to run efficiently, and that's why it's important to have a nutritious diet.

2. Don't use the giving or withholding of food as a reward or punishment, and don't endow it with symbolic meaning.

Food is not "evil," and eating is not a "sin." Neither should it be equated with love. All of these give food an inordinate amount of power over an individual, a power that she may never be able to shake. She deserves a better fate than learning to feel guilty every time she enjoys a meal or developing the habit of turning to food for the comfort and solace more reliably found in supportive relationships.

3. Love your daughter unconditionally.

Yes, you may have high expectations for her, but don't make your approval the carrot in front of the donkey, something that is always promised—and sometimes withheld. She will never tire of your praise, and it's impossible to tell her too often that you love her.

Never criticize your daughter's body or her eating patterns. Don't tease her about her figure, either. It may seem trivial to you, but to her it is deadly serious. She already has several multibillion-dollar industries aligned for the sole purpose of making her feel fat and ugly. What she needs from you is reassurance that she is neither.

Likewise, you may feel you're being helpful and supportive when you ask if she's lost or gained weight, what she had for lunch, or if she's sure she wants another plate of pasta. What you're really doing, though, is reinforcing society's messages that food is bad, hunger is a sin, and being thin is the highest good.

Yes, we know. Life isn't easy for overweight women. People are cruel. And obesity can create health problems as well. But in general many of the factors that lead to the development of eating disorders can also cause obesity: low self-esteem, a preoccupation with food, constant dieting, feeling unacceptable. Left to create her own relationship with food, your daughter may have some weight fluctuations, but eventually she will probably settle in at her biologically programmed best weight. Better still, she may be spared the preoccupation with food, weight, and body image that afflicts so many women.

4. Fathers, you have a special role to play.

As we've said, anorexia usually develops at puberty, and there is a high incidence of the disorder among young women who feel they've been abandoned by their fathers.

All young women, whether they are likely to become anorectic or not, need special attention from their dads at this crucial stage of development. Unfortunately many fathers become uncomfortable with their daughter's emerging womanly body, and, not sure how to act around her anymore, they withdraw. They don't love her any less, of course, but she doesn't know that.

To your daughter you are the most important man in the world, and at the moment when she is starting to take an interest in the opposite sex and establish her sexual identity, your approval or disapproval means everything. Tell her she's pretty, and she'll be on top of the world. Turn away from her, and she will feel that you are rejecting her new body as unacceptable and undesirable. When this happens, some young women will stop eating in an effort to regain your love by maintaining their emaciated boyish figure, while others will simply seek it somewhere else—from other males.

It may be necessary to reevaluate your physical relationship with your daughter when she enters puberty. Wrestling matches will have to stop, for example, and it's no longer appropriate for "Daddy's little girl" to climb on your lap. If yours is a huggy family, a family where members touch each other often to show love, withdrawing the hugs will send a negative message, so keep hugging away. In all families an arm around her shoulder, a kiss on the cheek, a pat on the back—accompanied by lots and lots of reassuring words—are just what she needs right now. Do see that she gets them!

5. Make peace with your own body.

Set a good example by eating a well-balanced diet and getting regular exercise, but don't talk about it all the time. Indicate by word and deed that there are more important topics in the world, better things to do.

6. Don't offer critiques of other women's bodies or point out their figure "flaws" to your daughter.

Be accepting of those who don't meet your ideal. Give your daughter an opportunity to see other women's bodies. (For example, take her with you into the adult locker room at the Y—or into one of those communal dressing rooms that some discount clothing stores have. Or just look around the next time you're at the beach or a pool together.) We don't mean this in a prurient way, but as an educational experience. When all the bodies she sees in the magazines and on the videos and in the movies are almost as identical as they are impossible to achieve, it's easy for a young woman to believe that there is an ideal, and she's the only one who doesn't meet it.

As Gloria Steinem said in a wonderful essay called "In Praise of Women's Bodies": "I know that fat or thin, mature or not, our bodies wouldn't give us such unease if we learned their place in the rainbow spectrum of women. Even great beauties seem less distant, and even mastectomies seem less terrifying, when we stop imagining and try to see them as they really are."

It has been suggested that some women pursue thinness and beauty because this has been a rare area open for female achievement. Praise and promote your daughter's other ambitions and achievements so she won't have to resort to this.

7. Give her access to information about real women's bodies with books like Our Bodies, Ourselves.

8. Developing—or underdeveloping—breasts are an issue of constant concern to young women.

Again, be sensitive to her feelings and offer reassurance. Since young men are often fixated on female breasts, your daughter may feel totally undesirable if she's slow to develop.

When Mindy was in ninth grade, she "put out the word" that she'd really like to go out with a certain handsome classmate (a common technique of indicating interest among adolescent females). She was devastated to learn his response: he wouldn't go out with her because she was "flat as a board." Even though she "developed" shortly after that, she continued to think of herself as flat-chested until her daughter was born years later.

If your daughter develops earlier than her friends, she may have a problem of a different sort: too much male attention. This may embarrass her, or she may learn to use her body to get the attention or acceptance she desires. If she gets acceptance at home—particularly from her father—she will be less vulnerable to these reactions. Do what you can to help her feel comfortable with her new body as well.

You should also be aware of the unfortunate tendency among many people of all ages and both sexes to equate large breasts with low intelligence. If your daughter is well endowed, she may have more of a conflict than other young women with the idea of achievement because of the way she may be treated, particularly by males. Make sure she understands that there is no connection at all between her appearance and her mind.

One woman we interviewed recalled one of her best friends in high school, who was very well endowed. It was a major source of her identity with the group. Because she was so large breasted she was teased, to the point where she would never stand up straight. When the guys paid attention to her, it was for this physical feature, not because she also was brilliant and a National Merit finalist. She once said sadly, "I don't know whether John likes me for me or because I am a full-breasted trophy." That was twenty-five years ago. What's sad is she didn't use her brilliance; when last heard of, she was just drifting through life.

Taking joy in life is a woman's best cosmetic.
—*Rosalind Russell*

How many cares one loses when one decides not to be something, but to be someone.
—*Coco Chanel*

9. Explain to your daughter the difference between image and substance, and encourage her to pursue the latter, even though it takes more effort.

Anyone can look tough, for example, by putting on a black leather jacket and a sneer. To be strong, however, takes courage and dedication. It's easy to display bravado, much harder to develop self-confidence. Girls, more often than boys, tend to feel that there is some physical ideal they must live up to, and this detracts from their ability to develop and revel in their own identity.

10. Work for women's equality.

When women feel valued and admired for what they do and who they are, they may finally stop being obsessed by how they look and whom they attract.

What new messages would you like to give your daughter about appearance? Include them in "Your Plan."

chapter twenty

I'm Nobody Till Somebody Loves Me

Your daughter will probably never be as aware of or concerned with her appearance as she's sure to be at adolescence, when she starts wanting to attract boys. It won't take her long to notice that they aren't interested in her grade-point average or her hardy personality. Adolescent males, insecure about their own sexual identity, are generally looking for reassurance that they are okay, and they gain confidence from the most traditional young women. A "feminine" girlfriend makes a boy feel like a man.

You won't have much luck trying to convince your daughter that she's wrong about what boys find appealing or that she shouldn't be interested in males anyway. "My daughter told me," Susan reported, "that her boyfriend, Joe, is 'really interested in girls. Whenever we bring anyone up, he asks, "Is she cute?"' When I demurred, she said, 'That's the way boys are, Mom. Face it.'" Here you're dealing not only with intense cultural and peer pressure, but with nature, biology, and instinct. What's more, your daughter will know you're not telling the truth and may have less trust in any advice you offer in the future.

Consider for a moment the world your daughter lives in. She doesn't have to look very far to find adult women who have made a career of trying to be attractive to men. And they can make it seem desirable or even glamorous. To the typical teen, a life of shopping for clothes, experimenting with makeup, and having weekly facials and manicures seems much more appealing than going to work every day.

Advertisements and popular culture tell her that being pleasing to men will be her most rewarding role. The rules for keeping a boyfriend haven't changed much over the years: Don't compete with him, or if you do, let him win. Be a good listener, but don't expect him to listen to you. Let him lead. Be supportive. Don't talk

With the boys, I aimed low and gave in, disregarding all my mother said, and only worried about my flat chest, presumably because that's what the boys were concerned with, and about being abandoned and left on the shelf at age fourteen! I allowed them to control me completely, to the point of physical abuse.

—Woman, 47

too much. Look good. And if you're smarter than he is, for goodness' sake don't let him know.

Female peers can be unrelenting enforcers of society's rules. For example, Dorothy Holland and Margaret Eisenhart note in their book, *Educated in Romance*, how one young woman tried to insult another female student by telling her, "You may be able to do calculus, but I'm dating a football player." Friendships among young women often center around discussions of what boys find appealing, trying to meet those standards, plotting how to meet boys, and judging the progress others are making in these regards. Achievement is disparaged. The only way to gain prestige is through the approval of men.

In all these ways, women learn how to see themselves as others—particularly men—see them. And what are the adolescent males in your daughter's life looking for? Because their own image is partially dependent on whom they go out with, they are concerned primarily with appearance and sex appeal (image over substance). Because their identity is still a little shaky, they want someone who will not question or challenge them. And to bolster both their image and identity, they are looking for a young woman who will be supportive and submissive.

Obviously these are not the traits of achievement, and this can be a terrible conflict for your daughter.

In 1960, when Susan was at Stanford, her boyfriend (who also attended Stanford) told her that he and a fraternity brother preferred San Jose State girls to Stanford girls because they were more "subservient." She noticed that he continued to hang around her, though. What disturbs her now is that she continued to hang around him for a year or so after that.

Why date?

Why not, you may be wondering, simply forbid her to date? While you may be able to delay her entry into the world of male-female relationships, you can't put it off indefinitely. Besides, the fact that she's not seeing anyone will not necessarily lessen her desire to attract male attention. On the contrary, it may even lead her to intensify her efforts in subversive and dishonest ways.

And there are some good things about dating: It will help your daughter learn how to handle herself in mixed groups. If she starts attending dances and parties at about the same time as her peers, everyone will share a certain amount of clumsiness and uncertainty at first, but all will become more confident and comfortable together. A latecomer to the scene must suffer these indignities alone.

Going out with a number of young men will also help your daughter begin to consider what qualities are most important to her, what she is looking for in a life partner (more on this in chapter 26). If she has learned to be discriminating, the more males she dates, the more likely she is to end up with a suitable and satisfying mate.

Finally, dating helps her get to know herself better. It lets her see a completely new side of her personality. How does she function in this world? How does she feel about her successes and failures? Does she have the strength to be discriminating and to be assertive about her own needs and wants, or does she feel she has to give in to the other person? Is she hardy enough to withstand the ambivalence of dating (will he call, will he call again, should I give in) and still maintain her own standards? Some of her experiences will almost certainly be painful (few things are more painful than breaking up with someone you really care about), but they may be interesting and instructive as well.

A woman has got to love a bad man once or twice in her life, to be thankful for a good one.

—*Marjorie Kinnan Rawlings*

Remember, though, that girls mature at different rates and have varying levels of interest in dating. There's no reason to be terribly concerned if your daughter lags behind her friends in this regard. If she is shy or introverted, it may take her more time to feel comfortable around young men. Or perhaps it's not that she's *less* interested in dating, but that she's *more* interested in something else: if she's a serious young athlete or musician, for example, she may find it more important or pleasurable to spend her spare time at practice.

If you sense that she wants to date but hasn't been asked out, be especially careful not to push, tease, prod, or offer unasked-for advice. She probably feels embarrassed and unhappy about the situation already. If she thinks you consider her a

302 WHAT'S A PARENT TO DO?

"failure" for not going out, her sense of rejection and inadequacy will only be magnified.

If she *tells* you she wants to date and wants to talk about it, listen empathetically and offer advice—if she asks for it. (Why not suggest that she be assertive and do the asking herself?)

Whether or not your daughter is dating, don't put too much emphasis on the situation. Young women need more encouragement and support for their efforts to achieve than for their relative "failure" or "success" at relationships. Your daughter will have plenty of time to develop her dating skills.

The importance of the first relationship

No one seems to have a solid reason for why it happens, but it seems that a young woman's faltering self-esteem makes a rebound when she has her first real boyfriend. Many girls report they feel so much more confident after their first boyfriend. It appears likely that this has something to do with the fact that, having given males the authority to judge her worth, she finally has visible proof of being desirable and therefore worthwhile.

Once she has established a first relationship, others are likely to follow. Perhaps this is because her attractiveness has now been validated by a male, or maybe potential suitors find her newfound desirability appealing. But this first male relationship is important, because the way he treats her often helps determine how she expects to be treated in future relationships.

If she is treated badly by her first love, she is more likely to be treated badly by his successors. Her expectations draw on the only experience she has. On the other hand, if her first relationship is with a young man who is well thought of by others, and if he treats her well, she will be allowed more freedom and given more respect. Once it has been determined that she is acceptable, what she does, says, or wears is likely to gain approval as well.

Your job

Adolescence and first relationships are a real test for every young woman's self-esteem. It is here, though, that your past efforts may truly pay off. If she knows who she is, likes who she is, and has developed the personal skills and been given permission to consider herself as worthy as any male, she is less apt to fall prey to the pressures of this difficult period.

A young woman's father can be a particularly valuable ally at this point in time. Since he is likely to still be the most important male in her life, his approval of both her "femininity" (relationship traits) and her achievements is essential. The balance is key. If her father praises and encourages only her relationship traits, she receives the message that her achievements are no longer important or even appropriate. And without his approval for her budding womanhood, she is likely to look elsewhere for the reinforcement she needs.

This is a time for both parents to be nurturing and nonjudgmental. You can't tell your daughter what to do. She won't listen. But if you've developed a good relationship and good communication techniques, you can gently guide her with your questions. And if she wants it, you can offer advice and information. Your own wisdom and experience are urgently needed.

Don't validate a male's right to pass judgment on your daughter, to determine if she measures up to his standards. Your goal should be to develop your daughter's self-esteem to the point where she is more concerned that he measure up to her standards.

—Nicky Marone, author, *How to Father a Successful Daughter*

Giving advice

There are probably few things parents would like more than to be considered "trustworthy" enough so that their daughters come to them to talk and get advice about dating, relationships, and choosing a mate. Unfortunately this doesn't happen as often as it should. Who, after all, is in a better position to understand these troubling times than a parent who's been through it and, somehow, survived? A young woman's friends are likely to be as confused or inexperienced as she is.

The trick to making your daughter understand that you are on her side is through open and effective communication.

Parents can only give good advice or put them on the right path, but the final forming of a person's character lies in their own hands.

—Anne Frank

At a certain point, at least by the time your daughter reaches eighteen or moves out of the house, you need to stop acting as a parent in some ways and become more of a consultant. Advice comes from consultants, people with certain experience or knowledge that allows them to handle particular situations or solve particular problems. The receiver of this advice has the option of accepting, modifying, or rejecting said advice without fear that her choice will affect her relationship with the consultant.

If you can put yourself into this new role and clarify what it means with your daughter, you have a good chance of keeping open the lines of communication as she enters her later teen years.

Here are some points to keep in mind:

1. *Always ask for permission to give advice before offering it.*

"May I offer some advice?" "Would you like some suggestions from me?"

2. *Remember that advice is just that.*

It's a gift that can be accepted or rejected. Just because mom or dad offers it doesn't mean it has to be accepted or followed.

3. *Never question whether your advice has been followed.*

Offer it, and then forget it unless your daughter raises the topic at a later time.

This may take some practice, but it could be rewarding for you and helpful for your daughter to give it a try.

Modeling healthy intimate relationships

One of the best ways to teach your daughter how to recognize a healthy relationship is to model one in your own home. If she sees that her mother is respected by the men in her life—particularly by her spouse—for her intelligence and assertive behavior, your daughter will expect no less from the young men she goes out with. If, on the other hand, she observes her mother constantly putting everyone else's needs and desires ahead of her own, she is more likely to defer to the men in her life, even when their wishes conflict with her own goals and dreams.

The major goal in my life had always been to graduate from college. But at the end of my junior year I basically handed my life over to my boyfriend, James. He decided that we should get married and I should give up my education and get a job so he could go to grad school. I remember taking my last final, then going over to the administration building to apply for a clerical job. As I walked home that evening, tears started running down my cheeks. It took me years to figure out why.

—Woman, 40

Maintaining her autonomy

Often a young woman confuses possessiveness with love. The more time her boyfriend wants to spend with her, the more he must care about her. In healthy couples, however, both partners also have a full existence outside the relationship. This is particularly important for young women, who are usually the ones to give up their own identity in favor of their boyfriends'.

Maria, the mother of two daughters, recalls, "When I started dating my first husband, he just sort of took over my life. He managed to alienate all of my friends, so very soon I had no one else to turn to. I had doubts about the wisdom of marrying him, but he convinced me I was wrong. I'd completely lost track of who I was by that time, and there was no one left around to remind me."

When you see this happening to someone you or your daughter knows, discuss the situation with her. If her friend Ellen, for example, isn't available to her anymore because she's spending all her time with her boyfriend, ask your daughter how that makes her feel. Is she envious of Ellen, or does she think Ellen's making a mistake? Who decides what they do on their dates? Is Ellen honestly interested in ice hockey and auto shows? Does she ever get to decide how to spend the evening? Does that seem fair? Is this relationship likely to last? What will happen to Ellen if it doesn't? Will her friends take her back, or will they feel resentful? Will she have fallen behind in school? Can she think of ways that Ellen could keep her boyfriend without giving up her other friends, responsibilities, and interests?

If she can't maintain her autonomy—her identity—in a relationship, your daughter will inevitably lose her self-esteem, and she may give up her ability to be self-sufficient as well.

Separating relationships and achievement

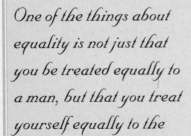

One of the things about equality is not just that you be treated equally to a man, but that you treat yourself equally to the way you treat a man.

—*Marlo Thomas*

"Boys like me because I am intelligent and fun to be around," says Caitlan, a college freshman. "I make my own decisions. I don't let anyone tell me what to do, how to think, or what to look like." While Caitlan successfully avoided the pressure to give up any part of her identity that is not stereotypically "feminine" (concerned with relationships), many young women do not. Scholastic achievers begin to let their grades slide. Outspoken young women suddenly don't have an opinion on anything more serious than lip gloss. Capable athletes become more concerned about the condition of their hair than the conditioning of their bodies.

As we noted earlier, these are the traits that attract adolescent boys, so don't expect your daughter to pass them by entirely. Do, though, remind her that this is not necessarily an either/or situation. She can be pretty and smart, strong and supportive, ambitious and caring. And so can her boyfriend. Review the exercise on the Australian study in chapter 2 ("What Attitudes, Experiences, and Feelings Do You Bring to Parenting?"), which shows how both men and women benefit from nurturing a wide range of personality traits, "masculine" (achievement oriented) and "feminine" (relationship oriented).

Trying to live up to some cultural ideal instead of taking pride in her own identity is another way she'll destroy her self-esteem.

One way women have found to keep their relationships and their achievements in balance is to separate the two. Authors Holland and Eisenhart reported in *Educated in Romance*, for example, that women dating men who attended a different school were able to concentrate on their studies without losing any prestige in the eyes of their classmates. This is a good argument for encouraging your daughter to consider a single-sex school.

Similarly, though there's no way to arrange it, if she should find a "summer romance" or become interested in a young man who does not attend her school, don't discourage the relationship. It will probably fade in time, but as long as it lasts, she can have the best of both worlds.

There are also coed schools where achievement is valued for all students. Or send her to computer camp or a summer session class in her area of special interest.

Establishing emotional connection before physical connection

The universal double standard that used to keep many young women at least technically chaste until late adolescence or even marriage is no longer in place. Many of today's young women are just as intent on losing their virginity by a certain age as their male counterparts. Over half of girls age seventeen are sexually active. Most have little understanding of the emotional connection required before the physical connection can be truly satisfying.

This is understandable: everywhere they turn, they are barraged by erotic images and messages. But it is also unfortunate: aside from all the other good reasons to avoid indiscriminate sex, it's been shown that women generally get little satisfaction from the act unless they have previously established a close relationship with their partners and feel valued by them.

Is your daughter aware of this, and does she know how to build a relationship, how to communicate with males? Once she is comfortable talking with the young man in her life, she is in a better position to judge how far this relationship should go. Does she genuinely like him, or is it just a physical attraction? What are his values? How does he regard women in general? What role does sexuality play in his relationships?

Communication skills don't come naturally (especially, it seems, to young men). Your daughter needs to learn the different levels of communicating and then to observe and practice until she can judge whether or not anything of importance is being said. She may actually have to teach some of her dates how to carry on a meaningful conversation. A few will be unable or unwilling to learn, and these she will probably want to remove from her list of potential mates.

In his book *Why Am I Afraid to Tell You Who I Am?*, John Powell lists the following as the five levels of communication:

Level five: Cliché conversation
Level four: Reporting the facts about others
Level three: My ideas and judgments
Level two: My feelings (emotions)
Level one: Peak communication

Cliché conversation is the kind of "Hi, how are ya?" talk that acknowledges another person's presence but doesn't go much beyond that. Level four conversation has some content—pieces of gossip, what was served for dinner last night—but is still impersonal and unrevealing. (It is also extremely boring. This is the level of the person who corners people at parties and tells interminable stories about the average annual rainfall in Poughkeepsie or the life expectancy of a gray squirrel.)

At level three, things start to get personal. Individuals begin to share their thoughts and ideas, usually quite hesitantly at first. If there is any sense of disapproval of what is being said, or if the individuals involved do not trust each other, the conversation can quickly shift back to more neutral ground (levels five and four). At this level speakers use phrases like "I think" and "it's my opinion."

Level two communication opens up even farther to include feelings and emotions. This is where real communication begins, where people start to tell each other who they are at their deepest level and how they feel about things. That phrase—"I feel"—will pop up consistently.

Finally, at level one, people are absolutely open and honest with each other. And in that honesty they feel safe that the other person will not make judgments about their true feelings. They are willing to share their deepest thoughts and dreams, no matter how absurd, frightening, or revealing. No one communicates at this level all the time, but among close friends and in couples, it is important to have this kind of verbal intimacy.

Help your daughter recognize, identify, and use the different levels. Use "gut level" communication (levels one and two) yourself, within the family, so she will feel more comfortable with the concepts. (Mom: "You really hurt my feelings when you said that." Dad: "I'm sorry. I had a rotten day because I lost a big account and I'm feeling frustrated, but I didn't mean to take it out on you.")

It's not important to identify or label any particular conversation as level two or level five or what have you, only to recognize when real communication is taking place. This will take awareness and practice. We suggest you share John Powell's book with your adolescent daughter and then practice this in the family so she can recognize the different levels of emotional commitment when she starts dating.

The young men she dates may be adept at joking around or telling entertaining stories, or they may have a smooth "line." Your daughter needs to see these for what they are. They may be enjoyable, and they are perfectly acceptable at times, but they do not constitute real communication or emotional commitment.

The following dialogues illustrate conversation at each of the different levels. Discuss them with your daughter and ask her to come up with other examples.

(Level five)

HE: Hi, nice dress.
SHE: Thanks. Good to see you. How was your day?
HE: Okay.
SHE: What did you do?
HE: The usual.

(Level four)

HE: What did you do today?
SHE: I went to the mall with my friend Lucy. She needed some new shoes for the party. It's hard for her to find any that fit because one of her feet is bigger than the other.
HE: I knew this guy once who had six toes on one foot. He had a hard time finding shoes, too.
SHE: I'll bet.

(Level three)

SHE: The shoes she bought were awful. They didn't have any heel at all.
HE: I like girls to wear flats.
SHE: Oh, me too. It's just that these were kind of a weird color.

(*Level two*)

SHE: Actually, I don't care about shoes at all. I'd rather spend my money on books, but I was afraid you'd think I'm really geeky if I told you.
HE: You don't have to pretend with me. I like your honesty.

(*Level one*)

HE: That's one of the first things I noticed about you. You're not phony like some of the other girls at school. I could never really talk to them, but I feel as though I could tell you just about anything and you'd understand.
SHE: I'm glad to hear you say that. My last boyfriend wouldn't talk about anything personal, and it made me feel like I couldn't be very important to him.

Acquaintance rape

Acquaintance rape, often called "date rape" by the media, is unwanted sexual contact with someone you know. According to Naomi Wolf, writing in *The Beauty Myth*, it "is more common than left-handedness, alcoholism, and heart attacks." She bases her statement on studies at a number of American colleges, including a 1986 study by Neil Malamuth at UCLA, which found that 58 percent of the college men surveyed said they would "force a woman into having sex" if they thought they could get away with it. In a survey commissioned by *Ms.* magazine in 1988, 25 percent of female respondents had experienced rape or attemped rape. Eighty-four percent of the rape victims knew their attacker. There is a good chance, therefore, that sooner or later it will happen to your daughter.

Obviously not all date rapes include violence or even threats of physical harm. But the young woman who is quietly coerced into having sex against her will is no less a victim than the woman with a knife at her throat. If she doesn't feel she has the right to say no, she is every bit as helpless.

Being raped leaves a woman feeling fear, shame, confusion, and guilt. Since the rapist was ostensibly someone who cared about her, it can also damage her ability to trust. Needless to say, it is toxic to her self-esteem.

To help your daughter avoid this situation:

1. Help your daughter understand that men and women tend to have different understandings of the terms sex and intimacy.

To many men, the two are virtually synonymous: sex equals intimacy, and intimacy always involves sex. To women, though, there's a difference. They often find conversation more intimate than sex and are most likely to find sex satisfying only if they have established an intimate relationship with their partner. If she clearly understands this difference, she may be able to avoid some painful experiences later on.

2. Give her permission to say no, to not be "nice."

If she doesn't tell her date to stop, he's not likely to do it on his own.

3. Teach her how to be assertive or, if you are not able to, make sure she receives some formal "assertiveness training."

She should practice these skills in all areas of her life—including with you. If she sees assertiveness as "unfeminine," help her understand the importance of being able to stand up for her rights. It is imperative that she knows her own feelings are more important than what her date wants her to do, no matter what the circumstances.

4. Suggest that she pay her own way on dates, particularly if she is concerned about a young man's intentions.

This eliminates the young man's "I bought you dinner, you owe me something in return" argument.

5. Have her take a class in self-defense.

Even if she never has to use what she learns there, she will feel more confident in her dealings with anyone bigger or stronger than she is.

6. While she has every right to say no to anyone, any time, encourage her to play it safe, and give her strategies for doing this.

Explain, for example, that she may be going with her date to that hotel room just to talk, but he is likely to have other ideas, and since he can probably overpower her physically, what he says may very well go. Young women can be extremely naive, and this trait can do them great harm. Explain things to her before she finds herself in trouble. (After she is assaulted is, of course, no time to tell her what she did wrong. The victim is not to blame.)

Add any messages you'd like to give your daughter about relationships to "Your Plan."

chapter twenty-one

Sex and the Teenage Girl

One topic that probably raises more anxiety for the parents of teenage girls than any other subject is sex. The subject of sexuality and teens makes some people so anxious, in fact, that they avoid thinking about it at all, let alone talking with their daughters about it.

Yet in a world where song lyrics blurt out "Let's Grind," and "I Want to Sex You Up," it is naive to think you can insulate your daughter from sexual information and misinformation, curiosity, peer pressure, and her own desires. Like it or not, society has changed in this area, and so must your parenting strategies. Basically you have two choices here: get actively involved in your daughter's sex education—or let the media explain it all, rightly or wrongly.

It is often helpful to set aside for a minute your moral values and personal feelings on the subject of sexuality and think practically about the ways that your daughter's sexuality will influence both her teen years and the rest of her life. For now, your daughter needs to handle well the adolescent stresses of dating and sex, because her success will greatly influence how well she will choose both her life partner and her life work. To have the best chance in life, she needs to avoid becoming one of the shockingly large number of teens who become pregnant every year. Sexual activity could also lead to severe health problems, of which the cruelest is AIDS. More than ever, her sexual decisions require responsible actions and maturity. It's a

My daughter's beginning to bloom into a sexual being. The thought of sending her to a strict girls boarding school or a nunnery has crossed my mind more than once. I panic when I think of what's ahead of us.

—Mother of a 14-year-old girl

My mother handed me a book when I was thirteen years old. It gave a great biological description of the sexual act but nothing on the emotional rewards and personal responsibilities. That was the extent of my sex education from my parents, and in hindsight I feel cheated.

—Woman, 37

matter of life and death. The teen years, and indeed all the years of growing up, are also times when she is forming attitudes and feelings about her sexuality. The ways she comes to think about herself as a sexual being will influence her fulfillment and happiness throughout her adult life.

So there are two broad areas of concern for parents. The first is forming a plan for sharing necessary information and values with your daughter so that she can deal well with the stresses of dating and sex. This chapter will address the key issues surrounding your plan for her "sex education."

In the next chapter we will move into a more personal, intimate area—how you can help your daughter develop healthy, self-aware, self-empowered attitudes about her future sexuality as an adult.

Your values

At the beginning of the book, when you were first thinking about your daughter's self-esteem, you began by thinking about yourself—your beliefs, your philosophies, your childhood. In the same way, the place to start thinking about your approach to your daughter's sex education is by exploring your personal values and experiences. Answer the questions in "Your Sexual Values," pager 315–316.

The (a) statements of the sexual values survey reflect what our society has come to call the "traditional values system," one that was commonly held until about the last thirty to forty years. It may be difficult to raise a daughter with this set of values, given the overt messages teens receive from today's society.

The (b) statements reflect fairly conservative values in relation to today's sexual code. This value system gets little support from the greater society (media in particular), therefore strong intervention will be required by parents who want their daughter to grow up with these values.

The (c) statements present a more progressive mind-set, one that has more visible societal support. Passing on this code should be easier for you, if you agree with it.

The (d) statements represent an independent sexual code. If you marked (d) in the majority of instances, you believe sexual values should be governed by each person's conscience. This is not a license to neglect discussions of sexuality with your daughter. Passing on this moral code will actually require the most intervention on

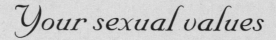

Your sexual values

These questions will help you articulate your values as you begin planning the ways you will talk with your daughter about sex.

Choose the statement below that best describes how you feel or act. Be as candid as you can. There are no right or wrong answers here. If none of the statements reflect your values, write your own statement by letter *e*.

My sexual values are:

    a. the same as my parents'; that area of my life probably mirrors theirs.

    b. similar to my parents'; yet in a few areas we differ.

    c. more contemporary than my parents'; in many ways we differ.

    d. very different from my parents'; I have created my own sexual code.

    e.

I believe

    a. sex outside of marriage is wrong.

    b. sex outside of marriage is acceptable for engaged couples only.

    c. sex outside of marriage is acceptable for committed couples.

    d. sex is acceptable for two consenting adults.

    e.

I believe

    a. couples should not live together outside of marriage.

    b. engaged couples may live together only in a trial situation.

    c. couples may live together in committed relationships.

    d. what other couples do is their concern alone.

    e.

When my daughter is an adult

    a. I believe she should not live with a man outside of marriage.

    b. I would accept her living with her fiancé as a trial relationship.

    c. I would accept her living with a man she loved and was committed to.

    d. I believe what she does with her life is her business, and I will accept and support her in all her decisions.

    e.

I will give my teenage daughter the following message:
  a. Any kind of sexual activity beyond kissing good night is wrong.
  b. Any kind of sexual activity beyond necking is wrong.
  c. Any kind of sexual activity is all right as long as it doesn't progress to sexual intercourse.
  d. If you are going to be sexually active, be sure to protect yourself.
  e.
I want my daughter
  a. to adopt my sexual values.
  b. to have sexual values similar to mine.
  c. to have sexual values that are acceptable to contemporary society.
  d. to follow her own sexual code.
  e.

your part as a parent. First, you will need to provide adequate sex information so your daughter can make informed and responsible decisions about her sexuality. Then, knowing you have done a good job, you will have to find the strength to step back and let her do what she thinks is best.

Travel back in time

Now that you've thought about your sexual values, let's explore your sexual past. What was sexual awakening like for you? Go back to your past, and you can better put yourself in your daughter's shoes. Your conversations will be better, and your thinking will be clearer.

What do you want to be different for your daughter?

Do you remember what it was like as a young adult exploring your sexual feelings and experiencing your first intimate relationships? Sit down in a quiet place, shut your eyes, and travel back to that time. "Your Sexual Awakening" (pages 317–319) can help you go back in time. (Look back at your answers after you read this chapter and the next, when you're putting together the whole picture for yourself and your daughter.) If you had a best friend in high school or college, one you shared almost everything with, call that person and reminisce.

Your sexual awakening

At what age did you first begin to "notice" the opposite sex?
What was the situation?

What were your feelings at the time?

When did you first want to date?
When were you first allowed to date?
If these ages are not the same, how did you feel about your parents' constraints?

At what age did you have your first "real" boyfriend or girlfriend?
What is your definition of "real"?
When did you first go "steady"?

What were your feelings at the time?

How old were you at the time of your first romantic kiss?
How did you feel about that experience?

At what age did you move beyond the kissing stage to petting?
Were you a virgin when you were married?
If not, how old were you when you lost your virginity?

If you had to make that choice again, would you do anything differently?
What?

How would you rate your sexual knowledge at the time you became sexually active?

Naive/Uninformed   Confident/Informed

Do you feel comfortable talking about sexual issues with your spouse? Yes   No
    your best friend? Yes   No
    your parent(s)? Yes   No
    your siblings or other relatives? Yes   No
    your counselor or religious guide? Yes   No
    your children? Yes   No
    others

Did you feel your parents were open to your questions or made it a point to educate you on sex and dating? Yes   No
Did you go to your parents for information on sex and/or dating? Yes   No

If you didn't go to your parents, where did you get most of your information on sex and dating?

Were you ever in conflict with your parents about your dating or romantic interests? If so, describe the situation. What were your feelings during this time?

Looking back as an adult, is there anything you wish your mother and/or father had talked to you about regarding sex that they didn't? What?

If you had to live that time of your life over again, how would you have liked your parents to handle sex and dating? What could they have done to make it a more positive experience?

If your daughter is being raised by two adults (natural parent or otherwise, living together or otherwise), be sure both partners in parenting take this survey. Compare your answers.

Where were your experiences the same?
Where were they different?
Why were they different?
In what areas might they have been different because of being female? Being male?

After you've looked at your own philosophies and your own past, you are ready to start formulating the approach you will take with your daughter. Look back at your personal inventory as you tackle the questions in "Your Approach" (on page 320).

Discussing sexual issues with your daughter

The best way to start discussing sex with your daughter is to begin when she is very young. In chapter 22, "Developing Healthy Sexual Attitudes," you will find many different ideas and activities that will help you formulate your plan.

If your daughter is a teen, it may be difficult to begin a dialogue on sex. She may want to avoid the topic for a variety of reasons (she thinks she knows it all by now, she doesn't feel comfortable with the topic, or whatever). She probably views her

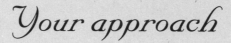

Your approach

YOUR PHILOSOPHIES

When it comes to dating and sex, do you want your daughter to grow up in the same way you did? Yes   No

In what areas do you want "things to be different" for your daughter?

Think about the societal changes since you were a child. Because of these changes, how will "things be different" for your daughter?

Have you and your daughter's other parent discussed your beliefs about how your daughter should be raised in relation to sex and dating? Yes   No

Do you and your daughter's other parent or guardian agree on how your daughter should be raised in this area of her life? Yes   No

If not, what are your plans for finding a middle ground on this important issue? Are you going to do more reading or seek the guidance of a counselor or religious professional?

mother as asexual (our society's standard for mothers), and even to consider the possibility of her mother as a sexual being may be very disturbing to her. If this is the case, take things slowly. Give her time to adjust, but be available for her. Spend more time together alone just talking, if you can. There are probably lots of things she'd like to tell or ask you, once she feels assured of your nonjudgmental support.

If your daughter is physically challenged, you may, like many people, tend to regard her as somehow asexual and, therefore, immune to the issues discussed in this chapter and the next. This is far from true. In fact, she is likely to be particularly sensitive about them, and extra attention is probably required on your part.

It should be acknowledged that a sizable number of young women are attracted to other females. If your daughter is among them, she is likely to suffer from most of the problems discussed here, as well as the additional stress caused by societal pressures, confusion, guilt, or lack of acceptance by peers or family. Most larger communities now have gay and lesbian help lines or special organizations designed to help homosexual adolescents get through this difficult time. Check your local phone book for listings under "Gay and Lesbian." You may want to provide your daughter with additional counseling. In many cases family counseling is in order.

Adolescence was a particularly difficult time for my daughter, a lesbian. She didn't discuss the matter with us at the time, but she did share with us a story she'd written, concerning a character who looked like everyone else, was expected to behave like everyone else, but knew inside that she was profoundly different. I can only imagine how painful and confusing it must have been for her.

—Mother of young adult lesbian

As you read through this chapter and the next, fill in "Your Plan for Discussing Sexual Issues with Your Daughter," on page 322. Write down when and how you will pass along important information as well as your feelings and philosophies about sex.

While your ideas may change as your daughter grows up and you can better evaluate her maturity level, it is helpful to review your feelings now so you can communicate them clearly to her before she becomes interested in boys. This will help assure that your expectations and hers are in line. Fewer conflicts will arise if everyone knows the rules ahead of time.

If your daughter is already an adolescent, complete the plan as if she were still an infant. Then, if you haven't already addressed these issues with her, set about the task of presenting them now. It's never too late, and it is so important to her future!

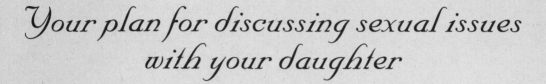

Your plan for discussing sexual issues with your daughter

At what age do you (or did you) begin your child's sex and dating education?
What topics do you want to address at which age?

Infant to two years old:

Three to five years old:

Six to eight years old:

Nine to eleven years old:

Twelve to fourteen years old:

Fifteen to eighteen years old:

At what age do you feel it is appropriate for your daughter to begin getting involved with boys?
    Attending boy/girl parties/dances? _____ years old
    Attending school dances as a couple? _____ years old
    Going on double dates unchaperoned? _____ years old
    Going on dates unchaperoned? _____ years old

Sex education

It is important in today's world that your daughter have a good understanding of the physical aspects of her sexual life. We can't do justice to these topics here, but there are many good books on the topic. Don't just hand her the book and look away in embarrassment, however, or leave it on the hall table and hope she picks it up. First read it yourself, then discuss it with your daughter as openly and honestly as you can, and *then* give her the book, along with some encouragement to come to you with any questions she may have.

It is essential to your daughter's safety and well-being that she thoroughly understand how her own body works, how the male body works, and what happens during sexual intercourse. Be your daughter's best source of information if you can.

Developing good medical habits

As soon as your daughter reaches puberty, allow her to choose her own gynecologist. Don't assume that she will want to go to yours. Their relationship, like any doctor/patient relationship, should be considered a private one. She and her doctor together will determine the best schedule of preventative examinations and regular checkups.

Before her first visit, tell her what types of services the gynecologist will provide for her at different stages of her life. If your clinic has an education department, see if they have pamphlets or other resources that can make your discussion more informative.

A key part of every sex-education plan—talking about AIDS

"Women either don't recognize the risk or they are not in a position where they can really enforce safe sex practices," Joseph Catania, an author of the largest national sexual survey since 1948, told reporters in 1992. He was referring to the survey's finding that 71 percent of women with sexual partners at high risk for AIDS say they do not use condoms.

In April of that same year Congress issued a report stating that the HIV virus is "spreading unchecked among the nation's adolescents, regardless of where they live or their economic status." They might have added that among young people, AIDS is striking more females than among any other group: while one out of nine victims is a woman among the general population in this country, one out of four thirteen- to twenty-four-year-old AIDS patients is female. Among fifteen- to twenty-four-year-olds, AIDS is the sixth leading cause of death. In its August 3, 1992, issue, *Newsweek* reported that "the ratio of female to male AIDS patients has doubled in the last four years, with females going from 17 percent of adolescent cases in 1987 to 39 percent of cases last year." In 1994 the Centers for Disease Control reported that the infection rate in women is increasing four times faster than that in men.

There seem to be four basic reasons teens get AIDS:

1. *They don't receive a proper education (permitted to be discriminating).*
2. *They don't believe it can happen to them (fantasy vs. reality).*
3. *They feel they'll be "rescued" (anxiety tolerance).*
4. *They don't know how to stand up to peer pressure and insist on abstinence or safe sex (assertiveness).*

Your daughter may receive AIDS education at school, but don't abdicate your responsibility for her education on this life-and-death topic. Give her the information she needs, as frankly and explicitly as you can. Many young people still believe that only gays or drug users are at risk for AIDS. Make sure she understands that this is far from true. Try not to frighten her or to be judgmental, and encourage her to ask questions—now and at any time in the future. If you don't know all the answers, make it a point to find out what they are.

As a rule, young people do believe that they are immortal, that nothing really bad can happen to them. Girls, especially, expect to be rescued. But if you have been diligent in helping your daughter develop a hardy personality, an honest discussion with you should be enough to help her separate fantasy from reality and realize that young women do get AIDS—often from young men who appear to be beyond reproach or suspicion—and that, so far, no one has been rescued from AIDS.

A young woman with a hardy personality should also be more adept at dealing with peer pressure, but again it's important for you to talk this through, perhaps even to do some role-playing, giving her an opportunity to practice being assertive.

Make sure that your position on sex and AIDS is clear and consistent.

Other sexually transmitted diseases

While the AIDS epidemic has increased awareness of the need to practice safe sex, other sexually transmitted diseases are seldom mentioned anymore. They should be. They're still around and are, in fact, flourishing. Your daughter is more likely to be infected with herpes or syphilis than she is with HIV, and while they can be cured or controlled, they can cause long-term health problems, especially if not detected immediately.

Be sure that knowledge of *all* sexually transmitted diseases is part of your daughter's sex education. She should know their names, how they are contracted, and what their symptoms are. Make sure, too, that she knows all the options for safe sex, including celibacy and/or waiting until she finds a committed (and tested) mate.

The other key part of every parent's sex-education plan—preventing teen pregnancy

One of every parent's greatest fears has always been teenage pregnancy. This is a legitimate concern for all parents because it knows no socioeconomic, ethnic, or religious boundaries. No one who is sexually active is immune.

The concern is so great because in today's world early parenthood has dire and long-lasting economic consequences. It hasn't always been this way. Throughout history, and still in many cultures today, females once mated or married shortly after puberty, the point when females are physically ready to become sexually active. After the Industrial Revolution, marriage and childbearing began to be delayed to allow workers time enough to acquire the skills or education now required for economic survival. Yet even as recently as the 1950s and 1960s, many couples married and started raising families right out of high school. Jobs were plentiful enough, cost of living low enough, and wages high enough so that even without vocational training, a young family could eventually aspire to a middle-class life-style. Many of these young couples started in minimum-wage jobs and eventually worked their way into a job that allowed them to purchase a home and establish a secure life-style.

But in today's technological era, education beyond high school is almost mandatory for individuals who want to compete successfully for jobs that support a family. Therefore, a female who bears a child before she has acquired marketable skills has financially handicapped herself and her baby, particularly if she is single or her mate is also young and uneducated.

In the United States today, each year more than a million teenage girls gets pregnant. See "The Numbers" box for other disturbing statistics on teen pregnancy.

Another difference today is that nearly 90 percent of teenagers giving birth keep their babies. In the 1950s and 1960s, if a teenager got pregnant and didn't get married, she quietly went off to visit Aunt Lucy across the country, had her baby, and returned home minus the baby, who had been put up for adoption. Because the stigma of being a single mother has lessened, teens keep their babies today—but often lose their futures.

The psychological and emotional costs for both the premature parent and her child are immeasurable. Most of these families will live much of their lives in poverty, with little hope of escaping its tragic consequences. Only half of those who

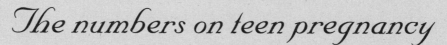

The numbers on teen pregnancy

- Each year more than a million teenage girls in the United States get pregnant. Of these, four out of five are unmarried. Thirty thousand are under fifteen.
- Five out of six of the pregnancies are unintentional.
- Forty percent end in abortion.
- Every sixty-seven seconds a teenager has a baby.
- One in six babies is born to a teenage mother.
- Forty percent of all young women will have been pregnant at least once by the time they turn twenty.

give birth before the age of eighteen complete high school, compared with 96 percent of the females who postpone childbearing. A person who drops out of high school because of parenthood will earn half as much money in her lifetime as a person who graduates.

The economic consequences are bad not only for the individual but for our society. Everyone foots the bill—taxpayers spend an estimated $8.6 billion a year on income support for families started by teens.

For the last decade our government, schools, nonprofit organizations, and churches have tried to find solutions to the critical issue of teenage parenting, but all have failed. In a 1989 survey of 4,241 teachers around the country, the Alan Guttmacher Institute reported that 93 percent said their schools offered sex or AIDS education in some form. With the majority of schools now providing sex education and the availability of contraception, the teenage birthrate should be on the decrease. But it is still increasing at an alarming rate. In 1987, 68.4 percent of the women between ages eighteen and twenty-four giving birth were unmarried.

Surveys show only 50 percent of sexually active teenage girls report using contraception at first intercourse. Given the risks and the consequences, why don't girls protect themselves?

And as a parent, what can you do to prevent your daughter from becoming a statistic?

One of the best teen pregnancy prevention strategies I use with my students is to bring in a panel of teen mothers to talk about their experiences. Although they love their children, they are candid about the difficulties and struggles. They are unanimous on one point: if they had it to do over again, they would not.

—High school home economics teacher

When I was seventeen, I was very much in love with my boyfriend, and I began to make noises about wanting to get married and have a baby. It all sounded so romantic and grown-up. I just loved babies. Well, my mother, wise woman that she was, somehow arranged for my older cousin to take a trip and then asked if I wanted to take care of her eighteen-month-old little boy for a week. I jumped at the chance. That was one of the longest weeks of my life. At the end of the week I was convinced that I was not ready to be a mother. I immediately went on the pill, signed up for junior college, and today at age thirty-three I have two lovely children, a devoted husband (different from the seventeen-year-old boyfriend), and a career I enjoy. Thanks, Mom, for being so strategic, because all the lecturing in the world would never have changed my mind. All it took was one active toddler.

—Woman, 33

There is little scientific evidence that sex education by itself makes any difference in the pregnancy rate. (But don't neglect the sex education, either—it's a necessary but not sufficient condition for preventing pregnancy.) However, studies show that there is a strong relationship between high career aspirations and the prevention of adolescent pregnancy. A girl who has goals for herself in a field of work and who sees herself working outside the home for a major portion of her adult life is much less likely to become a teen parent. In other words, developing your daughter's thinking and reasoning skills may be more important than sex education in preventing her from becoming pregnant.

Michael Resnick, a public health researcher at the University of Minnesota, and his research partner, Robert Blum, found that students who have the ability to project themselves into the future and understand how it will be affected by their actions today were far less likely to become teen parents. "Kids are ultimately capable of making decisions," Resnick wrote in his well-publicized report. "What's important is that they understand their own responsibility and the impact that decisions will have on their lives."

Does your daughter have the ability to visualize her own future? Does she understand what it means to raise a child? Does she have any notion of what it costs? Has she thought about what it would mean to raise a child and work at the same time?

As we pointed out in chapter 6, "Developing a Hardy Personality," many young people in our culture cannot think beyond next Saturday night. We are a society of instant gratification, from credit cards to fax machines. Do we plan for the

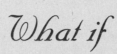

What if

Depending on your daughter's age, you can discuss a "What If" situation with her, act it out, make up a story about it, or simulate it in play.

Example: You have just read "Cinderella" to your four-year-old daughter. You ask, "Josie, *what if* Cinderella had not married the prince? What would her life have been like?" This discussion can lead in many directions. Your goal is to continue asking questions that keep your daughter thinking about Cinderella's future and understanding the possible consequences of each of her decisions.

Example: Your ten-year-old daughter announces she might want to be a politician when she grows up. You ask, "Cleo, *what if* you were president of the United States? What things would you hope to accomplish? What qualities should a good leader have? What kind of education should a politician have?"

Example: Your sixteen-year-old informs you that she is thinking of quitting school to get a job. You ask, "Stephanie, *what if* you do quit? What will your life be like in five years? In ten years?" Later ask, "*What if* you don't quit? How will your life be different?"

Pretty soon your daughter will begin asking "What if" of herself, without your prompting. This simple act will help her build a vision of her future, a very important skill for her lifelong success and for preventing unwanted pregnancies throughout her life.

future? A quick review of the average amounts people save for retirement shows graphically that we do not. How can we expect our children to be concerned about their future if it is not ingrained in the culture as a value?

Throughout this book you'll find strategies for helping your daughter make daily decisions based on future goals. These will help her prepare for a satisfying and self-sufficient life. During her adolescence they just may keep her from becoming a teen parent.

The United States has as much as seven times the teenage pregnancy rate of some European countries. The difference may be because we tend to stray beyond the practical issues when we talk to our children about contraception. A woman raised in Great Britain said, "The messages I received about sex while growing up were not clouded with the moralistic overtones I see in this country. The message was clear and simple. Don't get pregnant before you are ready to take care of a child because it could ruin your life."

The activity "What If" can help girls from age four to age twenty-four get in the habit of looking into the future and predicting the results of a particular action.

Be careful not to romanticize babies and motherhood. Your daughter will see enough of this on television, with the cooing model babies and serene mothers who look as if they just stepped out of the beauty parlor. This is not to say you want to downgrade motherhood, either. Just be sure to present it in a realistic light—the difficult times along with the joyous experiences.

Girls Incorporated's programs for preventing adolescent pregnancy are some of the most successful available. Based on a three-year research project, these programs help girls and young women build assertiveness, decision-making, and communication skills, and provide information on health services, responsible sexual behavior, and basic training in sexuality and life management. The comprehensive program has four parts:

Growing Together, for girls ages nine to eleven, is a series of parent-daughter workshops designed to increase positive communication about sexual information and values, helping to decrease adolescent pregnancy by delaying the onset of sexual activity.

Will Power/Won't Power, for girls ages twelve to fourteen, is an assertiveness training program that helps girls learn to say "no" while remaining popular with peers of both sexes.

Taking Care of Business, for girls ages fifteen to eighteen, is a structured program designed to increase teens' educational and career planning skills and to keep them motivated to avoid pregnancy.

Health Bridge, for girls ages twelve to eighteen, addresses the psychological and logistical obstacles many young people offer as reasons for not using contraceptives when they start having intercourse.

This program is available to community organizations. For more information, contact Girls Incorporated (see "Ordering Information," page 483).

What about birth control?

Your answer to this question will depend on your personal and religious beliefs, but if you do believe in using contraceptives, start discussing the matter of family planning early.

Mindy remembers her earliest experiences on the topic related to the family's numerous animals. She knew there was a time for them to breed because the topic was discussed openly by her parents. If they didn't want Susie, the family beagle, to have puppies, she had to be kept inside when she was in heat. Making sure she didn't escape was a responsibility shared by the children. While we don't advocate bringing unwanted animals into the world for the purpose of your daughter's education, you will probably have opportunities to share this kind of information with her. It's not too early to start even when she's a preschooler.

You might also comment, as Mindy's mother often did, that your children are "planned and loved." Hearing that message from the time she was very young made a huge impact on Mindy. She grew up determined that her children, too, would be planned.

Preventing pregnancy takes more than determination, however, and it is important that along with the sex education discussed earlier in this chapter you provide her with thorough information about the various methods of birth control—what they are, how they work, how reliable they are, and what risks they may entail. That way, when she decides to become sexually active, she will be able to make the best choice for herself and her circumstance.

With a good working knowledge of her menstrual cycle and how it relates to fertility and a thorough understanding of contraception, she will be better able to control her reproductive life.

However . . .

Encouraging abstinence

There is no failproof contraceptive. Be sure to make this information part of your daughter's sex education. If your own values include celibacy before marriage, and if you can provide a similar supportive community for your daughter, you have a fairly good chance of persuading her to follow this path. If she is surrounded by sexually active friends, though, or if the unmarried adults in her life have sexual relationships, she is unlikely to be convinced that abstinence is the answer for her.

Even so, it is the safest and, in most cases, the best course of action for teens. You can encourage it by promoting either fear or understanding. Fear may be effective, but it can have consequences for her future sexuality (see chapter 22). We recommend the other route—talking with your daughter, answering her questions, and withholding judgment. Discuss the fact that for most women sex is truly satisfying only when they feel secure within a committed relationship, when they trust and love their partner.

Even if your daughter is sexually experienced, help her understand that she is still free to say no, to take an extended break from sexual activity. It's been our experience that many young women, curious to find out what it's all about, willingly sacrifice their virginity. Once they've made this step, though, they can feel they have no right or no reason to abstain in any future relationship. This often leads to unhappy experiences, such as becoming deeply involved with an unsatisfactory partner.

The best way to make sure this doesn't happen to your daughter is to start discussing situations like this in her early teens, before she becomes sexually active. Give her opportunities to imagine herself in various situations and think through how she would react. Better yet, follow Girls Incorporated's Will Power/Won't Power model, and allow her to do some role-playing. This will help her feel secure about setting her own boundaries concerning sex—or anything else.

With luck and attention your daughter may have the type of hardy personality displayed by a young woman we know whose boundaries were strong enough to allow her to use the "three-month rule of thumb" while she was growing up: she insisted that a young man be exclusively attentive to her and treat her the way she wanted to be treated for three months before she would allow any physical intimacy beyond a good-night kiss. This made her much more discriminating about the young men she became involved with.

If your daughter gets pregnant

If your daughter does become pregnant, this is not the time to blame her, yourself, or your partner. Your main concern should be her welfare. She needs your support. If you feel professional counseling is needed, get it immediately.

While in the ladies' lounge of a major hotel a few years ago, Mindy overheard a telephone conversation between a teenage girl who looked approximately seventeen years old and her mother. The young woman had just found out she was pregnant and called her mother. Her mother had obviously told her what she must do. Mindy could tell from the one-sided conversation that if the girl did not comply, she was banished from her family. She listened as the frightened girl pleaded with her mother, sobbing into the phone and beseeching her over and over to let her make her own decision. Mindy has always wondered what terrible pain both the young woman and her mother have since suffered because of that afternoon's conversation.

Your concern should be for her emotional and physical well-being, not your moral code. It is encouraging that our society has evolved to a point that young people are no longer pushed into loveless marriages for the sake of appearances. Yet at the same time single parenting is not an ideal situation for the woman or for the child. Therefore it is important that your daughter manage her pregnancy and make hard choices with as much data and information as possible. This is not the time for her to take a passive role in making decisions.

The most important question to ask is "What do you want to do?" and then support your daughter in her choice. As she works out what she wants to do, continue only to ask questions *so her solutions are her own.* If you don't feel competent in doing this, seek professional help from trained counselors who are experienced in working with pregnant adolescent girls.

If your single daughter decides that she wants to keep the baby and raise it herself (over 90 percent of teens giving birth today make this choice), seek outside counsel (professional, favorite aunt, older sister) who will gently present the economic, physical, and emotional realities of this decision. If you know a single mother of a toddler, your daughter might agree to have a candid discussion with her.

Your local Planned Parenthood, Family Service agency, Catholic Charities, or other community service agency could be of help during this time. Call your daughter's school counselor, United Way, or your community information service for an appropriate referral.

Children raising children creates many problems in our society, from illiteracy to violence. It is a societal shame we cannot ignore and a reality we cannot afford to perpetuate. Yet to blame the young mothers is to ignore the fact that we have probably set them up by raising them in a way that does not recognize female sexuality and does not promote sexual parity and responsibility for women or men. Read on.

If you'd like to add some messages about sexuality, relationships, or family planning to "Your Plan," now's a good time to do so.

chapter twenty-two

Developing Healthy Sexual Attitudes

Throughout her years of growing up, and especially in the teen years, your daughter forms ideas about her sexuality that will influence her happiness and fulfillment for the rest of her life. As a parent there is much that you can do to help her develop healthy, self-aware, self-empowered attitudes for her sexual future.

The topic of sex is entangled with other ethically and politically charged issues: AIDS, pro-choice/anti-abortion debates, and the alarming rise in teenage pregnancy. Many people within the media, government, and religious agencies are pointing a finger at the "promiscuous 1970s and 1980s" and saying, "See, if we would have controlled ourselves in these times, we wouldn't be suffering today."

As authors and women we find it difficult to give this controversial subject the attention it deserves in a book meant for all parents. One of our fervent hopes as we began this book was that it would speak to all parents, no matter what their ideology. But as we delved further into our research on girls, teenage women, and young adults, it became apparent to us that failure to deal with the subject of sexuality in a direct and, for some, controversial manner would mean that "things would not be different" for most of our daughters. To think that economic independence is all it takes to build a satisfying and happy life, that financial, professional, and personal success would guarantee high self-esteem, is naive and perhaps even cruel. In chapter 21 we gave you the basics; now we want to address more intimate matters. If you are comfortable with what we have said so far, with the thought and care we have put in our guidance and support, read on.

If your value system views sex primarily as a procreative issue or does not believe women have a right to sexual satisfaction or a sexuality that should be nurtured, then you may choose to skip this chapter. It will not affect your understanding or appreciation of the balance of the book. Because this is such a sensitive subject, we don't want to offend those of you who don't share our views.

We knew from the beginning that we would have to deal with the topic somewhere in this book, but for a long time, we avoided it—just the way many parents do—and all but hoped it would go away. As we got deeper into the research, though, the issue of female sexuality began to "leap off the pages" as an important area requiring serious attention.

Human beings have basic needs, which include the need to survive, the need to develop a sense of self in relation to the world, the need to work at something productive, and the need to love. We have addressed the issues of economic survival, emotional development, and the ability to take control of life through the development of high self-esteem and a hardy personality. We would be remiss if we didn't give the same attention to the issues of love and sexuality, which are an important part of your daughter's identity search.

As a parent you will have a great impact on your daughter's ability to feel comfortable with who she is, to enjoy sex as an adult woman.

Oh, you're writing a book entitled Things Will Be Different for My Daughter? I know exactly what I want to be different for my daughter. I want my daughter to enjoy sex. I want her to grow up more open to her sexuality and less burdened with the messages I received when I was growing up. It has taken me years to move beyond those messages, and I have been very lonely because of it.

—*Divorced woman, 43, with daughter, 16*
(First interview for this book)

Sexuality (female) is a social construct mixing sensuality, reproductive life, eroticism, and gender-role performance, diffused throughout all social and personal life in activities, feelings, and attitudes.

—*Women's Studies Encyclopedia, volume 1*
Helen Tierney, editor

A female definition

It is difficult to define sexuality for women because each female has her own opinion, based upon her own experiences. She is influenced by the surrounding culture, by her family and especially her parents, and by her personal experiences. How a female is introduced to the notion of herself as a sexual being and what she experiences in her sexual moments (from earliest childhood self-exploration to her first adult sexual contacts) will affect her potential for developing a satisfying adult sexual identity.

The influences of a positive, satisfying adult sexual identity go far beyond the marriage bed. According to Leonore Tiefer, writing in the *Women's Studies Encyclopedia*, studies show that "sexual freedom and satisfaction for women are intimately connected to women's self-respect, self-knowledge, and the sense of having options in life, which are in turn directly related to women's socioeconomic opportunities."

How do you define sexuality?

What comes to mind when you hear the following term? Write your explanation below.

Female sexuality:

Male sexuality:

Which definition was easier to write? As you defined them, how are female and male sexuality different? How are they the same?

Physical differences in sexuality for men and women

It is widely accepted that men and women view sex differently. Until recently, however, sexuality has been defined almost exclusively in male terms. In the last few years more scholarly and popular attention has been drawn to female sexuality. Today the barriers to female sexual satisfaction are beginning to fall. From medical research and sociological studies we now know the following:

We all know that love leads to sex for girls and sex leads to love for men.
—*Overheard conversation of two late-adolescent girls*

1. *The clitoris is the center of pleasure for a woman, not the vagina.*
2. *Women place an emphasis on the emotional and physical closeness that comes with being sexual. Tenderness and loveplay (sometimes known as "foreplay," as if it were only a prelude to the main event) are important aspects of the female sexual experience.*
3. *A female's sexual identity, like a male's sexual identity, starts forming in the first years of life.*
4. *Masturbation provides the same opportunities for women as for men. It helps the budding adult learn how to experience orgasm in a safe, nonjudgmental way.*
5. *Reliable birth control has freed women to experience their sexuality without the fear of pregnancy.*
6. *Erotica is as valuable for the female sexual experience as it is for the male, although males and females are stimulated by different material.*
7. *A woman frequently reaches her sexual prime later than a man for two reasons:*
   • *She has less knowledge about her body and its sexual functioning.*
   • *Little attention has been paid to her sexual pleasure.*

Couple this with the negative messages described later in this chapter, and it is little wonder that some women never experience orgasm.

Where our attitudes about women's sexuality come from

Around the turn of the century, the Victorians believed that sexual desire or pleasure was inappropriate for all women, before and after marriage. Sexual intercourse was only for procreation. Young girls were raised to be passive observers of the courtship process and, once married, to never show desire lest they "lose control." While a woman was expected to submit to her husband, she wasn't supposed to enjoy it. "Close your eyes and think of England" was the motto of the day. Demure, coy, and, yes, prudish women were seen as paragons of virtue—totally asexual paragons, of course. Though these standards were often flaunted by "bohemians," it wasn't until the late 1930s and early 1940s that mainstream society began to challenge Victorian values.

In some ways the Victorians are still with us. Because most of us took on the sexual mores of our parents, who learned it from their parents, and so on, and because these ideas are deeply ingrained, it can take generations to make significant changes in our beliefs.

Our mothers were born and raised in the 1920s, 1930s, and early 1940s. We learned from our mothers' attitudes about sexuality as we grew up in the 1950s, 1960s, and 1970s. Think back to your own childhood. What messages did you receive from your family? Do the "Messages in My Childhood" checklist.

If you remember hearing many of the statements in the checklist, the Victorian era had an impact on your upbringing and therefore can affect the way you raise your daughter. But you've also been affected by the social and cultural changes of the past twenty years. Today's parents grew up in the 1960s, 1970s, and 1980s during the sexual revolution, yet were raised by a mother who received and probably passed on a Victorian code. Little wonder so many of us are confused. Will we pass this confusion on to our daughters? Probably.

It is no coincidence that the women's movement and the sexual revolution started at about the same time. As women became more vocal and assertive in their demands for economic, political, and social equality, they also sought sexual freedom. It was a time of experimentation and of attempting to break the moral codes that recognized male sexuality but refused to acknowledge female sexuality.

The pendulum is swinging back. During the sexual experi-

The pendulum always swings far to the left and then far to the right before settling back in the middle.

—Folk saying

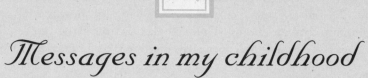

Messages in my childhood

Place an "M" in front of any message you received in some form from an important male in your life (father, grandfather, uncle, and so on). Place an "F" in front of any message received from an important female (mother, grandmother, aunt, and so on). This is not necessarily what you believe, but what your family believed.

If you are a female, did you receive any of these messages?
_____A nice girl doesn't call boys. She waits to be called.
_____Nice girls don't use those sexually explicit words.
_____Nice girls never show overt interest in boys.
_____Nice girls don't do that (as your hand was taken away from your genitals).
_____Your virginity is your greatest asset.
_____That's dirty (relating to a part of your body), don't touch it.
_____Playing hard to get is the way to attract a man.
_____Don't look too strong or competent. That is a man's role.

List below any other messages you received that might have an impact your sexuality. Note where those messages came from.

What year was the woman who raised you born? _____

What year was the man who raised you born? _____

If you are a male, do you remember receiving any of these messages? From a male or female?
_____A nice girl doesn't call boys. She waits to be called.
_____Nice girls don't use those sexually explicit words.
_____Males do the chasing; females wait to be chosen.
_____It is the male's job to awaken his wife sexually.
_____It is best to marry a virgin.

List other messages you received about women below. Note where those messages came from.

What year was the woman who raised you born? _____

What year was the man who raised you born? _____

mentation of the 1970s and early 1980s, many people believed that true sexual growth could not happen in a monogamous relationship. During this time countless numbers of women felt coerced into casual sex and were not comfortable with the new attitudes. Casual sex was not satisfying for most women, who felt a need fo committed relationships. The outbreak of the AIDS epidemic made one-night stands less desirable and downright dangerous for just about everyone. Promiscuity is out, commitment is back in.

And although women have come a long way in the last twenty years toward attaining economic and political equality, the same cannot be said about their freedom to value a female-defined sexuality. Today our society accepts the fact that a woman can climb a telephone pole, replace a kidney, pilot a 747, or run a country, but the collective consciousness is not yet comfortable with a woman who is a responsible and aggressive participant in her own sex life.

We may be able to change our attitudes quickly, perhaps simply by reading an article or a book or by having a conversation. It takes somewhat longer to change behavior. With concerted effort, behaviors will change to reflect the new attitudes. To change how we feel about something, however, especially something as important as sex, will take energy and work. The messages we received as children are fixed deeply in our psyches. If, after reading this chapter, you are convinced you want "things to be different" for your daughter, you will need to develop a plan and make a conscious effort to give her the precious gift of her sexuality, because you may be going against all your deepest feelings and conditioning.

A child develops her moral code in early childhood. The earlier you make the commitment to promote your daughter's joyful and responsible sexuality as a value in her moral code, the more ingrained these attitudes will be in her psyche. The more ingrained these attitudes are in her psyche, the more satisfying your daughter's adult sexual life will be. The more satisfying your daughter's sexual life, the more likely it is that she will develop a satisfying intimate adult partnership. And because relationships are important to most, if your daughter is successful in this area of her life, she has a greater probability of maintaining high self-esteem.

Please don't mistake this to mean that to have a satisfying life you must have a satisfying sexual life. Your support of your daughter's developing sexuality will allow her more life choices. Then, if having a satisfying sexual life is a high priority for her, if it is something she desires and wants, she will not have to try to erase any harmful messages from her past.

The old double standard

Your daughter is growing up in a hypocritical society. Sexuality is used to promote everything from toothpaste to automobiles. Everywhere she turns, from print advertisements, television commercials, and billboards to music, talk shows, and best-selling books, sexual messages are blaring at her. Yet there are troubling contradictions. Our patriarchal society views females as sexual objects, then tries to protect them from their sexual feelings by the denial of them.

Explore your feelings more in "How Do You Feel About . . ."

How do you feel about . . .

As you read through this list of questions, quickly jot down the first thing that comes to your mind. Do not read through the list of questions first; do not spend time thinking about your response.

How would you feel if you found your teenage son in bed with his girlfriend? What would you do?

If your unmarried teenage son got his girlfriend pregnant, how would you feel and what would you do?

Is masturbation a normal part of growing up for young men?

How would you feel if you found your teenage daughter in bed with her boyfriend? What would you do?

If your unmarried teenage daughter got pregnant, how would you feel and what would you do?

Is masturbation a normal part of growing up for young women?

Review your responses. Do you have a different standard for males than for females? How prevalent do you think the sexual double standard is today? Are teenagers, for instance, still more critical of promiscuous girls than promiscuous boys? (Susan reports hearing junior high school girls called "sluts" by their peers for the clothes they wore.) Could this have an impact on a girl's self-esteem?

The double standard is just one way girls are discriminated against when it comes to sexuality. It's difficult as a parent to think about challenging the attitudes and customs of a whole society that practices hypocrisy and the double standard. We don't expect you to challenge our entire culture single-handed, but throughout this book and particularly in chapter 27, "Advocacy for Girls," we will offer some ideas for becoming an advocate for your daughter and all girls growing up today.

There are things, however, that only you can do to teach your daughter: how to feel comfortable with her body and in control of her body and her sexuality. At home you can combat and defuse the negative messages she will receive in the greater society—using example, language, and empathy.

There are five messages that can split a girl from her sexuality, all extensions of "double standard" thinking that pits woman against woman, woman against herself. We will discuss each one and offer suggestions on what we can do to change it. The messages that limit a female's enjoyment of her body and sexuality are

the nice girl/bad girl split
the little girl syndrome
the dirty body image
confusing love and lust
the red light/green light game

The nice girl / bad girl split

Although it's seldom acknowledged, by and large our society still believes that the less sexual the woman, the nicer she is.

No, you say—not in this day and age! Consider some of the recent top-grossing movies: *Fatal Attraction, Basic Instinct, The Hand That Rocks the Cradle.* The female villains are driven by what appears to be insatiable sexual drives (a very primal fear indeed). They are not nice women. In movies like *The Good Mother,* a woman is forced to give up her child when she begins exploring her sexuality.

"A lady in the drawing room and a whore in the bedroom": most men in their forties, fifties, and sixties will nod in acknowledgment or grin when this locker room phrase is presented as the ideal woman. Yet they are ambivalent about the concept of the sexually open woman. When asked if this is the kind of woman they want to marry, many will gasp, shuffle their feet, and mutter something like "I want to marry a woman just like the woman who married dear old dad."

How are these attitudes changing for young men today? Nancy Friday reports in her 1991 book *Women on Top* that the number of men surveyed who report that marrying a virgin was important to them had stayed at a consistent 25 percent since she started taking her surveys in the early 1970s.

The message was that it's "bad" even to think about having sex. No wonder young women are reluctant to carry contraceptives—being prepared proves that they aren't "nice."

As a parent you can help your daughter get beyond the nice girl/bad girl split. First, change your language. Where you may have been tempted to use the words *nice* girl or *good* girl or woman, use the term *responsible* girl or woman.

Insist on having the same standards and rules of behavior for everyone in the family. If you wouldn't expect your son to "be nice" and jump up from the dinner table to wait on others, don't ask your daughter to do it, either.

Encourage your daughter to be discriminating in her relationships, beginning when she is very young. If she comes home and tells you she doesn't like Joanie anymore, help her explore these feelings by asking questions (not making judgments) about the other child rather than encouraging the Pollyanna posture. Don't insist that she be nice to everyone—some people are not worth being nice to—and don't insist that she be nice all the time. Encourage her to experience a wide range

> I know I should have used contraception. My gosh, I have had extensive sex education in school. I knew the risks. I even knew the dangerous times of the month. But I kept thinking if I acted prepared, I would be admitting that I wanted sex, and nice girls don't do that.
>
> —*Pregnant honors student, 17*

> I remember going to see the film *A Man and a Woman* with my boyfriend. There's this scene where the man and woman get into bed together, but the woman decides she can't go through with it, the memory of her dead husband is still too strong for her. So she gets up and goes into the bathroom to wash her face. At that point, my boyfriend leaned over and whispered to me, "I thought she was pretty before, but now she looks like a whore."
>
> —*Woman, 41*

of emotions, including anger and distrust, and encourage her to use her perceptions in choosing friends to spend time with.

You can also show her the example of yourself as a person who is sexual and also "good." Do not hide the sexual side of your personality from your daughter. This does not mean she needs to hear about or observe your private moments. She does not want to know the details of your sex life, any more than you want to know the details of hers. She'll be more comfortable with the topic, though, if she has seen her parents be affectionate and loving toward each other in gestures as well as in words.

If you are a single parent, you can still convey a sense of sensuality by the way you talk about and appreciate the opposite sex and by the way you articulate your feelings about all things sexual.

I was fourteen when I became sexually active. My boyfriend was nineteen. I'm surprised I didn't get pregnant, because we didn't use any contraceptives until he brought it up. I just assumed he knew what he was doing. I looked to him to teach me. Isn't that the responsibility of the man? Aren't they supposed to take care of us?

—*Honors student, 18*

Nowhere do we women act more like little girls than in our refusal to protect ourselves contraceptively.

—*Nancy Friday, Women on Top*

The little girl syndrome

You can see the little girl syndrome in the fashions promoted by top designers, in our society's obsession with youth, even among sixty-year-old women who refer to each other as "girls." While this may be innocent on the surface, it affects the way women think and feel about themselves.

Sexually the little girl posture means that women have been raised to view sex as the responsibility of the male. It is assumed that the man is supposed to bring the woman to life, make her a woman, and ignite her sexual fuse so this untapped energy can flow. It is also assumed by many females that the male will protect them. This may be a wonderful fantasy, but it is very far from reality. And believing it gets women into trouble. Only half of sexually active teen women surveyed reported contraceptive use at first intercourse. And when couples get pregnant, usually only the woman is blamed.

When a young woman maintains this little girl posture, she risks the possibility that little attention will be paid to her sexual satisfaction or pleasure. An inexperienced male knows little about pleasing women. If the female abdicates her role as an equal partner in the sexual act and waits for the male to discover what pleases her, both participants may become frustrated.

For many adults, good sex is playful, and we can use our childlike selves to enjoy sexual pleasure. Childlike openness, however, is very different from childish irresponsibility.

Many men are attracted to women who appear helpless. Perhaps this satisfies their need to protect. One study, for example, found that the more distressed teenage females appeared while watching a horror film, the more attractive the adolescent males found them. This is the result of cultural conditioning, however, and once males recognize the rewards of having relationships with females who are more responsible and mature, and less "little girlish" in all areas of their lives, including the sexual areas, this preference can change.

What's a parent to do? Don't perpetuate the "little girl" syndrome beyond the appropriate age. When your daughter begins to state emphatically that she is a "big girl," agree with her. (You don't necessarily have to agree to the course of action she wants to take when she tells you this, however.)

Dads, stop calling her "Daddy's little girl" about this time. She's not even Daddy's big girl. She is her own person, and it is vital to support this in every way. By perpetuating the limiting "Daddy's girl" image, you are implying she is owned by someone other than herself. By the same token, when she makes a good decision, don't tell her you are "proud," tell her you are impressed. Pride in her implies that she is an extension of you.

If you let her grow up and encourage and celebrate her independence and maturity, she will be less apt to fall into the trap of seeing herself as a child. She will take charge of her life, and that's the most important step to high self-esteem.

The dirty body image

Girls who are taught at a young age that their genitals are disgusting and nasty will become women who cannot enjoy the pleasures of adult genital sexuality with a partner. Furthermore, because they will feel detached from their sexual functioning, they will fail to take responsibility for it, which can lead to unwanted pregnancy as well as life-threatening sexually transmitted disease.

Perhaps these feelings started when she was a baby, when her mother took her hand away from her genitals and she saw the shocked look on her mother's face or heard the reprimand. Mother was all-knowing, and the child was driven to please her.

Toilet training is another critical time. When a parent approaches the subject with revulsion and tells a child that these parts of her body are "dirty," the lessons will be difficult to unlearn.

Good feelings about her body, and especially her genitals and sexuality, start early. While a boy learns the name of his penis at an early age, girls learn much later the names of their vulva and vagina, and usually the clitoris goes unmentioned, as if it doesn't exist. Parents who turn to children's books for assistance will usually find pictures of the reproductive organs—uterus, ovaries, and fallopian tubes—without complete representation of all the female genitals. A child who can name and explore her genitals with comfort at an early age is comfortable with herself as a sexual person. (Of course you can explain that genital exploration takes place in private.)

As a little girl I was taught never to touch "down there." Except for cleaning myself after using the toilet, I would have died before I dared touch "it." I was led to believe it was dirty and disgusting. I never relaxed about that area of my body, even after marriage. Intellectually I knew I should enjoy sex, but I just didn't. Today I'm divorced, and I can't help but think my attitude about sex had a lot to do with my failed marriage.

—*Woman, 35*

Upon viewing a mother nursing her infant on a park bench while in a conversation with another mother, a seventeen-year-old girl said, "Mom, you didn't do that in public with me when I was a baby, did you?" This is a sad commentary on how the sexual parts of the anatomy are viewed by our society. Even something as beautiful and natural as nursing a baby can create anxiety in a young woman.

With the onset of menstruation, your daughter faces another turning point. Becoming a woman should be an exciting stage in her life. In many cultures it is celebrated. In ours it is either ignored or looked upon as a curse or a shame. For the young woman who already views her female parts negatively, to bleed and be inconvenienced is one more reason to feel betrayed for being a woman.

So she begins to hope that no one notices these changes coming over her. Menstruation is not a subject discussed in polite society. Terrible cramps are endured because she can't bring herself to tell the teacher, and she suffers tremendous anxiety on the days when she might bleed through and spot her clothes.

Every child must learn to use the toilet and must also learn that there are certain things one does in private. In teaching these lessons, however, parents often pass on the message that there is something shameful about the activities and/or the parts of the body involved. This is usually effective in helping the child avoid social embarrassment, but it can have serious consequences for her emotional and private life.

The issue, really, is privacy, and privacy can and should be taught.

How can women think well of themselves, have high self-esteem, if they think parts of their bodies are dirty and repulsive? Men take pride in their genitals—encourage your daughter to do the same. Start early.

If you received the message that part of your body was untouchable, try to give a different message to your daughter. Don't react to the natural exploration of

My first period happened to start as I was getting ready for the weekly dance class I loved. My mother said I should skip class that night—saying something about how some girls bleed a lot at first. I remember thinking that this process of becoming a woman was going to cut into the things I liked to do. And I remember being a little scared of all that "gushing" that was supposed to start happening right away.

—*Woman, 36*

her body when she is small by taking her hand away, grimacing, or making a negative statement.

When she begins to get verbally curious about her genitals, explain them in a matter-of-fact fashion. She will probably be a preschooler when she starts asking questions and when you think she can understand simple answers. Tell her how unique women's bodies are and how the different parts function to provide pleasure and produce children. When she is little she will be receptive to these lessons. She has not yet learned to be ashamed of any part of her body.

Show her pictures in books depicting the different parts of her anatomy as her curiosity peaks. Use the anatomical names for her vagina, vulva, and clitoris. Explain the function of each.

Educate yourself on the sexual anatomy and physiology of the sexual response so you can give your daughter factual information as she grows. Look for appropriate books so when the time comes you can talk with her and then give her additional reading material.

Make puberty a time for celebration. In private, notice your daughter's budding sexuality and congratulate her on it. Share with her your memories of good feelings about growing up. You'll probably laugh together about your stories and how things are different for girls today. These stories are important because they will help her realize that other messages she may continue to get from society are "prehistoric" and not to be taken seriously.

When her period finally begins, make it a celebration and announce that she is taking another step toward becoming a woman. Don't make her hide this from the males in your family. Your sons will probably marry someday, and they should be knowledgeable and understanding about what's going on and not view it with contempt or disgust.

The father of a thirteen-year-old girl said, "We planted a tree in the backyard and had a ceremony to commemorate this important event in our daughter's life. I remembered reading that ancient tribes planted a tree over the placenta after the birth of a baby, and we thought it would be a fitting symbol." Another father, of a twelve-year-old, said, "I sent flowers to my daughter when I found out she had started her first period. I wanted to celebrate her womanliness." Close family friends may want to express their congratulations, too. A forty-three-year-old businesswoman said, "I remember the surprise and delight in the face of my friend's daughter when I congratulated her on getting her first period. I wish someone had congratulated me!"

Young women often feel frightened, confused, panicky, or ill at their first menstruation. To make things easier for your daughter, be sure she has enough information before her period starts. Today young women are more likely to learn about menstruation at school than from their parents. The clinical approach necessary in a sex education class doesn't do justice to the emotional side of menstruation or sexual activity. Get the jump on the school and make this a family responsibility.

Don't make snide remarks about the attitude of your daughter around the time of her period. And don't allow anyone else in the family to make derogatory remarks about it. It is not a time to tease or generalize.

If you teach your daughter to love her body, she will be more likely to put in a diaphragm or insist that her partner use a condom. The price for unprotected sex used to be pregnancy—traumatic, but not the end of life. Today, because of the AIDS epidemic, it may be a matter of life and death for your daughter.

Confusing love and lust

Another thing your daughter needs to do is learn to separate love from sexual feelings.

Gasp! Who would ever want to do that? you say. What would be the purpose?

Males learn to separate love and sexual feelings as adolescents. It starts with the comfort and knowledge they have about their bodies. From the time they are little boys, they learn to touch their penis, even if only to urinate. As they enter adolescence, masturbation is an accepted part of their growth process.

Later, when young men become sexually involved with females, they understand the ways their bodies react to the sexual stimuli. They have experienced these feelings when they masturbate, so they are comfortable with them. Because they know what causes sexual feelings, they are less likely to get sexual feelings mixed up with feelings of love.

Therefore they are not as likely to get involved in a long-term relationship that does not meet their intellectual, emotional, or spiritual needs. Only time will tell whether a relationship is an enduring and committed love—time to get to know the other person, to match their values, and to develop mutual respect. Boys are not as likely to let the rush of lust get confused with love. Perhaps this is why males are more comfortable, at least during the courting stage, with short-term relationships.

Not so for girls. The first rush of sexual feelings can be very confusing for them. Usually they are mistaken for love.

This confusion can lead to getting involved before she is ready or getting involved with the wrong young man. If girls were more experienced at recognizing the physiological responses of their bodies to sexual stimuli, they would be better judges of potential sexual partners and they might not rush into premature sexual activity or commitment.

Some parents fear that their daughters will become promiscuous if they are "awakened" sexually before they connect with their mates. Or that their capacity for multiple orgasms will make them sexually insatiable.

Unlikely. Most females still value monogamy and commitment over pleasure and adventure. The relational experience still seems to be the priority for women

> *With each of my sons, I knew when this time started. All of a sudden they wanted privacy. The bedroom door was kept shut and locked. My husband and I would wink at each other each time one progressed to this stage. It was a rite of passage that we accepted and even felt good about.*
>
> —*Mother of four young adult sons*

> *I'm so confused. There's this boy who really is trying to get involved with me. For weeks he has been calling and seeing me after class. We really don't have that much in common. But the other night at a party I finally gave in and we necked. It was wonderful. Is it love?*
>
> —*Virgin, 17*

over the physical experience. They will discover that their most satisfying sexual experiences occur in a relationship with someone they love and respect who loves and respects them in turn.

Some people consider masturbation to be sinful or unhealthy. Medically speaking, the American Medical Association defined it as normal in 1972. If it conflicts with your religious beliefs, ask your religious adviser to explain the church's reasoning, or do more reading on your own.

As a parent, what can you do to help? You can't teach your child to masturbate. That is something the child will discover for herself, in private, if allowed to explore her body. What you can do is not interfere when your young child is exploring, not get visibly upset if you discover her masturbating, and not condemn the act if it is brought up in conversation. Make sure your child has the privacy she needs when she enters puberty.

If your daughter understands the difference between sexual feelings and love, she may not feel compelled to act on her sexual feelings when these unknown and exciting sensations are first experienced. This is something you can discuss openly with her—physical pleasure is wonderful, but it isn't the same as love.

Teach your daughter that her body belongs to her alone. She is responsible for it, and she must give permission for and be an active participant in any activity that involves her body.

The red light / green light game

The failure to enjoy sex or be orgasmic as women is believed to be the result of repression of sexuality in girlhood.

We think that if we limit our daughters' exposure to sexuality and sexual feelings, we are protecting them from promiscuity and its consequences. So the message that sex is bad and off limits before marriage is deeply ingrained in many young women's minds.

When and if they do experiment with sex (which most do at some level before they are married), they feel a great deal of shame. Or they associate sexual excitement with something dirty, something forbidden. This is not conducive to a healthy sexual attitude. To become sexually alive, it is important to come to the experience with enthusiasm. If a woman's first experiences are negative, she may face a life of less than optimum pleasure.

To think that passion can be turned on and off like a light switch on the wedding night is unrealistic. Most young men are not the patient teachers portrayed in novels. And unless a woman knows what pleases her, she will never have the experience of complete passion. The woman must teach the man where to touch and how to please her; likewise, her partner can teach her what pleases him.

To many parents, though, there is something safe in encouraging their daughter not to become sexually active before her wedding night or at least until she has established a committed relationship. After all, the best way to prevent AIDS or any other sexual disease is to remain celibate until making a lifelong commitment to another person who is also a virgin.

But given that most young people do experiment, what's a parent to do? First, don't use negative statements about sex to convince your daughter to postpone sexual activity. Speak about it with the reverence that will lead to a healthy respect.

Looking back, I realize it was all very confusing. As a young woman I remember being told sex was off limits and given the impression it was something bad and disgusting. I'm sure this was done to keep me from experimenting. Yet on my wedding night I was suddenly supposed to think it was the most wonderful thing in the world. It took years of personal exploration and therapy to become a fully functioning sexual human being.

—Woman, 38

Reevaluate the messages you received from your parents about sex. Be particularly vigilant if those messages included the concept of sex as taboo or bad. Become comfortable in talking about sex. If you really aren't comfortable, however, admit it. Tell her your mother didn't tell you much and that you don't know how to talk comfortably about it, but that you will talk with her in the best way you can so she can have an experience different from yours. If your young daughter even senses that the topic is taboo—for instance, if you change the subject when the topic is raised, it will have an impact on her attitudes.

Reevaluate your own sexual history. If you are angry because it hasn't been satisfying, you haven't found a compatible partner, your upbringing was too restricted, or whatever, get some help and try to overcome your disappointment. Talk to a trained professional or become a student and read up on the topic. Your anger or dissatisfaction will spill over into your relationship with your daughter when you speak about sex. She will pick up the cues no matter how hard you try to hide them and receive the message that sex is bad or unpleasant.

If we help our daughters value their bodies, love themselves, and understand

352 WHAT'S A PARENT TO DO?

and learn about all their feelings, sexual as well as romantic, they will be much more likely to make the best choices for themselves and not feel pressured into an act or relationship they do not want or are not ready for.

Sexuality and the hardy personality

Allowing and encouraging the development of your daughter's sexuality should not lead to a promiscuous life-style if, along the way, you have also nurtured her self-esteem and encouraged her to develop a hardy personality. Because if you help your daughter

- *establish her identity* . . . it is not likely she will give herself up to the person she becomes intimate with.
- *learn to be discriminating* . . . she will probably be careful to choose a partner who matches her values, personality, and expectations.
- *learn to set boundaries* . . . she will set her own limits and not feel compelled to rush into sexual activity.
- *learn to be assertive* . . . she will feel comfortable saying "no" to sexual advances she is not ready for and still have the communication skills to maintain a relationship with a boy she cares about.
- *learn to set goals and priorities* . . . she will be conscious of when she wants to begin a sexually active life and will feel comfortable acting on her goals and priorities.
- *learn to distinguish fantasy from reality* . . . she will be less likely to get swept away by some vague romantic notion.
- *learn to tolerate anxiety* . . . she is less likely to become sexually active because she is afraid of losing the affections of the boy or because of peer pressure.
- *learn to project herself into the future and understand the consequences of her actions today* . . . she is less likely to become a teen parent because she will have thought about the consequences of too early parenting as it relates to her goals and dreams.
- *allow her to trust herself* . . . she will be her own center of authority and will gain confidence in herself as a woman as she grows and matures.

If the positive experiences described in this chapter are foreign to you, are not the experiences you have had, it will be more difficult for you to pass along the positive messages required. Are you willing to put in the effort required to change the parental and societal programming of your childhood?

If you hope that our daughters can be more sexually integrated, independent, and responsible than we were, if you want them to have an adulthood where they won't have to learn about sexuality by trial and error, then you need to get actively involved in this aspect of parenting. Difficult? You bet. But it should be well worth the effort. As fully integrated sexual human beings, it is more likely that women will have satisfying and loving adult relationships. And isn't that what we want for our daughters . . . and our sons?

Record any new messages you'd like to give your daughter about sexuality in "Your Plan."

chapter twenty-three

Getting Girls Ready for Career Education

When it comes to thinking about careers today, most girls and young women are confused. Not surprisingly. We tell them they can be anything they want to be, then buy sweaters for them and computers for their brothers. We say "Yes, you could be president of the United States," then criticize his wife for being too smart and successful. We get more excited when they make cheerleader than when they make the honor roll. We tell them it's important to be able to support themselves, but they learn from TV, newspapers, and magazines that if they earn too much money, they turn into shrews and their husbands abandon them. It's hard to know what to believe, much less how to act.

The next three chapters of this book, then, will be devoted to clarifying the messages young women get about careers. As your daughter enters adolescence, she will begin making some of the most important decisions of her life. Before she does, she needs to have a clear vision of what lies ahead, and you, too, need to reexamine the messages you are sending about her future.

Career planning and development is a more complex task for females than it is for males for a variety of reasons. We have been speaking and writing about this subject for over ten years and from our research, observations, and discussions recommend these special strategies for girls:

1. *Preadolescent girls require a special "precareer awareness" phase before beginning more traditional career education.*
2. *Career exploration and education must begin with an identity formation activity that helps the teenager first answer the questions Who am I? and What do I want?*

3. Strategies for mixing career and family must be addressed as part of the career exploration process.

These strategies are so important that we're going to devote one chapter to each of them—each full of ideas you can use in your daughter's education about careers.

The activities and exercises in this chapter are geared for your daughter, to help her develop the understanding and attitude she'll need *before* she starts seriously considering her future career.

Before career planning: precareer awareness

A few years back I agreed to take part in a career day sponsored by the Girl Scouts. They'd put together a group of women representing dozens of jobs: surveyors, engineers, lawyers, a composer, and a woodworker, you name it. We each had our own little booth in the auditorium, and the girls could walk around and talk to anyone they wanted. Hundreds of them turned out, so they must have had some career ambitions. For the better part of the day, though, the rest of us sat and watched as most of the girls lined up at the cosmetic representative's booth: she was doing makeovers.

—Advertising copywriter

"Precareer awareness" is something girls need to develop before they even start planning for a career. This crucial step is necessary because some girls are still not convinced that they even need to plan for a career. Without it many girls will let career planning information go in one ear and out the other, thinking, I won't be working when I have a family, therefore I do not have to get serious about career preparation, or, I don't have to plan for a career because someone else is going to take care of me.

Your daughter needs to learn differently and really internalize the messages before she enters high school and takes more traditional career education classes (those dealing with researching particular careers, examining educational requirements, and so on). We suggest precareer awareness opportunities for every girl between the ages of eleven and thirteen whether she is currently voicing the desire to be a clerical worker or a rocket scientist. This important developmental step is not provided in most schools, so it will be your responsibility to provide it.

If your daughter's school is an exception, be sure to show interest in and support for the class. Without encouragement, especially from her mother, your daughter is unlikely to hold on to the more ambitious attitudes instilled by the program.

Comprehensive career education is more important for girls

There are two general theories about why so many young women do not take career planning seriously or choose low-paying careers held traditionally by women. The first maintains that girls still do not believe they will have to work, despite all the evidence. "Most young women expect to work for pay, but many assume they will be able to choose whether and when to be in the labor force," says Dr. Heather Johnston Nicholson of Girls Incorporated. The second posits that young women have little faith either in their ability to succeed at nontraditional jobs or in society's willingness to allow them to try. "A discrepancy exists between what girls would like to do and what they feel is possible," wrote Pamela Trotman Reid and Dorothy Stenson Stephens in the journal *Youth & Society*.

There is undoubtedly a great deal of truth in both theories. Recent studies and surveys tell us that most teens think they will have the option to stay home with their young children, even though more than 50 percent of women with children under a year old are back on the job. It is predicted that by the year 2000, 80 percent of women aged twenty-five to fifty-four will work outside the home, and two-thirds of those entering the labor force will be women.

Many young women say they have career aspirations—in a 1994 *New York Times*-CBS News poll of young people aged thirteen to seventeen, "86 percent of the girls said they expected to work outside the home while married, while only 7 percent said they did not." Yet only 28 percent take the math classes they'll need to enter more than half of all college majors. The vast majority are still going into traditional women's fields like teaching and nursing—not surprising, since studies indicate that both boys and girls have placed limits on their occupational choices because of their gender by the time they enter first grade.

In fact, girls may have some good reasons for their choices: they are often discouraged, or even punished, by society for making nontraditional career choices, and there are still few female role models to follow and emulate.

Fortunately, girls can avoid the stereotypes and the dead-end jobs. What your daughter needs from you is support and encouragement, any possible exposure to role models, and information—ideally starting at the preschool level.

"We need to debunk the myth of Prince Charming in favor of the reality that most women will work outside the home for a large proportion of their lives," says Johnston Nicholson.

More girls are serious about preparing for a career today than in the past, and perhaps your daughter is one of them. Even if she has wonderfully high aspirations, however, it's important to reinforce her determination. Dorothy C. Holland and Margaret A. Eisenhart, authors of *Educated in Romance*, report that a very small percentage of women who enter college with career ambitions follow through and graduate with a degree in the field of their stated interest. Most backslide and change their major to something less challenging or drop out of school altogether. (We will discuss this more thoroughly later on.)

If your daughter is a teenager and you've only now come across this book, your daughter is likely to need some remedial work—not necessarily because you've done anything wrong, but because there are such strong cultural messages out there that need to be overcome and because there is such a serious lack of awareness among most teens and adults. Does she have any attitudes that might limit her aspirations? Is she conscious of them? Does she say one thing but do another (announce that she wants to be a psychologist, then not take the math and science classes she'll need, for example)?

In either case, the following activities should provide the precareer awareness that will help her benefit from and take to heart the career development education she ideally will get in school (or that you can provide for her).

Attitude survey and reality check

In many ways, you know your daughter better than anyone. You can see every single one of her younger selves in the face across the dinner table from you now. You can instantly recognize her voice, her smile, and her walk from those of a hundred other identically dressed teens in a crowded mall on a Saturday afternoon. Only you know about her habit of leaving spoons in ice-cream cartons or the way she opens her eyes just a little bit wider when she's not telling the whole truth.

Even in the closest families, however, some things are seldom discussed or remarked upon, and though it's not the least bit embarrassing or controversial, career awareness seems to be one of those things.

Do you know

- *what your daughter imagines a typical day in her life will be like when she's thirty-five?*
- *which three careers she is considering most seriously?*
- *what she would do with her life if she could wave a magic wand and have any career she wanted?*
- *whether she plans to work and, if so, for how many years?*
- *why, and for how long, she might want to leave the workforce?*
- *whether she plans to have children, and if she sees a conflict between her work and her family life?*

Think about your own adolescence for a few minutes. Could you have answered these questions when you were her age? What would your answers have been? Would it have been helpful if someone had asked you and then helped you work through your responses?

Most kids can use some help. Sitting down with your daughter for an interrogation session is probably not the best way to go about it, however. These things need time for thoughtful consideration. We recommend that over the next few weeks you set aside a few hours for discussion. You could do one of the four activities here each time.

Once you've done all four activities together, sit down and evaluate your daughter's position:

- *Was she able to project herself into the future and understand the consequences of her actions today?*
- *Will anxiety about not being smart enough or committed enough to achieve her goals get in the way of realizing her ambitions?*
- *Is your daughter's vision of her future realistic or based in fantasy?*

Picturing the future

Ask your daughter to describe a typical day in her life when she is thirty-five years old (or whatever adult age you think she can relate to). How will she spend most of her time? Who will be the primary people in her life? What will be her priorities? What will make her feel successful? (If you've been playing the "What if" game with your daughter, this will be an easier activity for her.)

If she finds it difficult to answer these questions, try another approach. Sometime when she's in the house with a number of her friends, suggest that they all do an art project. Get out a pile of magazines, scissors, glue, and paper, and have each girl complete a collage illustrating her ideal adult life. This should help you get a grasp on her sense of reality. If the collage is peppered with luxury cars and lavish estates, but she says she wants to be an aerobics instuctor, you have some serious explaining to do.

Another idea, good for older teens, is to ask your daughter (and friends, if you like) to write the autobiography she'd like to be able to submit for her twenty-year high school reunion.

Share your own feelings and experiences as you do these activities. How did you think your life was going to turn out when you were your daughter's age? Did it? If not, discuss with her why it did not. Be candid and direct.

Make it a habit, too, to *listen* to your daughter—all the time, not just during these activities. Be attuned to what she's saying, who or what inspires or excites her. Comment or query on what you hear. She may be looking for your reactions, or she may not be aware of the connection between her passions and the kind of career she might have someday.

What do you want to be when you grow up?

Ask your daughter which three careers she is most seriously considering. There's a good chance that one of her choices will be similar to your career or your spouse's. Another may have an element of fantasy about it—being a rock star, for example. Take the remaining choice most seriously; it's likely to be closest to her dream job.

"What would you be if you could wave a magic wand and have any job you wanted?" If your daughter's answer to that question is different from her responses above, investigate why. Does she feel this job is an unsuitable career for a woman or that she wouldn't be hired because of her sex? Is she afraid she doesn't have the talent or the intelligence? (Does she? There's a fine line between realism and pessimism, and you don't want to limit her aspirations unnecessarily, but if she's been taking voice lessons for five years and they still won't let her in the church choir, she's probably never going to sing at the Met. Perhaps she knows this, and that's why she didn't include it in her earlier responses. At any rate, if it is apparent to you that this is an unrealistic ambition for her, don't laugh or put her down.

Is she afraid the training would be too difficult or that she might fail? Does she think the required education would be too expensive? Whatever her concerns, if you get the feeling that this is really her ideal job and you believe she could do it, talk things through and try to resolve them. If she gives up on her dream without ever trying to achieve it, she may have lifelong regrets.

There's an interesting pattern in the way girls think about careers at different ages. Younger girls are likely to have the most gender-stereotyped ideas concerning which jobs are open to women. As they get older, nontraditional careers begin to seem more appealing and more possible. Then, when they start college, young women often begin to have doubts about their abilities, panic, and change their plans. Again, we will discuss downscaling thoroughly in the next chapter, "Helping Girls Realize Their Career Potential."

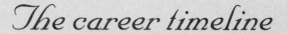

The career timeline

Ask your daughter how many years she plans to work outside the home between the time she is eighteen and sixty-five. According to the U.S. Department of Labor, the average woman today can expect to be in the workforce for twenty-nine years. Does she believe this fact applies to her, or do her eyes glaze over when you discuss the matter? Use the following tactic to make your point graphically.

Draw a timeline for a life span of about eighty years. Have your daughter divide it into five-year sections and mark where she thinks the important milestones in her life will occur. When will she graduate from high school? How long will she need for postsecondary education or training? Will she marry? When? Have children? Finally, have her highlight the line to indicate when she can expect to be in the workforce. Does she plan to leave her job temporarily at any time—for example, when her children are young? Have her leave gaps in the job line to indicate these periods.

You might even want to get the entire family in on this exercise. Use different-colored markers for each member. It can lead to interesting dinner conversation and may tell you some surprising things about your children's plans or expectations.

Changing your daughter's attitudes

A good precareer awareness plan should ultimately accomplish the following:

- *It should help your daughter resolve any conflict that she may feel exists between her gender and her career aspirations.*

What about kids?

Ask your daughter if she plans to have children. If so, how many? How old would she like to be at each birth? Does she plan to work when they are five years old or under? Eleven or under?

If she says she doesn't plan to have children, or she's not sure if she wants them, ask her how she came to that decision. Casually! Whether or not she has childen is a personal decision. Some women decide not to for very good reasons. Many young women wait to make this decision later in life.

In some cases, however, young women feel conflict about their ability to have both a career and a family. Men don't have this problem. For them, providing for a family has always been their accepted role. Thus, doing well at a job is doing well for their loved ones. Women, however, are more likely to feel guilty for leaving their children to go to work or to believe that if they can't devote their lives to their families, they don't deserve to have one.

Your daughter may have quite rightly observed that there is very little support for working mothers in our society. If most of the working mothers she knows are economically strapped and terminally exhausted, it's reasonable for her to want a different kind of life for herself. There are ways to combine career and family successfully, but it takes planning. We'll discuss this in detail in chapter 25, "Strategies for Mixing Career and Family."

- *It should teach her to separate fantasy from reality and provide solid information about the latter.*

A good first step is to have her complete the "Typical Male, Typical Female" survey you took back in chapter 2 (included again on page 363).

Go over together her answers to "Typical Male, Typical Female, for Daughters." If her charts show that she doesn't see much difference between a healthy adult and a healthy woman, or between a healthy adult and herself, your daughter probably won't let her gender get in the way of choosing her future career or feel that she is in any way unwomanly for selecting a nontraditional field of work.

Typical male, typical female, for daughters

Below, we've listed a dozen characteristics in the left-hand column and the opposite traits in the column on the right. There are seven spaces between each pair of attributes, allowing you to indicate how you feel a typical man and woman would rate on this scale. For example, if you feel strongly that a typical male is independent rather than dependent, put a check in the left-hand column provided on the male chart. If you strongly believe that the opposite is true, make your mark in the far right-hand column. If you think the answer lies somewhere in between, mark what you believe to be the appropriate column.

Do the chart for a woman twice, using different-color ink—one to indicate the characteristics typical of women in general and one to rate yourself.

TYPICAL MALE

Independent	_	_	_	_	_	_	_	Dependent
Self-reliant	_	_	_	_	_	_	_	Subservient
Aggressive	_	_	_	_	_	_	_	Submissive
Assertive	_	_	_	_	_	_	_	Yielding
Stoic	_	_	_	_	_	_	_	Emotional
Risk taker	_	_	_	_	_	_	_	Cautious
Competitive	_	_	_	_	_	_	_	Cooperative
Leader	_	_	_	_	_	_	_	Supporter
Strong	_	_	_	_	_	_	_	Gentle
Decisive	_	_	_	_	_	_	_	Indecisive
Forceful	_	_	_	_	_	_	_	Soft-spoken
Individualistic	_	_	_	_	_	_	_	Conformist
Analytical	_	_	_	_	_	_	_	Intuitive

TYPICAL FEMALE

Independent __ __ __ __ __ __ __ Dependent
Self-reliant __ __ __ __ __ __ __ Subservient
Aggressive __ __ __ __ __ __ __ Submissive
Assertive __ __ __ __ __ __ __ Yielding
Stoic __ __ __ __ __ __ __ Emotional
Risk taker __ __ __ __ __ __ __ Cautious
Competitive __ __ __ __ __ __ __ Cooperative
Leader __ __ __ __ __ __ __ Supporter
Strong __ __ __ __ __ __ __ Gentle
Decisive __ __ __ __ __ __ __ Indecisive
Forceful __ __ __ __ __ __ __ Soft-spoken
Individualistic __ __ __ __ __ __ __ Conformist
Analytical __ __ __ __ __ __ __ Intuitive

Okay, let's do this one more time, but with a slightly different angle. Complete the chart below in the same way, this time indicating how you believe a healthy adult would rate.

HEALTHY ADULT

Independent __ __ __ __ __ __ __ Dependent
Self-reliant __ __ __ __ __ __ __ Subservient
Aggressive __ __ __ __ __ __ __ Submissive
Assertive __ __ __ __ __ __ __ Yielding
Stoic __ __ __ __ __ __ __ Emotional
Risk taker __ __ __ __ __ __ __ Cautious
Competitive __ __ __ __ __ __ __ Cooperative
Leader __ __ __ __ __ __ __ Supporter
Strong __ __ __ __ __ __ __ Gentle
Decisive __ __ __ __ __ __ __ Indecisive
Forceful __ __ __ __ __ __ __ Soft-spoken
Individualistic __ __ __ __ __ __ __ Conformist
Analytical __ __ __ __ __ __ __ Intuitive

If there are sizable discrepancies, however, some remedial work is in order. The first step is simply and calmly to discuss the matter with your daughter. Ask lots of questions. (If necessary, review the section on parent/daughter communication in chapter 8, "Your Role.") How does she feel about the gender differences she perceives? Can she think of men or women she knows who don't conform to her societal norms? (Be prepared to bring up some names: Aunt Mary, who likes to camp alone in the wilderness; Bob down the street, who bakes bread every weekend; her female dentist; and so on.) What kind of jobs do they have? Do they seem happy about what they do and who they are?

Try to find out why your daughter feels the way she does. Where did she get these messages? Review the exercise "Message Center" in chapter 2 ("What Attitudes, Experiences, and Feelings Do You Bring to Parenting?"), and do an informal version with her. What messages has she received from her friends concerning what women can and can't be or do? How do her classmates feel? Has her teacher said or done anything to indicate there are jobs suitable only for one sex or the other? What messages has she received from you or your spouse?

If your daughter indicated in the attitude exercise above that if she could wave a magic wand and have any job she wanted, she would choose a nontraditional career, but she didn't list it as one of the three she is seriously considering, help her take a closer look at the dream job. What does an architect actually do, for example? Is there any physical reason a woman couldn't perform these tasks as well as a man?

Changing your daughter's attitude is likely to take time, but keep on trying. Try to expose her to more positive role models. Try to be a better role model yourself. Whenever you hear news that supports your position, bring it up in casual conversation: "I see that Betty Smith's construction company has been awarded the contract for the new high school," for example, or "My friend Linda says that the new Miss Springfield is planning to be an astronomer."

Telling it like it is

The inspiration for our first book, *Choices,* came to Mindy one evening at the (then) Girls Club of Santa Barbara when an obviously exhausted single mother came to pick up her young daughter. The woman had a clerical job that didn't support her family and was living with an emotionally abusive man because she needed the financial support. "Why didn't someone tell me what it was going to be like when I was growing up?" she asked. Ever since, we've made it our mission to do just that.

Now it's your turn. Reality can be a powerful motivating tool. The young woman we mentioned earlier in the book, for example, the one who thought that lifeguards earn $100,000 a year, has little reason to study her math instead of going to the tanning salon. But a lesson in reality could change her mind. "The Startling Statement Quiz" is a good place to begin. Quizzes are especially effective learning tools because they engage the reader and make her think. Reading or hearing the same information doesn't have nearly as much impact.

The startling statement quiz

The next time your daughter (age eleven to thirteen) has a group of friends in the house for a party, meeting, or the like, ask them to do this trivia activity. Hand out copies of the quiz and divide the young women into groups of two or three. Give them time (twenty minutes or so) to read the questions, discuss, and agree on the correct answer. By offering a nominal prize, you will probably encourage more energy and discussion.

Bring the group together and let them correct their own papers. Before you provide the right answer to each question, ask for a show of hands. Which answers do the girls support as true? Let them discuss or even argue if you like. Then give the correct answers and discuss some more. Which group did the best?

You can do the exercise individually with your daughter if you prefer, but it's not likely to have the same impact. As a group activity that promotes discussion, the lessons will be much more memorable.

These statistics can be a downer, so make sure you don't approach this activity with a defeatist "what's the point of trying?" attitude. Keep any anger or bitterness under control as well. Instead use the numbers to empower your daughter (and her friends), to make her a problem solver: "If women today can't count on being supported by someone else, what can you do to make sure you don't become one of these statistics?" "If you're going to have to work, what can you do to ensure you'll have a satisfying job?"

1. In 1991, for every dollar earned by an American man, women earned
   a. 59 cents.
   b. 74 cents.
   c. 85 cents.
   d. 98 cents.

2. The average salary for a man with four years of college is $50,000. The average salary for a woman with the same education is
   a. $30,000.
   b. $40,000.
   c. $42,000.
   d. $20,000.
3. Of women with full-times jobs, four out of five earn
   a. more than $25,000 a year.
   b. about as much as their husbands.
   c. less than $20,000 a year.
   d. more than $20,000 a year.
4. In 1991, of the forty highest-paid entertainers in the country, __ were women.
   a. 25
   b. 17
   c. 13
   d. 3
5. Child care for employees is offered by __ of private American companies.
   a. 1 percent
   b. 10 percent
   c. 25 percent
   d. 50 percent
6. Women are __ of all single parents.
   a. 50 percent
   b. 65 percent
   c. 87 percent
   d. 45 percent
7. In 1992, for every ten marriages, there were __ divorces.
   a. 10
   b. 5
   c. 2
   d. 1
8. Of divorced women, about __ are paid alimony.
   a. 5–10 percent
   b. 25 percent
   c. 35–50 percent
   d. 80 percent
9. Without post–high school education or training, a woman can expect to earn
   a. as much as a male high school graduate.
   b. less than a male high school dropout.
   c. more than a male high school dropout.
   d. about the same as a male high school dropout.

10. Of all women workers, about __ say they have been discriminated against or paid less because of their sex.
    a. 5–10 percent
    b. 20–25 percent
    c. 32–40 percent
    d. 80–95 percent
11. Of all adults living in poverty in the United States, __ are women.
    a. three-eighths
    b. two-thirds
    c. half
    d. one-third
12. Of all those entering the workforce in the year 2000, __ will be women.
    a. two-thirds
    b. one-fourth
    c. half
    d. one-third

Answers

1. (b) Women earned seventy-four cents for every dollar earned by an American man in 1991. In 1977 women earned only fifty-nine cents for every dollar earned by a man. According to Susan Bianchi-Sand of the National Committee on Pay Equity, "We are closing the gap. But it's not because women are making big progress, but because men are doing worse." Between 1988 and 1991 the economy slumped, and men's average wages dropped faster than women's.
2. (a) While men with college degrees averaged $50,000 a year, a woman with four years of college averages $30,000. What's more, for each year of work experience, men's earnings go up about twenty-four cents an hour, while women receive only a seven-cent pay increase for each year on the job.
3. (c) Of women with full-time jobs, four out of five earn less than $20,000 a year. One reason for this may be that nearly one-third of all working women are clustered in only six of the five hundred job categories: secretaries, elementary and high school teachers, semiskilled machine operators, managers and administrators, retail and personal sales workers, and bookkeepers and accounting clerks. When most of the workers in a career field are women, the pay level is almost always lower than comparable jobs most often held by men.

4. (d) In 1991 three of the forty highest-paid entertainers in the country were women: Oprah Winfrey, Madonna, and Janet Jackson. In 1989 the Screen Actors Guild reported that men earned 68 percent of total earnings from film, television, and commercials.

5. (a) Only about 1 percent of private employers provide child care for their employees. This figure has not increased for years, and it may even be declining.

6. (c) Women are 87 percent of all single parents. This figure has declined in recent years: it used to be 90 percent. If this trend continues, we might see an equal number of single moms and dads by about the year 2052. Until then women need to be especially well prepared to support their children.

7. (b) There is still about one divorce for every two marriages in the country. This figure, too, doesn't change much from year to year. The average single mother earns about $12,000 a year.

8. (a) Of divorced women, about 5 to 10 percent are paid alimony. The average child support payment is about $140 a month, and many men don't support their ex-families at all. Most divorced women, with or without children, are on their own.

9. (b) A woman with a high school diploma can expect to earn less than a male high school dropout. Since a woman needs more education to make less money, and since there is a good chance that she will have to support both herself and her family at some point in her life, education beyond high school is imperative.

10. (d) Of all women workers, about 80 to 95 percent say they have been discriminated against or paid less because of their sex. There have also been dramatic increases in charges of sexual harrassment and rape.

11. (b) Of all adults living in poverty in the United States, two-thirds are women. Women and their children make up 76 percent of the poor. Women also make up the fastest-growing segment of the homeless. Nearly half of these are the victims of domestic violence and of the severe cuts in funding for battered women's shelters.

12. (a) Of all those entering the workforce in the year 2000, two-thirds will be women. It is also predicted that among women between the ages of twenty-five and fifty-four, 80 percent will be working outside the home. The question remains, What kinds of jobs will these be, and will they pay a living wage?

Happily ever after?

Use news reports and magazine articles to continue your discussion of the real world. There's plenty of material, but—probably because it makes us feel so helpless—we usually don't stop to think about what it means. Next time you see a TV journalist interviewing a man who's lined up to apply for a job, and he tells the reporter he's been unemployed for two years, ask your daughter what she would do if she were that man's wife.

When a columnist for the local paper writes about the widow and children of a police officer who's been killed in the line of duty, ask your daughter how she supposes that woman will support herself and her family.

Ask her opinion about the family that adopted a child with AIDS. How will they pay for the huge medical bills? And what about the formerly successful businessman who lost everything during the recession or the aging homemaker whose husband left her for a younger woman?

You don't have to beat your daughter over the head with these stories—once you start looking, you'll probably come across dozens of them on any given day. Make it a practice, though, to have periodic discussions about these crisis situations. Pay particular attention to stories about

- *families in which the main provider died or left.*
- *families in which the main provider suffers long-term unemployment.*
- *families in which major health problems have caused financial burdens.*

These discussions will not only keep your daughter rooted in the real world, but will reinforce the theme that she needs to prepare herself for a career that can support a family if need be or contribute significantly to the family budget.

It will cause less anxiety for your daughter if you start your discussions with stories about people she doesn't know, but as she becomes more comfortable with the idea, you might bring in stories closer to home. If they're about people she knows, the lessons will have an added impact.

The cost of living

In one form or another we've been doing budget exercises with young people since 1976. Mindy learned it as a child from her parents and first started using it with her college students. At their suggestion ("Why didn't someone do this with me long ago?") we began including it in various formats in most of our books for young people.

They enjoy them, and they learn a lot, too. Most parents don't discuss finances with their children, and as a result, the younger generation grows up ignorant of what it costs to support their life-style. Oh, they know exactly how much the trendiest pair of athletic shoes costs, but they have no context in which to view that figure. Is it an hour's pay? A day's wages? Half the rent?

It's essential to do this exercise now, before your daughter starts her career exploration. A salary of $10,000 a year can sound like a fortune to someone with a $10-a-week allowance. By the time she's completed her budget, however, she will have a fairly sophisticated idea of what constitutes a living wage, and that will add an important dimension to her career search. (Do the exercise using current prices. They'll probably be higher by the time your daughter goes to work, but we're more concerned about relative costs here: about what percentage of income goes for housing, and so on.)

You are your daughter's designated resource center for this exercise. It's your job to provide her with the information she'll need or tell her where she can find it. This shouldn't be a major problem, assuming you have access to a variety of bills, grocery tapes, receipts, department store catalogs, want ads, and other assorted financial drains and obligations. You also need to explain the exercise to your daughter and, together, decide how you want to do it. (You may, for example, want to make it a day-long project for a rainy Saturday, or you might prefer to complete it in weekly segments. Whatever works best for you is fine.)

Okay, let's get started. Ask your daughter to think about the kind of life she hopes to have at a specific adult age—say, twenty-eight (many young people have difficulty imagining being any older than this). What kind of home would she like to have? What kind of car? Will she have children? How many? How old will they be then? Give her as much time as she needs to imagine in detail. Then help her get her dream down on paper. Since budgets are greatly influenced by the number of people in the household, be sure to include that information. If she says she'll have children, have her record how many and how old they will be at the time she is twenty-eight. Location is another important consideration. The cost of a condominium in Manhattan is in no way comparable to that of one in Dubuque. Where does she want to live? Use the budget form to complete the exercise.

372

Budget form

When I am _____ years old, I would like to be living in a _____ located in _____ with the following people:_____

_____.

I hope to have _____ children, who at that time would be _____ years old.
I will probably need to spend these amounts each month to have the kind of life I want:

Housing	_____	Vacations	_____
Transportation	_____	Child care	_____
Clothing	_____	Health	_____
Food	_____	Furnishings	_____
Sundries	_____	Savings	_____
Entertainment	_____	Miscellaneous	_____

Monthly Total: _____

Special note: After she has described her family, you may choose to suggest that for this activity she assume she is single for whatever reason.

Housing is the biggest item in most people's budget. Does she want to rent or own her own home? What amenities would this ideal home have? (A fireplace? A spa? A gourmet kitchen?) If she's planning to stay in the area, you can send her to the local classified ads and ask her to find a few places that seem to meet her requirements. What is the average rent or asking price? If your daughter wants to live in a different area, you'll need to consult ads from that place. You may be able to find newspapers at your library, or your librarian may be able to help you find the information you need in other resources.

The housing expenditure should also cover utilities: gas, electric, phone, water, trash, cable, and so on. You can use your own bills for these things to predict how much your daughter's will be.

Transportation usually means a car, except in some urban areas. Send your daughter back to the classified ads to discover how much the one she wants is likely to cost. There will be additional expenditures for insurance, license, gas, maintenance, and, perhaps, parking. How much do you spend on these? Share these figures with your daughter.

In considering costs for clothing, your daughter should assume that she needs only to replace items or supplement her wardrobe. She needs to consider, however, whether she'll need special clothes for the kind of work she might be doing. If she plans to have children, they probably will go through at least one wardrobe in a year. Clothing prices are easily available from catalogs.

Food costs vary widely. How big will her family be? Will she have a garden? Does she like to cook? Save some grocery tapes and let her determine a food budget from them. With the computerized checkout systems most stores have now, it's easy to tell exactly what each price on the tape was for.

Sundries include personal items like toothpaste, shampoo, deodorant, and makeup, services like getting a haircut, as well as toilet paper, laundry detergent, and so on. Tell your daughter roughly how often you need to buy these items.

Entertainment and recreation include movies, tapes, concerts, books, eating out, and so on. How much does your daughter think she'd like to spend on these?

We've found that by this time many young people start to panic. The numbers are adding up. With this in mind, your daughter may proclaim that she won't really need to take vacations. Remind her that they are important for her physical and psychological health. The Sunday travel supplement to most newspapers has lots of prices. You might pick up some brochures from a local travel agency as well.

Child care is a huge expense for most working families. What kind of care does your daughter most want to have? She can find out how much it costs by asking a parent with a similar arrangement or by calling a nursery or day care center like the one she'd hope to use.

Health care is usually subsidized by employers. Is yours? What kind of coverage do you have? How much do you pay for it each month? Share this information with your daughter.

Home furnishing costs should be for additions or replacements only. Department store catalogs are good sources for prices.

Saving a portion of each month's income is an important habit. Help your daughter decide what would be a reasonable amount for her to save.

Miscellaneous costs would be for things like charitable contributions, birthday and holiday gifts, pet expenses, newspaper subscriptions, and so on.

When all the figures are in, have your daughter add them up and announce the grand total. Is it more or less than she expected it to be? Are there any changes she wants to make? What has she learned?

The final step is to determine the gross salary she would need to earn to support this life-style. Explain to her that because of withholding for taxes and Social Security, she can't expect to bring home the figure listed as the annual salary for a job.

This is extremely important information for her to have as she begins her career search.

A much more extensive version of this activity is found in *Lifestyle Math: Your Financial Planning Portfolio* (Academic Innovations; see "Ordering Information"), a book Mindy wrote—with her mother as co-author.

Turn to "Your Plan" and add any new messages you'd like to give your daughter about career planning and economic self-sufficiency.

chapter twenty-four

Helping Girls Realize
Their Career Potential

S andy remembers baby-sitting for her nephew, Darin, when he was about four years old. His older sister was teasing him that he wanted to marry the little girl next door. When she refused to accept his vehement denials, he exclaimed in frustration, "I can't get married! I don't even have a job!"

Darin did have a career in mind, though, and had even found himself a role model: the garbage collector. He would get up extra early on trash collection day to wait by the curb so he could help empty the cans. Males, it seems, start to view themselves as workers at a very early age. It's not really so surprising. For them the messages have always been clear and direct: As a man, you will be the provider. You must do well at school so you can do well at work so you can support your family.

For girls, there is no similar chain of thought. Most feel they are supposed to do well at school and that they are expected to have a family, but they do not perceive the connections. What does school have to do with work? And doesn't work get in the way of having a family? In many ways, then, career exploration and development is more important for girls than it is for boys.

Why be in school?

In their book, *Educated in Romance*, Dorothy Holland and Margaret Eisenhart propose some interesting answers to questions that have nagged at us for years: On average, women get at least as much education as men. Why, then, do they do so poorly in the workforce? Is it all because of discrimination? Why do even the brightest young women scale back their ambitions during their college years? Why do so many female college graduates still end up in marginal or dead-end careers?

Holland and Eisenhart's findings seem to support our theories about the importance of developing a hardy personality and forming an identity as an achiever. What the authors have to say about achievement and careers is so central to our thesis that we want to discuss sections of their book in detail here.

Briefly, the book grew out of a study the authors did of women attending two (unidentified) colleges in the South, one largely African American, the other mainly white, beginning in 1979, when the group entered college, with follow-ups in 1983, when they were supposed to graduate, and again in 1987. The participants had all been good students in high school, and half of them entered college proclaiming math- or science-related majors.

Our discussion here will center around two chapters of *Educated in Romance*, "Schoolwork for What?" and "Pathways to Marginal Careers." Holland and Eisenhart found that for women college is more of a peer culture than an academic one. Men could gain status from academic success, participation in athletics, or other activities (achievement), but for women status could come only from social success (relationships). There was a great deal of peer pressure to date and socialize and almost no support for spending time on schoolwork or for dealing with problems concerning school.

According to the authors, each young woman approached her schoolwork in one of three ways: as "(1) work in exchange for 'getting over,' that is, finishing college and thereby obtaining college credentials; (2) work in exchange for 'doing well,' that is, receiving good grades and other academic accolades; and (3) work in exchange for 'learning from experts.'" Which interpretation she embraced had a profound effect on her potential for future success.

A majority of the women at "Bradford" (the name the authors applied to the African American college; the white college is known as "SU") fell into the first category. They felt they needed a college degree to get a good job, but they did not see any relationship between the content of their classes and their future occupations (inability to project into the future and understand the consequences of present actions). Therefore they were not motivated to work hard at their studies, and they were relatively unconcerned about their grades (did not set goals and establish priorities). Still, these women in the "getting over" category held steadfastly to their career goals and did not change their fields of study. They were more likely to leave school than to change.

A majority of the women at SU fell into the "doing well" category. Past success in school led these students to believe that they could achieve academically without having to work very hard (inability to separate fantasy from reality). They were likely to value their grades not for the achievement they represented, but for the rewards success at school brought from parents and teachers. These "people pleasers" tended to choose as majors subjects in which they had the most natural ability, assuming that they would also excel at careers in these fields. When these students discovered, much to their surprise, that college classes were more difficult than their high school studies had been, they began to question themselves and their suitability for academic work (no self-trust or anxiety tolerance). They were not interested in working hard or being challenged by their classes, only in getting good grades (inability to set goals, establish priorities, project into the future). Perhaps not surprisingly, a majority soon changed their majors to an area of study they thought would be easier.

A small minority of students from both Bradford and SU made up the "learning from experts" category. They came to college to learn (identified themselves as achievers), had a particular career goal in mind (ability to project into the future, set goals, and establish priorities), and expected to work hard (anxiety tolerance). Women in this group valued grades as an indication of how much or how well they had learned. Many also seemed to have a "cause" or a mission in life, whether it was to make sense of past experiences or advance a political belief. Interestingly, most of these women also changed or added to their majors, but they were scaling up rather than down.

Women in the first two categories did not take themselves seriously as workers or students. Only 18 percent of them pursued their college career interests after graduation, whereas 80 *percent* of the women with the "learning from experts" interpretation would go after their chosen careers after graduation.

Why? Holland and Eisenhart report that women in the first group could not visualize themselves in a career (project into the future), though they said they wanted to have one. The "doing well" group, on the other hand, didn't have a notion of themselves as significant breadwinners (inability to separate fantasy from reality).

The "getting over" group found schoolwork boring and unrewarding. With no support from their peers or their school (identified with relationships rather than achievement) in developing their careers, 40 percent left school before graduation. When the authors contacted women from this group in later life, the overwhelming majority were working at clerical or low-level technical jobs. The authors explain that women from this group looked at the worth of a degree in relation to its costs (time, energy, anxiety, money, other interests). When the costs were perceived to be too high, the education was abandoned.

The "doing well" women were largely disappointed with themselves. When they didn't achieve the academic success they were used to, they scaled back their ambitions and became less committed to school in general (didn't trust themselves or tolerate anxiety). Many became involved with other interests, especially romantic attachments. By devoting most of their time to boyfriends and other social activities, they had even less time for schoolwork. Most stopped thinking of themselves as either good students or serious workers (no identity as achievers). While most of these women graduated from college, the majority also ended up in clerical or low-paying jobs, with one notable exception, a young woman who received special support from her family in learning about her career choice, insurance specialist. Her father introduced her to several insurance specialists he knew, and her brother, a former math major at SU, gave her advice about courses and professors (family support can make a huge difference!). This young woman also did not have a boyfriend, as did most of the other women in her group.

By 1987 women in the "doing well" group were likely to be married and working at a low-paying job, in part, Holland and Eisenhart speculate, because they never really believed that they would have to support a family. Most of their mothers were homemakers. None of the students in this group ever spoke about the possibility of divorce (inability to separate fantasy from reality, project into the future).

Women in the "learning from experts" group did not feel a need to set aside their own priorities to meet someone else's expectations (identity as achievers, trust themselves). They all graduated from college, and nearly all pursued their final college majors into graduate work or jobs in their fields of study (set goals, established priorities, projected into the future).

As the results of this study make clear, it is essential that your daughter come to identify herself as an achiever by the time she enters college (and, preferably, before she enters adolescence). We've already discussed many ways for you to help her do this, but here are a few more suggestions:

- *When discussing her schoolwork, focus on achievement rather than reward: "What did you learn?" not "Did you get an A?" Praise effort and improvement.*
- *Take the same approach to other areas of her life. Ask if she played well, not if she won.*
- *Encourage her to take classes that challenge her abilities and make sure she understands that excelling at some subjects will take effort.*
- *Talk about the excitement of learning something new or taking on a challenge. Make it sound like adventure rather than duty or drudgery. Be a role model—take on a challenge of your own and share how rewarding it is to accomplish something difficult.*
- *Provide opportunities for her to achieve in many different ways. Teach her how to change a tire, catch a fish, bake a cake, hit a ball, sew a hem, build a fire, sail a boat, play a guitar, write a poem—the possibilities are endless. Don't step in to rescue her, though. Emphasize the satisfaction of doing a job well, no matter how long it takes.*

- *Teach her to appreciate the process of achieving, not just the end product— the doing, not just the having. "I took up sewing because I wanted to have a lot of clothes," says Louisa. "I didn't understand the artistry of sewing. I didn't enjoy it. That possibility never even occurred to me. I was, therefore, in a hurry to get done. I took shortcuts. When I made a mistake, I didn't bother to correct it unless I absolutely had to. I ended up with a lot of badly made, ill-fitting dresses, and I felt like a failure." Take the time to tell your daughter about quality and pride in craftsmanship. These lessons will spill over into every part of her life.*

If you can help your daughter experience the pride and joy that come from achievement, she'll soon be hooked. She will be motivated to work hard, set goals, and stick to them, and she will be well on her way to achieving her potential.

Career and identity

We spoke earlier, in detail, about identity and personality. In this section we will look closely at the relationship between identity and career exploration and development. How can you help your daughter discover who she is and what she wants and then see why this knowledge must be considered in choosing her future field of work? It is important for her long-term happiness and satisfaction that she do so. And in the shorter term this knowledge will motivate her to complete her eduction, as the previous section showed.

She should be well on her way to completing this process by the time she's fourteen. (You may want to review chapter 5, "Forming an Identity as an Achiever.") In fact, career exploration itself can be an ideal way to formalize an identity search.

Chances are your daughter will receive some kind of career guidance at school. Don't assume, however, that it will be as comprehensive as it should be. Check it out. Asking your daughter to research and write short papers about three potential careers, or giving her an interest test and telling her she should be a speech pathologist (the extent of most schools' career planning), won't help her form her identity, even if they do uncover her ideal job. It's the process that counts most.

A good career exploration curriculum should assess the following qualities in your daughter:

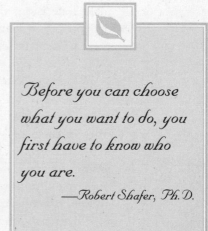

Before you can choose what you want to do, you first have to know who you are.

—*Robert Shafer, Ph.D.*

1. Her passions.

What does she truly love, or love to do? You could probably sit down right now and make a fairly accurate list for your daughter, but could she? Is she aware of the fact that you have to call her at least a half dozen times for dinner when she's working at her computer, or that she seems to go into a trance when she plays the violin? Does she think of these activities in terms of future careers? Those who can make a living from pursuing one of their passions are among the happiest people around.

2. Her values.

We're not thinking of values in the ethical sense here, but in terms of what is valued. Your daughter is not likely to find much satisfaction in a career that goes against one of her major values. For example, if she values privacy, she probably doesn't want to be a politician, and if she values money, she probably doesn't want to be a poet. Some of the most commonly held values include adventure, family, power, recognition, personal integrity and moral courage, money, security, creativity, helping others, knowledge and truth, friendship or companionship, beauty and aesthetics, or independence and freedom.

If your daughter has one overpowering value, it can simplify her career search considerably. She probably has several, though, and that makes things more complex. It's more difficult to come up with a job that combines adventure and power, for example, than one that is only adventurous.

3. Her personality traits.

Every once in a while we all come across someone who seems to have chosen the wrong job for his or her personality: the sales representative who isn't at ease with people, the accountant who can't be bothered with details, the manager who can't make a decision; all should probably have chosen a different career. What are your daughter's personality strengths? What kinds of work do they best suit her for? Are there jobs she should stay away from because of her personality?

4. Her skills and aptitudes.

These are usually the most obvious qualities and the most apt to be tested for. One word of caution: Many young women have a tendency to ignore all other factors and concentrate solely on this one when choosing a career field. As the "doing well" group of women from the Holland and Eisenhart study demonstrated, evidence of natural ability in a certain subject does not inevitably mean that subject should be chosen as a college major.

Many schools are using curricular materials like the book *Career Choices: A Guide for Teens and Young Adults—Who Am I, What Do I Want, and How Do I Get*

It? (Academic Innovations) to take students through these steps in identity development. Once students know who they are, they can begin looking for careers that match up with their personalities and preferences and also pay enough to support their life-style goals. This means they'll be more likely to see themselves achieving and stick to their goals. Available in bookstores, libraries, or through the publisher, this book is a journal that helps young people articulate their identities.

(Turn back to chapter 5, page 68, and have your daughter complete the personal profile activity, "Getting to Know *You*" to get her started on her own identity search.)

A recent article described a character in the TV series *Civil Wars* as "an independently wealthy bicycle messenger and poet." With independence and wealth, apparently, all things are possible. For most people, however, a perfect match is unlikely. It's almost always necessary to balance sacrifices and rewards, though giving up on a passionate interest entirely is seldom required. Your daughter's career education should provide a good balance of ambition and reality, providing encouragement, answering questions, and teaching a process she can repeat as often as she needs to throughout her life.

Does her school offer such a course? If not, consider discussing the topic with the principal or school board. A one-day career fair, including one or two self-assessment tests, could give your daughter and all of her classmates important information, *but it is not enough information to start planning for a satisfying work life*. A comprehensive career education class that includes a formalized identity search should be part of the school's curriculum. If it's not, ask why.

Role models and shadows

Your daughter needs to be able to imagine herself in a given career—to be able to see herself holding this job—before she can seriously consider it as an option for herself. We've already talked about the importance of providing female role models for her whenever possible and hope that you're continuing this process. The more jobs she sees women doing, the more possibilities she'll see for herself.

We've also discussed using gender-neutral labels for careers ("hairdresser," not "beautician" or "male hairdresser," and so on) and trust that you are vigilantly monitoring yourself and others in working toward this goal.

A further step that you can take, once your daughter expresses an interest in a nontraditional career, is to help her find a woman now working in that field who is willing to let your daughter be her shadow for a day. As a shadow she will simply quietly follow the woman around as she goes about her daily activities. As she observes the day-to-day tasks, she takes notes. Then, at the end of the day, the woman will spend a half hour or so with your daughter, answering questions and discussing what went on. It's as simple as that. But it's been shown to be a powerful tool in helping young women expand their options.

Betty Shepperd, national coordinator for the Women Helping Girls with Choices project, made the experience even more meaningful by having participants in her group report to the women's homes about the time the families were getting up in the morning so they could also observe how the women go about balancing their roles as worker, mother, and homemaker. We think this is a terrific idea, if you can find a woman who's willing to go along with it.

How do you recruit potential role models? Networking is probably the best way. Ask everyone you know if they know a woman in your daughter's preferred line of work. If you belong to any organizations or associations, make an announcement asking for help at the next meeting. If these steps fail, try calling the Chamber of Commerce or any associations for people in that profession.

The level of difficulty you encounter will depend on where you live and just how nontraditional your daughter's career choice is. Some compromises may have to be made. If she wants to be a U.S. senator, for example, the number of potential candidates is small, as are your chances of knowing someone who knows one of them. But it's quite likely that you could find a state senator willing to spend the day with your daughter.

Before your daughter goes off for her day as a shadow, make sure she understands that she is not to ask questions, make comments, or get in the way until the agreed-upon time for discussion at the end of the day. She is to pretend she is the person's shadow. She also needs to send a handwritten thank-you promptly after the assignment is completed.

Once your daughter has a career goal, one of the questions she has to answer is How do I get there from here? She can practice this kind of thinking with "The Career Ladder," a fun activity that encourages creativity, instills confidence, and demonstrates that problems can be solved, mistakes rectified, and heights climbed.

The career ladder

You can do this together with your daughter, or with two or three girls, or a larger group divided into teams of three. Discuss with your daughter, or have the group discuss and agree upon a dream job. Draw a ladder with seven rungs, and write that job title on the top rung. Then assign an entry-level job (receptionist, sales clerk, student) to be placed on the bottom rung. (If you have more than one team, assign different entry-level jobs to each.) Ask your daughter or the team or teams of girls to come up with a series of steps—professional or educational—that could lead them from the bottom rung to the top. If you have more than one team, have the groups share their schemes with each other when the plans are completed.

Traditional versus nontraditional jobs

A reporter once asked Tipper Gore whether she was raising her son to be a senator. "Actually," she responded, "I'm raising my daughter to be a senator." Mrs. Gore's quick comeback must have opened new possibilities for many young women, just as it made countless adults more aware of how deeply embedded these stereotypes are.

This is quite an accomplishment when you consider that only a few years ago the idea of female senators was a joke and we didn't even have a word for male flight attendants. Probably few people raised an eyebrow when, in 1956, the Minneapolis *Star Tribune* printed an article under the headline THIS ENGINEERING STUDENT KNITS—AND SHE'S A GIRL, TOO. Despite teasing from her "rugged male classmates," Jean Ann Olexa chose engineering because she loved math and wanted to become a designer for an aircraft firm, "doing rockets." Before her mother would go along with this plan, however, she insisted that her daughter learn to cook. She did and won a scholarship to engineering school.

Here's a candidate for the Hardy Personality Hall of Fame! What an extraordinary young woman Ms. Olexa must have been. In her story we see evidence of the best and the worst things about going after a nontraditional job. In many instances, even today, doing so can make a woman an object of ridicule or a freak. Ms. Olexa couldn't even count on her own mother for support.

But then there are the "rockets" and the love of math. Few would argue that the most challenging and most desirable jobs involving neither stretch marks nor diaper changes have traditionally been held by men. As we've seen, women tend to cluster in only a few of the hundreds of possible career fields. Doesn't your daughter deserve the right to choose her life's work from the full spectrum of possibilities? Isn't it in the best interest of society that all individuals be allowed to make contributions commensurate with their abilities?

Moreover, nontraditional jobs almost always pay more than those traditionally held by women. We've already seen that women tend to earn less, even compared with men in the same job, so it is essential that your daughter think about potential earnings when she chooses her career. If she's done the budget exercise, and if she's come to accept the fact that she must be prepared to support her family on her own, she should be more willing to give this factor its due weight.

Some young women will resist, saying they want to "help others," not work for their own financial gain or for power. This is a commendable philosophy, but a flawed one. Generally, the higher-paid jobs or the ones with the most power offer greater opportunities to help more people in more dramatic ways. We've done exercises around this issue, asking young women to choose a position of authority (head of a corporation, secretary of education, president of the United States, or whatever) and write a short description of the things they might be able to accomplish in that job. We've also asked them to consider who can do the most good: a nurse's aide or a surgeon? a legal secretary or a judge? a child care worker or the secretary of the Department of Health and Human Services? You might find similar exercises helpful with your daughter.

Another powerful argument for nontraditional careers is that they allow women more time and freedom to be mothers. Because they pay more, a woman doesn't have to work as many hours to earn a living wage. Higher-paying jobs are usually more flexible as well. A department manager may be able to work at home when her child is ill or leave early to attend a soccer match, but her secretary probably does not have the same freedom. We will discuss this concept in depth in the next section.

We'd like to make one more proposal, that people stop using the term *nontraditional* as it relates to careers. The term *nontraditional* is used throughout the educational system to denote careers where most workers are of the opposite sex (nursing is a nontraditional job for men, plumbing for women). It is a goal of some educational programs to recruit girls into "nontraditional" careers. Bad word if this is the

Whom would you hire?

This final exercise uses the lists of feminine and masculine characteristics from the Bem Survey described in chapter 3, "Redefining Femininity." The traits for employee A are usually considered "masculine," those for employee B, "feminine."

In column C make your own short list of jobs, some held mostly by men, some held mostly by women (be sure to include "mother"). Ask your daughter to play an employer. If column A represented the traits of one job candidate and column B the traits of another, which person would she hire to be the manager, secretary, doctor, nurse, journalist, mother, or whatever? In column D enter her chooses. In most cases she will choose candidate A, even for jobs usually held by women.

A EMPLOYEE A	B EMPLOYEE B	C JOB TITLE	D CANDIDATE HIRED
Acts like a leader	Affectionate	_____	_____
Ambitious	Cheerful	_____	_____
Assertive	Gentle	_____	_____
Competitive	Gullible	_____	_____
Defend my own beliefs	Loyal	_____	_____
Independent	Sensitive to the needs of others	_____	_____
Individualistic	Shy	_____	_____
Self-reliant	Soft-Spoken	_____	_____
Self-sufficient	Understanding	_____	_____
Willing to take risks	Yield	_____	_____

goal. Most adolescent females do not want to be "nontraditional" anything. Remember, as they struggle to form their identities, they are more apt to lean toward being like everyone else than toward being different. So instead, let's just call these nontraditional jobs for women what they really are—"higher-pay, higher-autonomy, and usually more fulfilling" careers.

"Whom Would You Hire?" will help your daughter see what the "right stuff" really is for jobs both traditional and nontraditional for females.

Turn to "Your Plan" and add any additional messages you'd like to give your daughter about career planning, the importance of education, or achievement.

chapter twenty-five

Strategies for Mixing Career and Family

*D*uring the summer of 1992, the whole country was caught up in the saga of Murphy Brown and her fictional single motherhood. When millions of people tuned in to view the opening episode that fall, there was plenty of material for laughter and debate, but underneath it all came a subtler and probably unintended message: Successful career women make bad mothers. Murphy was totally inept at caring for her new baby and frantic about it all. For all Murphy's fame, power, and wealth, she needed men—two men—to teach her how to hold and feed the baby.

The myth that real careers, requiring training and commitment, are incompatible with family life is one of the most pervasive and damaging messages young women receive. Since nearly all of them plan to marry and have children, the idea of a career is the easiest thing to give up or scale down.

Researchers at the University of Illinois, in a ten-year study of eighty high school valedictorians, found that the women in the group, even though they were doing better academically than the men, scaled back their ambitions as they moved through their college careers. These women differed from the "doing well" women we discussed earlier in that they were top achievers and undoubtedly had worked for the high school honors accorded them. Nor did they seem to be faltering in college: the women in the study had a 3.7 grade-point average as compared with a 3.5 for the men.

Still, they reported that their self-esteem was falling. While 21 percent of the women said they felt "far above average" intellectually when they graduated from high school, by the time they were seniors in college none considered themselves better than their peers. (For men the percentage increased, from 23 to 25 percent.)

Researcher Karen D. Arnold, now associate dean of students at Reed College in

Oregon, explained to *The New York Times* that forming an adult identity is more complex for women because they see a conflict between success at home and achievement on the job. When they begin to worry about these dual roles, usually during their college years, they tend to scale back their professional ambitions.

When the study followed up on students who had entered the workforce, most of the men had entered professional careers, while the women were working at jobs well below the level they had aspired to originally. Some young women voice concerns about mixing career and family at an even earlier age.

A counselor at one prestigious West Coast prep school told us, "One thing I've noticed seems different about the girls attending this school: when asked about children, most respond that they don't think they'll have children because they don't know how they will reconcile this with their career aspirations. They seem confused and even somewhat depressed about this issue."

No doubt they are. Most schools offer no advice on mixing career and family, although about 90 percent of high school women say they expect to be wives, mothers, and workers. At that age males and females can be equally serious about career planning, and expect to attain about the same level of education. Both girls and boys also expect that the women will carry most of the responsibility for child care and housework.

Looking at their own mothers and other adult women, teens see that they receive very little support from their employers and/or spouses. If young women ask how they're supposed to balance dual responsibilities, they're likely to be told that "things work out somehow" or "you just do the best you can." It's sort of like that cartoon where the mad scientist scrawls his formulas across the board and reaches his solution by stopping at the tricky part to write, "And then a miracle happens." Girls aren't buying it.

To many of them the most obvious solution is to scale back their career ambitions, but there are obvious flaws in this plan.

Young women need a strategy

Scaling back is not the answer, nor are most jobs traditionally held by women. Instead young women need a strategy for mixing career and family. The most workable plan, it seems to us, is to aim for a higher rung on the career ladder. Let us explain.

In most families the resources for which demand usually outruns supply are time, money, and flexibility. Time is the finite resource. There are twenty-four hours in a day, and that's it. When you consider all the things working parents have to fit into that day—getting the children dressed and fed, getting themselves ready for work, commuting to day care, commuting to work, working, picking up the kids, driving home, making dinner, eating dinner, bathing the children and putting them to bed, doing laundry, cleaning the house, getting a few hours' sleep—it becomes obvious that time is invaluable. Too often it is also the resource that is, like most parents, exhausted.

This is not news. Trying to buy time is the reason most women give for choosing less demanding jobs. It's easy to find work as a part-time salesclerk. If a secretary wants to quit for a while, she can find a similar job when she's ready to go back to work. Teachers get the whole summer off. These statements are all true, but what about that second resource, money?

The fact that low-level or traditional women's jobs do not pay enough for most families to live on quickly becomes clear when a family tries to do it. If a man loses his job for some reason, or if there is a divorce, the family will not be able to survive economically on the woman's salary. She will have to put in more hours or get a second job. And where is she supposed to find the time to do that?

What if, instead of becoming salesclerks and secretaries, women became accountants and chiropractors or auto mechanics and electricians? They would earn so much more money per hour that they could buy time. With a higher salary they would need to work fewer hours to earn a living wage. Or they might choose to hire a housekeeper or a nanny. Either way they gain time to spend with their families and lose the stress of financial insecurity.

Raising my children has always been a priority for me. I chose teaching because I wanted to be home after school and when my kids were on vacation. I also thought it would be easier to get another assignment if I decided to stay home for a few years when they were small.

The facts are, though, I usually don't get home till late afternoon because of meetings and job requirements. The day-to-day flexibility of my job is almost nil. I can't just take a few hours off in the afternoon to attend my daughter's school recital. If Tommy got sick in the middle of the day, I can't pick up my work and take it home with me.

But the cruelest fact of all is that my traditional female career, the one I spent five years of college preparing for, will not support my family financially. My husband left us last year, and I have been struggling to make ends meet. I'm going to have to sell the house because I can't make the payments, and we're going to have to move to an area I would never have considered living in before. I'm looking for a second job to supplement our income. That means even less time with my kids.

—Mother, 37, of two grade-schoolers,
and a teacher for 15 years

Three months after my first son was born, I set up shop as a book developer and producer, using skills and contacts acquired over a dozen years as a book editor in publishing houses. Way back in college, one thing that had first attracted me about publishing was that I thought I could do a little proofreading or something on the side while my future children were young. My husband was very supportive of the idea of launching out on my own at the time. It has worked out even better than I planned. My flexible schedule makes life much less stressful for the entire family. It made it possible for the older boy to go to the preschool I chose (with hours ending at three). My husband often has to leave for work at seven, but I can get the kids organized by a much more leisurely eight-thirty. I can be there for the class field trip to the zoo or when the baby has one more ear infection. The real kicker—the one I love to add as a punch line when people ask me how I managed all this—is that I make much more money than I ever did working for someone else. And I love my work, something I'm afraid I can't say about many of my friends.

—*Book developer, mother of a 5-year-old and a 2-year-old*

The higher-paying, autonomous careers also offer the most opportunities for self-employment, which millions of women have found to be the ideal solution for working mothers. With the right education or training and a few years of experience, women can take control of their own lives. Professional women and skilled workers can set up their own practices or businesses. Those with specialized knowledge often choose to become consultants. Writers, photographers, graphic designers, and the like can freelance their work. Those with a talent for sales might go into real estate, insurance, securities, and so on.

Women who work for themselves not only decide for themselves when and how much they will work, but they also get around the "glass ceiling" that has halted the advancement of so many of their sisters.

Finally there's the issue of flexibility. We tend to think of flexibility in terms of the ease with which a person can leave and reenter the workforce or the availability of part-time jobs. The truth is, though, that parents are more likely to need day-to-day flexibility. They want to be able to stay home with a sick child or to attend school conferences and activities. Which jobs allow them to do these things? Almost without exception, the higher-paying nontraditional jobs offer the most autonomy.

She will have to make one sacrifice: because she needs to have her career in place before she starts her family, child-bearing will have to be delayed. But that may not be a bad idea in any case. When *Working Woman* magazine polled 4,900 of its readers, it found that the most satisfied women were those who had established their careers before having children (80 percent said they were "very happy" with their lives, as compared with 53 percent of those who began parenting at an early age).

Tape this to your mirror:

> The higher your daughter's aspirations for educational and professional achievement, the more freedom she will have for parenting in later life.

What you can do to help

It is unfortunate that most schools continue to separate career education and family education (home economics, parenting, family life) in separate classes, as though there were no connection between these two major spheres of life. Does your daughter's school offer family life and career planning as one unit in the same classroom? If not, bring the problem to the administration's attention. Be an advocate for getting a combined curriculum into the home economics department or the career education curriculum.

Our book *More Choices: A Strategic Planning Guide for Mixing Career and Family* was written to help young women work through their own planning process. The concepts summarized in this chapter are presented in depth in a self discovery format. You may want to get her a copy.

You can also help your daughter make the best decisions for her future in the following ways:

1. Make sure she understands the concepts we've discussed thus far, and that she views work and family life as interconnected parts.

2. Give her a realistic picture of motherhood.

Many young women are so wrapped up in the fantasy of the cuddly, cooing infant that they overlook the more stressful aspects of parenthood. Talk to your daughter about the sacrifices involved as well as the rewards. Be sure she understands what mothering entails on a minute-to-minute, day-by-day basis. Some of the facts she should accept before deciding to have a child are that

a) she is likely to carry most of the child care responsibilities in her family;

b) the demands of motherhood will mean less personal time and less privacy; and

c) parenting may take a toll on her ability to achieve at work.

3. Encourage her to select a satisfying career.

Many young women feel that in some way they are cheating their families if they train for and work at a job they find meaningful, especially if it has higher demands. But motherhood is not a lifetime job, and since the great majority of all parents are likely to be working for pay most of their lives, family happiness can be greatly enhanced if both parents like what they do for a living and come home with a smile on their face.

Your daughter should remember, too, that she is most likely to succeed at a job she loves. A bond trader who really wants to be an English teacher is unlikely to be either happy or successful. That's one reason why the process of becoming identity achieved is so important.

4. Make sure that the following questions are included on her career research surveys:

What is the day-to-day flexibility of this job? What is the salary potential for this job? Will that salary support a family on one income? Are there part-time or freelance opportunities within this career?

We've already discussed the importance of flexibility. Your daughter also needs to look at the salary potential for careers she is considering. Some offer relatively high starting salaries, which may be fine when she's single or newly married. If there is little room for salary advancement, however, she may find herself in economic difficulty later on, when growing families lead to increased expenses.

Due to the rapid advancements in technology, some job categories face extinction. Your daughter needs to look at this factor to avoid training for a job that may not be around for long.

5. Help your daughter choose her partner wisely, not by choosing for her or by giving unasked-for advice about her current boyfriends, but by starting a dialogue about marriage and relationships in general early.

While doing research for another project, we asked women why they had married when and whom they did. Some of their responses: "To get away from home," "For security," "I didn't know what to do with my life," "I didn't want to disappoint him," and "I thought he was the ideal man to build a family with. No, no, no, I fell in love with him, and that was it."

Your daughter needs to understand that her best shot at happiness is with someone who shares her values and aspirations about both professional and family matters. More on this in chapter 26.

6. Encourage her to think seriously about whether and when she wants to have children.

It is so often assumed or expected that women will be mothers that many do not really consider their own feelings in the matter. If she does expect to have children, what kind of child care would she like to have? Does she see how her preferences relate to her career aspirations, as well as to when she might plan to give birth? (If she wants live-in help, for example, she will need to be earning quite a lot of money, something it is unlikely she will do at twenty-one.)

7. Help her learn to set priorites, starting now.

Working parents who can't weed out the unimportant events or activities in life are likely to end up frustrated and exhausted. But it's difficult to focus on long-term goals when faced with a messy house, a child needing help with her math, and a note demanding delivery of five dozen cookies for the bake sale tomorrow. By learning now to ask herself what's most important, what will help her achieve her goals, your daughter will also have an easier time avoiding the distractions that can deter her from her studies.

Are there further messages you'd like to add to "Your Plan" about economic self-sufficiency, family planning, career planning, relationships, marriage and children, or achievement?

chapter twenty-six

Out into the World

Whether your daughter is entering college, getting her first job, or going on to technical school, the period following high school graduation is one filled with change and growth. If you and your daughter have five or six years to plan and prepare for this important time, it can be even more exciting and fulfilling.

Start now to think about what you want from her, what you expect from her, and how you will go about giving her her independence. No matter what her present age, it's not too soon to start talking to her of the wonderful time when she will be grown and able to take care of herself.

The worksheet on page 395 will help you answer the question "What Are Your Expectations?" Have you discussed these expectations with your daughter? They should be made clear to her years ahead of time so that the entire family can plan for her eventual emancipation (the legal term for releasing a child from parental care and responsibility) and transition into adulthood. This should be approached as an exciting, positive step for her. And by making it a gradual process, you are able to provide her with the information she'll need, while she has time to develop the skills of independence and to prepare herself for the responsibilities of adulthood. This is not "getting rid of" a child. It is a loving letting go. By allowing your daughter to experience this transition in a successful way, you are also bolstering her self-esteem.

She flies by her own wings.

—*Latin proverb*

What are your expectations?

EDUCATION

Do you hope your daughter goes on to college or vocational school after she completes high school?

If so, do you expect her to assume any of the costs for that education?

How much money are you prepared to contribute? (This information may help determine her choice of schools.)

HOUSING

Do you expect your daughter to live at home after high school or to move into a dorm or apartment?

If you expect her to move, who will pay the rent? Who will pay for food, utilities, and the like?

If your daughter continues to live with you, will you expect her to make a financial contribution to the household? How much? What do you expect this money to cover?

If you plan to continue supporting your daughter, how long do you think this support should last? Are there circumstances under which this support would be extended or withdrawn? What are they?

Once she's moved out, will she be welcome to move back home at her own discretion or do you expect her to be on her own after that time (unless there is a crisis)?

FINANCES

At what age or what point in her life do you expect your daughter to be financially independent of you?

Under what conditions would you agree to be responsible for all or part of your young adult daughter's expenses?

Freedom and responsibility

Traditionally, women in our society have been denied their full freedom because, it is said, they must be "protected." This protection, however, often leads to a different kind of freedom: the freedom of irresponsibility. A young woman we know who was "protected" from the financial realities of life, for example, ran up a five-hundred-dollar phone bill her first month at college because she had no idea how much it cost to make a long-distance call. Another bright college student risked the scholarship she needed to remain in school because, finally away from her family's "protection," she was too caught up in her newfound liberation to do her class assignments.

Allowing your daughter to be irresponsible is also a way of keeping her dependent. Even if you can afford it, and even if you have all the best intentions, it is not wise to give her money whenever she requests it, no questions asked, no accountability required. If you do, what is her motivation to become self-sufficient or to learn to live within a budget? Negotiating an allowance with her, on the other hand, allowing her the freedom to spend that money as she wishes, and then refusing to rescue her the first time she makes a mistake teaches her not only the connection between freedom and responsibility, but self-reliance, creativity, and pride as well.

One of the greatest dangers in withholding freedom from your daughter is that she will become accustomed to living within your restraints and protection. It will feel comfortable for her. This situation is not conducive to building healthy relationships with men in her adult life. As Nicky Marone says in her book *How to Father a Successful Daughter,* "Since she will have already learned how to adapt to limitations set by others, it will not feel uncomfortable, and she will not put up a fight when her rights are threatened. She will not even know that her rights are being threatened." The potential hazard is that she will leave home only to go into a marriage or job where she gives up her personal rights.

Emancipation

Plan to begin giving your daughter her freedom as she enters adolescence. Your own expectations and your daughter's level of maturity will determine when she is to be wholly emancipated (able to make all her own choices without consulting you). Will it be when she starts college? When she finishes her education? On her eighteenth or twenty-first birthday? When she is financially independent?

Each year up until then, negotiate with your daughter the freedoms to be given and the responsibilities to be taken on. There should be at least one of each concerning her curfew, finances, education, and dating or friendships. Consider having an annual lunch or ceremony of some sort, perhaps on her birthday, to celebrate the occasion and make it more meaningful. You might even make up a Declaration of Independence–type document on parchment paper, tie it up with a ribbon, and present it to her.

As you negotiate with your daughter, ask yourself if you'd be doing things any differently if you were discussing your son's freedom. Resist the temptation to make different agreements with girls than with boys.

Use the following worksheet to brainstorm by yourself the freedoms and responsibilities you will gradually give your daughter, then negotiate with her to reach their final form.

Less than two weeks after he got his driver's license, my brother was allowed to drive at night. Even though I've always been more responsible than him, my parents made me wait six months. As a male, they told me, my brother was simply more capable than me.

—Hispanic honors student, 18

Sample plan

AGE THIRTEEN

Freedom: *To go on outings with friends within the community, providing she is home by a stated curfew and she conducts herself responsibly.*

Responsibility: *To let her parents know where she is at all times and to follow safety rules, obey the law, and respect other people's property.*

AGE FOURTEEN

Freedom: *To receive a weekly salary to cover bus fare, school lunches, personal needs and sundries, weekly entertainment, and personal phone calls, as well as an annual clothing allowance.*

Responsibility: *To live within her means, understanding that additional funds will not be given or advanced.*

AGE FIFTEEN

Freedom: *To have her curfew extended to midnight on weekends.*

Responsibility: *To make every effort to be home by curfew and to call if she will be more than five minutes late; to maintain a certain grade-point average.*

AGE SIXTEEN

Freedom: *To drive the family car.*

Responsibility: *To maintain a clean driving record; to pay for any increase in insurance rates due to her driving violations; to give up driving privileges until age eighteen if she receives two tickets.*

AGE SEVENTEEN

Freedom: *To choose the college she wants to attend or the vocational training she wants to receive.*

Responsibility: *To plan within the budgetary constraints of the family; any additional money required must be raised by scholarships, loans, grants, or working.*

AGE EIGHTEEN

Freedom: *To make all decisions concerning her life, without parental interference.*

Responsibility: *To be either economically independent or in college or vocational school full-time as a dedicated student.*

Your emancipation schedule might include some of the freedoms and responsibilities included in our example.

By granting your daughter gradually increasing levels of freedom and by acknowledging her growing independence, you can greatly lessen the stress and tensions associated with a young person's separating from her parents. If she knows you champion her growth and are not trying to control her, she will feel free to talk with you about her concerns and to come to you for advice. You can be a friend as well as a mentor throughout her adolescence and into her adult years.

Emancipation plan for your daughter

AGE THIRTEEN

Freedom:

Responsibility:

AGE FOURTEEN

Freedom:

Responsibility:

AGE FIFTEEN

Freedom:

Responsibility:

AGE SIXTEEN

Freedom:

Responsibility:

AGE SEVENTEEN

Freedom:

Responsibility:

AGE EIGHTEEN

Freedom:

Responsibility:

Basic skills of living checklist

Before your daughter goes out on her own, she should know the following:

LIFE SKILLS

❏ How to shop and cook
❏ How to do laundry and maintain her wardrobe
❏ How (and how often and why) to clean her apartment
❏ How to negotiate with roommates, if she will have one
❏ How to maintain an automobile (if she will have one)
❏ How to get from point A to point B on public transportation (bus, train, or airplane)

FINANCIAL MANAGEMENT

❏ How to live within a budget
❏ How to be a savvy consumer
❏ How to balance a checkbook
❏ How to negotiate the lease on an apartment
❏ How to negotiate a salary and ask for a raise
❏ All about credit, credit cards, and credit ratings
❏ All about savings, personal and retirement

PERSONAL SECURITY

❏ Family planning information
❏ AIDS information
❏ Drug information (including tobacco and alcohol)
❏ Breast self-examination techniques
❏ Preventative health care (nutrition, diet, annual physicals)

- ❏ Stress-reduction techniques
- ❏ How to test smoke alarms and change their batteries
- ❏ Self-defense and safety requirements for women alone

CITIZEN RESPONSIBILITIES

- ❏ How to file income taxes
- ❏ How to register to vote

The big decisions

Quick: What are the two most important decisions your daughter (or anyone else) will make in her lifetime?

When Mindy conducts workshops, she always asks this question, and without hesitation most of the audience responds that choosing a career and choosing a life partner are the "big two."

Although we've discussed these issues earlier, here are a few additional thoughts and activities that are appropriate for your emerging adult daughter. You are entering a time when you are even less likely to speak with your daughter on a regular basis—she is busy, living away from home, or both. When you do get together or talk on the phone, try to work the following points into the conversation.

Big decision number one:
choosing a career

We have dealt extensively with career decisions and relationships throughout the book, but here are a few more points that you should especially focus on with an older daughter preparing to go out into the world.

If your daughter loses sight of how essential it is for young people to have some kind of job training or education beyond high school, have these statistics at your fingertips. The William T. Grant Foundation's report, "The Forgotten Half: Non-College Youth in America," states that this group of young adults faces some extremely unfavorable odds:

- *With the greatly changing job market, there is little opportunity for obtaining "a job with a future" without advanced education.*
- *Unemployment among Americans aged twenty to twenty-four is higher than that for other age groups, and real income is declining.*
- *Between 1973 and 1986 there was a decrease of 27 percent in the real median income of families headed by a twenty- to twenty-four-year-old.*
- *"Between 1974 and 1986, the proportion of married twenty- to twenty-four-year-old males living with their spouses plummeted by almost one-half, from 39.1 to 21.3 percent."*
- *In 1986 the poverty rate for families headed by a person under twenty-five (32.6 percent) was three times as large as the rate for all American families.*

In 1992, when *Money* magazine published "The American Dream and Today's Reality," Denise M. Topolnicki wrote, "If there is one overriding lesson of our research, it is this: Today's economic winners are those with the most schooling; the losers tend to have the least." She added that "the only sure tickets to prosperity are a solid education and a valuable skill."

The article went on to state that low-skilled jobs offering relatively high pay have been decreasing in numbers since 1979, and that this trend is expected to continue into the next century. Today the wage gap between high school graduates and college graduates is bigger than the often mentioned gap between earnings of men and women at the height of the women's movement: at that time, women earned only fifty-nine cents for every dollar paid to men; today, those with a high school diploma earn only fifty-seven cents for each dollar paid to a college grad.

404 WHAT'S A PARENT TO DO?

College life is dominated by gregarious activity, very little of which focuses on academic excellence. By the time your daughter graduates from high school, she should have a clear understanding of why she is continuing her education (to learn and prepare for a career, not just to get a certificate or a good grade), and how her performance relates to her future on the job. She should also be strong enough to turn down social invitations if they interfere with her work, even if she's teased about being too serious.

Many young people become nervous and uncertain about their goals and their future during this time. If your daughter has learned to tolerate anxiety, it should be easier for her to hang in there, but you and she should also be aware of some of the most common symptoms of anxiety overload. Then, if they occur, you will be more likely to see them for what they are and deal with them accordingly. The most serious symptoms are wanting to change her major, wanting to quit school, or deciding to get married. There may be good reasons for making any of these decisions, but talk things through with her before she takes action, or urge her to talk with her adviser or a school counselor. Would she really rather be a dancer than an archaeologist, or could that D she got on her last exam have something to do with her decision? Are there less drastic steps she could take? Is she willing to give herself some more time or to take a different approach to her studies?

"During my last year in college, I would have married anyone who asked me," says Clarice, a brilliant woman who went on to earn two master's degrees before settling down. She is hardly the only woman who felt that way. While college life offers some of the same comforts of home, going out into the "real world" can be frightening. Marriage can suddenly seem like a refuge, even for those who have always aspired to careers.

Of course, many people do meet their future spouses in college, but if your daughter's decision comes about quickly and/or entails giving up her own goals, there is reason to be concerned. Again, without being judgmental, you can ask questions and, giving advice only if it is requested, talk the matter through with her.

Two years or less of vocational training can also lead to lucrative careers—more lucrative than some jobs requiring a college degree. Many plumbers, for example, earn more than most teachers. Once again, the highest-paying jobs tend to be those most often held by men, so urge your daughter to look beyond the cosmetology and secretarial programs many young women think of when they consider vocational school.

The military, although cutting back, still offers opportunities for job training, particularly in technology, though the problems with sexual harassment that have become known is something to consider before recommending this option to your daughter. Some people elect to make it their career, retire before they're forty with an adequate pension, and have the rest of their lives to pursue whatever interests them.

Some fields still offer apprenticeships or on-the-job training. You and your daughter can consider whether she has any special talents. If she's outgoing and persuasive, for example, she might do very well at commissioned sales.

Remember that the final choices—what she will study, where she will study, and what she will do with her education—are your daughter's. Your job is to listen and to offer support, information, and advice, if it's requested. Try not to impose your own ideas and values. If she has been educated about the need to be self-sufficient, the opportunities available to her, and the options for mixing career and family, chances are good that she will choose wisely.

Big decision number two: choosing a mate

Choosing a mate is also entirely up to your daughter, but you can help her think about and describe the kind of a person she's looking for by initiating conversations on the subject. *These must begin before she falls in love.*

The conversations should be low-key and comfortable. Initiate them when you'll have some time alone together: in the car, over lunch or dinner, on vacations. It is essential that you not impose your own feelings or try to direct her thoughts. If this is difficult for you, practice your approach with friends before you begin.

Your goal is to help your daughter clarify her own desires by gently asking questions to guide her along.

Start by asking the broad questions: Does she want to get married? Does she want to have children? What kind of a relationship would she like to have with her husband? Where you go from here will depend on your daughter's answers. She may change her mind, perhaps several times, but this process will help her understand the importance of continually examining what and who it is she's looking for.

In general terms there are three kinds of heterosexual relationships. Traditional relationships are just that: the man earns

As a general thing, people marry most happily with their own kind. The trouble lies in the fact that people usually marry at an age when they do not really know what their own kind is.

—*Robertson Davies*

the money, and the woman cares for the home and children. Most of the male's attention is focused on his work, and there may be little time to build or maintain relationships with the family. Gender roles are rigidly enforced.

Contemporary relationships are more pragmatic. Both partners are likely to work outside the home, but the male expects and is expected to be the prime support for the family. The wife is still responsible for most housework and child care, but the husband is more involved with family matters than the "traditional" male. Decisions are made on the basis of what works or what makes sense instead of what is expected or what has always been done. Gender roles apply somewhat but are not strictly enforced.

In egalitarian marriages both partners are expected to contribute equally to the family's finances and to share equally in housework and child care. Neither partner has more power than the other. Maintaining the relationship, too, is the responsibility of both individuals. Gender roles are not enforced.

The survey "What Kind of Relationship Do I Want?" might help your daughter begin to consider the kind of relationship that would be most satisfying to her.

In "What Kind of Relationship Do I Want?" did your daughter lean strongly toward one of the relationships? Which one? Her choice will probably mirror the relationship she sees between her parents or stepparents.

That raises another point: People have an unconscious tendency to re-create the marriage of their parents. It is often noted, for example, that the children of alcoholics are more likely than others to marry an alcoholic. But the pattern is much more complex than that. Maggie Scarf describes it thoroughly in her book *Intimate Partners*. If, for whatever reason, you think it would be a mistake for your daughter to re-create your marriage, we recommend that you read the book to get a better understanding of the process and then discuss it frankly with your daughter. (Again, this must be done before she gets involved with someone.)

While it is more permissible than it used to be for young women to initiate a relationship, it doesn't often happen. When we ask groups of college students which ones would ask a boy for a date, nearly all raise their hands. When we ask how many have, however, most of the hands are lowered.

It's not difficult to understand why. All those cultural myths about girls being pursued and/or rescued are still around. Parents who grew up in a different era may be passing on the message that "nice" girls don't make the first move. And then there's all

If mothers raise their girls to take the initiative rather than wait, we may eventually have a generation of women more responsible for their sex. When you set your sights on the man you want, know why you want him, and accept that he might reject you, you are already more in charge than the woman who waits to be picked like a cookie on a platter.

—Nancy Friday,
Women on Top

What kind of relationship do I want?

Ask your daughter which statement under each heading is most in line with her own thinking.

CHILD CARE:

☐ 1. It is the mother's responsibility to care for the children.
☐ 2. Mothers should be primarily responsible for child care, but fathers should offer some relief.
☐ 3. Parents should share child care tasks equally.

IF MY HUSBAND WERE OFFERED A PROMOTION THAT REQUIRED MOVING TO ANOTHER PART OF THE COUNTRY:

☐ 1. I would go along with his decision.
☐ 2. I would probably agree if it meant a significant raise in pay or authority and it was what my husband really wanted.
☐ 3. I would expect to have an equal voice in the decision, and I would be comfortable saying I don't want to go if, after serious thought and discussion, I thought it would be an unwise move.

I BELIEVE:

☐ 1. my husband will be the sole support of our family.
☐ 2. I will have a job, but my husband will probably earn more money than I will.
☐ 3. my husband and I will be equal partners in the financial support of the family.

I EXPECT MY MAIN ROLE TO BE:

☐ 1. taking complete responsibility for the household and child care tasks and for maintaining relationships within the family.

☐ 2. working outside the home, but also taking most of the responsibility for household tasks and child care. My husband will offer some help.

☐ 3. acting as an equal partner with my husband in all aspects of our marriage, financial and personal.

I BELIEVE THAT CARRYING OUT HOUSEHOLD CHORES:

☐ 1. is a woman's job.

☐ 2. is the wife's responsibility, but the husband should help.

☐ 3. should be shared equally by marriage partners.

COMMUNICATION:

☐ 1. Since men are not good at communication, I will take responsibility for maintaining it within our relationship.

☐ 2. My husband will struggle with communicating his feelings and needs, but the majority of the responsibility of maintaining open dialogues will be mine.

☐ 3. I expect my husband to work as hard at keeping the lines of communication open as I do.

MY PERSONAL ASPIRATIONS ARE:

☐ 1. to support the goals of my husband and children.

☐ 2. to follow my own dreams, but only after my children are grown.

☐ 3. as important as my husband's, now and into the future.

Key: Statements numbered "1" reflect the traditional view; those numbered "2" are contemporary; those numbered "3" are egalitarian.

that anxiety and fear of rejection that males have always had to deal with. What if he says no?

If your daughter is looking for a "traditional" relationship, she will probably want to follow the traditional "rules." Otherwise, feeling free to ask for what she wants in the complicated sphere of dating and choosing a mate can be a big step toward her future happiness.

You can help by not making negative or judgmental statements to her—or to your sons—about girls who take this step. Better yet, encourage her to do it.

Encourage your daughter to develop her own strategies for initiating friendships and relationships with men. Some young women will be more comfortable with direct methods, while others will want to be less direct but at the same time proactive. You can help your daughter distinguish between freely initiating a relationship and acting needy and desperate to have one. With experience she will be more comfortable making these kinds of decisions and moves on her own.

Emphasize that the idea is not to see how many hearts she can capture, but rather to take a serious look at herself and the young men she knows and to choose those who appear to meet her standards.

During the fall of 1992 Mindy interviewed nine freshman women at a prestigious college on the West Coast. When she asked about careers, they easily came up with the "right" answers. But when the questioning turned to dating, there was clearly more energy in the room; nervous voices rose in pitch and tone. Question: What are the traits you are looking for in your ideal man? Silence. When one young woman volunteered that she had a long list, the others quickly silenced her, saying it was unrealistic to expect so much. Question: Okay, what five nonnegotiable traits would any male have to demonstrate before you could get seriously involved with him? Silence. Fine, Mindy said, think about that and we'll come back to it. About five minutes later she raised the question again. More silence. Finally one young woman came up with a characteristic: honesty. Still more silence. When it became obvious that this line of questioning was only making everyone nervous, Mindy reluctantly moved on.

When you think about it, it really doesn't make much sense for "a cookie on a platter" to set boundaries or make demands. Most young women want desperately to be chosen, and their only requirement may be that they don't find the young men in question physically repugnant. They may have long lists of "ideal" traits, but these are mainly fantasies and

You're writing a book about daughters. I hope you talk about the importance of being able to get out of a bad or less satisfying relationship before getting in too deep. Young women have so much trouble with that.

—Father of young adult daughters

In order that she may be able to give her hand with dignity, she must be able to stand alone.

—*Margaret Fuller*

are recognized as such. They would like to marry a Tom Cruise or a Denzel Washington, but they don't really expect it to happen.

Has your daughter given this matter any thought? As she moves through adolescence and into adulthood, she should. This is an ideal topic for your ongoing conversations with her. What traits are absolutely essential in any man she would get seriously involved with? There may be five or six, perhaps fewer (and realistically, not many more). Set up a series of luncheons with your daughter to brainstorm and discuss this. If she begins to articulate her list, she will be much more likely to choose wisely.

"It took me eight years to leave a bad relationship," says Beth, "mostly because I thought what he wanted was more important than what I did." Because women often see themselves as having less power or less worth within a relationship, they may feel it's not their place to decide to end it.

This is an empowering skill that every young woman should have. It can make the difference between a life of success and satisfaction or one of pain and struggle. Can your daughter tolerate the anxiety of being alone? For many women, the thought that there might not be anyone else out there for them holds them in unsatisfactory situations.

If you've raised your daughter to have a hardy personality, she will be in a good position to choose the right life partner for herself:

Because she can be discriminating, establish boundaries, and set limits, she is less likely to get involved with an individual who does not meet all her nonnegotiable standards.

Because she is assertive and sets her own goals and priorities, she will be more comfortable being an active participant in the process of choosing a mate and is therefore more likely to find her relationship personally fulfilling.

Because she knows the difference between fantasy and reality, she won't let myths and fairy tales color her decisions but will see the situation clearly and act accordingly.

Because she has her own goals, she will be willing to wait for the right relationship before getting married.

Because she can tolerate anxiety and act anyway, she will be willing to risk rejection if it means having a more active role in the courting process.

Because she can project herself into the future, she will be more likely to consider the consequences of a commitment and to ask herself if this is the person she wants to spend the rest of her life with.

Because she trusts herself, she will not be manipulated or talked into acting against her will or against her own best interests.

With your daughter's emancipation, your official job is over. Relax. She can take it from here. Of course, you'll continue to give her your love and support. In return she will give you a feeling of unprecedented joy as you stand back and watch her soar.

Are there any final messages you'd like to add to "Your Plan," perhaps about achievement or marriage and family?

iv.
Everybody's daughter

chapter twenty-seven

Advocacy for Girls

U p to this point we have discussed ways to influence your daughter's future within the family. Now it's time to talk about moving into the wider world and making a difference for everybody's daughters. We're not asking you to be entirely selfless here. Unless we see substantial changes in the way society operates, the potential is great that most of your efforts on your daughter's behalf will, sooner or later, be undone by outside forces. In this chapter and the next we will present strategies for becoming an advocate for girls within your community—and beyond it. We will also provide a comprehensive plan for setting up small groups of mothers and daughters to provide support networks for both populations during the difficult period of your daughter's adolescence.

> *Never doubt that a small group of thoughtful committed citizens can change the world; indeed, it is the only thing that ever has.*
>
> —*Margaret Mead*

Becoming an advocate

Former AAUW national president Sarah Harder became an advocate for girls when her teenage niece was raped and murdered. The incident took place in a populated area where the young woman might have been saved if she'd called out, but

> *Don't just change the girls; change the rules!*
> —*Heather Johnston Nicholson,
> Girls Incorporated*

> *When our daughters ask why they may never see a woman president . . . we have no good answers for them. That is because there are none.*
> —*Anna Quindlen*

she kept her silence. Talking about the murder later, Sarah and her sister decided that they probably wouldn't have called for help, either, and that something needed to be done about that fact.

For Penny Paine, formerly of Advocacy Press and now a regional consultant for the California Department of Education's Office of Gender Equity, a degree in embroidery was the ticket to advocacy. Asked to teach needlework at what is now Girls Incorporated of Carpinteria, California, she soon became executive director, and she's been working for girls' equity ever since.

Betty Shepperd was looking for a project that would be a break from her job directing a hospice when she wandered into one of Penny's workshops and, before long, became national coordinator of the Women Helping Girls with Choices program.

In the 1980s there were rumors that activism for girls' and women's rights was dead. Don't believe it. It never died, it simply changed direction. Once a movement of mass action and visible protest, it is now a network of small groups and individuals working within the system, more quietly but more effectively, for change.

There are many ways to advocate for girls' equity. What you choose to do is your decision, but it is important that you do something: things will not be measurably better for your daughter until they are better for everyone's daughters. In recent years we have relearned the lessons of interdependence. And as columnist Ellen Goodman says, "A family also thrives or shrivels in the larger human environment."

Ways to be an advocate for girls' equity

You might want to make advocacy a full-time job, as many people have done. Some have gone to work for organizations that are geared toward making social changes for girls and women. Some have been elected to political office. Others have turned their traditional jobs into advocacy positions: counselors specialize in clients with eating disorders or survivors of incest, for example; writers concentrate on women's issues; attorneys handle cases dealing with sex discrimination, sexual harassment, or violence against women; financial advisers offer seminars to teach investment strategies to women.

Can you think of ways to be an advocate within your present line of work? If you're in a position of authority, you might start by examining your employment policies. Do you give the women who work for you an equal chance at advancement? How flexible are the jobs? What are your policies on family leave? Can you help with day care?

No matter what your line of work or your position within the organization, it is essential that you become an advocate for women in the workplace. This is one action that will speak volumes to your daughter about the value you place on women's equality.

Could you teach a Saturday morning computer class for girls? Volunteer to paint walls or fix the plumbing at a battered women's shelter? Transport the girls' volleyball team to out-of-town games in your van?

You might want to tie your advocacy efforts to issues of particular concern to your daughter. Is she an athlete attending a school with an inadequate athletic program for girls? Has she been harassed on the bus or in the halls at school? Has she wondered out loud why there are so few women in government?

Early in the book we suggested that women form Mothers for Daughters support groups. Similarly, we urge men to form Dads' committees to serve as advocates for girls within the community. Perhaps you will want to make a presentation about the needs of girls in today's world to your Rotary Club, Lions Club, or other service organization. A young woman who receives visible support from her father has a real advantage both in terms of her self-esteem and her potential for achievement.

Whatever else you decide to do, speak up for the rights of girls and women. Act as a mentor and/or role model. On an individual basis, try to raise the consciousness of those around you. One woman we know, for example, listened to a male acquaintance tell her that his dream was to send his son to college, even though he had just explained that his daughter was brighter and more ambitious. "Shouldn't she have an opportunity to get an education?" our friend asked. Her question at least gave him something to think about.

On a larger scale, attend meetings and write letters. Make financial contributions to organizations you believe in. Support political candidates who support women's issues. And don't forget to vote.

If you hear a sexist comment or joke, speak up and defend the reputation of women even if it appears unpopular with the group. Dads, if you do this in front of your daughter, she will love and respect you for it.

A "to do" list

Girls Incorporated offers the following suggestions any individual can follow to make things better for all our daughters:

IN THE FAMILY

- *Watch your language; watch other people's. Don't talk in sexist stereotypes.*
- *Try some role reversal at home. Let Dad do the dishes; son bathe baby; and daughter mow the lawn or take out the garbage.*
- *Read what children are reading. Point out sexist messages/advertising. Write protest letters together.*
- *Encourage girls to talk as much as boys; and listen just as intently to what they say.*
- *Watch TV with the children; help them analyze what they are seeing.*
- *Praise nonsexist programs and protest stereotyping to networks, program producers, and sponsors.*
- *Include boys in discussions about sexual responsibility. Your expectations for responsible sexual behavior of both sexes should be equal and explicit.*
- *Encourage and praise risk taking in female children and caretaking in boys.*
- *Avoid rescuing girls.*
- *Demonstrate to your daughters the math and science in everyday activities.*
- *Use the language of skill and success to compliment girls.*
- *Talk to girls and boys about balancing family responsibilities.*
- *Introduce girls to women and men in the world of work in both traditional and nontraditional jobs.*

IN THE SCHOOLS

- *Work with other parents and teachers to foster nonsexist environments from nursery school forward.*
- *Urge educators to introduce career awareness and information in elementary school.*
- *Look at textbooks: are there women in history, science, and art? If not, talk to the board of education; create a committee for change.*
- *Do girls have equal access and time on the computers and other high-tech equipment? Ask school administrators to develop viable programs to assure girls access and time.*

- How many girls are enrolled in advanced math, science, and computer courses? Work with school committees to develop a plan to register girls in these courses.
- Is there equal emphasis for girls and boys on sexual responsibility in human sexuality classes? If not, talk to the teachers and school administrators.
- Is there a stay-in-school program for teen mothers? If not, find out how you can start one.
- Are there organized, funded, team sports programs for girls? Talk to the principal, the coaches, the press.
- Are girls encouraged to participate in nontraditional vocational training? Help counselors get girls interested and enrolled.
- How many female counselors are there in vocational education programs? Campaign for more.
- Do teachers and counselors route girls to traditional jobs or none at all? Develop a network of working women to supplement the schools' efforts in career guidance.
- Recommend awareness training for faculty and staff on stereotyped language, books, and programming that slow girls' progress.

IN THE COMMUNITY

- Review and audit services for girls in your community. Work with women's organizations and political groups to strengthen and expand them.
- Are your United Way allocations distributed equally between programs for girls and programs for boys? Go to meetings. Make yourself heard on behalf of equitable funding for girls and boys.
- Are girls' programs designed to meet their needs? Make sure the funded programs actually serve girls, not just count them.
- Raise the issue of adequate and equitable funding through every affiliation you have.
- How many women are on the board of your United Way? Be the first (or the second).
- Get more women on the boards and allocation committees of funders— foundations, United Ways, service organizations—that help young people.
- Are advocates for girls involved in allocating resources for youth employment programs? Be one.
- Work for adequate community funding of teenage pregnancy prevention programs.
- Lobby to get girls' issues on the agenda of public commissions and private women's organizations.
- Advocate equal athletic and recreation opportunities for girls in schools and community programs.

- *Volunteer your time and expertise in programs serving girls.*
- *Contribute financially to programs serving girls.*
- *Start a Girls Incorporated center.*

IN THE WORKPLACE

- *In your advertising portray real people, not stereotypes.*
- *Develop and publicize interest in girls' programs.*
- *In your community relations programs, address girls' needs both through giving and volunteering.*
- *Check that programs you fund are serving girls, not just counting them.*
- *Make sure females participate in decisions about corporate giving.*
- *In summer hiring, open nontraditional jobs to girls and boys alike.*
- *In entry-level positions and promotional practices, give girls equal opportunities.*
- *Serve as mentors to girls and young women in your employ.*
- *Provide special support to young women faced with discrimination or sexual harassment on the job.*
- *Strengthen flexible schedules, day care provisions, and parental leaves to deliver the message that workers, female and male, are equally important family members.*

IN THE NATION

- *Support only candidates for public office who support equal opportunity for girls and women.*
- *Contribute time and dollars to candidates running for office who support women's issues.*
- *Be the liaison between organizations for girls and political campaigns and lobbying efforts to help girls develop political skills and awareness.*
- *Get involved in women's commissions and put girls' issues on the agenda of national women's organizations.*
- *Support teenage pregnancy prevention initiatives.*
- *Write your Washington representative in support of equal access for girls to vocational and professional schools, athletic programs, and scholarships.*
- *Support job development programs designed for female teenagers.*
- *Communicate with your representatives in Washington in support of the Women's Educational Equity Act to combat stereotypes in education.*
- *Write your elected representatives in support of the Equal Rights Amendment. (ERA has been reintroduced in Congress; it is not a dead issue.)*

Organizations for girls

Girls Incorporated was formed in 1945 (as Girls Clubs of America), dedicated to helping girls and young women overcome discrimination, to developing their capacity to be self-sufficient, responsible citizens, and to serving as a vigorous advocate for girls. Today Girls Incorporated serves over 250,000 young people between the ages of six and eighteen through three hundred centers across the country. In order to meet these goals, it has developed a number of innovative programs: Operation SMART encourages girls to get involved with math, science, and technology; Friendly PEERsuasion works to convince girls to avoid drugs and alcohol; Sporting Chance teaches basic athletic skills and exposes girls to a variety of sports, as well as to women athletes; Teen Connections focuses on health issues; Preventing Adolescent Pregnancy motivates girls to avoid pregnancy.

In 1981 Girls Incorporated founded its National Resource Center in Indianapolis, Indiana, in order to research problems and develop and evaluate new programs to help solve them. The nation's most extensive clearinghouse on girls, it also collects, analyzes, reports, and publishes research on girls and young women for use by the public as well as by the organization.

If you think you might like to start a Girls Incorporated center in your community, it's not a complicated process. According to the organization, Girls Incorporated affiliates can be started by one or two individuals who see the need for such a program in their community. Like you, they might be parents looking for an innovative afterschool program, a counselor who is seeking a new way to help prevent teen pregnancy, or even a local politician or community leader just trying to make a difference in a young girl's life. One thing these people all have in common is that they feel strongly about girls' special needs and want to make a difference.

To take the first step, call the national office of Girls Incorporated ([212] 689-3700). They will give you the phone number for the service center director who works with centers in your geographical region. Call her and discuss what you have done so far. From this conversation she will know how to proceed. Along with some advice, she may send you materials that describe more fully what the organization is and what they do and ask you to examine them more fully. Or she may send you a kit that will include the specific steps for you and your community to make. Just by beginning the process, you've already taken the most challenging step.

Addresses for the largest agencies with a priority of serving girls are as follows:

Girls Incorporated
30 East 33rd Street, 7th Floor
New York, NY 10016

Girl Scouts of the U.S.A.
420 Fifth Avenue
New York, NY 10018

YWCA
726 Broadway
New York, NY 10003

In recent years a number of agencies that formerly served only boys have gone coed. But do they really serve girls? It's best not to make any assumptions. Before sending your daughter—or your check—make some inquiries: How many girls does the agency serve? How many boys? Are all the programs coed, or are some for boys or girls only? Which ones?

It may be that a coed photography class is just what your daughter is looking for. Because girls have special needs, however, she may have a better experience within an all-girl environment. As far as we can tell, few of the coed agencies specifically address girls' issues. A call to the administrative office of the Boys and Girls Club in a metropolitan area, formerly a Boys Club, for example, uncovered only one program just for girls: a basketball league.

Then there's the matter of funding. Your local United Way or other funding source has probably made progress in distributing its monies more equitably. (Don't take this on faith, however. Check it out.) In 1990, for example, the YMCA received $207,372,958, as compared with $185,600,000 for the YWCA—not quite equal, but certainly getting closer.

Remember, though, that there are more agencies serving boys only or coed agencies serving mostly boys. When *The New York Times* listed eighteen leading recipients of charitable contributions for 1990, the list included the YMCA (see above), Boys Scouts of America ($194,941,000 received), and Boys and Girls Clubs of America, formerly Boys Clubs of America ($157,319,431 in support). The only agency primarily serving girls on the list was the YWCA (see above).

One more thing: Many organizations have other sources of income besides the private support they receive each year. This includes money from investments, fees, tuition, and so on. Who would you guess has been in a position to bequeath the substantial amounts of money that lead to additional income for an institution, men or women? And do you suppose these individuals favored agencies serving men or women? Looking again to *The New York Times*, we see that while private support was almost evenly divided between the YMCA and the YWCA, total income for the former was $1,438,455,518, while the latter earned just $323,570,000, less than one-fourth the earnings of its predominantly male-serving counterpart.

Keep these figures in mind next time you plan your charitable giving.

Organizations for adults

"Joining NOW is one of the most important things I've ever done," says Lorette, who was active in that organization for several years in the late 1970s and early 1980s. "When you feel that huge social changes need to be made, and you're just one individual, everything seems hopeless. In a group there's a real sense of empowerment, as though you're part of something important. I remember being at the NOW National Convention in Washington during the fall of 1978. The Senate, that day, had voted for ERA extension, and there was a celebration at the hotel that night. The lights were turned down in the room, and suddenly I found myself standing a few feet away from Betty Friedan. Our eyes met and we both grinned, and I felt at that moment that anything was possible.

"I'm still a member of NOW, though I'm no longer active. Belonging to an organization, I think, serves two purposes: it helps accomplish the group's goals, which is extremely important, and it is also a growth experience for the individual members—assuming they really get involved. Many of the women I met in NOW found new confidence there, or new interests and skills that they went on to use in their own ways to work toward equality for women."

There are dozens of service organizations with thousands of local affiliates dedicated primarily to improving the lives of girls and women. We've listed a few of them here. Why not write to the ones that sound most appealing to you and ask for more information? There may already be a group in your area working on a project you support. Or you might have to convince the membership that they should be working on such a project. At least you'll find an organized group that, quite often, is more effective at getting things done than a lone individual.

Alpha Kappa Alpha
5656 Stony Island Avenue
Chicago, IL 60637

Altrusa International
332 South Michigan Avenue, #1123
Chicago, IL 60604

American Association of University
  Women
1111 16th Street N.W.,
Washington, DC 20036-4873

American Business Women's
  Association
9100 Ward Parkway
Kansas City, MO 64114

Association of Junior Leagues
  International
600 First Avenue
New York, NY 10016

B'nai B'rith Women
1825 L Street, Suite 250
Washington, DC 20036

Child Care Action Campaign
330 Seventh Avenue, 17th Floor
New York, NY 10001

Church Women United
475 Riverside Drive, Room 812
New York, NY 10001

Delta Kappa Gamma Society International
P.O. Box 1589
Austin, TX 78767

Delta Sigma Theta Sorority, Inc.
1707 New Hampshire Avenue N.W.
Washington, DC 20009

Displaced Homemakers Network
1411 K Street N.W., Suite 930
Washington, DC 20005

General Federation of Women's Clubs
1734 N Street N.W.
Washington, DC 20036

Hispanic Women's Council
5803 East Beverly Boulevard
Los Angeles, CA 90022

The League of Women Voters of
the U.S.
1730 M Street N.W.
Washington, DC 20036

The Links, Inc.
1200 Massachusetts Avenue N.W.
Washington, DC 10005

Mexican American Women's National
Association
1030 15th Street N.W., Suite 468
Washington, DC 20005

Ms. Foundation for Women
370 Lexington Avenue
New York, NY 10017-6503

National Association for Female Executives
127 W. 24th Street
New York, NY 10011

National Association of Commissions
for Women
YWCA Building, M-10
624 9th Street N.W.
Washington, DC 20001

National Committee on Pay Equity
1201 16th Street, N.W., Room 422
Washington, DC 20036

National Conference of Puerto Rican
Women
812 West 181st Street, #63
New York, NY 10033

National Council of Jewish Women
53 W. 23rd Street
New York, NY 10010

National Council of Negro Women
1211 Connecticut Avenue N.W.,
Suite 702
Washington, DC 20036

National Federation of Business and
Professional Women's Clubs, Inc., of
the U.S.A.
2012 Massachusetts Avenue N.W.
Washington, DC 20036

National Hook-up of Black
Women, Inc.
517 South University Avenue
Chicago, IL 60615

The National Organization for
Women
1000 16th Street, #700
Washington, DC 20036

National Women's Law Center
1616 P Street N.W., Suite 100
Washington, DC 20036

The National Women's Political
Caucus
1275 K Street N.W., Suite 750
Washington, DC 20005

9 to 5, National Association of Working Women
614 Superior Avenue N.W., Room 852
Cleveland, OH 44113

Organization of Chinese American
Women
1300 N Street N.W., Suite 100
Washington, DC 20005

Organization of Pan-Asian Women
1220 L Street N.W., Suite 555
Washington, DC 20005

Women's Action Alliance
370 Lexington Avenue, Suite 603
New York, NY 10017

Women's Campaign Fund
120 Maryland Avenue N.E.
Washington, DC 20002

Women's Legal Defense Fund
2000 P Street N.W., #400
Washington, DC 20036

Zonta International
557 W. Randolph Street
Chicago, IL 60606

Other organizations

While women's service organizations are a natural focus for programs aimed at girls, there is no reason why men's or mixed groups couldn't perform the tasks just as effectively.

Also, think locally. Consider all the local organizations you currently belong to or know of: professional groups, service organizations, church groups, and school alumni or parent groups. Are they looking for new projects or in need of some new cause to energize the membership? Who are the members? What special resources, talents, or concerns do they have? How do these match up with possible programs for girls? (A group of business executives might start a summer jobs program in which both boys and girls would work at nontraditional jobs, for example. Or a group of displaced homemakers might go into the schools to talk about the importance of career planning with young women.)

Does the makeup of your organization lend itself more readily to direct service projects or advocacy projects? In direct services projects, members work face to face with the girls they are trying to help. Teaching girls to use computers or setting up a mentor program so that girls can spend a day on the job with a member of your group are examples of direct service. Advocacy projects, on the other hand, work more indirectly to expand opportunities for girls. Raising funds for a girls' athletic program or sponsoring equity training sessions for local teachers involve advocacy. Which type of program do you think your fellow members would feel more comfortable with or do best?

Think, too, about what's happening in your community. Are residents alarmed about a skyrocketing teen pregnancy rate, for example, or about an increase in reports of violence toward women? If so, you may want to set up a project that uses your group's particular strengths to address the issue. Or you might be inspired by what some other groups have done.

The American Association of University Women is as good a group to emulate as any. In the past few years it has started a new national dialogue about girls, self-esteem, and equity by conducting and reporting on the surveys we have discussed throughout this book. In addition, the AAUW has initiated Choices for Tomorrow's Women programs in branches across the country to empower women and girls to make appropriate life choices. Its Eleanor Roosevelt Fund for Women and Girls has, among other things, awarded fellowships to public school teachers in order to improve the way math and science is taught to girls. AAUW has always awarded grants and fellowships to women scholars, and now its Selected Professions Fellowships "combat discrimination by assisting women who are pioneers in fields traditionally dominated by men."

The AAUW Initiative for Educational Equity is designed to bring about change at the personal, community, and systemic levels. The organization is also conducting research on how women and girls think, learn, and play. Its Legal Advocacy Fund presents an annual Progress in Equity Award to recognize a higher education program "that has resulted in significant progress toward educational equity for women and girls." AAUW also sponsors Educational Equity Roundtables so that educators, policymakers, corporate leaders, and members of the media can work together to develop programs for combatting gender bias in education.

Business and Professional Women (BPW)/USA has also done a tremendous job, particularly through Women Helping Girls with Choices projects. In 1984 the BPW of Nashua, New Hampshire, collaborated with Girls Incorporated to build a program for local girls around the Choices curriculum. It was so successful that soon many other BPW branches wanted to bring similar projects to their own communities. By 1987 a pilot program involving ten states and 127 projects was in action, thanks largely to the work of ten state coordinators and National Coordinator Betty Shepperd. Again, the programs were so well received that by 1989 funding was available to publish the *Women Helping Girls with Choices* handbook for community service organizations.

The book contains detailed information on making a presentation to your organization, building coalitions with other groups in your community, publicity and promotion, and fund-raising, as well as everything you need to know to organize five different projects: starting a Choices/Challenges program in your school; setting up a Mother-Daughter Choices program; holding a career planning symposium for mixing career and family; presenting a math-science fair; and starting an Operation SMART program in your community.

Free to improvise, some groups came up with ideas of their own:

In West Virginia, Debbie Davis applied for and received Carl D. Perkins funding (see below) that has allowed junior high home economics to offer the Choices curriculum on an ongoing basis since 1988.

In Indiana the BPW conducted a "Leap Conference" for young women from all parts of the state. With a grant from the Lilly Endowment, and working closely with the Girl Scouts, they were able to stage a well-publicized event that graphically demonstrated to participants the need to consider nontraditional careers. At the beginning of the conference young women went through the Envision Your Life exercise from the Choices curriculum and then made a career choice. Each girl was then given play money equal to the average salary in her career field and sent on her way to booths around the auditorium, where she had to give up part of her "cash" in return for housing, transportation, insurance, and so on. The young women quickly learned that most of the jobs they were considering did not pay enough to support their preferred life-styles. Career counselors, representatives from various career fields, and bankers were also on hand to provide information and offer advice.

In Willmar, Minnesota, a group of BPW women decided to take the Choices program to adolescent daughters of clients at the local battered women's shelter. Each woman also became a mentor to one of the adolescents and contracted to spend time with her in various personal and professional activities over the coming year. The relationships could be extended if both parties agreed.

We don't have the space to highlight all of the innovative work that's been going on, but you can see that there is no shortage of possibilities.

Gender equity in the schools

Many people are not aware of an important resource for increasing gender equity in the schools: in 1984, Congress passed the Carl D. Perkins Vocational Education Act, which funds vocational training for underserved populations, including single parents and young women aged fourteen to twenty-five. The monies can be awarded to community-based organizations as well as to school districts.

The Arizona New Frontiers Project, for example, obtained Carl Perkins funding for its "Parents as Partners" program, which involves training high school counselors to get parents involved in career planning. The counselors go back to their schools and offer evening sessions where parents first take an interest inventory, then discuss values and how their own may differ from those of their children. They learn about the importance of math and science, especially for girls, and talk about sex stereotypes and how enforcing them can put their daughters at a financial disadvantage.

Every state, by law, has a gender equity coordinator to allocate and monitor the funds. Contact yours through your state Department of Education, Vocational Education Division. The coordinator can help you identify gender equity resources locally and share information of projects around your state. This is a good person to keep on your mailing list if you begin an advocacy project for girls in your community.

One person can make a difference

If you think that one person can't make a difference, or if you maintain that you're simply too busy to try, consider Betty Shepperd.

You think you're busy? Betty is married and has three children, all now young adults. For ten years she has been coordinator for a hospice program that works with clients at five sites covering hundreds of square miles in west central Minnesota. Although she's phased out one of the businesses she used to run in her spare time (managing rental property), she still has another—conducting seminars on educational advancement.

Betty has long been involved with BPW and serves as state chair for that organization's Council on the Future of Women in the Workplace. She is a member of the National Hospice Board of Directors and has served on numerous other boards as well as on her local police commission. Always involved in some kind of "political stuff" or church activity, she is also an advocate for girls.

Betty hadn't really thought about being an advocate for girls until 1986, when she first heard about the Choices program. "I immediately thought of all the women

I'd heard complain about their low-paying, low-level jobs. As an RN, I'd also worked in obstetrics and had been concerned about the number of teens having babies." The program, she says, "just made so much sense."

One of Betty's first achievements was to arrange for Mindy to address the BPW National Convention in 1987. It was at that meeting that Mindy, Betty, and Penny Paine began organizing what would soon become Women Helping Girls with Choices, with Betty as national coordinator.

In that position she was responsible for recruiting ten women from across the country to serve as state coordinators. Over the next four years she organized, energized, supported, lobbied, and cajoled, raised funds, raised spirits, and raised hopes for hundreds of projects and thousands of young women. Over 12,500 young women were part of the program that first year. It is largely because of her efforts that BPW has written Women Helping Girls with Choices into its three-year-plan as a national project.

On the local level, Betty started a Mother-Daughter Choices program in her church and still conducts it annually. She also recruited and trained men to conduct a similar program for fathers and sons. It, too, is an ongoing project. She has organized and conducted career conferences in numerous locations in her area, trained teachers, and placed articles in the local paper. It was Betty who started the program with girls from the shelter mentioned above, and she continues to mentor one of the young women. She has promoted advocacy projects with the Minnesota Extension Service and trained women from nine counties to carry them out. We could go on, but you get the general idea.

"One person can make a difference," according to Betty, "and it doesn't take as much time as you might think." Even better, she says, hook up with a group: the additional bodies along with the financial and political help an organization can bring to an effort make big changes possible.

"Start small," Betty recommends, "but always keep the vision. Just keep plugging away." She clearly follows her own advice. Since we first interviewed her for this project a few months ago, she learned that grant money was available to begin an Operation SMART program in her area and went to work putting together a collaborative group from the BPW, AAUW, local vocational school, and local junior college. The group has hired a part-time coordinator to organize a science-oriented summer camp for fourth-grade girls.

One final bit of advice from Betty: "Realize that you can do it, and don't be intimidated by 'experts.' Sometimes it's outsiders who are the vehicles for change."

Thousands of parents have also found that they don't need to be experts to form extremely beneficial support groups for themselves and their daughters. The following chapter explains how you can join them and why you should.

chapter twenty-eight

Forming Mother-Daughter Groups

S hould you take it upon yourself to form a mother-daughter group? "Definitely do it! No question," advises Nancy Marriott of Santa Barbara, who organized a group in the fall of 1987 when her daughter, Danielle, was in the sixth grade. "There aren't that many opportunities to spend time with your daughter focusing on careers and life satisfaction. It's a meaningful way to do things together rather than going shopping or to the movies."

Nancy's group was one of the earliest in a program that has now reached thousands of mothers and daughters across the country. The first was organized by Mindy in the spring of 1986, at the request of Diane Talley and Joyce Sitzer, the mothers of two of Wendy's sixth-grade classmates.

Graduates of those early programs are now young women, and most of the ones we've been able to keep track of are doing very well in college (many are attending top-rated schools) and pursuing dreams of achievement. "I don't know how much the group affected her," Nancy says of Danielle, "but as a tenth grader she decided she wanted to spend her junior and senior years at a special performing arts high school in San Francisco, where she could study dance. She graduates this spring, and has been accepted into the dance program at SUNY Purchase, in New York, which also focuses on the arts." She's been awarded two scholarships based on her skills and talents, Nancy reports, especially proud of the fact that Danielle actively pursued them, as she has her other goals. "She's worked hard to make this happen," her mother says.

Nancy adds that the group was also beneficial to her and the other mothers. "We were all hungry for that chance to share and talk," she says, noting that although all the mothers had jobs outside the home, they always found time for the group. In fact, they kept meeting for an entire year even though the program itself ran only six weeks.

The program we'll be describing in this chapter is ambitious in scope. It includes exercises and activities for girls in grades four through six, to be completed in small groups of young women and their mothers or other significant women in their lives. The purpose is to nurture the skills of the hardy personality, encourage young women to see themselves as achievers and maintain their self-esteem as they move into adolescence, and to solidify the relationship between parent and child *before* adolescence, so you can keep the lines of communication open, even during those turbulent teen years.

If your daughter has already passed fourth grade, you'll want to look at the suggested session agendas later on in this chapter, evaluate your daughter's maturity level, and decide for yourself where to begin, or which activities are appropriate. It is quite possible that she and her friends can benefit from all three years' worth of activities, even if they are already adolescents. (For groups of older girls, you might want to combine sessions, or complete the entire program over the course of a single year.) Use your own judgment in this, as in utilizing all of the information in this chapter. We're only offering suggestions. You are in the best position to decide what's best for your daughter.

Don't be intimidated. The whole program is surprisingly easy to organize (we'll tell you how Mindy did it), and once you get going, momentum and enthusiasm will carry you through. You don't need experience, just an honest desire to help your daughter and other young women.

The first thing you'll need is a group. Since Mindy had been approached by the mothers of Wendy's classmates, hers was ready-made: all the girls were members of Wendy's class at school. Nancy and Danielle's group, too, was made up of classmates and their mothers; this often works well because the girls have ongoing relationships that provide support outside the group, where peer pressure can work against the traits and skills you're trying to instill.

There are many other places to look for a suitable group, however. Think of your daughter's various activities. Is there a church group? A scout troop? An athletic team? Just be sure the girls know each other, are the same age (they change so quickly during these years that even a difference of one grade in school is significant), and will probably continue to see each other after your program concludes.

Consider the size of the group, too. Five to eight mother-daughter pairs is ideal. It's best to divide into smaller groups if you have more than this number of participants.

Once Mindy identified her group, she checked with Wendy's teacher to see if there were any problems. If, for example, one mother couldn't always attend, another adult would be needed to act as the girl's partner. Aunts, older sisters, stepmothers, and family friends have all made excellent replacements when a mother is not available. Some *father*-daughter groups have been formed, and you're free to try it, but we've found that an all-female group generally works best. Some girls are more comfortable discussing the topics you'll be covering in the company of women and girls, and there is also great value in the sharing of experiences from one generation of women to the next.

The mothers' meeting

Once Mindy had her list of names, she invited the mothers to a meeting at her house to explain the idea, get their endorsement, and begin making plans. She asked each mother to bring along her appointment calendar—and her daughter's—along with a self-addressed, stamped envelope. If you don't want to have the meeting at your house, schedule it elsewhere, but make sure it's a place where you're unlikely to be interrupted.

The meeting will probably take about two hours. Mindy invited her group to come half an hour early for coffee and snacks to help assure that everyone would arrive before the real business began. Since the women already knew each other by sight, at least, she didn't ask them to wear name tags, but you might want to if your participants are unacquainted.

Even though the women were enjoying casual conversation over coffee, Mindy started the meeting on time. (She made this a rule for the mother-daughter meetings, too. The program is unlikely to succeed if meetings don't begin when they're supposed to, or if they drag on long past the scheduled closing time.) As an ice-breaker, she paired off the participants and gave them five minutes or so to get to know each other. Then she asked them to introduce their partners to the group.

Next, Mindy passed out copies of a "Women Today" quiz, similar to "The Startling Statement Quiz" on page 366. Again, she had the mothers work in pairs to discuss the questions and agree on the correct answer. She allowed about ten minutes to complete the activity, then revealed the right answers and let the group discuss them. This is a good way to identify some of the problems women face today, make sure everyone is thinking along the same lines, and motivate the group to try to improve matters for their daughters.

PRESENTATION AND DISCUSSION

After the quiz, Mindy made a short presentation to the group, focusing on the special needs of girls today and why mother-daughter groups are helpful in meeting those needs. You should be able to find plenty of information for your presentation in this book, but consult other sources, too, if you like. (Be sure to include some positive statements and success stories. The idea is to get your group excited, not overwhelmed by the size of the task.)

Once Mindy spelled out the problem and what she thought her guests could do about it, it was easy to get group agreement to proceed with the plans. That's why Mindy had asked them to bring their appointment calendars along. Knowing how busy women and girls are these days, she felt it was essential not only to commit to doing a group "someday," but to set a starting date and decide where and how often they would meet. Her group decided to get together weekly, during the same evening each week, at the homes of the participants—but a different arrangement may be better for yours. (By rotating the setting, everyone shared in the effort. Those who didn't or couldn't host a meeting at their homes took turns helping to set up and serve the refreshments and cleaning up afterward. This was an informal arrangement in Mindy's group, but you may want to formalize it in yours.) Evening or weekend hours seem to work best for most people, but you may have to do some juggling to find times when everyone can attend. It's okay to skip a week, or to vary the days and times of your meetings.

There are many possibilities for meeting places, as well. Would the group prefer a home setting, or perhaps a community center? Homes may be more comfortable and usually are preferable. On the other hand, they may be more prone to interruptions, or it may be difficult to displace the rest of the family for the evening. Remember that privacy is an important consideration. Where are you most likely to find it? If you think a community center may be better for your group, do a little research before the meeting if you can. Find out what kinds of facilities are available in your area, when they are open, and so on. The teachers' lounge or library at your daughter's school is often a popular choice. Public libraries, churches, and recreation centers usually have private meeting rooms, too.

After Mindy's group decided when and at which homes they would meet, Mindy asked each of the hosting mothers to draw a map or write directions to her home. She collected these, along with the self-addressed stamped envelopes, and, the next day, made copies of the schedule, the addresses, and the directions and sent a set to each participant. (You won't, of course, be able to schedule more than a few months' worth of meetings. Plan to have a mother's meeting at the beginning of each year.)

Getting going

Once you bring in the girls, the first rule, according to Nancy Marriott, is "Make it fun!" She also suggests choosing, early on, a special event that will mark the completion of the program, giving the girls something to look forward to, talk about, and plan for. "It helped us bond," says Nancy. Their group went on an overnight camping trip, where the mothers and daughters had an opportunity to sit around the fire, talking and sharing stories for hours. It was a special experience they'll always remember.

But let's not get ahead of ourselves. Here are some hints from Mindy and Nancy on how to work through the program.

THE MOTHER-DAUGHTER RELATIONSHIP   If you are the group facilitator, remember that you are also one of the mothers. Don't neglect your own daughter. Mindy remembers Wendy becoming quite upset in the car after one of their meetings, claiming rightly that Mindy was so concerned about everyone else, she had virtually ignored her own daughter. To make sure this doesn't happen in your group, you might want to share the leadership position with other mothers. Another good idea is to play a sort of musical chairs with your mothers and daughters. Nancy says the girls in her group really enjoyed "trying on" the other mothers.

It's likely that every mother will not be able to make it to every meeting, but allow daughters to come on their own if they can. The other mothers can fill in quite easily. There's another side to this coin. It's also quite likely that one of the moms' child care arrangements will fall through, and she will ask to bring her daughter's siblings to the meeting. This is *not* a good idea. It usually leads to interruptions, disruptions, and/or total chaos. Better to let the daughter come alone. (Or your group may decide to arrange shared child care for anyone who needs it. This is a good thing to discuss at the mothers' meeting.)

STARTING THE MEETINGS   In Mindy's group, the host was responsible for providing refreshments, which were served between 6:15 and 7:00 P.M. The mothers decided on this arrangement because it allowed time for socializing before the meeting, which began at 7:00. It was understood that those coming straight from work could bring their dinner to eat during this time. Mindy and Wendy often arrived with a bag of take-out food. Another benefit of this arrangement is that it helps assure that everyone will be there when it's time to start the real business of the session.

QUESTION OF THE WEEK   Once you get your group together in a room, you may experience one of two problems: there may be an uncomfortable silence, or the girls and women may be having such animated conversations that you have trouble getting their attention. Either way, Mindy and Nancy agree that a good way to start your meetings is with the "Question of the Week." Divide the group into adult-girl pairs, and allow about five minutes for interviews. The mothers will be asked one question, the daughters another. You'll want to have ideas about these for the first week or two, but if your group is anything like Nancy and Danielle's, the daughters will soon be coming up with their own questions for the moms. When, after all, are they likely to get another opportunity to learn, risk-free, "everything they've always wanted to know but were afraid to ask" about their mothers? Nancy's group was particularly interested in hearing about their mothers' first kiss. Some of the answers were touching, some funny—and all helped the young women realize that their moms had once been girls like themselves who, perhaps, really *did* understand what it was like to be young.

Try to think of questions for your group that will get the girls to explore their future ("Describe your dream career") or their identity ("Tell me about an accomplishment that made you feel proud of yourself"). Questions for mothers might also relate to the future ("Tell me what you want to be doing when you're sixty-five"), or they might provide an opportunity to look back to their youth ("If you could be a teen again, what one decision would you make differently?").

After the interviews are completed, have participants share with the group what they learned. ("I talked to Wanda Davis. She says the worst job she ever had was cleaning rooms in a hotel. She did it to make money for college, though, and now she thinks it was worth doing.") These interviews often allow daughters to see their mothers in a new light and can make future communications about sensitive topics much easier.

PERSONALIZING THE AGENDA   As we said before, it's okay—it's desirable—for you to change the agenda to meet the needs of your group, giving more weight to the topics you are particularly concerned about, skipping those that seem irrelevant. Feel free to bring in your own activities. Nancy's group, for example, spent considerable time working on "priority ladders," a good tool for making decisions. The girls once went through the exercise to decide which boys they would most like to date. Each girl listed the names of ten boys she liked, and was then asked, "Would you rather date Larry or Timmy?" If she said she preferred Timmy, the questioner proceeded through the list: Timmy or Ahmad? Ahmad or Lee? And so on. Mothers went through the same process, making decisions about their ideal jobs.

Mindy's group, originally set up for six meetings, decided during the third week to include an additional session for a presentation on sex education.

Design your agendas however you like. Mindy and Nancy recommend, however, that each meeting be at least two hours long if you hope to get much accomplished.

GETTING ALONG, GETTING INVOLVED   To make the meetings productive and enjoyable for everyone, discuss some basic rules at your first session. Stress the need for common courtesy, making it clear that it is not appropriate to make judgments or put down anyone else. Likewise, agree that everyone will be allowed to talk without interruption.

Confidentiality should be discussed and agreed upon by the entire group at the beginning of the first session. Spend some time brainstorming why it is important to guard other people's privacy. You might even ask the girls to come up with some assertive responses to anyone (sibling, father, other friends) who tries to get them to reveal what is discussed within the group. Learning to keep quiet about what's been said in confidence is an important trait for young women to acquire.

To avoid pandemonium during brainstorming sessions, when participants are to share ideas on a given topic, allow a minute or two for thinking before you begin. Make sure to acknowledge everyone's ideas by writing them on a flip pad or chalkboard, no matter how far out they sound. (A flip pad on a stand is an important piece of equipment—perhaps the only one you'll need. If you don't already have one, see if you can borrow one from a school or bank.)

If you steadfastly apply the rules above, you're likely to have an environment that makes everyone comfortable and communicative. Nudge anyone who's particularly reticent by asking open-ended questions, ones that require more than a simple "yes" or "no" answer, and being supportive of her replies. Keep the atmosphere friendly and informal and make sure the activities are relevant to everyone.

Keep in mind the comfort level of the daughters as well as that of the mothers. Nancy's group of mothers, for example, thought it would be interesting and informative to have a session on sex education, complete with guest speaker and slide show. This might work well in some groups (Mindy's found it helpful), but for Danielle and her friends it was a bit intense and, as Danielle put it, "gross." Again, this demonstrates the need for mothers to assess what's right for each group.

Session agendas

Below are our suggestions for activities for the mothers' meeting discussed earlier in the chapter, and for discussion topics in mother-daughter meetings, week by week.

An active group is an involved group, so it is important that each mother be assigned tasks that meet her talents and skills. Some may want to facilitate meetings, others would rather make phone calls or arrange for supplies.

You may want to suggest that each of the mothers read *Things Will Be Different for My Daughter* before the sessions begin. If so, be sure to allow sufficient time before the first session. (You might even decide to have a second mothers' meeting before the program begins to discuss the book and reevaluate the agenda in light of what's been learned.)

Mothers' meeting

This is a very important meeting, as we've already noted. Do your best to schedule it at a time when everyone can attend. You'll want to have a mothers' meeting before each of the three years of mother-daughter sessions.

Agenda:
- Pre-meeting social hour
- Introductions
- Awareness activity (quiz)
- Presentation about program
- Ask for a decision: who wants to participate?
- Decide on meeting details and arrangements:
    - Dates, times, and locations of meetings
    - Persons in charge of refreshments
    - Topics for each session
    - Facilitators for each meeting
    - Pre-meeting social time
    - Supplies and cost sharing (if any)
- Decide on meeting etiquette and ground rules:
    - Arriving and starting on time
    - Substitutes for mothers who can't attend
    - Privacy and freedom from interruptions
    - Shared child care for siblings, if desired
    - Brainstorming rules
    - Preserving confidentiality

MOTHER-DAUGHTER MEETINGS

Year One   Activities for the first four meetings center around building the traits of the hardy personality. Girls will learn how to resist "losing their voice," as Carol Gilligan and her associates put it. During these weeks, girls will learn authentic communication skills and how to appreciate each other's unique identity. Again, the ideal time to learn these skills is as a preadolescent, but older girls need them desperately, and the activities can be adapted for them. If the adults participate actively, the girls will, too.

Session one

After reviewing the ground rules (we suggest asking questions and brainstorming rather than lecturing), introducing everyone, and completing the Question of the Week activity, you might do the following activities:

1. "Appreciating Her Uniqueness" (chapter 12, page 172)
2. "Liking Herself" (chapter 12, page 171)
3. "Making Her Own Designer Label" (chapter 12, page 172)

Hardy personality traits practiced:

Trusting herself and her own perceptions
Forming an identity as an achiever

Session two

The purpose of this session is to help each girl recognize and celebrate her unique identity. These self-esteem-building activities help participants articulate their individual traits and skills and begin a formalized identity search. (You might ask mothers to review chapter 11 of this book before they arrive for the meeting.)

Get started with the Question of the Week.

1. The following activity is based on "You at Nine" on page 147 of chapter 11. Ask the mothers to think about themselves the way they were when they were nine. You might help them by asking them to sit quietly with their eyes closed, breathing deeply, and visualizing the year they were in fourth grade. As they relax, ask them:

> *To see themselves at that age*
> *To see their bedroom*
> *To picture their parents, teachers, and friends*
> *To remember a special day*
> *To relive the activities they took part in*
> *How they felt about themselves*
> *What they wanted to be when they were that age*

2. Then have the mothers share their thoughts with their daughters or, if the group is comfortable doing it, with everyone. Finally, ask them to share their thoughts on the following topics:

> *Did you live up to the image you had of yourself at that time?*
> *If so, in what ways? If not, why not?*

3. As a group, discuss how individuals can help each other be true to their authentic selves.

4. Next, create an art project, "My Ninth-Year Album." Mothers and daughters each make a scrapbook or journal with a cover that reflects their identity when they were nine years old. Supplies needed are sturdy paper board for the front and back covers (punch three holes in each so rings can be inserted), materials for a collage on the cover (use pictures from magazines, personal photos, etc.), decoupage glue, scissors, three-hole-punched notebook paper, and rings. Encourage participants to fill with journal entries, copies of schoolwork, photographs, certificates, letters from friends, etc.

Hardy personality traits practiced:

Tolerating anxiety and acting anyway
Separating fantasy from reality
Settling goals and establishing priorities
Projecting into the future and understanding how today's choices
    affect the future
Learning to be discriminating
Trusting herself and her own perceptions

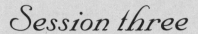

Session three

The purpose of this session is to help both daughters and mothers learn to take risks within relationships. When we take risks with people we love and respect, we form stronger and more satisfying and lasting bonds of friendship and intimacy, yet females in our culture are usually not exposed to the important skills involved.

After the Question of the Week, we suggest one or all of the following activities:

1. Review the section entitled "Help Your Daughter Develop Good Friendships" on pages 169 to 175 in chapter 12. Then ask the group to list qualities or traits of a truly good friendship. Discuss the difference between friends and acquaintances.

2. Ask group members to think of situations in which they have had to risk displeasing someone with whom they had a relationship. Have the mothers go first. After each has told her story, ask:

> *Did you take the risk?*
> *If so, how? If not, what did you do instead?*
> *What was the outcome?*
> *How did you feel about it?*

3. Complete the activity "Learning to Give and Take Criticism" (chapter 12, page 173).

4. Complete the activity "Learning to Discern Between Friendly Criticism and Abusive Behavior" (chapter 12, page 174).

5. Discuss the section "Learning to Disagree" on pages 182–183. What activities there would the group like to try?

Hardy personality traits practiced:

Tolerating anxiety and acting anyway
Separating fantasy from reality
Learning to be discriminating with choices
Setting boundaries and limits
Asking assertively for what she wants
Trusting herself and her own perceptions

Session four

The purpose of this session is to help participants learn and practice the skills of assertive communication.

After the Question of the Week, review the section "Learning to Be Assertive" (pages 178–182) and complete the activity "Passive, Assertive, or Aggressive?"

When the group feels that it understands and can identify each of the different modes of communication, try the following role-playing activities:

1. Ask each mother-daughter pair to think of a situation and write it on a piece of paper. Put all the papers in a hat, pair up the girls, and have them role-play assertive, passive, and aggressive responses to the situation they draw.

2. Have the mothers pair up and follow suit. We suggest drawing on the following situations, with one mother playing the aggrieved person, the other responding as might be expected to the various communication styles:

- *Your daughter has just arrived home from a date one hour past her curfew.*
- *Your boyfriend is trying to pressure you to do something you don't want to do.*
- *Your teacher has given you a final grade lower than the one you think you deserve, considering your performance on tests and assignments throughout the year.*
- *Your college-age daughter has run up a high balance on her new credit card. She asks you for a loan you do not want to give her.*

Ask the girls to think of other situations for the pairs of moms. As a group, discuss which type of response usually led to the most desirable outcome—passive, assertive, or aggressive?

Hardy personality traits practiced:

Tolerating anxiety and acting anyway
Setting goals and establishing priorities
Projecting into the future and understanding how today's choices
    affect the future
Learning to be discriminating in making choices
Setting boundaries and limits
Asking assertively for what she wants
Trusting herself and her own perceptions

Year Two The purpose of these four sessions is to help both mothers and daughters evaluate their attitudes concerning their own potential, consider any self- or societally imposed limitations on their aspirations, and begin to develop identities as achievers.

Session one

This session is designed to examine the ways in which our culture—particularly the media—affects attitudes about being female.

1. After the Question of the Week, complete the activity "Fairy-Tale Messages" (chapter 14, page 204) as mother-daughter pairs. Then, as a group, share your observations.

2. Next, divide into groups of four (two mother-daughter pairs) and ask each group to pick a favorite fairy-tale and revise it so that it supports the message that girls are capable, confident, and skilled. Allow twenty to thirty minutes, and then have each group tell or act out its "new, improved" story.

3. As a group, brainstorm other ways in which the media present limiting images of women. (You will want to review chapter 15, "Lessons Learned from the Media," beforehand.)

4. Break the group into two or three teams, leaving out one individual who will act as timer and referee. You may want to make this a mother vs. daughter exercise, though the daughters will probably have an advantage. Provide a large sheet of paper and markers or crayons for each team. Set a timer for ten minutes, and ask the teams to identify and list all the female TV characters they can think of who exhibit the traits of the hardy personality. When the timer goes off, ask each group to share the list. Give one point for each character found to have a truly hardy personality. If another team can point out evidence that the character is less than hardy (in one episode, she gave into peer pressure against her better judgment, for example), that team gets *five* points. The referee decides, if the group can't come to agreement. The team with the most points wins.

5. If you can get a copy of *Father Gander Nursery Rhymes* by Father Gander (Dr. Douglas Larche) (Advocacy Press, 1986), you may want to end the session by reading a few favorite rhymes.

Session two

The purpose of this session is to evaluate individuals' and society's attitudes about what it means to be female and to start developing the vocabulary that will help each person articulate her own identity.

1. Following the Question of the Week, have daughters and mothers individually and privately complete the "Typical Male, Typical Female" survey that appears in chapter 2 (pages 36–37). As a group, discuss the results and see how many of the surveys match the findings of the Brovermans (page 37).

> Note: You may need to define some of the terms on the list for younger girls. This in itself is a good thing to do because it increases their vocabulary and allows them to articulate the traits they want to develop as they form their own identities.

2. Explain to the group that the characteristics on the left have traditionally been considered masculine, while those on the right were thought to be feminine by many people. Review the sections "Either/Or Thinking" and "Changing Our Language and Labels" on pages 55 and 57 in chapter 4, and discuss whether or not it's a good idea to assign personality traits to a person based only on his or her gender. Then ask the group to think of new labels for the lists of characteristics.

3. Assign each girl to a woman *not her mother* and have each pair discuss the activity "What to Do?" on page 59 of chapter 4. When they've completed it, ask them to assign a term from the Broverman lists to each response.

   Finally, ask each participant, privately, to list:

> The personality traits she feels she currently has
> The traits she would like to develop

Session three

When asked what they want to accomplish on a job, many girls reply that they "want to help others." While this is a laudatory goal, it is unfortunate that they tend to feel they can meet it only by acting in supporting roles (nurse's aide rather than surgeon, for example). During this session, girls will come to see how they will have more power to help more people if they aim for more ambitious careers.

1. After the Question of the Week, read the picture book *My Way Sally* (Advocacy Press, 1988) aloud and discuss the questions at the end of the book.

2. Ask the girls to list all the tasks that must be completed to make this a better world (feed the hungry, clean up the environment, etc.). Then have them come up with and list jobs that would help accomplish these tasks. Next, have the *mothers* come up with careers not traditionally held by women that would meet the same goals. Write those job titles next to the ones on the girls' list. As a group, decide on and circle the career in each pair that offers the opportunity to help *more* people, or to have *greater impact* on them.

3. Finally, divide participants into groups of four (two mother-daughter pairs) and ask each group to complete the "Career Ladder" exercise (chapter 24, page 383), using one of the high-impact careers from the exercise above, starting as a high school student on the lowest rung of the ladder.

Session four

The purpose of this session is to combat any societal messages or images that prevent girls from seeing themselves as achievers.

1. Following the Question of the Week, pair off the girls with women who are not their mother and ask each pair to complete The Message Center activity from chapter 2 (pages 23–24). Then ask them to identify any negative messages they've received and write a positive affirmation to counteract each of them (See "Seeing Herself as Successful at Math," chapter 17, page 254). Hand out 3 x 5 cards and suggest that individuals write their affirmations on them. Post the cards on a mirror or other location where they'll be reminded to repeat the new positive statements daily.

2. Next have the pairs complete the activity "Math and Future Earnings" (chapter 17, page 262). Would anyone like to add some affirmations about liking math and being good at math to her list?

3. While they remain with the same partners, ask the pairs to complete the activity "Whom Would You Hire?" (chapter 24, page 385). Tell them to imagine that they own a large company (let them decide what kind), and they need to hire a completely new staff. What jobs must they find employees for? (Add "child care worker for company nursery" to the list if no one else does.)

   On a flip pad, list the characteristics from columns A and B in the above exercise, labeling them employees A and B. Going through each of the job titles, ask the group to decide which candidate they would hire. Except in the case of the child care provider, most of the jobs will go to candidate A. Ask if the group recognizes the lists of traits and where they came from. A lively debate should follow.

4. To conclude, ask group members to expand the list of traits they want to acquire that was begun in session two. This list will provide the girls with a set of healthy goals to work toward as they enter adolescence.

Year Three The next group of sessions is designed to expand girls' precareer awareness, as discussed in chapter 24. (This was the theme of Mindy's first group.) A comprehensive 144-page guide covering these six sessions in great detail has been published. The six-week program helps participants begin to envision their future lives, look at the realities of the working world, evaluate their future economic requirements, assess their work values so they can choose a satisfying career, learn to set quantitative goals and make considered choices, and practice asking for what they want. The activities are built around our first book, *Choices: A Teen Woman's Journal for Self-awareness and Personal Planning.*

We suggest you get a copy of *Mother-Daughter Choices: A Handbook for the Coordinator* (Advocacy Press, 1988), in which all the planning has been done for you and a minute-by-minute agenda is supplied. You'll find ordering information on page 482.

Another good program for mother-daughter groups is Girls Incorporated's "Growing Together." Contact Girls Incorporated (see "Ordering Information") to learn how to start or locate a program in your area.

As Nancy noted, her group went on meeting far beyond the scheduled six weeks. If your group makes a similar decision, in addition to using some of the other activities from this book you might consult two of our other texts. *More Choices: A Strategic Planning Guide for Mixing Career and Family* (Advocacy Press, 1987) or *Career Choices: A Guide for Teens and Young Adults* (Academic Innovations, 1990). These contain lots of relevant activities, especially for older girls. We urge you to use your imagination and come up with your own ideas, as well. Just remember that you need to keep participants active and involved. Lectures don't work in mother-daughter groups.

Special note: If you conduct a group, whether you use our suggestions or come up with your own agenda, let us know how it goes! Send your comments to Mindy Bingham and Sandy Stryker, 3463 State Street #267, Santa Barbara, CA 93105. Your experience and ideas could help us develop new materials to share with mothers and daughters across the country.

chapter twenty-nine

Letters of Healing,
Letters of Dreams

You have just become the beneficiary of information and advice gathered and developed by hundreds of people over dozens of years. Yes, it is overwhelming, but no, you don't have to deal with it all at once. We do hope that you will make a genuine effort to change any of your own attitudes and behaviors you now perceive to be counterproductive to fulfilling your wishes for your daughter, and we suggest, too, that you keep this book and your plan close by as a reference.

The one section of the book we urge you to take especially to heart is that dealing with the hardy personality. The traits or skills associated with that term are, we believe, absolutely central to changing the lives of girls and women. Since you will probably have daily opportunities to encourage or discourage their development in your daughter, please take the time to memorize them. Carry a list in your wallet, if you think it will help, or tape one to your mirror for a few weeks. Before long, we're confident, acting in accord with their development will become second nature.

We want to remind you, too, that if things are to be different for our daughters, they must also be different for our sons. It would take another book to fully cover this theme, but we hope that you will begin to treat any young men in your lives as you do young women, encouraging them to develop both the achievement and relationship sides of their personalities. We would like to see you assign them household or child care chores instead of just yardwork. And we trust that you will teach them to think of women not as sex objects, not as people to be considered worthy or unworthy according to their appearance, but as full-fledged members of society, due all the rights and respect that title carries.

Consider some other words
of wisdom—your own

Before we close, on the following pages or on separate pieces of paper, we suggest you write three letters. They are meant not to be shared with the addressee, but only to help you clarify your thoughts, set your priorities, and personalize much of the material you've just read.

The first letter is to your parents. Knowing what you know now, think back to the way you were raised. Reconsider your past triumphs and mistakes. What role do you think your upbringing played in bringing these about or in determining the way you dealt with them? What are you grateful for? What do you wish had been different?

We hope that this letter will help you put your past in perspective and help heal any pain you may have incurred while reading this book. It might also help you empathize with your daughter—and your parents—and remember how very difficult it is to grow up, no matter when you do it.

The second letter is to yourself. You decide what should be in it. Perhaps you want to outline some goals and plans to improve your own life and make you a better role model for your daughter. You might want to write about your response to this book and which parts of it seem particularly important to your family. Or you might want to attempt to make peace with your past—perhaps you'll address your letter not to the adult you, but to you at four, or you at eleven, or you at sixteen. What can you tell that struggling child that might bring about comfort, acceptance, or reconciliation?

The final letter, of course, is to your daughter. Tell her not what you expect from her, but what you hope for her. We're talking big picture here. Turn back to this page whenever you lose sight of your goals or aren't sure how to proceed. Let it remind you what you're trying to do and why it's so important. Make it your guide as you move through the challenging and rewarding years to come.

We wish you all the best!

Letter to my parents

Letter to my parents

Letter to myself

Letter to myself

Letter to my daughter from her mother

Letter to my daughter from her father

Your plan

Here's where you begin planning how to assure that things will be different for your daughter. (Turn back to page 129 for explanations and examples.)

1. "feminine" and "masculine" stereotypes

INFANT TO FOUR-YEAR-OLD
Verbal message:

Action message:

FIVE- TO EIGHT-YEAR-OLD
Verbal message:

Action message:

NINE- TO TWELVE-YEAR-OLD
Verbal message:

Action message:

THIRTEEN- TO SIXTEEN-YEAR-OLD
Verbal message:

Action message:

SEVENTEEN YEARS AND UP
Verbal message:

Action message:

2. achievement

INFANT TO FOUR-YEAR-OLD
Verbal message:

Action message:

FIVE- TO EIGHT-YEAR-OLD
Verbal message:

Action message:

NINE- TO TWELVE-YEAR-OLD
Verbal message:

Action message:

THIRTEEN- TO SIXTEEN-YEAR-OLD
Verbal message:

Action message:

SEVENTEEN YEARS AND UP
Verbal message:

Action message:

3. *learning to tolerate anxiety and act anyway*

INFANT TO FOUR-YEAR-OLD
Verbal message:

Action message:

FIVE- TO EIGHT-YEAR-OLD
Verbal message:

Action message:

NINE- TO TWELVE-YEAR-OLD
Verbal message:

Action message:

THIRTEEN- TO SIXTEEN-YEAR-OLD
Verbal message:

Action message:

SEVENTEEN YEARS AND UP
Verbal message:

Action message:

4. learning to separate fantasy from reality and to act on the reality

INFANT TO FOUR-YEAR-OLD
Verbal message:

Action message:

FIVE- TO EIGHT-YEAR-OLD
Verbal message:

Action message:

NINE- TO TWELVE-YEAR-OLD
Verbal message:

Action message:

THIRTEEN- TO SIXTEEN-YEAR-OLD
Verbal message:

Action message:

SEVENTEEN YEARS AND UP
Verbal message:

Action message:

5. *learning to set goals and priorities*

INFANT TO FOUR-YEAR-OLD
Verbal message:

Action message:

FIVE- TO EIGHT-YEAR-OLD
Verbal message:

Action message:

NINE- TO TWELVE-YEAR-OLD
Verbal message:

Action message:

THIRTEEN- TO SIXTEEN-YEAR-OLD
Verbal message:

Action message:

SEVENTEEN YEARS AND UP
Verbal message:

Action message:

6. learning to project into the future

INFANT TO FOUR-YEAR-OLD
Verbal message:

Action message:

FIVE- TO EIGHT-YEAR-OLD
Verbal message:

Action message:

NINE- TO TWELVE-YEAR-OLD
Verbal message:

Action message:

THIRTEEN- TO SIXTEEN-YEAR-OLD
Verbal message:

Action message:

SEVENTEEN YEARS AND UP
Verbal message:

Action message:

7. learning to be discriminating

INFANT TO FOUR-YEAR-OLD
Verbal message:

Action message:

FIVE- TO EIGHT-YEAR-OLD
Verbal message:

Action message:

NINE- TO TWELVE-YEAR-OLD
Verbal message:

Action message:

THIRTEEN- TO SIXTEEN-YEAR-OLD
Verbal message:

Action message:

SEVENTEEN YEARS AND UP
Verbal message:

Action message:

8. learning to set boundaries and limits

INFANT TO FOUR-YEAR-OLD
Verbal message:

Action message:

FIVE- TO EIGHT-YEAR-OLD
Verbal message:

Action message:

NINE- TO TWELVE-YEAR-OLD
Verbal message:

Action message:

THIRTEEN- TO SIXTEEN-YEAR-OLD
Verbal message:

Action message:

SEVENTEEN YEARS AND UP
Verbal message:

Action message:

9. learning to be assertive and ask for what she wants

INFANT TO FOUR-YEAR-OLD
Verbal message:

Action message:

FIVE- TO EIGHT-YEAR-OLD
Verbal message:

Action message:

NINE- TO TWELVE-YEAR-OLD
Verbal message:

Action message:

THIRTEEN- TO SIXTEEN-YEAR-OLD
Verbal message:

Action message:

SEVENTEEN YEARS AND UP
Verbal message:

Action message:

10. learning to trust herself

INFANT TO FOUR-YEAR-OLD

Verbal message:

Action message:

FIVE- TO EIGHT-YEAR-OLD

Verbal message:

Action message:

NINE- TO TWELVE-YEAR-OLD

Verbal message:

Action message:

THIRTEEN- TO SIXTEEN-YEAR-OLD

Verbal message:

Action message:

SEVENTEEN YEARS AND UP

Verbal message:

Action message:

11. the importance of education

INFANT TO FOUR-YEAR-OLD
Verbal message:

Action message:

FIVE- TO EIGHT-YEAR-OLD
Verbal message:

Action message:

NINE- TO TWELVE-YEAR-OLD
Verbal message:

Action message:

THIRTEEN- TO SIXTEEN-YEAR-OLD
Verbal message:

Action message:

SEVENTEEN YEARS AND UP
Verbal message:

Action message:

12. *the importance of math and computers*

INFANT TO FOUR-YEAR-OLD

Verbal message:

Action message:

FIVE- TO EIGHT-YEAR-OLD

Verbal message:

Action message:

NINE- TO TWELVE-YEAR-OLD

Verbal message:

Action message:

THIRTEEN- TO SIXTEEN-YEAR-OLD

Verbal message:

Action message:

SEVENTEEN YEARS AND UP

Verbal message:

Action message:

13. sports and physical fitness

INFANT TO FOUR-YEAR-OLD
Verbal message:

Action message:

FIVE- TO EIGHT-YEAR-OLD
Verbal message:

Action message:

NINE- TO TWELVE-YEAR-OLD
Verbal message:

Action message:

THIRTEEN- TO SIXTEEN-YEAR-OLD
Verbal message:

Action message:

SEVENTEEN YEARS AND UP
Verbal message:

Action message:

14. appearance

INFANT TO FOUR-YEAR-OLD

Verbal message:

Action message:

FIVE- TO EIGHT-YEAR-OLD

Verbal message:

Action message:

NINE- TO TWELVE-YEAR-OLD

Verbal message:

Action message:

THIRTEEN- TO SIXTEEN-YEAR-OLD

Verbal message:

Action message:

SEVENTEEN YEARS AND UP

Verbal message:

Action message:

15. relationships / dating

INFANT TO FOUR-YEAR-OLD

Verbal message:

Action message:

FIVE- TO EIGHT-YEAR-OLD

Verbal message:

Action message:

NINE- TO TWELVE-YEAR-OLD

Verbal message:

Action message:

THIRTEEN- TO SIXTEEN-YEAR-OLD

Verbal message:

Action message:

SEVENTEEN YEARS AND UP

Verbal message:

Action message:

16. marriage and children

INFANT TO FOUR-YEAR-OLD
Verbal message:

Action message:

FIVE- TO EIGHT-YEAR-OLD
Verbal message:

Action message:

NINE- TO TWELVE-YEAR-OLD
Verbal message:

Action message:

THIRTEEN- TO SIXTEEN-YEAR-OLD
Verbal message:

Action message:

SEVENTEEN YEARS AND UP
Verbal message:

Action message:

17. sexuality

INFANT TO FOUR-YEAR-OLD
Verbal message:

Action message:

FIVE- TO EIGHT-YEAR-OLD
Verbal message:

Action message:

NINE- TO TWELVE-YEAR-OLD
Verbal message:

Action message:

THIRTEEN- TO SIXTEEN-YEAR-OLD
Verbal message:

Action message:

SEVENTEEN YEARS AND UP
Verbal message:

Action message:

18. economic self-sufficiency

INFANT TO FOUR-YEAR-OLD
Verbal message:

Action message:

FIVE- TO EIGHT-YEAR-OLD
Verbal message:

Action message:

NINE- TO TWELVE-YEAR-OLD
Verbal message:

Action message:

THIRTEEN- TO SIXTEEN-YEAR-OLD
Verbal message:

Action message:

SEVENTEEN YEARS AND UP
Verbal message:

Action message:

19. career planning

INFANT TO FOUR-YEAR-OLD
Verbal message:

Action message:

FIVE- TO EIGHT-YEAR-OLD
Verbal message:

Action message:

NINE- TO TWELVE-YEAR-OLD
Verbal message:

Action message:

THIRTEEN- TO SIXTEEN-YEAR-OLD
Verbal message:

Action message:

SEVENTEEN YEARS AND UP
Verbal message:

Action message:

20. mixing family and career

INFANT TO FOUR-YEAR-OLD
Verbal message:

Action message:

FIVE- TO EIGHT-YEAR-OLD
Verbal message:

Action message:

NINE- TO TWELVE-YEAR-OLD
Verbal message:

Action message:

THIRTEEN- TO SIXTEEN-YEAR-OLD
Verbal message:

Action message:

SEVENTEEN YEARS AND UP
Verbal message:

Action message:

To Learn More

Listed below are supplementary resources—books, videos, organizations, and so on—to help you expand your knowledge. We've included only those that we feel are exceptionally good but recognize that many more are out there. For those items that may not be readily available at your library or bookstore, ordering information follows on page 482.

We hope you will not consider it presumptuous of us to have included some of our own books in these lists. We struggled with the issue and finally decided that since we wrote the books because we thought the material was important and we couldn't find it anywhere else, you should at least know these resources exist. If you decide to implement the program we've outlined here, they might make your job easier.

CHAPTER 1
SELF-ESTEEM: A KEY TO UNLOCKING
YOUR DAUGHTER'S FUTURE

The Six Pillars of Self-Esteem by Dr. Nathaniel Branden, Ph.D. (Bantam, 1994).
Trusting Ourselves by Dr. Karen Johnson (Atlantic Monthly Press, 1991).
Learned Optimism by Martin E. P. Seligman (Pocket Books, 1990).
Women and Self-Esteem by Linda Tschirhart Sanford and Mary Ellen Donovan (Penguin, 1984).
Women and the Blues by Jennifer James, Ph.D. (Harper & Row, 1988).
"Shortchanging Girls, Shortchanging America" (AAUW, 1991). Available as a full report, summary, action guide, or video. (See "Ordering Information.")

"Past the Pink and Blue Predicament: Freeing the Next Generation from Sex Stereotypes," Girls Incorporated National Resource Center. (See "Ordering Information.")

CHAPTER 2
WHAT ATTITUDES, EXPERIENCES, AND FEELINGS DO YOU BRING TO PARENTING?

Chiquita's Cocoon: A Cinderella Complex for the Latina Woman by Bettina R. Flores (Pepper Vine Press, 1990).
Backlash: The Undeclared War Against American Women by Susan Faludi (Crown, 1991).

CHAPTER 4
RESOLVING THE CONFLICT WOMEN FEEL BETWEEN FEMININITY AND ACHIEVEMENT

How to Father a Successful Daughter by Nicky Marone (Fawcett Crest, 1988).

CHAPTER 5
FORMING AN IDENTITY AS AN ACHIEVER

Interventions for Adolescent Identity Development edited by Sally Archer (Sage Publications, 1994).

CHAPTER 10
INFANT, TODDLER, PRESCHOOLER

Your Child's Self-Esteem by Dorothy Corkille Briggs (Dolphin Books, 1970). Briggs's ideas about sexual identity are outdated (her book was written more than twenty years ago), but her other suggestions to parents are clear and still quite useful.
Facts and Reflections on Careers for Today's Girls (Girls Incorporated, 1985). (See "Ordering Information.")
The Psychology of Women: Behavior in a Biosocial Context by Juanita H. Williams (W. W. Norton & Company, 1987).
Know Your Child: An Authoritative Guide for Today's Parents by Stella Chess, M.D., and Alexander Thomas, M.D. (Basic Books, 1987).

CHAPTER 11
AGES SIX TO TEN

The Girl Within by Emily Hancock (Fawcett, 1989).

My Way Sally by Mindy Bingham and Penelope Colville Paine, illustrated by Itoko Maeno (Advocacy Press, 1988). (See Academic Innovations, "Ordering Information.")

Feelings About Friends by Linda Schwartz (Learning Works, 1988).

I Am Special by Linda Schwartz (Learning Works, 1978).

An Income of Her Own, a board game for young female entrepreneurs. (See AIOHO, "Ordering Information.")

CHAPTER 12
ADOLESCENT

How to Say No and Keep Your Friends by Sharon Scott (Human Resource Development Press, 1986). This is reading your daughter might enjoy.

CHAPTER 15
LESSONS LEARNED FROM THE MEDIA

Media & Values, a quarterly publication by the Center for Media and Values. (See "Ordering Information.")

Still Killing Us Softly, a video on sexist advertising, Cambridge Documentary Films. (See "Ordering Information.")

"Media Guide for Black Girls," National Black Child Development Institute. (See "Ordering Information.") Many other publications are also available.

CHAPTER 16
LESSONS LEARNED IN SCHOOL

Failing at Fairness: How America's Schools Cheat Girls by Myra and David Sadker (Scribner's, 1994).

A New Curriculum for Girls: Horizons 2000 by Cheryl G. Bartholomew (B. L. Winch and Associates).

How Schools Shortchange Girls, AAUW report prepared by the Wellesley College Center for Research on Women. This comprehensive book examines how girls are at a disadvantage in the schools and includes recommendations for educators and policymakers. (See "Ordering Information.")

School Girls: Young Women, Self-esteem and the Confidence Gap by Peggy Orenstein in association with the American Association of University Women. (See "Ordering Information.")

CHAPTER 17
MATH, SCIENCE, AND COMPUTERS

The Scientist Within You: Experiments and Biographies of Distinguished Women in Science by Rebecca Lowe Warren and Mary H. Thompson (ACI Publishing, 1994). (See "Ordering Information.")

CHAPTER 19
MIRROR, MIRROR, ON THE WALL

The Beauty Myth by Naomi Wolf (Doubleday, 1992).

CHAPTER 20
I'M NOBODY TILL SOMEBODY LOVES ME

Why Am I Afraid to Tell You Who I Am? by John Powell (Tabor Publishing, 1969).
Sexual Harassment and Teens by Susan Strauss (Free Spirit Publishing, 1992).

CHAPTER 21
SEX AND THE TEENAGE GIRL

"Guidelines for Comprehensive Sexuality Education," a fifty-two-page booklet for kindergarten through twelfth grade, from SIECUS. (See "Ordering Information.")
Parents and Friends of Lesbians and Gays. For information, write Parents FLAG, P.O. Box 27605, Washington, D.C. 20038-7605
Preventing Adolescent Pregnancy Program, Girls Incorporated National Resource Center. (See "Ordering Information.")

CHAPTER 23
GETTING GIRLS READY FOR CAREER EDUCATION

Choices: A Teen Woman's Journal for Self-awareness and Personal Planning by Mindy Bingham and Sandy Stryker, with Judy Edmondson (Advocacy Press, 1983). (See "Ordering Information.")

Lifestyle Math: Your Financial Planning Portfolio by Mindy Bingham, Jo Willhite, and Shirley Myers (Academic Innovations) (See "Ordering Information.")

CHAPTER 24
HELPING GIRLS REALIZE THEIR CAREER POTENTIAL

Educated in Romance: Women, Achievement, and College Culture by Dorothy C. Holland and Margaret A. Eisenhart (University of Chicago Press, 1990).
Career Choices: A Guide for Teens and Young Adults—Who Am I? What Do I Want? How Do I Get It? by Mindy Bingham and Sandy Stryker (Academic Innovations, 1990). (See "Ordering Information.")

For information on an eighth-, ninth-, or tenth-grade comprehensive career education component designed to be taught in the Department of English/Language Arts, write Academic Innovations. (See "Ordering Information.")

CHAPTER 25
STRATEGIES FOR MIXING CAREER AND FAMILY

More Choices: A Strategic Planning Guide for Mixing Career and Family by Mindy Bingham and Sandy Stryker (Advocacy Press, 1987). ("See Ordering Information.")

CHAPTER 26
OUT INTO THE WORLD

Are You the One for Me? Knowing Who's Right and Avoiding Who's Wrong by Barbara De Angelis, Ph.D. (Dell, 1993).
Intimate Partners by Maggie Scarf (Random House, 1987).

CHAPTER 27
ADVOCACY FOR GIRLS

Women Helping Girls with Choices: A Handbook for Community Service Organizations by Mindy Bingham and Sandy Stryker (Advocacy Press, 1989). (See "Ordering Information.")

CHAPTER 28
FORMING MOTHER-DAUGHTER GROUPS

Mother-Daughter Choices by Mindy Bingham, Lari Quinn, and William P. Sheehan (Advocacy Press, 1988). (See "Ordering Information.")

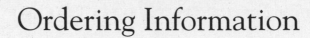

Ordering Information

Here are addresses for the publishers and organizations that produce the books, videos, pamphlets, and other resources mentioned throughout the book, particularly in the "To Learn More" section. Most of the books are also available in bookstores.

AAUW Publications
1111 16th Street N.W.
Washington, DC 20036-4873
(202) 785-7743

AAUW Sales Office
P.O. Box 251
Annapolis Junction, MD 20701-0251
(for videos)

Academic Innovations
3463 State Street, Suite 219T
Santa Barbara, CA 93105
(805) 967-8015, ext. 892
(for titles published by Advocacy Press or Academic Innovations)

ACI Publishing
P.O. Box 40398
Eugene, OR 97404-0064

Advocacy Press (See Academic Innovations.)

AIOHO
P.O. Box 8452
San Jose, CA 95155-8452

Annick Press
15 Patricia Avenue
Willowdale, ON M2M 1H9
Canada

B. L. Winch & Associates
2675 Skypark Drive, Suite 204
Torrance, CA 90505

Cambridge Documentary Films
P.O. Box 385
Cambridge, MA 02139
(617) 354-3677

Carolrhóda Books
241 First Avenue North
Minneapolis, MN 55410

Center for Media and Values
1962 South Shenandoah Street
Los Angeles, CA 90034

Direct Cinema Ltd
P.O. Box 315
Franklin Lakes, NJ 07417
or
P.O. Box 69799
Los Angeles, CA 90069

FASE Productions
4801 Wilshire Boulevard, Suite 215
Los Angeles, CA 90010

Girls Incorporated
National Resource Center
441 West Michigan Street
Indianapolis, IN 40202
(317) 634-7546

Human Resource Development Press
22 Amherst Road
Amherst, MA 01002

Ishtar Films
P.O. Box 51, Route 311
Patterson, New York 12563
or
6253 Hollywood Boulevard, Suite 623
Hollywood, CA 90028

The Learning Works
P.O. Box 6187
Santa Barbara, CA 93160

Lodestar Books
375 Hudson Street
New York, NY 10014

National Black Child
   Development Institute
1023 15th Street N.W., Suite 600
Washington, DC 20005

Orchard Books
387 Park Avenue South
New York, NY 10016

Pepper Vine Press
P.O. Box 2017
Granite Bay, CA 95746

Sage Publications, Inc.
2455 Teller Road
Thousand Oaks, CA 91320

SIECUS
130 West 42nd Street, Suite 2500
New York, NY 10036

Tabor Publishing
25115 Stanford Avenue, Suite 130
Valencia, CA 91355

University of California at Berkeley
Lawrence Hall of Science
Berkeley, CA 94720

Index